No Depression in Heaven

No Depression in Heaven

The Great Depression, the New Deal, and the Transformation of Religion in the Delta

ALISON COLLIS GREENE

OXFORD
UNIVERSITY PRESS

OXFORD

UNIVERSITY PRESS

Oxford University Press is a department of the University of Oxford. It furthers
the University's objective of excellence in research, scholarship, and education
by publishing worldwide. Oxford is a registered trade mark of Oxford University
Press in the UK and certain other countries.

Published in the United States of America by Oxford University Press
198 Madison Avenue, New York, NY 10016, United States of America.

© Oxford University Press 2016

First issued as an Oxford University Press paperback, 2017

Library of Congress Cataloging-in-Publication Data
Greene, Alison Collis.
No Depression in Heaven : the Great Depression, the New Deal,
and the transformation of religion in the Delta / Alison Collis Greene.
pages cm
Includes bibliographical references and index.
ISBN 978-0-19-937187-7 (hardcover : alk. paper); 978-0-19-085831-5 (paperback : alk. paper)
1. Arkansas Delta (Ark.)—Religion—20th century. 2. Memphis (Tenn.)—Religion—20th
century. 3. Arkansas Delta (Ark.)—Race relations—History—20th century. 4. Memphis
(Tenn.)—Race relations—History—20th century. 5. Depressions—1929—Arkansas—Arkansas
Delta. 6. Depressions—1929—Tennessee—Memphis. 7. New Deal, 1933–1939—Arkansas—
Arkansas Delta. 8. New Deal, 1933–1939—Tennessee—Memphis. 9. Social change—Arkansas—
Arkansas Delta—History. 10. Social change—Tennessee—Memphis—History. I. Title.
BL2527.A63G73 2015
277.67'8082—dc23
2015018302

For my parents,
Larry Joe Greene
and
Margaret Collis Greene

Contents

Acknowledgments

MY DAD WAS once a Southern Baptist preacher who thought too much, read too much, and talked about hell too little. Then suddenly he wasn't a preacher anymore. He drove a school bus and pruned Christmas trees and delivered heating fuel on icy mountain roads for the rest of my childhood, and he did it all with an uncomplaining kindness that I wish I'd inherited. Meanwhile, my mother proved that no one in the world is more important than a good public school teacher. She was an even better parent, who never once made me quit reading that book or come down out of that tree. This book is for them, and that's why.

I'm thankful for many extraordinary mentors. Ruel Tyson was the reason I landed at the University of North Carolina, a timid and insecure kid he refused to believe was either of those things. Ruel might be the only scholar of religion I've met who can believe a thing into being. There is no livelier mind, no more committed teacher, no more gracious friend.

Glenda Gilmore has read more drafts of this work—first as a dissertation and again as a book manuscript—than anyone else. She is the best sort of mentor: honest, generous, thoughtful, and eloquent in person and on the page. I have learned always to trust her advice. Jon Butler is one of the kindest, fairest, and toughest scholars anywhere. Because he did not tell me my work was good when it was not, I trusted his praise when it came. Skip Stout told me when I first arrived at Yale that it was a lot easier to teach history than writing, which I think was his gracious way of telling me that I had an especially long road to learn the former. But with good humor and a great deal of kindness, he taught me both. Beverly Gage was a new professor when I was a new graduate student. I watched her navigate the start of a spectacular career, and though her grace and wit are inimitable, she has nonetheless provided a wonderful model for many new scholars.

I am grateful for the warm atmosphere in the Department of History at Mississippi State University. My colleagues have been almost universally welcoming and encouraging from the moment I set foot on campus, and have also become good friends. My department head, Alan Marcus, has been supportive all along and creative in helping me carve out time and resources to write.

Many, many friends and colleagues have helped me along the way. I have had the remarkable good fortune to work on parts of this book as part of three different writing-and-eating-and-drinking groups, all of them wonderful: Julia Irwin, Grace Leslie-Waksman, and Eden Knudsen McLean; Sarah Brauner-Otto, Shalyn Claggett, Devon Brenner, Alix Hui, Anne Marshall, and Amanda Clay Powers; and Heather Curtis, Jonathan Ebel, Jennifer Graber, Kip Kosek, and Tracy Fessenden. Jon Ebel read this book first as a dissertation and then as a much-revised book manuscript, and he has become a good friend, endlessly generous and always encouraging. I am grateful to Jon for the conversations that have helped shape this book, and I eagerly await his forthcoming book on religion and the Great Depression in California. Ed Blum and Matt Sutton read a full draft of this book when it was a dissertation and when they certainly did not have the time, and their thoughtful feedback helped me restructure the narrative. I am grateful to several more people who have read or heard portions of the book in its various forms and provided opportunities for me to share it: Wallace Best, Jessica Delgado, Darren Dochuk, Elizabeth Fones-Wolf, Ken Fones-Wolf, John Giggie, Paul Harvey, Kevin Kruse, Ted Ownby, Bruce Schulman, Stephen Tuck, Judith Weisenfeld, and Julian Zelizer. Finally, I thank the two anonymous readers at Oxford University Press for their incisive commentary and critiques.

The 2013–2015 Young Scholars in American Religion mentors Robert Orsi and Courtney Bender, and my colleagues Shelby Balik, Rosemary Corbett, Omri Elisha, Kathleen Holscher, Hillary Kaell, David King, Anthony Petro, John Seitz, and Josef Sorett, have made this whole enterprise simultaneously more fun and more awe-inspiring. Hillary read two chapters as I worked to revise and made some wonderful suggestions. Bob and Courtney have gone above and beyond their responsibilities to us in many ways, but I'm especially grateful that they both took time to read a penultimate version of the manuscript. Bob's wonderfully thoughtful response helped me see the big picture and figure out how to end, all while reassuring me at a low moment.

I'm also grateful for other wonderful colleagues in Mississippi and across the country, especially Kathryn Barbier, Caitlin Casey, Kat Mellen Charron, Rob Ferguson, Jim Giesen, Julia Guarneri, David Huyssen, Mark Hersey, Adriane Lentz-Smith, Kathryn Gin Lum, Anne Marshall, Jessica Martucci, Robin Morris, Julia Osman, Brendan Pietsch, Steve Prince, Brenda Santos,

Dana Schaffer, Sam Schaffer, Kirsten Weld, and Molly Worthen. Several other good friends either put me up or put up with me as I researched and wrote: Devon Myers, Charity Taylor Grindstaff, Laura Willard Tucker, and Jane Buchanan Williams. To my friend Sarah Hammond, whose bright light drew me to Yale in the first place—I miss you so.

I visited two dozen archives and libraries in pursuit of this story, and I enjoyed working in every single one of them. More than fifty different archivists and librarians helped me along the way, and I'd like to thank all of them, especially Mattie Abraham, who knows the Mississippi State archives inside and out and is now enjoying a well-deserved retirement. History librarian Nickoal Eichmann arrived at Mississippi State just in time to help me chase down images and answer convoluted copyright questions. I am grateful for support from the two institutions that have allowed me to complete this work, Yale University and Mississippi State University, and to the Charlotte W. Newcombe Foundation, the Franklin and Eleanor Roosevelt Institute, the Louisville Institute, the Richard J. Franke Fellowship, and the Woodrow Wilson Foundation, which helped fund it at various stages.

I also appreciate the support of the presses and journals that have allowed me to try out in draft form some of the ideas that appear in this book. Those are "The Faith of the 'Flotsam and Jetsam,'" *Journal of Southern Religion* 13 (Fall 2011); "The End of 'The Protestant Era'?" *Church History* 80, no. 3 (September 2011): 600–610; "The Redemption of Souls and Soils: Religion and the Rural Crisis in the Mississippi Delta," in *Gods of the Mississippi*, edited by Michael Pasquier (Indiana University Press, 2013), 130–160; "'A Divine Revelation'?: Southern Churches Respond to the New Deal," in *Faithful Republic: Religion and American Politics*, edited by Andrew Preston, Bruce Schulman, and Julian Zelizer (University of Pennsylvania Press, 2015), 56–70; and "The Welfare of Faith," in *Faith in the New Millennium: The Future of Religion and American Politics*, edited by Darren Dochuk and Matthew Avery Sutton (Oxford University Press, 2016).

Susan Ferber has shepherded this book through three rounds of revisions, and at the last stage she helped to speed a lagging process and saved me from several narrative and structural errors. I am grateful for her incisive feedback and for her encouragement throughout the process. My production editor, Maya Bringe, painstakingly read the entire manuscript. She caught several lingering inconsistencies in style and helped me clean up muddy prose.

Of course, remaining blind spots, interpretive errors, and other mistakes are entirely mine.

And now back to the beginning: Apart from my family, a few adults made a rocky adolescence a little easier. Mary Sue Ledford, my high school English teacher, introduced me to Richard Wright and Zora Neale Hurston and Thomas Hardy and a host of other writers who helped me to see the world differently. She also listened, and encouraged, and taught me how to write. Bob Ballance never treated me like a kid or a nuisance, and he always took my questions seriously. That is what I wish for my own children as they grow to adolescence: that they find adults who will push them to work hard and think for themselves, who will allow them to speak aloud their fears and their dreams, and who will encourage them to seek kindness and justice.

Charley and Cynthia Nash first showed up on White Oak shortly after we did, and we claimed them immediately. Later, I babysat their son Christopher, who now has two little girls of his own. When I ventured off to college, Charley wrote me clever, insightful letters and brought me jugs full of fresh mountain water. They are all family. I landed in another wonderful, and large, family as an adult, and I thank all of the Morgans and Wards for their warmth, good humor, and generosity. A special thanks to Tim Tyson, who has taken many an afternoon to talk me through a stuck spot. Mike and Hope Morgan Ward are just astonishingly good people who care in all the right ways and fight for all the right things. Brooke Morgan Ward holds together this whole universe of people with her sharp insight, her gentle humor, and her innate kindness.

Miranda Callis knows how to grab hold of joy and pull anyone around into a swirl of fun and laughter. She is magnetic, but also kind and smart and thoughtful—and one heck of a good sister. I am thrilled that Tom Callis has joined the family to ensure our visits are full of interesting conversation, good food, and yeowling cats. My uncle Mike doesn't give a fig about this book or anything else that keeps me so many miles from home, but he keeps me stocked with good fiction and great talks. He's the contrariest person I know, which means he thinks for himself, consequences be damned, and I love him for it.

This book is for my parents, Larry Joe Greene and Margaret Collis Greene, but the two people who have most steadily endured its making are Jason Morgan Ward and our son Amos. Without Amos, this book would have appeared well before now, but Amos brings joy and magic to our lives every day. His brother Theodore arrived just ahead of the finished book and has already expanded both the happy chaos and the magic of our universe. As much as Amos and then Theo slowed this work, their father sped it. How to thank someone who does not acknowledge the sacrifices he makes for those he loves, who perhaps does not deem them sacrifices at all, who shrugs off gratitude? Thank you, Jason. For carving out more space and time for me to write than you ask for yourself, for talking me through thorny patches, for imagining with me all the fun places we will one day hike and swim and eat and laugh. And thank you most of all for your unswerving sense of what really matters.

Abbreviations

AAA	Agricultural Adjustment Administration
ABA	American Baptist Association
AME	African Methodist Episcopal Church
AMEZ	African Methodist Episcopal Church, Zion
ASWPL	Association of Southern Women for the Prevention of Lynching
CCC	Civilian Conservation Corps
CIC	Commission on Interracial Cooperation
CME	Colored Methodist Episcopal Church (now Christian Methodist Episcopal Church)
COGIC	Church of God in Christ
CWA	Civil Works Administration
FCC	Federal Council of Churches
FERA	Federal Emergency Relief Administration
FSA	Farm Security Administration
MECS	Methodist Episcopal Church, South
NBC	National Baptist Convention
NCNW	National Council of Negro Women
NIRA	National Industrial Recovery Act
NRA	National Recovery Administration
NYA	National Youth Administration
PCUS	Presbyterian Church in the United States (southern Presbyterians)
PCUSA	Presbyterian Church in the United States of America (northern Presbyterians)
PWA	Public Works Administration
RFC	Reconstruction Finance Corporation
REA	Rural Electrification Administration
SBC	Southern Baptist Convention
SCS	Soil Conservation Service

STFU   Southern Tenant Farmers' Union
TVA   Tennessee Valley Authority
WPA   Works Progress Administration

A note on quotations: Whenever possible, I have quoted individuals precisely as they wrote or spoke without using [sic] to draw attention to unconventional spelling and usage. When the original spelling or punctuation significantly impedes clarity, I have replaced it with the corrected word or words in brackets.

No Depression in Heaven

INTRODUCTION

We Didn't Know We Was Poor

MY GRANDMOTHER WASHED out used paper towels and hung them on the clothesline to use again. She spent painstaking hours piecing quilts of mismatched and worn-out fabric scraps or odds and ends from the knitting mill where she worked because she could not fathom buying new material. "We didn't know we was poor," Grandma said nearly every time she told us a story about her childhood. It was not a boast. It was an apology: an apology because she had to quit school after sixth grade and never again felt smart; an apology because she spoke in a mountain accent so thick that my friends from college scarcely understood her; an apology because she was a child of the Great Depression. Those words also acknowledged the still deeper poverty that Grandma knew surrounded her, the real and urgent need for outside help as hunger and despair crept into households once happy and humming.

By the twenty-first century, the depression generation would become the Greatest Generation, idealized in the popular consciousness as plucky, selfless, and self-sufficient. They grew their own food. They went to church every Sunday. They helped their neighbors. They defeated Hitler. Maybe they suffered some deprivation during the Great Depression, but that just taught them the value of saving and thrift. "We didn't know we was poor," or some variation of it, became a common phrase, a badge of honor that set the Greatest Generation apart from their spoiled offspring, who turned to the government instead of one another when things got rough.

This rendering of history erases one of the most traumatic episodes of twentieth-century American life and turns it instead into a morality tale about the value of family and community. There is no room in Great Depression nostalgia for parents forced to abandon their children to orphanages because they would otherwise starve, for communities fractured as their residents fled in the vain hope that any place had to be better than where they were, or for evicted farmers forced out of their homes onto frozen soil. That sanitized narrative of the depression erases the voiced suffering of millions, the murmurs of revolution that swept Franklin Roosevelt into office. That is, in the end, the point of it.

This book tells a story that the myth of the redemptive depression obscures. There is truth in the myth, of course: members of families and communities indeed turned to one another in their hardship, and many also turned to their churches for solace, for support, for meaning. Yet that turning together revealed only the inadequacy of families, communities, and churches full of poor people to aid one another in their time of mutual distress. The Great Depression gave lie to the toxic notion that responsibility for poverty lies with the poor rather than with systems of oppression that make a mockery of the American dream. Members of families, communities, and churches turned to one another, and then they turned together to demand more of their political system, more of their federal government. The greatest power of the Greatest Generation was their collective acknowledgment that they could not go it alone. Nowhere was this transformation more dramatic than in the South. For a moment, the southern Protestant establishment faced the suffering that plantation capitalism pushed behind its public image of planters' hats and hoopskirts and mountains of pure white cotton. When starving white farmers marched into an Arkansas town to demand food for their dying children, when priests turned away hungry widows and orphans because they were no needier than anyone else, and when visitors claimed that moonshiners did as much as churches to feed the hungry, southern clergy of both races spoke with almost one voice to say that they had done all they could. Their churches and their charities were broke. It was time for a higher power to intervene. They looked to God, and then they looked to Roosevelt.

When Roosevelt promised a new deal for the "forgotten man," Americans cheered, and when he took office, the churches and private agencies gratefully turned much of the responsibility for welfare and social reform over to the state. Yet Roosevelt's New Deal threatened plantation capitalism even as it bent to it. Black southern churches worked to secure benefits for their own community members, while white churches divided over their loyalties to Roosevelt and Jim Crow. Frustrated by their failure to alleviate the depression and split over the New Deal, leaders in the major white Protestant denominations surrendered their moral authority in the South and then blamed the federal government for its loss.[1]

THE GREAT DEPRESSION revealed the inability of American religious institutions to care for the needy in the midst of crisis, and it opened new opportunities for the state to take on the burden instead. From the poorest sharecropper in Arkansas to the wealthiest philanthropist in New York, depression-era Americans re-envisioned the relationship between church and state and re-evaluated the responsibilities of each for the welfare of the nation and its people. Yet the Great Depression was a profoundly local experience that affected each region of the nation and its residents in distinct ways.[2]

In Memphis and the Arkansas and Mississippi Delta, economic crisis compounded an ongoing agricultural depression and coincided with a devastating drought. Together, Memphis and the Delta make up a single economic and social region—an urban center with a distinct rural periphery (Figure I.1). Nowhere did the depression strike more swiftly or more savagely, and nowhere was the wholesale transfer of charity and reform from church to state more complete. The Great Depression and the New Deal remade this southern region, a place with striking religious, ethnic, and political diversity.[3]

In 1930, Memphis was the nation's thirty-sixth largest city and the South's ninth largest. Home to more than 250,000 people, just over a third of whom were African American, Memphians oriented toward the vast cotton plantations that spread out on both sides of the river south and west of the city, in Arkansas and Mississippi. Delta planters sent their crop to Memphis, an important inland port and the nation's largest inland cotton market. The predominantly African American sharecroppers and tenant farmers who cultivated the cotton often fled to Memphis as well, either to escape racial violence or to seek work away from the fields. Fierce racial repression and widespread suffering among the poor of both races provided the pillars of the region's plantation capitalism. After all, given a choice, no one would farm cotton on someone else's land for pennies a day. Hard times came early to the region, as cotton prices fell after the Great War and a 1927 Mississippi River flood inundated the flat Delta.[4]

Memphis and the Delta graphically illustrate the broader transformation of American religion and culture in these turbulent years. A land of extremes, the Delta endured a devastating drought in 1930, before its residents could recover from the flood. The Delta became the locus of national debates about voluntary aid and federal responsibility for the suffering, and its hungry and homeless residents represented the face of rural poverty to millions of distant Americans. The elite white businessmen and religious leaders who both emerged from and reinforced the region's fierce commitment to white supremacy called for federal aid even as they worked to bend its distribution

FIGURE I.I Map of the Delta region, spanning Memphis and the upper regions of the Delta in Arkansas and Mississippi.

Map by Alice Thiede.

to the region's racialized economic system. By 1933, their steady and essential support for Franklin Roosevelt and the New Deal meant that elites in Memphis and the Delta helped to set the terms and constraints for the transfer of charity and reform from voluntary and religious organizations to the federal government.[5]

Religious elites in Memphis and the Delta emerged almost entirely from the southern Protestant establishment, the wealthy and middle-class members of the region's major denominations. These white Protestant leaders represented a powerful social and political force in Memphis and the Delta, and together with businessmen drawn from their ranks, they shaped the region's major benevolent and service efforts. Episcopalians represented less than five percent of the region's churchgoers, but they sat atop the social hierarchy, with influence and wealth disproportionate to their numbers. Methodists followed, with just under a third of all white churchgoers but a larger proportion of the middle class. The Protestant establishment also included wealthy and middle-class Southern Baptists. That denomination claimed more than half the region's white churchgoers, and its size lent its elites considerable political heft, however powerless and disconnected its largely rural and poor masses might have been. Wealthy and middle-class Disciples of Christ, Presbyterians, and Congregationalists also played an important social role even though together those denominations represented only about ten percent of churchgoers, most of them in Memphis and larger Delta towns.[6]

The Protestant establishment faced competition and criticism from within and without. The ethnic and theological diversity of Memphis and the Delta belies stereotypical portrayals of southern homogeneity and regional isolation. Although Jim Crow circumscribed their broader political and social authority, black baptists and Methodists exercised tremendous power within their communities, and their tradition of self-help and social outreach ran far deeper than that of their white counterparts. Memphis and the Delta were also home to the fundamentalist Churches of Christ, a number of pentecostal and holiness denominations, a small but disproportionately influential Jewish community, and a thriving minority of black and white Catholics. The region's preeminent homegrown denomination, the Church of God in Christ (COGIC)—one of the largest global religious denominations in the twenty-first century—watched the established denominations struggle through the 1930s as its own influence grew.[7]

While *No Depression in Heaven* stresses the power of the Protestant establishment, it also incorporates the beliefs, critiques, and aspirations of those outside the establishment, especially as they took advantage of the establishment's faltering social power and moral authority in the waning years of the Great Depression. Church records and government files provide the backdrop for interwoven narratives drawn from oral histories, denominational papers, charity files, letters to public officials, union records, songs, social science surveys, and the personal records of the region's charitable and religious leaders.

When the Great Depression began, southern white Protestants stood at the peak of their power. They had spearheaded a drive for national prohibition and concluded that they possessed considerable political clout, at least on moral issues. Southern Protestants believed themselves to be the conservative moral compass of the nation, and they found it natural to take up campaigns for comprehensive education, public health, labor reform, racial reconciliation, and moral legislation. Southern churches were the only source of charity and social services for many rural people and were a significant charitable resource for city dwellers as well.

Yet the Great Depression and the New Deal transformed southern Protestantism. Religious leaders struggled to respond to a crisis that no one yet understood. Many staked their hopes at first on a great revival, confident that people chastened for their excesses in better days would turn to the church in their anguish. But the revivals did not come, and the crisis only deepened. Premillennialists declared the end near, radicals called for revolution, and both seemed to have a better grip on the sorrows of their people than did the Protestant establishment. Denominational leaders struggled to keep churches open and charities afloat, turning away many more needy souls than they helped. They clamored for the federal government to intervene.

When Franklin Roosevelt took office on the promise of abolishing Prohibition and establishing a social welfare program, southern Protestant leaders recognized the threat to their power. But the magnitude of the economic crisis had overwhelmed their resources and their ability to define poverty as a moral problem. Many remained preoccupied with a futile attempt to salvage Prohibition, but the majority of southern religious leaders praised Roosevelt for alleviating the widespread suffering and easing the burden of charity on struggling churches. Roosevelt's ability to frame the depression in moral and spiritual terms encouraged them, and many soon claimed the New Deal itself as a religious achievement.

Southerners in Congress helped to shape the region's new federal programs to the contours of Jim Crow, and white Protestant clergy often declared themselves its local guardians. Yet fissures in Jim Crow appeared as black southerners made their own appeals to the state. Black and white people who once had nowhere to turn save the churches could now take their troubles to the federal government instead. White clergy nonetheless expressed enthusiasm for New Deal relief and works programs, and they overwhelmingly endorsed the 1935 Social Security Act. For the time being, most white clergy trusted that they still held enough moral and social authority to guide the course of the New Deal in the South, while black clergy fought to ensure that the New Deal benefited their members as well.

The Great Depression and the New Deal fractured the southern Protestant establishment. Many liberals and moderates found a home in the New Deal coalition, often as agents of the state rather than of the church. They helped to shape New Deal policy and in so doing forged tenuous relationships with the region's displaced black and white sharecroppers and the Christian socialists who publicized their cause. The southern Christian left operated largely outside the region's churches, but it claimed a hold on the New Deal and pressured the Roosevelt administration to address the region's deep-seated racial and economic injustices. At the same time, members of the growing Church of God in Christ allied with mainline black activists who also pushed the federal government to address the needs of black southerners.

The conservative Democrats who made up the majority of the Protestant establishment could not decide whether the expanded federal government was their partner or their competitor, but by the late 1930s, they began to lean toward the latter. Although they maintained a strong presence in the New Deal coalition, many white baptists and Methodists turned away from reform and instead sought to preserve white supremacy in the region and in their churches. They crafted protests against federal power in terms of religious freedom and surely were surprised to find themselves in agreement with the barbs launched at Roosevelt by their tendentious fundamentalist rivals.

By the end of the 1930s, conservative elites within the southern Protestant establishment had already begun to rewrite the story of the Great Depression. No more had their churches faltered in the face of suffering, bewailing a spiritual famine and ignoring a physical one. No more had they cried out, overwhelmed by the sorrows around them, for the federal government to intervene where they could not. No more had they heralded Roosevelt's New Deal as the embodiment of biblical ideals.

Now the New Deal represented a threat to white supremacy, a danger to the very foundation of white southern Christianity. Most white Protestants would not yet abandon the New Deal outright, nor would they pull their churches away from the Democratic Party, in part because their allies in Congress had already begun to gut the New Deal's works and relief programs to fund the war. But those who suffered the least in the Great Depression's darkest years chose to pretend that no one had really suffered all that much, that there was no need for the federal government to step into a world so self-sufficient and serene that "we didn't know we was poor."

PART I

Crisis

End of October, 1929

Farm families across the Arkansas and Mississippi Delta dragged long canvas sacks between waist-high rows of cotton, plucking the white fluff from the prickly burrs beneath. A whisper of a chill in the air and the bare cotton stalks offered the clearest signs of autumn on the plantations. As the sun dipped low, families of pickers finished off their rows and made their way home. Those lucky enough to farm their own land might look forward to a supper of fresh fish or cold chicken with sweet potatoes and biscuits. Forbidden from growing food crops where cotton could flourish, many sharecroppers would settle for cornbread with molasses, dried field peas, and maybe a bite of salt pork. Perhaps those families that began the meal with a blessing thanked God for two years of good crops and rising prices. Or perhaps they prayed to end the year with a handful of twenty-dollar bills rather than in debt to the landlord or the bank. Perhaps they looked forward to the year's end and to the promise of a new decade of prosperity. The past decade had brought plummeting cotton prices, a flood that burst through the Mississippi River levees and filled the Delta like a bathtub, and a rash of deadly tornadoes that ripped through the buildings the flood left standing. The year 1930, hoped many desperate Delta farmers, just had to bring better luck than the 1920s.[1]

In Memphis, Tennessee, the Delta's commercial hub and the nation's largest cotton market, businessmen prepared for the season's last shipments of cotton. They went home to dig in to a hearty dinner, perhaps prepared by a cook who had grown up picking Delta cotton before moving to Memphis in search of a better life for her children. As they looked forward to a prosperous holiday season to follow the year of good crops, Memphis businessmen kept an eye on events in New York. The stock market dipped to an all-time low on Monday, October 29, and Memphis bankers and investors began to worry that the season would not end as well as they had anticipated. The local papers reassured them, however, supporting President Herbert Hoover's pronouncement that the slump was temporary and the markets would soon recover. Events in distant New York mattered little to Memphians, whose fortunes lay more in the agricultural market than the stock market. Like the Delta farmers whose crop they marketed, Memphis businessmen breathed a sigh of relief that the 1920s were drawing to a close. The new year and those that followed, they dreamt, would bring riches untold.[2]

For a moment, it seemed that they might be right. As the winter weather gave way to spring, farmers prepared the fields and planted the year's crop. Spring rains proved lighter than usual, and a spate of tornadoes put rural residents on edge. But it did not prepare them for the looming crisis.[3]

I

Depression-Whipped

THE SUMMER OF 1930 brought a blazing sun, a cloudless sky, and months of dust and despair. Farmers poured sweat into the earth that was not theirs as if their bodies could quench the thirsty soil and nurture the stunted cotton plants. The Great Southern Drought parched the earth from the Appalachians to the Ozarks, but it crouched longest over the Arkansas Delta, a flat expanse broken only by the Mississippi River and the low, arched spine of Crowley's Ridge. There the sun burned hot and long. The thermometer hit 113 degrees in July and stuck. Scattered clouds sometimes offered hope of rain but instead evaporated into the hot, dry air. The cotton plants hunkered low, brittle, withered. Farmers who scraped for long days at the dusty fields found little more sustenance than the cotton they tended. Even those farmers whose landlords allowed them to garden could salvage only a few root vegetables, protected beneath a layer of crumbling earth. Across the river in Mississippi, Coahoma County bluesman Son House sang, "It have been so dry, you can make a powder house out of the world." Indeed, the drought proved explosive. No crop meant no income and, for sharecroppers whose labor proved unnecessary, no shelter for the coming winter.[1]

The year 1930 brought hunger. In August, people robbed a Pine Bluff, Arkansas, store for provisions. In November, the largest banking system in the state failed, and the few farmers who had managed to save up for winter lost what they had in the bank. No one could buy anything on credit. The Red Cross stepped in to save livestock first and then freed up a few resources for hungry families. But many of the planters who administered the aid deemed hunger a lesser evil than charity. By January, tens of thousands of Arkansans were starving. Black and white farmers outside the town of England took up arms and marched into town to demand food. Thousands of Delta refugees made their way to Memphis, where they hoped they might get a bowl of soup from the Salvation Army if city officials did not chase them out first.[2]

The year 1930 brought desperate hope. "The year 1930 will long be remembered as the year of depression, of hunger, of distress, and of ill fortune," predicted the editor of Mississippi's *Ruleville Record* on Christmas Day. "Surely now we have reached the nethermost bottom of the depression that has so sorely hit us." The year was almost over, and a new year meant an opportunity to "set your eye ahead, begin over again, work and save," so that "in the end all will come right." The new year brought no better news, though, and still southerners had not hit the "nethermost bottom." A decade later, an observer in the Delta would declare the place "depression-whipped." Yet those first two years of the Great Depression proved perhaps the most shocking and the most disorienting, both for the few who had prospered in the 1920s and the many who had already lurched from crisis to crisis for a decade now. It seemed, over and over, that things could not get worse. And then, over and over, they did.[3]

"The Great Depression would not have been so bad if it hadn't come in the middle of hard times." This sober quip by a prominent Arkansan became a depression truism in the richer years that followed. Its promoters stressed the second half of the statement, that times were always hard, to argue that the depression really had not been so much different from what came before— even to claim that it bypassed rural America altogether. They did so perhaps to forget the trauma the depression brought, or to stress the greater horror of simultaneous events in Europe and the war that followed, or to downplay the fault lines in American capitalism that the depression laid bare.[4]

Taken as a whole, however, the quip was accurate. It gave the lie to a roaring twenties narrative that never made sense in rural America, where crop prices fluctuated wildly before angling downward for good at the end of the decade. The Great Depression came in the middle of hard times for farmers, for workers, for African Americans, for poor southerners. That is precisely what made it so devastating. For many Americans, the Depression was not just a story of financial ruin, because they already had little. It was a story of pain and suffering, of stunned agony. There was bad and there was worse, and the Great Depression was worse. It was deeper, longer, more all-encompassing than the precipitous dips of the unsteady 1920s. The scant sources of material assistance and social support available a decade earlier evaporated like a cloud in the Arkansas sun. "An' the people are driftin' from do' to do,'" sang Son House, "can't fin' no help, Lord, I don' care where they go."[5]

The "Middle of Hard Times" in Paris and the Plantation Country

Memphis and the Delta had a long-standing reputation as a hard place. Memphis, "the Paris of the plantation country," in the faintly mocking words of one journalist, sits atop a bluff in the southwest corner of Tennessee, bound by history, culture, and economics to the cotton country below and west of it. The Delta region broadens as the Mississippi River flows south of Memphis, where flat floodplains extend as far as seventy miles in each direction beyond the riverbanks. Memphis and its rural periphery span substantial portions of three states but operate as a coherent economic region, whose residents have for a century and a half moved across the countryside, to the city and back like the eddying river that flows through the Delta's heart. Residents of east Mississippi and western Arkansas, on poorer land outside the Delta, resented the Delta planters' growing political control in both states. Yet for the first half of the twentieth century, they were powerless to stop it, particularly because of the Delta's ties to Memphis wealth and markets.[6]

Memphis's fortunes have been intertwined with the Delta's since Andrew Jackson forced a treaty with the Choctaw and Chickasaw Indians who inhabited the region, claimed their lands, and then became president and signed the 1830 Indian Removal Act. As soon as the Choctaw and Chickasaw began moving westward on the deadly Trail of Tears, wealthy planters swarmed the Mississippi Delta and Memphis merchants began laying plank roads to haul cotton and supplies between the countryside and the rough river town that would become the nation's largest inland cotton market.[7]

The richest earth by the river remained buried beneath a dense tangle of forest and swamp, full of bears and panthers and seasonal floods. But the dark, deep, soft alluvial topsoil deposited by thousands of years of floods also extended along the river's tributaries and plains. Between 1830 and 1850, wealthy white settlers from the East Coast brought slaves to Mississippi to clear the dense undergrowth and drain the swampy bottomland for cultivation. Five times as many slaves as whites lived in the Mississippi Delta by 1850, and they worked the nation's most prosperous, vastest, and deadliest plantations. The Arkansas Delta, dominated by lumber rather than cotton in the nineteenth century, grew more slowly, but as the lumber companies cleared the land, they sold it in large parcels to outside investors. Thus, the frontier wilderness gave way to plantation capitalism: landscapes commandeered by powerful whites and remade by the toil of slaves. It was a world rife with malaria, malnutrition, and typhoid, a world built on captive labor, a world threaded with terror and violence.[8]

Memphis became a conduit and, eventually, a destination for the region's raw materials and the labor force that produced them. At first a rudimentary and notoriously violent port town, Memphis soon drew steamboat and rail traffic to link Deep South lumber and cotton to the urban Midwest and Northeast. In the 1850s, the city erected a slave market alongside its cotton market, an important step from barbarism to genteel society by antebellum white standards. Soon, German and Irish immigrants who had arrived to work the docks began to establish small businesses, and by 1860, foreign-born Memphians made up thirty percent of the city's population. A small manufacturing sector emerged, and Memphis grew steadily.[9]

The Civil War and the end of slavery seemed briefly to spell the end of the plantation empire. Freed slaves hoped that they might make some claim on the land they had cleared and cultivated, and black men anticipated access to the polls upon ratification of the Fifteenth Amendment. But Mississippi and Arkansas planters quickly re-established control over both land and labor with vagrancy laws, voter restrictions, and other legislation that circumvented the stipulations of Reconstruction and forced African Americans back to the plantations. Former slaves who resisted and dared to organize in their own defense, or who managed economic independence against the odds, faced fraudulent arrest and a hard labor sentence if they first managed to avoid vigilante violence. White Memphians and Union officials provided minimal help to African Americans who had fled to the Union-occupied city during the war. Instead, they pushed former slaves back toward the plantations with promises of pay for the same labor they had performed as slaves. Tensions in the city exploded in an 1866 massacre that followed a fight between white city police and black soldiers. Forty-six African Americans and two whites died during a three-day white rampage through black neighborhoods. Memphis and the Delta soon became a stronghold of the Ku Klux Klan.[10]

Out of this postwar context emerged new patterns that would define life in Memphis and the Delta right up to the Great Depression: a transition from slave barracks to tenant shacks on the plantation, a slowly crystallizing Jim Crow order that separated the races in new ways, a revised form of plantation capitalism that concentrated land and power in the hands of fewer and more distant owners. Many of these arrangements represented a negotiation of sorts: black workers refused to labor in gangs reminiscent of slavery and insisted on living with the families that slaveholders so relentlessly separated. They sought protection from exploitation and terror in black churches, fraternal orders, separate neighborhoods in the city, and even a few black towns like Mound Bayou, Mississippi.[11]

Yet whites held the upper hand in these negotiations, and the family-based sharecropping system that soon defined plantation labor in the region allowed black families to stay together but isolated one family from another in scattered shacks. Segregation allowed for the formation of black community on the one hand, but on the other, it policed that community, cut off its access to economic power and public services, and denied constitutional rights to a majority of the Delta's population. It also divided the black and white poor and working classes and ensured that the only employment open to the majority of black workers was in a cotton field or in the household of a white family. Thus, Delta elites created the conditions for what Greenville, Mississippi, native David Cohn called "the bitter and melancholy struggle of the poor against the poor, of poor whites against poor Negroes in an environment that had provided little for most of them and promised less so that the hungry fought the hungrier over already gnawed bones."[12]

Through all these patterns ran another. African Americans, and to some degree poor whites, sat poised on a razor's edge between hope and despair. Their fate in a given year depended not only on their own actions but also on the weather, the health of family members, the sturdiness of the mules, the absence of pests like the boll weevil and the army worm, and the honesty of the landlord. They farmed a profitable crop in lush, deep soil. The prospect of claiming a bit of that fecund earth for one's family, of attaining economic independence even against ever longer odds, was enough to keep many farmers at the plow for another year, particularly when alternatives were few. Freedom brought with it a hope not easily vanquished, a hope that echoed from pulpit and pew, from juke joint and field shout.[13]

In part, this hope reflected the gambling culture of Memphis and the Delta, and it crossed borders of race and class. Delta planters and farmers gambled on a single crop season after season and proved unwilling or unable to detach their fortunes from the cotton that had made them. Even those farmers who wished to try something new first had to break free of lenders who would support only cotton farming. Delta residents ignored the anti-gambling tirades of local preachers and played poker or cards in the evenings. Both the wealthiest and the poorest lived in a cycle of debt, either because of a bad year that left them reeling or a good one that persuaded them to go all in for the following year. Memphis businessmen, equally dependent on the Delta's white gold, followed suit. "Everybody agreed, when times were tough, that times were tough," explained David Cohn. "But they also agreed that the next cotton crop would bring high prices and prosperity. The future was an inexhaustible bank upon which we drew constantly to make up the deficits of the present."[14]

But if hope united rich and poor in the Delta, despair divided them. The hungry labor system of the region and the men who ran it traded on unattained hopes. They sent agents far and wide in the former slave states to recruit black workers and later whites too, who would abandon their worn-out farms and rocky soil for the Delta's famously deep, soft earth. During the nineteenth century, loggers cleared more of the riverside wilderness, European investors bought up vast tracts of the land for new cotton plantations, and the railroad arrived to connect the Delta more closely with Memphis, New Orleans, and other cotton markets. At the turn of the century, some Arkansas planters experimented with rice cultivation, but the region as a whole committed to the cotton monoculture.[15]

A few of the new farmers who arrived purchased property outright. Most began as sharecroppers or tenant farmers, who worked a designated portion of someone else's plantation land and accepted housing and sometimes tools in exchange for a portion of the cotton they produced. But small farmers in the Delta moved down the economic ladder more frequently than up it. Tenant farmers could rarely save enough to purchase their own plot of earth or even their own livestock. Small farm owners who fell ill or saw their season's work wash away in the floods that marked a regular part of life in the Delta too often found themselves among the landless, working someone else's soil. Meanwhile, planters and cotton corporations consolidated their holdings in the Delta, relying on the labor of the region's growing population of sharecroppers.[16]

Planters quickly learned to profit from the labor arrangement by removing opportunities for their sharecroppers to do business off the plantation. Tenant farmers could often market their own crop, but sharecropping soon became far more common in the Delta. Sharecroppers received supplies from the planter and turned over the crop to him, forced to trust that they would receive their fair share of the profit. Planters set up on-site commissaries that lent supplies and food to workers at high interest rates, and some planters paid their workers in scrip worthless outside the commissary. Sharecropping families routinely ended a year of backbreaking work without a penny to show for their efforts. Even honest planters sometimes had little profit to divide among their workers, because they in turn owed money at high interest rates to their creditors. Smaller planters in particular struggled to balance debts to creditors with payments to laborers, and the temptation to skim profits from workers was high for those who feared the loss of their own land as cotton prices plummeted. As a Cleveland, Mississippi, minister explained it, when a planter came to the end of a season facing loss rather than profit, "He can do one of two things: He can take the loss, or he can take what his tenants have honestly made for themselves." Many chose the latter, particularly since they believed that poverty kept their workers loyal. Sharecroppers who complained risked eviction or even whipping.[17]

Sharecroppers could move from a farm if they wished, but planters shared blacklists of uncooperative workers. If they owed money to the planter, then sharecroppers either had to work off the debt or leave under the cover of darkness, abandoning their possessions as they fled. Nonetheless, sharecroppers moved frequently from one farm to another within the Delta, clinging to the hope of a good season and an honest planter. Their mobility also served notice to planters that though their labor too often went unpaid and their backs too often bore marks of the whip, they were not slaves.[18]

Those who broke free of cotton country's seductive promises often sought a better life and future in the city. Although many would find their way along the Great Migration routes to Chicago or Detroit, Memphis was generally the first stop. Yet Memphis brought its own hazards. Widespread municipal corruption in the aftermath of the Civil War left the city in debt and unable to provide basic sanitation. Epidemics of yellow fever, a mosquito-borne virus that can cause kidney and liver failure, struck repeatedly in the late nineteenth century. More than half of Memphis's forty thousand residents permanently evacuated when the virus swept through the South in 1878. Five thousand more Memphians died of the disease that summer. The survivors who remained by the end of the epidemic were primarily African Americans who had nowhere else to go.[19]

In the aftermath of the epidemics, Memphis drew its population largely from the rural farmlands around it. By 1900, the city had grown to 100,000 residents, large by southern standards, and almost evenly divided between black and white. Yoked ever more closely to the Delta's raw materials, Memphis became one of the nation's largest cotton, hardwood, and mule markets. Its growing manufacturing sector produced hardwood flooring, wooden car bodies, and shoes. Memphis elites' anti-union politics and the city's large African American population guaranteed a ready supply of low-wage workers. Infamous for its regular appearance at the top of the nation's homicide list, Memphis seemed to have all the problems of a big city and few of the advantages. Despite the growth of industry, much of the city's population traveled back and forth from the countryside in sync with the growing and picking seasons, creating what writer and satirist H. L. Mencken disparagingly but rather accurately characterized as "the most rural-minded city in the South."[20]

Yet Memphis also had a thriving black business and political sector, even though most of its black residents could only find work in cotton-related industries or as domestic servants. While the black population of the city squeezed into overcrowded black neighborhoods across its landscape, Beale Street stood at the center of black life. There, Robert R. Church opened his first saloon just after the Civil War and eventually became one of the city's wealthiest landowners and the South's first black millionaire. Beale Street boasted black-owned hotels, restaurants, and shops. But it was most famous for its music. Delta-born blues flourished there, and famous singers like W. C. Handy and Lizzie Douglas (Memphis Minnie) played in clubs and on street corners. Beale Street Baptist Church, one of the city's most vibrant black congregations, stood over the business district. If weekday work, in poor conditions and for paltry wages, sapped body and soul, weeknight music and weekend dancing or worship—sometimes both—provided sustenance.[21]

The richest and poorest black Memphians all congregated on Beale Street, where gamblers and prostitutes rubbed shoulders with preachers and politicians. But there too, the city's notoriously corrupt police force descended periodically to sweep up black men and women in mass arrests, and Boss Crump's henchmen could make a person disappear forever. Those swept up in the arrests had no opportunity to protest their innocence: they had to pay a fee to the police and the judge or else pay those fines not with jail terms but with free labor in the cotton fields. Those who dared defy Crump's power, especially if they tried to organize workers or protest injustice, enjoyed no such option. They simply vanished. Memphis was an escape from the Delta and a place where an enterprising African American might have a chance, but it was no less dangerous than the countryside.[22]

In an era of famous city bosses—Richard Daley of Chicago, Huey Long of Louisiana, Tom Pendergast of Kansas City—Edward Hull Crump stood out. He singlehandedly controlled every Memphis mayor from 1910 to 1954, and he wielded enough control in the city to shape Tennessee politics and, later, the fate of the New Deal in the South. The man who ruled Memphis for the first half of the twentieth century hailed from Mississippi. Seventeen-year-old Ed Crump left Holly Springs for Memphis in 1894, and he began his first term as the city's mayor in 1910. Crump soon made a fortune in real estate and insurance, and he began to build a political coalition that took full control of city politics in 1927. He served in Congress from 1931 to 1935, but otherwise he chose to command city and state politics through hand-picked mayors, congressmen, and governors. The boss and city police took hefty bribes from the city's liquor, prostitution, and gambling establishments and allowed the Memphis underworld to thrive in exchange for its loyalty. Memphians who sought success in business, politics, or civic life first had to acknowledge Crump's authority, whether they purchased insurance policies from him, hired the men he sent their way, or promised their future allegiance. Crump consolidated power outside Memphis by increasing the city's voter turnout enough to influence statewide races. Memphis became one of the only cities in the South with a significant proportion of African American voters, because Crump's machine paid the poll tax for black and white Memphians alike and then told them how to mark their ballots.[23]

Ed Crump's control over city politics made Memphis a hostile place for dissenters, who faced fabricated fines or arrests, harassment, and outright violence at the hands of the city's law enforcement. At the same time, men—and a few women—who demonstrated their support for Crump could expect to gain a modicum of power, regardless of their religion, race, or nationality. A Democrat, Crump often allied with Republicans in city and state offices, and in 1923, he helped defeat the city's surging Ku Klux Klan in several municipal elections. African American ministers and businessmen who abided by Crump's demands could likewise expect to receive support for their own programs: Crump's machine built parks in black neighborhoods and provided jobs to the parishioners of his allies' churches. Such efforts did not extend to equal housing, city services, or employment options, but Crump paid lip service to black interests when many of his contemporaries failed to do even that. Those alliances made Memphis a simultaneously dangerous and hopeful place for black southerners in the coming years.[24]

"Stormin' Like It Never Did Before"

While Ed Crump rose to power in Memphis, large landholders consolidated their power in the Delta. Cotton farmers on the brink of despair in 1914 seemed vindicated in their single-minded pursuit of the crop as prices that had bottomed out at seven cents a pound rebounded and reached thirty-five cents a pound by harvest time in 1919. But the very next year, as wartime production ended and international supplies recovered, prices plummeted to fifteen cents a pound. An agricultural depression thus kicked off the 1920s in the Delta, and the region's economy lurched through the decade. Each year that prices dropped, farmers had to plant more of a crop to make the same amount of money they had made the previous year. But increased crop production flooded the market, pushed prices still lower, and created a surplus for the following year, dropping prices yet again, until disaster or pests reduced supply. Cotton prices shot back up to thirty cents a pound in 1923 and then fell as low as twelve and a half cents a pound in 1926. The price drop in 1926 wiped out several Delta banks, which crippled small planters, as well as religious and civic organizations, and foreshadowed what was to come in the next decade.[25]

Even the good years were hard. The high prices of 1919 should have made that one of the most hopeful years in cotton country, but instead it was one of the most terrifying. That summer, a group of black sharecroppers began to meet in a church in the community of Hoop Spur, near Elaine, Arkansas. They anticipated the high prices for cotton that year, and they also anticipated that they would once again end the season in debt to landlords who seemed always to find a way to deny them cash at the harvest. This time, they decided to protest the injustices of the white plantation aristocracy, and they organized the Progressive Farmers and Household Union of America. On September 30, in the midst of harvest season, the union met in the Hoop Spur church to discuss hiring an attorney. Armed guards stood outside to prevent white spies from hearing and reporting on the proceedings. Those spies arrived and confronted the guards, and in the ensuing shootout two white men died, one a railroad security officer and one a deputy sheriff.[26]

Local whites declared an insurrection, and a mob descended on Elaine, followed by five hundred troops dispatched by the governor. Two days later, scores of African American men, women, and children lay dead and another 285 sat in jail. Estimates of the final body count ranged from just under two hundred to more than eight hundred. The Elaine massacre resulted in part from nationwide racial tensions in the wake of a war that had armed black men in defense of their country and then returned them home prepared to defend their rights. It followed a number of white race riots across the United States that summer, as well as growing hostility to labor organization in the wake of the Russian Revolution. But it also resulted from a white Delta power structure determined to preserve its exploited and underpaid labor force at any cost.[27]

The Elaine massacre presaged a decade of routine violence against African Americans and a surge in lynchings across the Delta. Even before the Great War, Delta farmers joined the exodus of 1.2 million African Americans to the north, moving in ever-growing numbers to seek safety and economic opportunity in Chicago, Detroit, and other cities outside the reach of Jim Crow. Planters relied on an oversupply of labor, and with the departure of African Americans in the 1920s, they turned increasingly, albeit reluctantly, to white families pushed off their own soil. Still, outside the overwhelmingly white counties of northeast Arkansas, the majority of Delta sharecroppers were black. Small-scale white farmers and the black landowners who remained found it harder than ever to hold on to their property as planters and landholding corporations like the 38,000-acre Delta Pine and Land Company consolidated their holdings through foreclosure sales on their neighbors' farms. Corporations owned 8.5 percent of Mississippi farmland by 1934, most of them land banks that foreclosed on bankrupt owners. By 1930, more than half of southern farmers worked as tenants on someone else's land, but in the Delta, the tenancy rate was at ninety percent, the nation's highest (Figure 1.1).[28]

The exodus of black sharecroppers from the Delta meant a marginal improvement in daily conditions for those who stayed, because planters had

FIGURE 1.1 Plantation buildings and sharecroppers' cabins at the edge of a cotton field outside England, Arkansas. The building on the far right is a church.

Photo by Dorothea Lange, 1938, courtesy of the Library of Congress Prints and Photographs Division

to compete for their labor. During the planting season of 1927, a detailed study of eighty black tenant families on eight plantations across four Delta counties found that a minority of planters had begun to pay their tenants in cash instead of scrip, while others expanded the supplies available at the plantation commissaries. Some replaced one-room shacks with rough three-room cabins or added a coat of whitewash to existing structures. Under the management of Mississippian Oscar Johnston, the British-owned Delta Pine and Land Company imitated the welfare capitalist efforts of southern industrialists by building a school, a church, and a hospital for its one thousand black tenants.[29]

Yet more than half the families studied in this moment of relative ease suffered from malnutrition, severely deficient in protein, calcium, iron, and phosphorus. Children languished from famine-related diseases, and childhood hunger marked their parents as well. Toddlers with rickets—a disease that results from deficiency of vitamin D, calcium, and phosphorus—wobbled on bowed, brittle legs that could barely support their weight (Figure 1.2). In 1928, an estimated sixty percent of black children in the Mississippi Delta lived on less than two-thirds the minimum dietary requirement, as compared to thirteen percent of children nationally. An estimated twenty-five percent of sharecroppers black and white suffered from pellagra, a preventable disease that killed more than a thousand Mississippians each year in the 1920s. Pellagra results from niacin deficiency, and it progresses from diarrhea, skin lesions and discoloration, and confusion to dementia and, eventually, death. Even before the Great Depression, then, the Delta's tenant farmers and sharecroppers were starving to death. Malnourished families also proved more susceptible to malaria—so common in the region that it was simply known as "chills and fevers"—as well as hookworm, tuberculosis, typhoid fever, and other infectious diseases.[30]

Planters either denied that their tenants were hungry or attributed their hunger to laziness and complained that sharecroppers ate too much meat, not too little. Yet that "meat" was only salt pork, a high-fat and low-protein tissue that was all most sharecroppers could afford, apart from the game—opossum, rabbit, fish—that they could catch in the off-season. Sharecroppers grew less than half the vegetables they needed to survive the year because planters resisted granting them that rich cotton-growing soil for food crops and because vegetable gardening competed with the busy spring cotton-planting days. Even those sharecroppers who could find a patch of soil often could not find the time to grow a garden. Researchers also found that many of these expert cotton growers knew little about how to cultivate food crops for

FIGURE 1.2 This child's bowed legs, barrel chest, and rounded stomach indicate rickets and malnutrition. The child's parents sharecropped on the Wilson cotton plantation in Mississippi County, Arkansas.

Photo by Arthur Rothstein, 1935, courtesy of the Library of Congress Prints and Photographs Division

themselves. So cotton grew almost to the door of many tenant cabins, chickens often lived underneath, and there was nowhere left to plant a garden. A new coat of whitewash on a tenant cabin could not fill a hungry stomach, and it was not enough to stem the tide of weary and fed-up sharecroppers out of the Delta.[31]

Memphis absorbed many Delta refugees, and between the Great War and the Great Depression, the fortunes of city and countryside diverged. Cotton still dominated Memphis business, but the city expanded both its borders and its industrial base. The city's population of just over 162,000 in 1920 ballooned to more than 250,000 people by 1930, thirty-eight percent of whom were African American. Some of the men and women who fled the Delta sang of their woes on Beale Street, where blues singers gained fame in the wake of the Harlem Renaissance and the nationwide fascination with black music. Black politicians thrived too. Robert R. Church Jr. followed in his father's footsteps to ally with Crump and in 1916 he formed the Lincoln League, a regional alliance of black Republicans that expanded nationally three years later. Following a gruesome lynching outside Memphis in 1917, Church also founded Tennessee's first NAACP chapter, and in 1927 he helped Crump organize a coalition of black leaders to sway the Memphis mayoral election. Black and white churches and community organizations grew apace with the population in the 1920s, none more dramatically than the Memphis-headquartered Church of God in Christ. In many respects, Memphis seemed to be a city on the way up.[32]

Yet for all its wealth and growth, Memphis also remained a desperately poor city. Its homicide and infant mortality rates were the nation's highest, clear indicators of the sharp divide between rich and poor and the unlivable conditions that many Memphians endured. If Delta residents in the 1920s tipped toward despair, residents of Memphis held to a frenzied, crushing hope of better things soon to come, fed by the tantalizing proximity of vast wealth.[33]

The illusion of imminent success was washed down the hungry river in 1927. Minor flooding was a regular part of life in the region, and rising waters caused localized damage in 1912, 1913, and 1922. In the summer of 1926, rain began to fall again. It kept falling through the winter and spring and into the following summer—"stormin' like it never did before," in the words of blues singer James Crawford. From April through June, the Mississippi surged over its banks, backed up its tributaries, and burst through the levees built to contain it. Soon, 2.3 million acres of Mississippi and 5.1 million acres of Arkansas lay underwater. The flood of 1927 devastated Delta farmers black and white, and it blanketed in sludge the homes, churches, and businesses that it did not wash away altogether. At least 250 people died in the flooding, and hundreds of thousands more lost their homes and livelihoods. Refugees camped out on the broken levees for months, where they lived in tent colonies segregated by race. White refugees received the lion's share of Red Cross supplies and support. Fearful of losing their already-dwindling labor supply, planters patrolled the black tent colonies and restricted the movements of men in particular, even forcing some into fenced-in camps that provided a ready and captive workforce. Those who escaped often vowed never to return. Memphis avoided the worst of the flood's damage, and many Delta residents resettled there or left the region for good. "Heaven's angry," sang Crawford, "someone's done some wrong."[34]

But then things seemed to right themselves again. Delta farmers missed out on the twenty-cent cotton prices the year of the flood, but 1928 and 1929 were good growing seasons, and prices remained high. Even a rash of violent tornadoes that ripped through the region in early 1929 could not dim the enthusiasm of farmers who desperately needed a few good years to recover their losses from the flood. As hopes turned downward elsewhere after the 1929 stock market crash, they remained high in much of Memphis and the Delta, where cotton prices stuck at just under seventeen cents a pound. It seemed that the worst might finally be behind.[35]

"Our Children Are Crying for Food"

Spring planting in 1930 went well enough, with a few light rains. But that was the last rain for months, and the mild spring gave way by summer to one of the longest, most severe droughts in American history. The drought covered much of the South, from Virginia to Texas, but the hottest temperatures and driest days settled over the Mississippi River's now-parched floodplains, and across west Mississippi and east Arkansas. By the end of the summer, half the region's cotton was scorched dry—and cotton, a relatively drought-resistant crop, outlasted corn and other food crops, which withered and died altogether. Without a crop to harvest or food to gather, Delta sharecroppers sat with empty stomachs or lay dying of typhoid, pellagra, and other diseases that stalked the hungry. Planters could not get credit to feed their tenants in the coming months, and small farmers could not get loans to feed themselves. Even large plantations teetered on the precipice. Some collapsed. The state of Arkansas was broke and could do nothing to assist its suffering residents; Mississippi politicians refused to acknowledge that anyone needed aid at all. Arkansas agricultural officials and legislators pleaded for help from President Herbert Hoover and the quasi-public, privately funded American Red Cross, which had intervened during the flood four years earlier.[36]

Determined that voluntary self-help would resolve the crisis, Hoover held off direct aid from the Red Cross and instead offered seed loans, for which farmers had to mortgage their upcoming crop and sign an agreement to accept no other loans. But many cotton farmers could not accept Hoover's loans, because they already owed their crops to the planter or the furnishing merchant, and they also needed food and tools and livestock to start their year's crop—all excluded from the government loans. Only 22 of 5,500 Lee County, Arkansas, farmers qualified for these loans, for instance, and the proportions came out about the same in other counties as well. "Once more in its anxiety to escape 'the un-American system of the dole,'" one observer noted, "the government is falling into the curiously American system of advancing money to those who need it least. To the others it says, in effect, 'You are too hungry; therefore, we can't give you food.'" Indeed, an official with the Arkansas Extension Service warned that the state's families and their livestock faced a winter of starvation.[37]

Then, in November 1930, the Caldwell investment banking firm of Nashville, Tennessee, collapsed. The long agricultural recession and the Great Southern Drought together undermined the bank, which already teetered precariously after a decade of bad investments and fluctuating prices. The disaster spread rapidly across the South, as banks that held stock in Caldwell crumbled too. By the end of the month, seventy Arkansas banks shut their doors, most of them banks that served the hard-hit agricultural regions of the state. Altogether, Arkansas lost 134 banks in 1930—compared with an average of 10 a year over the previous decade. Mississippi lost 59 banks that year—twenty-three percent of its total. By 1932, 127 of Mississippi's 307 banks had collapsed, and with them Mississippians' meager provisions against hard times.[38]

Thus, planters who might have provided for their tenants from what they had in the bank, farmers who had scraped together a pittance each year to put toward the hope of land ownership or expansion, and churches and civic organizations that might have helped feed the hungry now saw their own savings wiped out as well. The banks that survived stopped lending to farmers, who relied on credit to get through even a good winter. "Since the landlords have no credit," one observer explained, "the tenants are on charity." Meanwhile, struggling farmers in Mississippi defaulted on mortgages and tax payments at such a high rate that by 1932, national newspapers announced that on a single day in April, "one-fourth of the entire area of the state went under the auctioneers' hammers." Each crisis seemed to spin out a new one in those hard years, with no relief in sight.[39]

The fall of 1930 had been bad enough, but winter was much worse. Farmers had already consumed their scant food crops and had none to spare for the cold months to come. The half crop of cotton that survived in the Delta brought a paltry five and a half cents a pound—less than a third of the previous year's prices. Yet planters had spurned any discussion of food aid for their workers until the harvest was in. Local Red Cross committees helped as they could, but only in December, as their fields stood empty and their tenants sat emaciated and unfed, did planters allow the agency to help. Finally, at the end of the month, the Red Cross began a food distribution program in Arkansas. Hungry families had to fill out ration cards and submit those to local committees that determined their merit before receiving the basic staples they needed to survive. Reports soon emerged of people walking miles for food, their feet wrapped in sacks, and of "frantic women begging for medical aid for babies dying of malnutrition or the many forms of disease that attack the underfed and underclothed." Some of those people arrived only to find that their townships or county Red Cross chapters had run out of ration cards and refused to provide aid without them.[40]

On January 3, a neighbor approached white Lonoke County tenant farmer H. C. Coney. In tears, she told him that her children had had no food for two days and asked, "Coney, what are we a-goin' to do?" Coney later explained that "somethin' went up in my head," and he told the woman to "just wait here. I'm a-goin' to get some food." Coney and his wife drove to the home of the nearest Red Cross chairman, who reiterated that he would not provide aid without ration cards. Coney invited the hungry men and women waiting there to join him, and with nearly fifty new companions, he drove to the town of England. There, the crowd grew larger as both the chief of police and mayor told them to wait. "Our children are crying for food," members of the crowd responded, "and we are going to get it." When it became clear that the farmers would go nowhere until they could feed their families, the Red Cross sent an agent to distribute provisions to the five hundred hungry farmers waiting. They took their rations and dispersed, but the march on England made national headlines.[41]

The England food march brought home the severity of the drought to Americans far from the hungry states. The notion that, as one relief worker put it, "people could hunger with the bountiful soil immediately underfoot" was unfathomable outside the region. City dwellers and rural elites had just assumed that farmers had "only to decapitate another hen or pull up some produce from the garden." But the hens were long gone, and the gardens cold and bare. By February, more than half a million Arkansans—more than a quarter of the state's population—relied on the Red Cross for food.[42]

Conditions in the Mississippi Delta received less attention but were nearly as dire. The Red Cross began distributing aid there in January, and by February, thirty thousand Mississippi families lined up for Red Cross rations. Meanwhile, Mississippi governor Theodore Bilbo refused to act in response to the drought, because to do so would require a special session of the state legislature, which Bilbo feared would impeach him. Mississippi had no centralized relief organization and no data on the condition of its residents. Reporters noted that the Red Cross spent about the same amount of money per month to feed a mule as it spent to feed an entire family in the Delta. Red Cross officials simply explained that "the human ration is fixed locally" and moved forward with plans to end all aid in Mississippi by March 1—long before that year's crops would be ready for harvest.[43]

A woman who worked with the Mississippi Baptist orphanage described the home's most recent additions that March. "The widowed mother was committed to the Insane Asylum," she began, indicating that the children had no other means of support. "There were three children between the ages of two and five. The youngest was so underfed and undernourished it had the rickets, could not stand alone or hold its head up, and cried constantly." When her new guardians brought out something to eat, the toddler "could not restrain herself and became frantic, trying to get the food." Her siblings were only a little better off and "displayed all the eagerness for food of children who had not had food for days." Insulated from suffering herself, this middle-class woman reported with dismay, "here were little children—babies—actually and really starving."[44]

Memphis again absorbed rural refugees, but the city offered them little. Altogether, Memphis welfare agencies reported to local papers that they cared for 45,000 drought refugees, though the Memphis Community Fund's records suggest a more modest effort. Most of those served received only a meal and, for those who fled from the countryside, a bus ticket back home because "in times like this people are better off in their own communities where they are known than as strangers in our city." Many of those who stayed lined up outside the city's hospital kitchens, hoping for leftovers, or appeared at the Salvation Army's headquarters. In December of 1929, the Salvation Army served 1,700 meals; by December of 1930, that number ballooned to 6,500. The drought and the flood of hungry men and women into Memphis continued that winter, peaking in March, when the Salvation Army served

10,250 meals. But the Salvation Army—like many of the city's agencies—primarily served whites.[45]

The city's black men, women, and children were hungry too. In April of 1931, a columnist for the local black paper described a scene he witnessed at Booker T. Washington High School, which had begun operating a cafeteria to ensure that the school's 1,800 students had at least one meal a day. The reporter noted that the school's students were in no position to be picky about what they ate and that very little food went to waste. But one afternoon after school, the reporter heard "a slight rustling" in the trash cans beside the school cafeteria. Looking down, he "was shocked to see a ragged, ash-colored little Negro boy of about seven digging in the mire of the containers." The child "had a paper box at his side and in it was very carefully placing pieces of old bread and other particles he had found . . . taking time to wipe each piece against his dusty trousers leg before depositing it." Another reporter described a fourteen-year-old who tried to steal an apple from his school cafeteria. Caught and questioned about the theft, the boy explained that his mother was dead, that his father was gone, and that the man he lived with had left three days before. He had not eaten since. City or countryside, the winter of 1930–1931 was a desperate, hungry one.[46]

BY THE SPRING of 1931, hope wore thin and rumors of revolution swirled. The region and the nation sank more deeply into crisis, even as President Herbert Hoover proclaimed yet again that the slump was over. Children who lived on topsoil deeper than they were tall strained weakly, frantically, for food, hunger twisting their limbs and swelling their hollow bellies. Youth wandered city streets in search of edible trash. More than a year after the *Ruleville Record* predicted that the region—the nation—had hit the "nethermost bottom," Americans' hopes and fortunes continued to plummet.[47]

The Delta had drawn the attention of the nation, its grinding poverty on display and its breadlines as infamous as those in New York City. "I tell you that there's sure goin' to be somethin' tearin' lose 'round here someday," England farmer H. C. Coney told reporter Lement Harris. Yet outbreaks of protest remained sporadic and unorganized. The rich and the poor, the powerful and the powerless, from the Arkansas sharecropper on up to the president of the United States, in those first bad years seemed suspended in stunned inertia. No response seemed adequate to the unfolding crisis.

PART II

Depression Religion

March to August 1931

Memphis businessmen responded to the Depression in characteristic fashion: they threw a party—an expensive, exclusive party with southern belles in hoop skirts, planters with hats and pipes, and cotton, cotton everywhere. There were galas and parades and business meetings, and a king and queen of cotton crowned to preside over it all. Like the mythic Old South it mimicked, the Memphis Cotton Carnival included only wealthy whites and their invited guests, with a few African Americans cast as slaves. Select black men were allowed to perform in a more visible role: they stood alongside horses and mules in traces to pull the floats carrying the gussied-up masters and mistresses of Memphis.[1]

The Cotton Carnival, an event modeled on Mardi Gras, represented the Memphis cotton interests' most enthusiastic effort to address the agricultural crisis swirling around them. The city's businessmen decided that demand, rather than supply, was the problem they could solve. Although Delta farmers, and thus Memphis cotton marketers and clothiers, had missed out on the meager profits of the 1930 crop because of the drought, cotton had flourished elsewhere even as demand dropped. Thus, heading into the 1931 season, ten million bales—more than half the total of an annual yield—sat unsold. Prices dropped from thirteen cents a pound at the end of 1930 to ten at planting time in 1931. The Federal Farm Board, a weak body that could only beg farmers to limit production in an oversaturated market, tried to persuade southern officials to plow under a third of the cotton crop. It failed. Where austerity fell short, Memphis businessmen believed, excess and indulgence would surely succeed.[2]

While wealthy white Memphians rode in carnival wagons pulled by mules and black men, Delta farmers harnessed their mules to the plow and dug long furrows for the seeds. The season of hunger was not yet behind, and farmers began the planting season frantic to make up the lost year. This year, the rains came and the sun relented. But cotton was at a dime a pound and dropping. Farmers would have to grow twice as much cotton as they had in 1929 to bring home the same income.

As the seeds sprouted, farmers and their families thinned the plants, built up the rows, and chopped away weeds with a hoe. Chopping cotton was hard, stooped, summer-long work, and farmers breathed a sigh of relief when the cotton grew broad enough to form a canopy between rows, smothering the weeds in darkness and bringing a brief respite from long days of labor.

Lay-by season, a moment to lay by and let the cotton mature, came in late July. White cotton flowers emerged and turned briefly pink, then withered to reveal the tight green fruit beneath. The soft, snowy fibers fattened inside, swelling and then cracking the bolls. It was a few weeks yet until the first bolls would burst open. For the farmer, it was a time to rest, to visit, to fish. This year, it was a time to worry. Prices for the hard-won white fluff continued to fall, hitting six cents a pound as the August harvest began, and falling still.[3]

It was revival season.

2

A Spiritual Famine

FIGHTING JOE JEFFERS was mesmerizing, funny, violent. No one expected him to come back that August. He had first arrived in Jonesboro, Arkansas, the previous summer to preach a revival in a big tent on Main Street, sponsored by First Baptist Church. The church was one of the largest in Arkansas, its members the elite of the community, but it was a town of ten thousand and there was inevitably some riff-raff too. A thirty-two-year-old who left behind a vaudeville career to preach, Jeffers (Figure 2.1) had gotten himself shot at twice in St. Louis when he stood over a card table and denounced gambling. He had preached the gospel by parachute over Washington, DC, and he claimed to have saved a thousand souls in a week in Oklahoma City.[1]

Fighting Joe was a big catch for Jonesboro. The summer of the 1930 drought was a desperate and idle one, and he had begun preaching at the end of June and stayed through August. Jeffers had trained with fundamentalist J. Frank Norris, nicknamed the Texas Tornado because of his penchant for fireworks in the pulpit and temper tantrums out of it. Jeffers filled the tent night after night, and the church on Sundays. In August, the sitting pastor at First Baptist left. Some church members held an unofficial meeting to elect Jeffers as their new pastor, and he agreed to stay. But others in the church cried foul, and soon First Baptist was in just the kind of uproar for which baptists are famous.[2]

By the end of August, it was clear that Jeffers's opponents would keep him out of the pulpit, and he prepared to leave town. In a parting shot to his detractors, Jeffers boasted that he had drawn twenty-five thousand people to his services in this town of ten thousand, saved four hundred, and baptized sixty. Then he left. The church called as its new pastor a young Texan named Dow Heard, who probably would have stayed home had he known what was coming.[3]

Keystone

FIGURE 2.1 Joe Jeffers, a traveling evangelist who frequented Jonesboro, Arkansas, in the early 1930s.
Photo courtesy of *Outlook and Independent*, September 23, 1931

For the next year, church members squabbled. Towns across eastern Arkansas crackled with tension through those long months: the drought persisted through winter, the Red Cross showed up only to do the bidding of the planters, sharecroppers rioted for food, and the price of cotton kept falling. The church controversy seemed to carry the weight of everything gone wrong. Business owners who took a side lost already-scarce customers. The fault lines were not clear, but many of the elite lined up behind their new pastor, while the poor tended to favor Jeffers.[4]

At the start of August 1931, Jeffers announced his return to Jonesboro. He set up his tent just a quarter of a mile from First Baptist, and it filled as before. Men, women, and children from every denomination in town, from the surrounding countryside, and from across the state line in Missouri poured downtown to hear the famous revivalist. A fiery preacher on his first visit to Jonesboro, Jeffers now declared himself a prophet and announced that the world would end in May of 1932. His proclamations drew scorn, but they also drew ever-bigger audiences.[5]

Pressed close in a tent that smelled of sweat and dirt, Jeffers's listeners learned about the evils that would bring Christ roaring back. The "dens of vice and crime" that Jeffers described were bad enough; worse were the secret sins of Jonesboro's leading lights. Between pleas for donations and plaintive renderings of "Lamb of God, I Come," Jeffers regaled his audiences with lascivious tales of Dow Heard's alleged misdeeds in Texas. If Jeffers was ambiguous about the nature of such behavior, he promised photos that were not. Jeffers also accused a distinguished local physician of murder. And in handbills posted all over town, he promised that his sermons would answer such pressing questions as "How many children in Jonesboro call Mayor Bosler 'Daddy'?" With each passing week, Jeffers's list of sinners grew longer and more specific.[6]

Though he had the bombast of a tent revivalist, Jeffers still had his eye on the pulpit at First Baptist. By September, tempers in the church were hotter than the air outside it. After a Wednesday meeting, several of Jeffers's followers abandoned the war of words and started a fistfight with members of the church who were ready to be rid of the evangelist. Local police broke them up and hauled two of Jeffers's supporters and one of Heard's off to jail on assault and battery charges. Jeffers's remaining followers marched on the jail, singing "Thy Blood Was Shed for Me." Authorities released the men and set the trial for the following day.[7]

That gave Jeffers time to prepare for his biggest show yet. Shortly before the trial began, he gathered five hundred followers on the courthouse steps and led them in song. Mayor Herbert Bosler, one of Jeffers's favorite targets, stepped forward to clear the crowd. Jeffers agreed to disperse his flock after "a moment of prayer." His moment soon dragged into several minutes, and the exasperated mayor interrupted and again asked him to leave.[8]

Head still bowed, Jeffers promptly instructed God to "strike the mayor dead with a bolt of lightning." When God did not oblige, a member of Jeffers's faction took a less supernatural approach: he punched Bosler in the jaw and knocked him flat. Two more men attacked the chief of police, who stood by the mayor's side. Rescued by a third officer, the mayor escaped and telegrammed Little Rock for help: "Thousands of lives are endangered. . . . Declare martial law now or shoot down 1,000 church members with machine guns."[9]

Governor Harvey Parnell activated several dozen national guardsmen. For four days, armed troops patrolled the streets of Jonesboro and stood inside Jeffers's tent. Five thousand people stood to applaud Jeffers as he took the platform the first evening. Jeffers glanced through his round spectacles at the men holding bayonets and machine guns in the recesses of the tent and then launched into a message on "Law and Order." The next day, an anonymous prayer aimed at the evangelist appeared around town: "O Lord, help me to keep my nose out of other people's business."[10]

For Jeffers, it was more bait. He replied with a sermon, "My Business in Jonesboro," and followed that with an even more pointed message: "Babel, Booze, Bootleggers, Preachers, Politics, and Religion." Jeffers's crowds grew larger and his list of sinners longer. He began to single out Catholics, and even dressed up as a priest and persuaded a local youth to play an altar boy with whom he mockingly dramatized Catholic rituals. One afternoon, the boy ran into the street in front of a car and was critically injured. Onlookers rushed him to the only hospital in Jonesboro: St. Bernard's, operated by a group of Benedictine nuns. The boy died that evening in their care, and soon the nuns topped the long list of Jeffers's targets. Finally, someone retaliated: Jeffers's tent burned to the ground in the October twilight after a Sunday meeting. Jeffers stuck around long enough to replace it with a rough wood structure, and then he invited his friend Dale Crowley to take the pulpit at the new Jonesboro Baptist Tabernacle and resumed his itinerancy.[11]

Revival season in Jonesboro proved magnetic to Fighting Joe, however, and in 1933 he returned with a new message. He pushed what locals called the "Jewish Israel doctrine," more commonly known as British Israelism: an anti-Semitic, British-born theology that claims whites of European descent to be one of the lost tribes of Israel. Jeffers and his remaining supporters lined up against the fundamentalist Crowley, and the two dueled from across the dirt floor in the Jonesboro Baptist Tabernacle. For weeks, they shouted out simultaneous Sunday morning sermons. When the preachers fell silent, two choirs sang competing hymns at ever-louder registers and intermittently chucked hymnals at one another. This time, Jeffers did not grow bored. He stayed while the courts worked to resolve which congregation could claim the church. Crowley won, and almost immediately he found himself in a shootout inside the church with Jeffers's loyalists, who refused to leave. Crowley mortally wounded an elderly custodian. As if he anticipated Crowley's eventual acquittal, Jeffers lit out for Florida and then California, never again to return.[12]

The tale of Joe Jeffers's adventures in Jonesboro is so outrageous that it seems almost meaningless, the kind of bizarre anomaly that could happen in any place, at any time, if it could happen at all. Yet Jeffers's four years of sporadic and dramatic sojourns in Jonesboro appear less fantastic when the landscape and people surrounding the Delta town come into focus. Perched on Crowley's Ridge and situated seventy miles northwest of Memphis, Jonesboro was the largest town in Craighead County and one of its two county seats. In contrast to most of the Delta, Craighead County was ninety-six percent white and boasted more small farms than large plantations. By the early 1930s, however, those farms were failing fast, their evicted owners now forced into tenant farming. The Delta was a region in motion, a few wealthy landowners and a few hundred professionals and small farmers the anchors in communities whose workforce shifted with the cotton season. Ephemeral and even invisible churches, traveling revivalists with widely varying theologies, and religious seasons determined as much by the height of the cotton as by the days of the week defined the ebb and flow of religious life in this region. If men—and a few women—like Joe Jeffers were not exactly ordinary, neither were they all that extraordinary.[13]

Yet Jeffers's message sparked like lightning in the dry Delta. Whether they spoke from the pulpit or between cotton fields, Delta clergy of both races had to choose their words carefully. Yankees, distant politicians, and Satan made fair targets, but preachers who spoke too plainly about injustices closer to home risked their pulpits—and if they were black, their lives. Though the vast majority of the sermons that rang across the region in those hardest, driest, most desperate years—including Jeffers's—are lost to the historical record, what remains suggests that neither big downtown churches nor short-lived tent meetings departed significantly from the kinds of messages or services they had delivered in better times. To the degree that they spoke of the deepening depression, clergy framed it as a religious crisis with religious solutions.

Such impulses played out across the nation. Between 1929 and 1932, religious leaders tried to make sense of economic and social conditions that seemed to get steadily worse even as politicians promised that recovery had already begun. The clergy often were not so optimistic, but they followed a predictable pattern: they declared that a revival of religion would propel the nation toward unparalleled prosperity. Whatever their theological or political perspective, clergy across the nation agreed on the connection between depression and recovery, punishment and redemption. A nation brought to its knees, they reasoned, would have to start praying.

This is not to say that churches had nothing to offer to their members in this moment of crisis. Clergy and church members in Memphis and the Delta, like Americans across the nation, struggled together to understand how the world had gone so wrong so quickly. Revivalism was a default response to crisis, based on the simple belief that stronger churches meant a stronger nation and on the evangelical desire to expand the fold. Some churches provided a place for people to express the sorrow and pain they experienced, to seek comfort, to fumble together toward an understanding of what it all meant and how they might get through it. If clergy failed to create that opportunity, church members often found it in fellowship with one another. Yet the revivalist message could also paper over the very real troubles people faced, stressing individual responsibility and ignoring broader social concerns.

That religious leaders at the dawn of the Great Depression judged themselves qualified to address a worldwide economic crisis is hardly surprising. American Protestantism was at the apex of its power. Despite some losses in the 1920s, Protestant churches had demonstrated a remarkable ability to shape public opinion and public structures in modern America. They faced the Great Depression as they had faced the Great War—as an opportunity to expand the influence of Protestantism and reshape the nation's fortunes. But they also faced it with deepening anxiety about their ability to control individual behavior through institutional means.

The Protestant establishment had as many critics as promoters, and Fighting Joe Jeffers belonged squarely in the former camp. Critics from the left fought to break the bond between Protestantism, modern capitalism, and sometimes Jim Crow; those from the right accused the establishment of abandoning any interest in individual salvation. Many fundamentalists, like Jeffers, contended that the Protestant establishment's ease with power was as clear an indication of the world's imminent end as a plague of locusts. But Jeffers differed from his counterparts in one key respect.

Fighting Joe named names and set dates. He picked on distant politicians, the pope, and major Protestant leaders. But he also picked on the mayor, local planters, and other members of the Jonesboro elite unused to hearing criticism from their inferiors. Jeffers recognized that a world already hard had gone even more terribly wrong. When he denounced those who suffered least and promised an end to it all, he acknowledged the unfathomable sorrow and misery of the people who stood in his tent with bellies empty of food and legs bowed by hard labor and malnutrition, their children dying of malaria and typhoid and hunger. Joe Jeffers appealed to the people of Jonesboro and surrounding farmlands because he was charismatic and daring, but also because his Protestant counterparts in the pulpits and papers rarely faced so directly the suffering before them.

Redrawing the Religious Landscape

Plantation capitalism depended on the willingness of its participants to ignore one another. "The best way I can think of to describe our lives and those of the people around us in those days is to think of our inhabiting different spheres that behaved like bubbles," recalled a white woman who grew up in Desha County, Arkansas. "There were spheres for landowners, black tenants, white tenants, et cetera, that coexisted sometimes as discrete entities and sometimes merged." The region's churches followed those demarcations, especially in Memphis and large towns like Jonesboro. The bubbles occasionally adhered to one another at revival time or at festivals, when entire communities gathered under one big tent. Even those events reinforced hierarchies of race and power, however, with distinctions among groups all the clearer as they eyed one another and then turned from one another in the shared space.[14]

Joe Jeffers understood the religious landscape of the Delta well enough to know that August was the time of year to appear, and reappear, because the region's religious life followed the rhythms of the farm and the plantation. Some revivalists arrived in the fall during picking season, when farmers were likeliest to have cash in hand. But revivals during lay-by time benefitted from warm weather and the hope of a good harvest. If the revivals went well, their effects lasted well into picking season. One Delta preacher later recalled, "[M]any times that we would be picking cotton and we would see some young person coming off the field hollering out, 'I know I have been redeemed.'" Sometimes, other pickers would "pull off the sacks and go from field to field" to preach or report on the newest converts.[15]

To the casual or distant observer, church life in Memphis and the Delta would have looked much like it did in the rest of the South. It is imprecise at best to count church members across faith traditions, as different churches report membership differently, but the 1926 Census of Religious Bodies provides an adequate overview of the region's religious distribution. Baptists and Methodists predominated among both races, composing eighty-seven

percent of the churchgoing population of Mississippi, seventy-five percent of the churchgoing population of Arkansas, and sixty-two percent of
the churchgoing population of Memphis. African Americans and white
Mississippians were likeliest to be some sort of baptist; in Memphis and
Arkansas, whites were about equally likely to be Methodist. Catholics and
Jews accounted for the two remaining largest populations in Memphis, with
about ten thousand adherents—just under ten percent of the city's churchgoing population—each. Most of the remainder of the region's believers
attended Presbyterian churches, Churches of Christ, Episcopal churches, or
one of the growing number of holiness and pentecostal churches. The 1936
Census of Religious Bodies shows a marked drop in the proportion of baptists
and Methodists, but these numbers are of little use for this region, as many
Southern Baptists and Methodists boycotted that year's count. The underfunded census takers also overlooked or undercounted many fast-growing
black denominations like the Church of God in Christ.[16]

The bird's-eye view shows the contours of the region's religious landscape,
but it captures the religious variety and creativity of the region's mobile
workforce little better than a snapshot of the ocean captures the life teeming
below. In a place where planters and merchants kept records as mendacious
as they were meticulous, many workers refused to keep any church records at
all. But for the work of a few public employees at the end of the 1930s, those
worlds obscured from prying eyes would also be lost to the historical record.

While the churches of the wealthy and middle class sat prominently in
the Delta's towns and villages, the religious world of the Delta's poor was
less visible. In part, this resulted from denominational divisions: most Delta
towns had at least one white Episcopal, Presbyterian, and Methodist church,
dominated by the middle class and wealthier community members. Black
Methodists tended to be more middle class and town centered as well. People
of all classes attended the more numerous baptist and holiness or pentecostal churches, though often in congregations divided by class—and always
divided by race. The larger towns also included a Catholic church for whites,
a Catholic mission for African Americans and Italian or Mexican migrant
workers, and sometimes a synagogue. Baptists, holiness believers, pentecostals, and independents of both races dominated the countryside, often disconnected from their parent denominations (Figure 2.2).[17]

Wealthy and middle-class residents of the region often assumed that the
migratory labor force and the working poor did not care for church because
they did not attend regular services or fill the pews of the buildings they had.
Even sympathetic observers lamented, "[T]he great masses of cotton workers

FIGURE 2.2 A black church outside Greenville, Mississippi.
Photo by Dorothea Lange, 1936, courtesy of the Library of Congress Prints and Photographs Division

are unchurched." A Presbyterian missionary in the Delta reported "ten miles square with thousands of rural people without a Church or Sunday School" and "boys twelve and fourteen years of age who had never heard the name of Christ except in connection with an oath." Certainly, many rural people—like many town and city people—chose not to attend church, but this claim was groundless. It reflected the scorn and ignorance of middle-class churchgoers regarding the faith of the rural poor, whose informal churches and distinctive religious traditions bore little resemblance to the Sunday morning services in the town churches.[18]

Between 1936 and 1942, a cadre of Arkansas researchers, trained and supported first by the Works Progress Administration (WPA) and then by the University of Arkansas, fanned out across the state with the mission of locating and documenting each of its churches. They interviewed church founders, clergy, secretaries, and members and compiled histories, often just a couple of lines penciled hastily on a worksheet, less often a handwritten page or more. These yellowed remnants of the New Deal bureaucracy thrum with life, and they crack open a window into a complex, adaptable, evolving web of religious worlds that left little visible imprint on the Delta terrain. Scattered news clippings and church histories from Mississippi and Memphis—whose congregations the WPA enumerated but did not examine—suggest that this web extended across the region, crafted primarily by the poor of both races.[19]

For poor whites, churches stood squarely at the center of this religious world. For African Americans, who had established their own networks during Reconstruction and maintained them as the new, segregated plantation order emerged, churches by turns blended and competed with fraternal orders. Segregated though they were, the churches of the mobile black and white workforce had more in common with each other than with established churches of either race. Less than twenty percent of Mississippi and Arkansas sharecroppers and tenant farmers stayed on the same plantation for five years or more, and more than thirty percent moved after only a year. Many spent the off-season or the weekends in Memphis, a city famous for its ever-shifting population of rural refugees. Men and women on the move needed a religious life that they could carry with them.[20]

"Church" for Delta tenant farmers and wage laborers often required neither an edifice nor a preacher. What they lacked in physical accommodations, they made up in theological creativity and variety. Even conservative Southern Baptist theologies appeared far too worldly to the fundamentalists who broke away because they opposed denominational centralization and the social gospel. Holiness and pentecostal churches split from baptists and Methodists, and from each other, to seek a purer and closer experience with God through ecstatic worship and separation from secular pursuits. These new churches often adopted oppositional and critical attitudes toward those outside them, belying characterizations of Delta religion as passive and dull.[21]

Religious controversies burned brightly in the Delta, and major religious movements grew from them. Charles H. Mason founded the Church of God in Christ (COGIC) in Holmes County, Mississippi, in 1907 and simultaneously held revivals in Memphis, which became the church's headquarters. William Christian established the Church of the Living God in nearby Leflore County. In Little Rock, Arkansas, in 1920, fundamentalist activist Benjamin Bogard created the American Baptist Association (ABA). The first two were predominantly black pentecostal denominations, although COGIC included white participants in its early years. Most white COGIC members departed for the Assemblies of God before the 1930s, but a few remained. The white ABA had strong roots in the Arkansas Delta, where Bogard began his career, and it continued to divide the region's white baptist churches in the 1930s. Bogard himself was a contentious and controversial figure who invited his rivals to debate him on questions of theology and practice and whose virulent anti-Catholicism rivaled that of Joe Jeffers. Indeed, Bogard's anti-Catholicism ran as deep as his racism, and both likely deepened during the 1920s when he joined the Ku Klux Klan. His aggressive and confrontational style was not unusual in the Delta, and his outspoken presence in Arkansas paved the way for men like Jeffers to sweep through in similar fashion.[22]

While the Delta proved fertile ground for new denominations, the poor and mobile population of sharecroppers and tenant farmers rarely connected with larger denominational bodies, even when they called themselves baptist, Methodist, holiness, or pentecostal. Even those who attended denominational churches often remained largely disconnected from their counterparts in middle-class and wealthy churches of the same denomination—a matter of much concern to Southern Baptists and National Baptists, whose congregations predominated in the rural Delta. Sharecroppers sometimes attended church in solid frame buildings, often funded and controlled in part by the plantation owner on whose land the church stood. Even those buildings might be baptist one year and holiness the next—or both at the same time. The difference mattered only on the rare Sundays when an itinerant pastor made an appearance, if it mattered at all.[23]

For many landless residents of the Delta, the cost of a church building was too great, both in material terms and in terms of independence. Instead, schools and vacant tenant cabins, as well as private homes or abandoned stores, moonlighted as churches and operated independently from prying employers. Brush arbors, temporary structures made of posts and branches and most often associated with slave churches, remained popular meeting places among both black and white congregations in the region. When rural workers in the Delta spoke of "church," they referred to a body of people who worshipped together rather than the building they occupied. Participants in the church service took turns leading hymn or gospel singing and prayer, and sometimes they read or recited scripture. As Delta believers moved from one such church to another, they created a common canon of song and a shared worship style that bound them together in a larger religious community even as they parted ways with a particular church.[24]

While some poor congregations considered the acquisition of property and shelter an important milestone, others declined to attend church in a building at all. Drucilla Hall, the white pastor of an Assemblies of God church in Poinsett County, Arkansas, explained to a visitor that her church had once worshipped with another organization, the Free Outside Pentecost. The Assemblies of God members, who met in a private residence before building a simple, unpainted frame church, grew frustrated with their coworshippers not over theology but over construction. True to their name, adherents to the Free Outside Pentecost "did not believe in an organized church and would not keep any records." Perhaps members of the Free Outside Pentecost—most of them probably tenant farmers—saw only trouble in record-keeping and chose to dispense with what made their daily lives most difficult: property and records.[25]

The preacher of a black church in the large town of Helena, Arkansas, explained this logic in a way that both echoed scripture and reversed the priorities of the plantation. They met in a small, unpainted building that they simply called a meeting house because "your body is the church and the house is only a place to meet." The church refused to adopt a formal name or keep records, and yet it had survived for sixteen years. Its members simply called themselves Sanctified—a common appellation for pentecostals. Their focus on the body over the building stood as a powerful critique of a world where property and production mattered most and black bodies mattered least.[26]

The Delta's working poor also differed in their attitude toward authority in the church. Some, like those who supported Joe Jeffers, rallied behind religious authority as an alternative to the plantation boss. The Church of God in Christ prized its clergy and honored their authority from the start. Other Delta believers seemed determined to avoid any religious authority at all. The Free Christian Church of Christ in England, Arkansas, met for four years in the 1920s and never called a minister. Instead, the group of black men and women who founded it "preached and exhorted" by turns—perhaps one reason that the baffled census taker who inventoried the church declared them "similar to Holy Rollers only worse." Churches like these, with fluid membership and shared leadership, often ignored the rules that governed established churches and flipped the hierarchies that shaped their working lives.[27]

In other ways, their religious choices followed the rhythm of their work, particularly when it came to women's leadership. Women in farming families planted and hoed and picked cotton, cooked meals, bore children, and founded churches. They also preached revivals and stood in the pulpit—or at the front of the brush arbor or the center of the living room. Perhaps the only consistent feature of the Delta's churches across lines of race and class was the disproportionate participation of women. Many churches, including most baptists and pentecostal denominations like COGIC, allowed only men in the pulpit, though women claimed other forms of leadership. But women like Drucilla Hall stood frequently enough in Delta pulpits to make their presence unremarkable to the WPA surveyors and to their own communities. Another white Assembly of God church in the town of Wynne organized in 1910 after a traveling woman evangelist held a revival, only one of its ten founders a man. The church grew slowly until 1931, when "two Canadian girls went through the country preaching" and stayed in Wynne long enough that the church had to build an addition. Women held leadership roles even more frequently in black churches. One of the most respected ministers among African Americans in Leflore County, Mississippi, was Cindy Mitchell, whose followers called her the Good Shepherd. Members of the Delta's Church of the Living God, the region's first holiness church, embraced founder William Christian's wife, Ethel Christian, as head of the denomination after he died in 1928.[28]

The churches of the poor accepted women in the pulpit more readily than did their middle-class counterparts, and sometimes those women gained influence and acceptance outside their small communities. Elder Ida M. Collins led white congregations in two rural communities before moving to Jonesboro in 1930, around the same time that Joe Jeffers first appeared. There she became founder and pastor of the town's Original Church of God (Holiness) mission. Despite the church's small membership of twenty-five, the local newspaper featured photographs of seventy-two-year-old Collins and her church in a 1937 article that boasted, "Church of God Is One of Most Active Institutions in City."[29]

Memphis churches followed much the same pattern as Delta churches. When they made their way to Memphis, men and women from the Delta sometimes visited one of the city's established churches, but many found a more familiar and welcome home alongside other recent and temporary migrants in its storefront, tent, and house churches. The Church of God in Christ maintained storefront locations even as its larger congregations moved to brand new buildings. New churches borne of tent revivals or conversations on the sidewalk and housed as casually as those in the Delta appealed to men and women who were on the move and uneasy in the city (Figure 2.3).[30]

The middle-class notion of church was not enough to contain the religious lives of the working poor. For the poor, the very definition of church spilled over rigid middle-class meanings of the term, and for African Americans in particular, it swirled into the other available means of community interaction and expression. Fraternal orders formed during Reconstruction weakened

FIGURE 2.3 This newsstand in Memphis, Tennessee, also featured Christian messages and art. Note the Red Cross symbol at the top, above the inscription for Peter's Chapel Baptist Church.

Photo by Russell Lee, 1938, courtesy of the Library of Congress Prints and Photographs Division

significantly and often failed during the 1920s and 1930s, but they too hosted religious meetings and helped shape and support black churches' relief work and community programs. Blues musicians, often characterized as antagonistic to organized religion, just as often imitated clergy and prodded the churches to attend to the immediate pain around them.[31]

If churches pushed black workers in Memphis and the Delta to imagine a better world, the blues provided a language and a rhythm to describe the one they inhabited. The two worked in tandem and in tension. Bluesmen like Son House and Charley Patton started out as preachers, and though their blues and preaching careers did not overlap, they bled into each other in both the style of delivery and the language of the music. The gospel music so important to black church life differed from the blues primarily in its lyrics, and sermons often took on a musical form as well. Many preachers delivered their messages in a sing-song, call-and-response style, and music leaders likewise chanted, or "lined out" the hymns and spirituals and gospel songs to be echoed by a congregation without songbooks or the education to read them. Other churches prized their songbooks. The most popular, *Gospel Pearls*, produced in 1921, incorporated hymns, spirituals, and pentecostal-inflected songs soon sung in churches all over the country. The saints danced and played instruments on Sunday mornings, as did the sinners in the juke joints on Saturday nights. Blues singers condemned the preachers, preachers condemned the blues singers, and they all damned the devil. Sometimes blues singers damned God too, but they also sang to him and pleaded for a better world even when they did not expect a response. Delta religion was no more complete without the blues than without churches, each an antagonist and accompanist to the other.[32]

Poor white believers shared with poor African Americans a mobile, oral religious culture with distinctive musical traditions. While black churches had *Gospel Pearls*, two shape-note songbooks, *Sacred Harp* and *Southern Harmony*, circulated widely among southern whites. Touring quartets taught church members how to sing and provided entertainment at all-day meetings. Some of these meetings overlapped with revivals, while others convened just for the purpose of singing together and training new song leaders in the shape-note tradition. These songs, like those in *Gospel Pearls*, provided the Delta's mobile believers with a shared tradition of song and worship that provided a comforting familiarity in each strange new home.[33]

In this multitude of ways large and small, Memphis and Delta believers and unbelievers circumvented, defied, and sometimes even mimicked the hierarchical, racially defined plantation culture of the region. They did so in ways that their wealthier counterparts often did not understand or recognize. If planters and tenants and wage laborers, black and white, inhabited separate bubbles, the bubbles of the poor proved opaque to those wealthier than them—even to the most well-meaning reformers.

Religious boundaries of class and race were difficult to bridge. A Mississippi Delta woman recalled that her mother, a prominent Methodist in the town of Sherard, "tried very hard to nurture the families" who worked at a local barrel stave mill and hoped "to assimilate them into the Sherard Church life." But the families "didn't want to come, and the establishment didn't want them either." One Delta visitor noted that tenant farmers, like the millhands, were "considered mere outsiders, and are hardly recognized as a part of the community." The churches of the poor and the not poor were different, not just in structure or standards of dress and behavior, but also in their openness to critiques of the region's power structure.[34]

The Protestant Establishment

By the end of the 1920s, wealthy and middle-class white leaders in the South's major Protestant denominations—the Protestant establishment—controlled many of the region's charitable and service institutions and much of its legislation. Yet these Protestant leaders worried that their power was under attack from immorality and irreligion on one flank, and from fundamentalist, pentecostal, and holiness groups on the other. During the previous two decades, Protestant activists in Memphis and the Delta, and across the nation, had successfully pushed for a range of social legislation, rallied support for an unpopular war, pushed ratification of the Prohibition amendment, and campaigned against Catholic anti-Prohibition Democrat Al Smith. At the same time, they had failed to maintain wartime levels of growth, squabbled incessantly about the role of church in modern society, and fallen deeply into debt. Thus, Protestant leaders faced the depression with both a strong awareness of their own importance and a deep sense of anxiety.

From the mid-nineteenth century to the Great War, Protestant leaders campaigned for a variety of progressive reforms. They argued that state and federal officials must work to regulate business, prevent labor abuses, create an educated populace, build a transportation infrastructure, ensure public health, and regulate private behavior. In the South, white Protestants also worked to build and police a society segregated by race and divided by class. Protestant leaders neither agreed amongst themselves about such reforms nor claimed exclusive responsibility for promoting progressive policies. Nonetheless, belief in the social gospel, or the notion that the church could solve the structural problems of society in preparation for the earthly return of Christ's kingdom, pervaded nineteenth- and early-twentieth-century Protestantism and helped shape the ethic and substance of progressive reforms.[35]

In the South, Protestant leaders emphasized the primary importance of individual salvation, but their rhetoric did not always match their actions. Even as they deplored the social gospel, they conceded that the church must play a role in addressing or ameliorating social injustice. More limited in scope and more hotly debated than in much of the nation, progressive reforms nonetheless reshaped southern life in the early twentieth century. The activism and support of southern Protestants, particularly the black and white women's societies that led many progressive campaigns, were essential to the establishment of public schools, public health programs, and laws controlling prostitution and the distribution of alcohol in the region.[36]

Between 1916 and 1919, Protestants' central role in shaping American life seemed secure. Americans led the way to victory in the War to End All Wars, the economy boomed, church membership grew, and the states ratified Prohibition. Although many religious people initially opposed involvement in the Great War, by 1917, American clergy enthusiastically campaigned for the Allied effort. Religious leaders described the Great War as a Christian crusade for democracy, and the churches established large missionary and relief organizations for soldiers and civilians around the world. The only major denomination in Memphis and the Delta to offer less than full support for American entry into the war was the Church of God in Christ. Though Charles H. Mason publicly backed the war effort, he also sought conscientious objector status for the church and was arrested on accusations that he obstructed the draft. Most African American denominations joined their white counterparts in supporting the war effort, hoping to win respect by acquitting themselves well in the name of democracy and Christianity.[37]

The 1919 ratification of the Eighteenth Amendment, prohibiting the sale of alcohol, seemed to provide further evidence of the Protestant churches' growing influence in American society. Protestant women, particularly members of the Women's Christian Temperance Union, spearheaded the decades-long temperance campaign, arguing that alcohol turned good men into poor workers, abusive spouses, and absent fathers. Banning the "matchless evil" would restore families and remove irresistible temptation from the weaker classes and races. White southern Methodists and baptists considered the passage of Prohibition a clear indication of their prominence in the region and importance to the nation. The churches celebrated Prohibition as an essential step toward creating a socially responsible and morally upright population.[38]

Religious leaders expected that their postwar influence would continue, and in the 1920s many denominations launched ambitious campaigns to support expanded programming in missions, education, social work, and publishing. In 1918, the southern Presbyterians played a key role in promoting a short-lived attempt to unite the missions programs of all American Protestants into one operation. The following year, the Southern Baptists consolidated their fundraising efforts into the Seventy-five Million Campaign, asking their churches collectively to pledge seventy-five million dollars to support the denomination's various agencies. The pledges came through quickly. The Southern Baptist leadership pronounced the drive a success, and they set about spending the money before seeing a dime. Confident that they were well on the way to making America a nation of Christians, if not a Christian nation, southern Protestants faced the 1920s with enthusiasm.[39]

That enthusiasm faded quickly, however, with a brief but deep recession and a corresponding dip in church finances in 1921. Postwar deflation proved particularly damaging in the South because the price of cotton and other crops fluctuated wildly throughout the decade. Churches had blown through the money pledged to them, and when receipts fell far below expectations, they blamed their members. In return, members began to complain about their denominations' perpetual fundraising campaigns. Growing divisions within some churches deepened members' frustration.[40]

Debates about the relationship between science and religion had raged among American Protestants for decades, and these debates intensified in the 1920s. Particularly troubling for theological conservatives were Darwin's ideas about human evolution and the growing popularity of Biblical criticism, which proposed reading the Bible as a historic and literary document, and not just as a religious text. Theological conservatives in the northern denominations, including baptists, Presbyterians, and the Disciples of Christ, denounced theological liberals as heretics and attempted to expel them from the churches. Because theological conservatism dominated southern churches, such debates in the region were generally one-sided, and few churches could find a liberal to expel.

The debate over evolution captured the attention of the southern churches, however, and many joined a crusade to ban teaching evolution in schools. The southern Protestant establishment had supported the expansion of public schooling in the South, and many religious leaders understood the schools to be an extension of their own work and power. They intended to control what happened in the classroom and pushed legislation to do just that. Their legal victory in the Scopes Trial of 1925 seemed hollow after a thorough defeat in the national press, however, which characterized the antievolutionists in Tennessee as ignorant hillbillies. Nonetheless, Mississippi and Arkansas voters soon passed their own antievolution statutes, an issue that further divided the states' churches. In Arkansas, the bill languished until Ben Bogard launched a campaign for its passage.[41]

If they could not agree on theology, Protestant churches could generally agree on the importance of maintaining and enforcing Prohibition. Democratic presidential nominee Al Smith's openly wet candidacy in 1928 provoked an outpouring of Protestant opposition for both Prohibitionist and anti-Catholic reasons. Southern Baptists and Methodists abandoned their long-standing Democratic allegiances and led the charge against Smith.

This time, their influence was not enough. Although Hoover won the general election in a landslide, both Mississippi and Arkansas remained loyal to the Democrats and voted overwhelmingly for Smith. Much to the joy of many Tennessee clergy, that state voted Republican for the first time since Reconstruction, led by the Republicans in the eastern part of the state.[42]

Even as white southern clergy celebrated Hoover's victory in the 1928 election, they warned of a deep moral decline in the years after the Great War. Their denominational institutions and legislative campaigns to remove liquor, police classrooms, and rehabilitate the needy or fallen were supposed to shepherd southerners toward salvation, or at least to remove the most tempting alternatives to righteous behavior. Yet the twenties brought images of young women wearing short dresses and shorter hair and of men and women skipping church because they were out late dancing and drinking bootleg liquor on Saturday nights. The New Woman and the New Negro, largely apocryphal characters in the tightly policed Deep South, nonetheless horrified southern clergy with their open transgressions of the racial and gender proscriptions that undergirded Jim Crow. As one observer explained of a Mississippi revival, the preacher "does not preach against sin. He preaches against sins, and he names them: drinking, gambling, fornication, card-playing, dancing, and stealing." The Protestant establishment fixated on the individual behaviors that it failed to control in the 1920s, and this preoccupation with personal sin shaped its initial response to the Great Depression.[43]

"Nobody Is Starving in America"

"Nobody is starving in America," scoffed Southern Methodist bishop Horace Mellard DuBose in a Christmas Day column in 1930. "To know and correct the cause of poverty is just now more important than the ability to maintain soup houses," he went on, including poverty among numerous evils that resulted from the state's failure to enforce Prohibition and moral uprightness. Nine days later, farmers outside England, Arkansas, banded together and marched into town demanding food. Their families were starving, and Americans were stunned.[44]

DuBose and other white southern Protestant leaders were neither willing nor able to see the suffering around them as a product of the Jim Crow economic system that they had worked to create and maintain and that reinforced their own power. Instead, some attributed the Great Depression to individual moral failures and a general lack of commitment to Christianity.

Others, particularly men and women who worked among the poor, worried that the wealthy lacked Christian charity but not that they profited from a system unfairly stacked in their favor. While they vaguely denounced distant greedy capitalists, their commitment to Jim Crow capitalism at home left them a limited range of responses to the Great Depression. What emerged from many southern Protestant quarters was a curious combination of denial and desperation—a refusal to acknowledge the immediacy of the sorrows before them even as they proclaimed the nation in a crisis so deep that only a wave of revivalism could save it.

So adamantly did many white southerners emphasize the importance of evangelism over charity that they spoke with little irony of the "spiritual famine" sweeping the nation at the same time that news headlines warned of a physical famine in their midst.[45] Southern Methodist leaders often took positions to the left of the region's other major Protestant denominations, but the Committee on Spiritual Interests in the North Mississippi Conference preferred to discuss physical hunger only as a metaphor for spiritual hunger. In the fall of 1931, just months after the England food riot, the committee reported, "Adversity brings most sharply to the attention of man, his spiritual dependence." And in response to adversity, "Religion should furnish a reply to the insistent demand of humanity for food for hungry souls." The committee recommended that clergy emphasize the "simple, always welcome story of Jesus and His love—His sympathy for the poor, the distressed and oppressed—His willingness and ability to help and cure and save." Despite Jesus' more comprehensive model, these Methodists determined that it was more important to save the souls than the bodies of "the poor, the distressed and oppressed."[46]

With the weapons of denial and revivalism, religious leaders faced the drought in Arkansas. Unable to do anything tangible to alleviate the environmental crisis, clergy across the nation instead weighed in on the appropriateness of praying for rain in the drought-stricken regions. Ministers across the South and Midwest followed the example of a Helena, Arkansas, Episcopalian who convened a special service in July to pray for rain after fifty-seven straight dry, hot days. It was the only relief they could offer. Lest Americans think they could simply beg their way out of punishment, religious leaders also warned that "repentance of sin" was "the need of the hour" and a necessary corollary to any prayers for rain. In September, nine nationally prominent clergy weighed in on the question "Does Prayer Change the Weather?" Only two answered in the affirmative, and renowned liberal

Harry Emerson Fosdick denounced the "crude, obsolete supernaturalism which prays for rain" as "a standing reproach to our religion."[47]

Southerners begged to differ. A Mississippi baptist declared in response, "If God cannot and does not hear prayer then the whole Bible is a farce" and blamed the drought on "the unbelief among those who claim positions of religious leadership." For Delta clergy, the drought's meaning was clear. It was "a national chastisement to make men think of Him." An Arkansas Delta baptist explained, "Many prayed for rain, but no rain came because it was not in our hearts to do the right thing by the cause of Christ." Another announced, "Nothing possibly causes man to feel his own helplessness and his entire dependence on the Lord [more] than a severe drought." Indeed, "the Lord gives or withholds rain as we may please or displease Him. . . . The present drought is one way the Lord has of telling us that our lives do not please Him." The clergyman's emphasis on helplessness perhaps betrayed his deeper feelings about the crisis—it was beyond human control, but no minister dared imagine that it was beyond God's. If God refused to let the rains fall, then there must be a good reason. Frightened and powerless clergymen announced that the drought was another manifestation of God's displeasure. Yet for all their talk of the drought as just punishment, they avoided speaking publicly of the deep suffering the drought brought, or of its disproportionate effects on the poorest farmers.[48]

While clergy prayed for rain and helped the Red Cross determine who deserved aid and who might work better with an empty stomach, Will Rogers reported at length on "a moonshine still working as a schoolhouse soup kitchen." The humorist and actor, who took a deep interest in drought-stricken Arkansas, quipped, "Even the bootleggers donate down here." He offered nary a word about similar aid from religious sources. Certainly, some churches provided assistance to those in need, and donations trickled in from around the country. But surely it stung the fiercely Prohibitionist clergy to imagine that moonshiners stepped in to help where they stepped back.[49]

Soon, however, the immediate crisis of the drought was behind them. Though the men and women who tilled the fields the following spring did so with shrunken stomachs and weakened bodies, the Protestant establishment turned its attention once again to the evils it judged most pressing and the revivals that would set things right again. Americans had gambled away their prosperity, individually in the back rooms of speakeasies and collectively in the halls of Wall Street, the clergy warned. An Episcopal priest in Mississippi suggested that Americans were better off when they had nothing left to gamble. "Was the 'prosperity' of 1929 REALLY PROSPERITY?" he asked. "Was it not rather one vast orgy of gambling in fictitious values? Money, profit quickly gained, was our national obsession." The priest concluded with his interpretation of the real meaning of the depression: "All of us, affluent and humble, share in the debasement of spiritual character caused by a prosperity induced by such means. The 'depression' is only a disclosure of realities. Now our eyes are opened."[50]

Southern clergy eagerly denounced Wall Street gambling and corruption, but few dared criticize its local version: the Memphis Cotton Exchange. The agricultural market proved every bit as much a gamble as the stock market, and trade in cotton futures—which meant trade based on projected costs of a crop that fluctuated wildly and unpredictably from year to year—particularly so. But Memphis cotton boosters only doubled down on their commitment to the crop, and to the Jim Crow capitalism it represented, as its price plummeted. In March 1931, with the enthusiastic support of Ed Crump and the Memphis Chamber of Commerce, Memphis Cotton Exchange president Everett Cook opened the city's first Cotton Carnival, its theme "The Old South." Black women could portray mammies and black men could pull floats, but otherwise only elite whites participated. The Cotton Carnival grew only more popular each year, and Memphians turned out in large numbers to watch its parade, one of the only events open to the public. When a local black dentist took his family to watch and asked his nephew what he thought of the event, the child replied, "I didn't like the parade, because all the Negroes were horses."[51]

Cook and Memphis Chamber of Commerce businessmen trumpeted the Cotton Carnival as a secular festival that would bring people to the city to spend money and buy cotton. Yet the Cotton Carnival spun off exclusive secret societies, re-enacted Old South weddings, brought in black choirs to sing spirituals, and displayed all the features of a southern civil religion built on the Lost Cause. David Guyton, a white Southern Baptist layman, banker, and English professor in Mississippi, wrote a paean to cotton later that year that demonstrated the way that white residents of Memphis and the Delta wove together their Christianity and their commitment to cotton culture. "We who strut in silk and satin, While their weavers feast and fatten" Guyton wrote, are "Worse Than Weevils"—referencing the boll weevil that decimated cotton crops across the South. "We can eat it, we can wear it, If we have the wit to dare it," he wrote. "Cotton stands our sole salvation. In these times of tribulation." He concluded, "Let us bear our cotton banners, Shouting, singing glad hosannas, Till they float from every steeple, O'er a proud and happy people." The Cotton Carnival might have been a secular event, but it was also a clear reflection of what Memphians—at least white, wealthy ones—most valued. Indeed, it represented a corporate parallel to the region's religious revivals.[52]

Too broke to initiate new campaigns that required any outlay of funds, southern denominations quickly discovered that they could promote revivalism at minimal expense. Like their parishioners, clergy struggled to make sense of the pain that surrounded, and sometimes engulfed, their communities. Some confronted that sorrow and wrestled with questions about a racial and social order that allowed it, but more fought to define the suffering itself as redemptive. Thus, many clergy nationwide and even more in the South continued to campaign for religious revivals to end the depression. The Southern Presbyterians declared 1932–1933 their "Evangelistic Year," encouraging ministers to focus on "straightforward evangelistic preaching" and instructing each church to conduct at least one weeklong revival. Southern Baptist leaders in Arkansas informally encouraged their own rallies, proclaiming repeatedly that their deeply indebted state convention was in the midst of "mighty tidal waves of revival."[53]

The revivalist enthusiasm among members of the Protestant establishment in the early 1930s transcended political and theological boundaries, marking a rare point of agreement between social gospelers and social conservatives, evangelicals and liberals. Even some modernists who had advocated a rational religious faith and declared revivalism dead spoke in abstract terms of awakening deeper religious feeling, which might happen in union meetings or seminary classrooms rather than under circus tents or in open fields.[54]

The emphasis on revivalism as a primary response to the depression did not always preclude discussions of more concrete policy solutions or social action among church members, but it distinguished religious solutions from social ones and privileged the former. At the end of the summer of 1931, a Southern Methodist minister warned, "We look for a political upheaval in this nation within a year or two ... [caused] by such ordinary and fundamental things as hunger, cold, and want ... and the maddening absurdity of poverty in a land reeking with wealth." But this minister dared push no further, proposing a solution that required no action from human quarters: "The congealed and frozen assets of wealth must be melted down by the warm rays of the Son of Righteousness." Only "a revival of pure religion" would "lift the clouds and let the sunlight of a better day shine upon us." The minister did not explain how his weather metaphors translated to the political scene, but his message was clear: only a revival could prevent a revolution.[55]

Clergy across the nation cited historical precedent for the connection between depression, revival, and recovery. The nation had endured periodic depressions since the Revolution, most recently in 1921. Those depressions generally proved brief, and religious leaders attributed their end to religious revivals. Roger Babson, a Massachusetts entrepreneur and evangelical beloved among southern Protestants, linked both the first and second Great Awakenings to economic crises, and he published a chart mapping a series of peaks and valleys in the nation's economic health over the course of the previous two centuries. He also mapped the peaks and valleys of church attendance in several major denominations. Lo and behold, he found, the two rose and fell in tandem. Thus, he concluded, depressions were caused by falling away from church, and in turn caused people to return to church. Babson explained, "Just as a great spiritual awakening followed similar conditions in previous times, so a great spiritual awakening is now ahead. All signs indicate that America will soon again be swept by a spiritual revival."[56]

Although Babson did not publish his complete study of depressions and revivals until 1936, the notion that depressions bred revivals was widespread by 1931. The following year, the former governor of Arkansas assured the state's Southern Baptists that the Great Depression would not last long. "These panics occur with startling regularity every 10 years," he contended, counting off the years in intervals: "1837, 1847, 1857, 1873, 1893, 1907, 1914, 1921, and 1929-32." He offered a long list of economic causes of the Great Depression, capped with "the tendency of people in times of prosperity to forget God and follow off after false gods, even as the children of Israel in ancient times worshipped the golden calf." The depression, therefore, should "spur us on 'toward the mark of the prize of our high calling in Christ Jesus.'" The governor instructed his listeners to "strike the three letters 'die' out of the word 'depression', leaving as our shibboleth the inspiring motto, 'Press On.'" The depression, he concluded, was a test of Americans' faith in God, which they would soon prove by filling the churches to overflowing.[57]

The white southern Protestant establishment clung to the revivalist response to the depression in the early 1930s as threats to its carefully constructed social order materialized from every direction. Shaken by the England food riot, by rumors that Communists were trying to organize southern African Americans, and by the ongoing collapse of southern agriculture, white Protestant leaders doggedly insisted that southerners must turn to religion rather than radicalism to recover. "We cannot deny the ghastly fact of economic evils," conceded one Southern Baptist. "But false or inadequate economic measures are fruits, rather than roots of evils that have come upon us. They are symptoms, not causes." The depression would end when a "deeply penitent and full-throated return to God" ushered in "an era of greater prosperity that will be both spiritual and material." Unable to offer a clear program for reform as it had done with Prohibition in 1918, the Protestant establishment simply insisted repeatedly that religious revivals were the first step toward economic recovery.[58]

From Social Gospel to Socialist Gospel

Revivalist language and rhythms permeated the lives of Memphians and Deltans, and residents of the region outside the Protestant establishment also spoke of the Great Depression in terms of redemption and revival. Yet many African American Protestants, Catholics, and other dissenters had no illusions that a nationwide religious revival would alone ease their woes. They spoke more pointedly and frequently of the suffering that surrounded them, and they demanded a response both within the church and without.

"Man's extremity is God's opportunity," declared an African American Methodist in Mississippi at the end of 1931, as he described how the drought and depression had crippled the churches' work in his district. "In the midst of good times, many people usually forget God. But many now see the folly of it all, and are ready to hear what God has to say about things." The language sounded similar to that of white Protestants in the period, and indeed, many African Americans who lived on the margins of the Protestant establishment argued that the most urgent need of the depression was to return to God. But what they thought "God has to say about things" in the Jim Crow South was often quite different from what their white counterparts thought.[59]

Black Protestants followed the same revival seasons and sometimes even attended the same revivals as whites. But their members were likelier to turn to one another for aid, and many had established informal networks of support alongside formal networks like fraternal orders and women's societies. Though they had to speak carefully when offering even implicit critiques of the region's segregated economic order, few African Americans had much desire to protect that order. They did not deny the suffering before them, but instead wove it into their songs, their sermons, and their relationships. Some spoke forcefully about the sources of their troubles.

Recalling the previous winter's misery, one black Methodist expressed concern about the coming winter during the warm summer months in 1931. "The populace will be shivering from cold, and the army of millions of unemployed will be augmented by other millions who will want, but can find no work," he worried. Particularly aware of African Americans' difficulty in finding work during a depression in an economy that prioritized white workers, the church member asked, "Isn't it better to give the people work at good wages than to drive them to desperation and crime from hunger? The jails can't hold them all, and our foolish capitalists seem not to have thought of that." Though they risked more than their white counterparts when they questioned the Jim Crow order, African American religious leaders nonetheless proved more willing to criticize the "cold blooded capitalism" that "ignore[d] human values and service" and judged people only by their race and riches.[60]

Catholic leaders too offered an energetic critique of capitalism in general and southern capitalism in particular. In 1931, Pope Pius XI issued *Quadragesimo Anno*, an encyclical that denounced unregulated capitalism and Communism as equally unjust and called for the state to take control of social reform. The encyclical provided Catholics in Memphis and the Delta with the impetus and the language to speak clearly about the necessity of reform. Shortly after the release of the encyclical, a Little Rock priest wrote "Capitalism is quite evidently on trial and should put its house in order." At the very least, he continued, "The capitalist system prevalent in the majority of the civilized world today is due for a thorough housecleaning." Particularly in Arkansas, where virulently anti-Catholic fundamentalists like Joe Jeffers and Ben Bogard were more numerous than in Memphis and Mississippi, Catholic leaders tended to be circumspect in their critiques of capitalism, and they conceded to the dictates of Jim Crow. Nonetheless, they made space to acknowledge sorrow and suffering and to speak in terms of immediate experience, as well as to call for action. They also spoke clearly and frequently about the depression as an economic crisis rather than just a spiritual one.[61]

What Catholics said carefully, a group of southern Christian radicals proclaimed loudly and forcefully to all who would listen—which for a time, was virtually no one. As the economy collapsed around them in the early 1930s, Americans from a range of political perspectives questioned the viability of capitalism. Many proposed to reform the system by regulating the distribution of wealth or the relationship between capital and labor. Christian socialists instead anticipated capitalism's demise and scorned the "cheap and futile optimism" of the Protestant establishment, which encouraged "people to smile and rejoice without prompting them to think profoundly upon the tragic aspects of life and to engage in its difficult tasks." A tiny coterie of socialists and Communists in the South claimed theologian-activist

Reinhold Niebuhr as their guide in crafting a radical Christian critique of modern America.[62]

Niebuhr argued in 1932 in *Moral Man and Immoral Society*, "Human society will never escape the problem of the equitable distribution of the physical and cultural goods which provide for the preservation and fulfillment of human life." Yet the Christian must nonetheless fight social and economic injustice. Niebuhr, a socialist at the time, further argued that "Marxian politics" were "identical with the most rational possible social goal, that of equal justice." Two of Niebuhr's southern students at Union Theological Seminary in New York, Myles Horton and James Dombrowski, joined forces with several students of social gospel advocate Alva Taylor during the early 1930s.[63]

A Disciples of Christ minister and professor at the Vanderbilt School of Religion, Taylor encouraged his students to become involved in interracial organization and labor activism. Taylor believed earnestly in the importance of the labor movement, which he termed "the zeitgeist of humanitarianism surging up through the social order to set free the last and least of men from the leftovers of the slave system." Taylor argued that Jesus, "the real progenitor of democracy," should be "at the head of these vast, marching columns of labor that are moving on to claim their part in the common heritage of the earth." He encouraged his students to become involved in the South's fledgling labor movement, a kind of activism that proved transformative for many of the young seminarians.[64]

During the early 1930s, four of Taylor's students, Don West, Howard Kester, Ward Rodgers, and Claude Williams, concluded from their work with southern churches and labor unions that capital denied black and white southern workers their basic human needs and civil rights. All four men embraced Christian socialism, and West and Williams also flirted with Communism. Kester formed a close friendship with Niebuhr, who drummed up support for his work when he joined Claude Williams and Ward Rodgers in the mid-1930s to support the Southern Tenant Farmers' Union.[65]

Meanwhile, in Memphis and the Delta, radicals kept quiet. After the 1919 Elaine massacre, a local form of black nationalism had swept the Delta, and rural workers signed up as members of the Universal Negro Improvement Association, led by Marcus Garvey. The movement died in the 1920s, but black Deltans held to a strong tradition of resistance. Arkansas had also been home to a small but active Socialist Party unit since the early twentieth century. Its numbers grew, mostly among whites, and increasingly included Delta residents and African Americans, in the early 1930s. In Memphis, members of a Jewish fraternal order, an Episcopal priest, and a group of college professors supported Socialist and even Communist political candidates and in 1932 helped organized the Unemployed Citizens League of Memphis, a short-lived cooperative society with socialist principles. Crump's response was swift and fierce, and the group's organizers fled town. But only when the homegrown radicals in Memphis and the Delta joined forces with the Christian radicals from Vanderbilt later in the decade did they link religious principles with political activism in a way that gave meaning to the growing troubles of thousands of Delta sharecroppers. The leftist Christian framework that blamed capitalism for the depression and proposed socialism as the just alternative proved powerful to suffering Americans in many parts of the nation. It would soon gain ground in Memphis and the Delta as well.[66]

The End of the World

For Christian radicals and dissenting liberals, the prescription for a rotten social order was to rebuild a new one from the ruins of the old. But for many residents of Memphis and the Delta, there was nothing to salvage. Mississippi Bluesman Son House captured the sentiment of drought-stricken poor black and white Deltans in "Dry Spell Blues." "Well, it has been so dry, you can make a powder house out of the world," he sang of both the severity and potential explosiveness of the drought. "I stood in my backyard, wrung my hands and scream/And I couldn't see nothing, couldn't see nothing green." A preacher before he sang the blues, Son House did not deem the church worth mentioning when he sang, "Hard times here an' everywhere you go/Times is harder than ever been befo'." The church was no help, but God might be: "Oh, Lord, have mercy if You please/Let your rain come down and give our poor hearts ease." Son House prayed for rain with one breath and doubted it would come with the next: "Oh, it's a dry old spell everywhere I been/I believe to my soul, this old world is bound to end." The song is a lament, a catalog of hardships, a desperate prayer for relief, and an acknowledgment that the future was in God's hands.[67]

Son House, Joe Jeffers, and many clergy in fundamentalist and pentecostal churches took seriously, and often shared, the hunger and fear that pervaded Delta life in the early 1930s. Many preached that such suffering signaled the world's imminent end. While mainline clergy tried to balance prayers for rain and calls for repentance with business as usual, prophets of the apocalypse stressed the unique struggles of the day. Son House's songs, Jeffers's sermons, and the end-times musings of many Delta clergy gave voice and meaning to

Delta residents' sense that they were in the midst of an unprecedented and uncontrollable catastrophe.

Premillennialist theology provided many Memphians and Deltans with space to acknowledge suffering and an explanation for the crises multiplying around them. By the 1930s, this newer theology had begun to replace post-millennialism in the region. Postmillennialists, who predominated in the nineteenth century, anticipated a millennium of progress toward Christian ideals before Christ's return. Premillennialists believed that Christ would return before the millennium, defeat an antichrist, and then establish a king-dom on earth. Although they often disagreed about the timing and nature of those events, premillennialists shared an emphasis on human depravity and the imminent return of Christ, first to punish the world and then to perfect and rule it.[68]

Independent and pentecostal churches in the South embraced premillen-nialism, as did many baptists. The theology surged during the Great War and held steady in the 1920s. The 1929 stock market crash, combined with chaos in Germany, Bolshevism in Russia, and Fascism in Italy, seemed a fulfill-ment of prophecy. Conservative critiques of capitalist greed and corruption, along with a host of new potential antichrists, provided ample fuel for the newfound fire in prophecy belief. In 1931, Philadelphia Presbyterian Donald Grey Barnhouse launched a monthly prophecy magazine, *Revelation*, which applied prophetic scripture to current events, and Texan John R. Rice soon followed with *The Sword of the Lord*. Prophecy novels, which offered mor-alistic, fictionalized accounts of the end times, appeared during the 1930s as well.[69]

Whereas wartime premillennialism focused on international events, depression premillennialism paired an international focus with an emphasis on domestic troubles. An Arkansas Church of Christ member wondered "if [the depression] is not one of the vials of wrath being poured upon the world as a just punishment for the sins of which we have been guilty." This specula-tion drew on a literal reading of Revelation 16, each of seven vials of God's wrath bringing mass suffering and chaos.[70]

Premillennialism flourished more in white churches, but African American pentecostals and some baptists embraced its premises as well, even as they maintained deeper commitments to postmillennialist-oriented social and self-help organizations within the church. A member of the Church of God in Christ recounted an apocalyptic vision that incorporated the passage from Revelation 16. The woman and her husband were walking down the road when she looked heavenward and saw "an exceedingly large and bright star." Soon, "an exceedingly large man stepped in front of it." The man leaned forward, "pointed his index finger towards the earth, then he would raise his hand palm upward as though being filled, then he would empty it on the earth." The man repeated the motion "6 or 7 times" before the woman "heard these words, that he was pouring out the wrath of God on the earth." The vision ended with the man "enveloped in smoke." God had made it clear that he would soon punish a sinful world, the woman warned. Prophetic visions like this one made future punishment as real as present suffering and demonstrated how much worse life could be without downplaying how bad it already was.[71]

Premillennial imagery vividly captured the misery and fear that many people felt at the start of the depression, and the notion of the economic crisis as the first sign of apocalypse soon made its way beyond the men and women who believed strictly in premillennial theology. In 1932, James D. Vaughan, songwriter for the premillennialist Church of the Nazarene, offered his own interpretation of the crisis in "No Depression in Heaven." Vaughan described the depression as evidence that the end was nigh: "For fear the hearts of men are failing/For these are latter days we know/The Great Depression now is spreading/God's word declared it would be so." The chorus sang of heavenly reward: "I'm going where there's no Depression/To the lovely land that's free from care/I'll leave this world of toil and trouble/My home's in heaven, I'm going there." In heaven, there would be "no hunger/No orphan children crying for bread/No weeping widows, toil or struggle/No shrouds, no coffins, and no death." But on earth, "the dark hour of midnight nearing" meant "tribulation time will come" to "sweep lost millions to their doom." Vaughan's song became popular across the South, particularly after the Carter Family recorded it in 1936. The song gave voice to suffering and sorrow, even as it promised an end to both. Premillennialist language thus became a part of southern culture, even for those southerners who did not embrace the elaborate end-time predictions of apocalypse devotees.[72]

For the most part, premillennial predictions and prophetic visions tied national and international events to scripture, but the 1930 drought briefly put the Delta at the vortex. Perhaps this was part of Jonesboro's fascination with Joe Jeffers. The evangelist had a knack for making scripture immediately and locally applicable. Jeffers predicted that the end would come less than a year after his 1931 trip to the Delta town, yet he found it of utmost importance to ferret out every local instance of immorality. When Jeffers accused local leaders of sins of biblical proportions and declared it essential to cleanse the town before Christ's return, he not only vindicated his followers' frustration with the authorities but also made their small Arkansas town an important player in the last days. Jeffers did not expect his flock to sit on their hands and wait for the end. He expected them to clear the way.[73]

While many Protestant clergy responded uncertainly to the Great Depression, premillennialists declared it the work of God and explained how men and women of faith should respond. They were not a fatalistic bunch; indeed, some suggested that it was the rest of the world that remained suspended in inaction. "Those who are waiting for the world to be converted will be caught in the tide," warned a Mississippi baptist. Unlike their postmillennialist counterparts, the premillennialists knew they did not have long to act: "The end of this age is approaching; and we should warn the people. But they will not heed." The closer the end, the more urgent the need was to pluck to safety those few who might listen.[74]

Premillennialists appealed to suffering Americans in the early 1930s in a way that many other Protestants did not (Figure 2.4). Premillennialists found cosmic meaning in the Great Depression, they set to work denouncing sin and demanding repentance before it was too late, and yet they still had the satisfaction of knowing that the men and women who caused trouble on earth would soon face punishment. While the Protestant establishment proposed a way out of trouble, premillennialists like Jeffers engaged with the troubles and the sorrows of those around them as they sought evidence of the world's end. In this way, depression-era premillennialism took on a militant, almost radical edge. For the time being, the emphasis was on personal salvation more than political revolution—after all, Christ would come soon enough to lead the revolution himself. But the acceptance of suffering and the social critique implicit in premillennialism lent it a widespread appeal that only grew as the depression wore on.

When Joe Jeffers stood on his rough wood platform and enumerated the failings of local preachers and professionals, he voiced a bitterness that others dared not. He did not tell his listeners that they were fine, or that things would soon be right again. Jeffers arrived at that rare moment each year when farming men and women had time to lay down their tools and face their sorrows and their fears. His messages were no balm but instead salt for wounded souls. He cast a wide net, and he undoubtedly captured some fair prey. But he targeted Jews and Catholics as well, and he stressed the salacious over the serious. He also embraced that most damnable of all the Delta's evils: the Jim Crow capitalism that arbitrarily designated some souls worthy and others worthless.

FIGURE 2.4 This photo shows an open-air meeting of Pilgrim Holiness Church, Blytheville, Arkansas. On the platform stand several of the church's organizers and its first minister, who left for a nearby church in 1940, and his wife, who took over as pastor upon his departure. The congregation later bought an old Church of God to house their services.

Photo from the Arkansas (WPA) Church Records, courtesy of Special Collections, University of Arkansas Libraries, Fayetteville, Arkansas

Others who scorned the Protestant establishment's response to suffering in the first years of the Great Depression offered deeper understanding. Many premillennialists—particularly the poor men and women who held one another up in their shared sorrow—treated the broken body and the wounded soul as one and acknowledged both. Black and white radicals and some southern liberals beheld the pain around them and demanded that white southerners recognize the segregated economic order that caused it as the root of the region's sin and degradation. They fought for a peaceful revolution, a more just social order.

Men and women in the pews and the missionary societies that gave the Protestant establishment its heft also suffered drought and hunger and loss, or reached out to those who did. Yet the southern Protestant leaders who spoke with the greatest confidence and to the broadest audiences often closed their eyes to the deepest pain. Many sought to protect their own power, their churches and their fortunes bound inextricably with the segregated economic order they had helped to build. Others could not fathom how things had gone so wrong so quickly. The future was uncertain, the present bewildering. Revivals provided a touchstone, a path many Protestant leaders believed showed the nation's surest way out of trouble. Revivals also served a practical purpose: they won souls for heaven, and they won donations for religious agencies that could provide physical relief to the suffering. But soon many of those would be gone too.

3

Where to Send People for Help

"DEAR REV. BISHOP," wrote Kate Abraham in March of 1933, "I lost every thing that I own the house which I live in caught a fire." A member of Greenwood's Syrian Catholic community, Abraham asked the Mississippi bishop for "anything that you will do to help me." Abraham doubtless understood the church's solicitude toward widows and their children when she explained, "I haven't got nothing to eat and no body help me, my husband have been dead eleven years." She pled again, "me and my son is starving to death, my son have to go to school without breakfast and dinner."[1]

Bishop Richard Gerow referred Abraham's request to her priest, Father John Clerico. Clerico replied immediately and defensively to warn Gerow that Abraham "quite exaggerates her conditions. Besides she has been given help by her own people, Syrians, by the Red Cross, by the R. F. C., and I too have been fleeced one way or another at different times." Clerico reported that Abraham had also received aid from Leflore County, written to the governor of Mississippi for help, persuaded a local Southern Baptist minister to write to the Extension Society on her behalf, and appealed to the Knights of Columbus in nearby Greenville. "I do not say all this to cool down your charitable feelings towards this party," explained the priest, "but to the credit of those who have been doing for her. Many people here are in difficult conditions, and I do not know that she is any worse than the others." According to her priest, Kate Abraham had appealed to nearly every public and private source of relief available in the Delta, and still she asked for more.[2]

By the time Abraham wrote her letter, neither revival nor relief had come. Religious organizations struggled to bear the burden of need in the region even before the depression began. Now many collapsed under that weight. Between 1929 and 1932, one third of private relief agencies in the United States folded. The demands on mutual aid societies and religious groups that served their own members likewise proved crushing. Clergy like Father Clerico grew weary of turning down pleas for assistance even from those people they judged worthy. His frustration with Abraham's case was not just that he believed she exaggerated her suffering—it was also that so many others suffered too, and no one could help them all. Religious leaders like Clerico continued to proclaim the need for religious renewal, but they also began to seek new ways to provide for the needs of the body as well as those of the soul.[3]

Since the end of Reconstruction, southern Protestants had claimed some responsibility for helping those at the bottom of the capitalist economy, while the region's Catholics and Jews worked to provide for their own communities and for many outside them as well. Even as they emphasized the primacy of evangelism, black and white religious societies in the region established orphanages, hospitals, schools, and settlement houses. Women's organizations fed and clothed local families, determined especially to reach the widowed women and fatherless children they deemed particularly vulnerable. Black denominations and fraternal orders built on a long-standing tradition of uplift and mutual aid, working sometimes in cooperation with white agencies and sometimes in defiance of them. White denominational and nonsectarian charities in Memphis and the larger Delta towns embraced relationships with professional social workers and municipal and state social agencies in the 1910s and 1920s, but even those relationships generally reinforced voluntary bodies' central place in charity and social service. Because southern charity followed the dictates of Jim Crow, the limited public support available went almost entirely to whites. In the rural Mississippi and Arkansas Delta, which lacked organized charities and municipal relief, churches were the primary—often the only—places where those in need could turn.[4]

Kate Abraham's desperate plea to her bishop and the defensive response from her priest together illustrate the breakdown of private and religious relief in the early years of the Great Depression. Religious aid organizations, denominational charities, and church members who provided informal assistance to struggling community members had neither the infrastructure nor the will to meet the growing needs of Americans. Conditions in Memphis and the Delta were particularly dire and public resources there virtually nonexistent. In addition to the drought in the Delta, the nation's unemployment rate surged from just three percent in 1929 to twenty-five percent by 1933. Several of the region's major Protestant denominations and the entire state of Arkansas teetered on the brink of bankruptcy, and the Memphis Community

Fund—which centralized the city's charitable fundraising—faltered as need soared.[5]

The places with the fewest public services did not compensate for that lack with private aid. Indeed, Memphis and the Delta ranked near the bottom of the nation in both public and private support for the needy. The region's wealthier residents and policymakers proved indifferent to the suffering around them and readily described poverty as a necessary part of the region's low-wage economic system. Local churches and charities failed to keep up with need even in good times. Now, as the depression dragged on, those organizations encountered a flood of new demands from once-healthy men and women who could not find work or even a place to live and whose families faced starvation. The numbers and needs of the poor and suffering grew too rapidly to ignore. Yet to acknowledge them was also to acknowledge the inability to help them. Homeless, widowed mothers like Kate Abraham found little support even in better times, and by 1933, her voice was just one in a chorus of desperate pleas for assistance. The Great Depression thus exposed the inability—and often the unwillingness—of religious and voluntary organizations to address the suffering that surrounded them.

As a result, the Great Depression prompted a new openness among the members of private aid organizations to a federal role in social service and reform. Now, southern religious activists began to join the black leaders and white liberal reformers who had long pushed the federal government to help the poor. As President Herbert Hoover continued to promote the piecemeal forms of voluntary aid that characterized his response to the 1927 flood and then the Great Southern Drought, southerners of both races pushed the federal government to do more to address the crises of unemployment, hunger, and displacement that threatened to unmake the nation. Indeed, discussions among religious leaders increasingly focused on how, and not merely whether, the federal government should intervene in the deepening crisis.

"A Taste of Charity Is as Dangerous as the First Shot of Dope"

The newfound interest in federal aid marked a sharp departure from southern church leaders' response to the crises of the 1920s. Then, in a social environment that often counted charity a greater evil than poverty and suffering, those who stepped in to help often had to defend the minimal resources they offered. Just after the 1927 flood, the head of Nashville-based Goodwill

Industries, a Methodist home missions organization that provided jobs for "the needy, the handicapped, the unemployed" in workrooms and stores where they repaired and sold used goods, sent out a plea for donations. Goodwill's slogan, "Not Charity but a Chance," encapsulated much of the southern progressive approach to social services in the years before the Great Depression. The organization's head took pains to distinguish Goodwill from a charity, explaining, "The further away from charity we get the surer we feel of our ability to be of real service to the individuals and families with whom the Goodwill comes in contact." Lest that message seem too soft, he clarified his point: "a taste of charity is as dangerous as the first shot of 'dope.' Therefore, we should not subject anyone unnecessarily to anything so dangerous."[6]

White, middle-class southerners deemed charity—particularly in the form of direct financial support for those in need—a threat to the social order. They inhabited a capitalizing and industrializing society built on the notion that anyone who worked hard enough could succeed and that labor itself was a sacred pursuit. Many southerners believed that the poor could blame only themselves for their suffering. The only assistance they deserved was assistance finding God, who would make them productive members of society. Public charity in particular galled middle-class and wealthy white southerners, who regarded it as a tax on the hardworking to support the shiftless. At their crassest, warnings about the addictive and demoralizing consequences of charity masked a defense of capitalism and a fear of losing control of workers—particularly nonwhite workers—who tolerated inhumane conditions only because they had no alternative.

Even progressives and advocates of social Christianity, like the Goodwill Methodist, often characterized dependence as a consequence of charity as much as of poverty. They pointed to the injustices of the industrializing Jim Crow South to describe poverty as a social rather than an individual evil and charity as a temporary necessity on the way to dramatic social reform. Yet these reformers repeatedly characterized even temporary charity as addictive. Rather than helping the poor get on their feet, they imagined, a single donation might instead render them unable or unwilling to lift a finger to help themselves and their families. It might even undermine the desperation that drove people into demeaning and dangerous work—though some progressives deemed this a positive outcome. Only with careful monitoring and correction would recipients of charity find the motivation to pursue better, more wholesome lives for their families. In other words, the poor could not possibly make the right decisions about how to spend money without coaching and supervision from the middle class. Even if social and economic ills created poverty, they also degraded the poor, who without help would drink too much alcohol, have too much sex with too many people, and abandon their families for lives of degeneracy and violence. Thus, progressives and advocates of social Christianity deemed it necessary to save both the individual and the social order.[7]

The aftermath of the Civil War set the stage for a distinctly white and southern vision of charity, welfare, and social reform. Whites in the South demanded broad public support from the Confederate states during the war. In the war's wake, both public and private relief agencies poured into the region from the North to aid recovery and to protect African Americans from the southern whites who resented their freedom. Northern missionary societies helped cities and towns rebuild and provided charity to both black and white southerners, while the Freedman's Bureau represented the federal government's most comprehensive effort to help former slaves transition to freedom. The bureau provided rations, clothing, and education to former slaves and to many whites and also worked to help African Americans find work at fair wages.[8]

When the South forced a formal end to Reconstruction in 1877, the states pared public aid to a minimum and the federal government curtailed its protection of African Americans. Only a few forms of public support survived in Memphis and the Delta: prisons and correctional institutions for juveniles; poorhouses, which housed indigent, elderly, and disabled people; asylums for the blind, the deaf, and those deemed insane; and pensions for Confederate veterans. Confederate pensions, correctional facilities, and some asylums operated at the state level, while counties and municipalities supported poorhouses and local asylums. The South's only real form of welfare went exclusively to white men who had fought in the war and, when they died, to their wives. The remaining burden of relief fell to private and religious charities, which proliferated in southern cities like Richmond and New Orleans, and to a lesser degree in Memphis, but were sparse in the countryside.[9]

Shut out from everything but prisons and poorhouses, African Americans in the postemancipation South quickly developed new resources for mutual aid and protection. Between 1865 and World War I, black fraternal orders created burial and mutual aid societies, while women's clubs and women's societies in the churches established networks of community support, built schools and hospitals and children's homes, and worked to provide some protection from white violence and intimidation. In an increasingly hostile atmosphere for black southerners, these organizations advocated for the safety and basic rights of black families, fought against lynching, and sometimes joined with white reformers to push for public health and sanitation measures that affected city dwellers of both races. Although fraternal orders and women's clubs often operated apart from churches, their memberships overlapped and their immersion in religious symbols and themes demonstrated the power of religion in everyday life.[10]

Black churches and welfare and self-help networks often divided by class. In an effort to carve out a livable world within the confines of the hardening and violent Jim Crow order, many black middle-class reformers policed the behavior of poor blacks. The small and increasingly threatened black middle class adopted forms of respectability and religious restraint that defied white caricatures of African Americans, and they pushed poor black southerners to do the same. Black workers resentful of middle-class meddling in turn formed their own mutual aid societies and community networks, the poor aiding one another as best they could. Thus, complicated class relationships, alongside a constant battle for survival and a measure of justice in an unjust system, shaped southern African American forms of charity and social activism.[11]

White southerners too developed a form of social Christianity, albeit with a lot more handwringing. In the aftermath of Reconstruction, white churches denounced the northern social gospel, which attributed poverty and suffering to systemic social problems rather than individual failings and therefore worked toward both individual and social salvation. But as the South's cities and towns grew, its industries expanded, and its plantations too followed a capitalist labor model, the region's religious and community leaders struggled to balance a sense of individual responsibility with their growing unease over the exploitative working conditions of industrial and agricultural capitalism.[12]

In particular, members of women's clubs and church societies demanded basic protections and services for children and mothers whom they saw as the most innocent victims of the industrializing order—and whom they wished to keep at home, together, in an attempt to preserve an idealized white family. While these women often remained skeptical about direct charity, they worked to reduce the need for it. They spearheaded fundraising drives to establish schools, hospitals, orphanages, and settlement houses. Memphis's largest and most elite women's club, the Nineteenth Century Club, supported two settlement houses where young white working women in the city could live. The club also pushed for better working conditions for white women and spoke out against child labor. In 1907, club members even supported a telephone operators' strike—likely a controversial decision given their husbands' prominent roles in industry.[13]

Clubwomen and members of denominational societies like the Southern Baptist Women's Missionary Union soon campaigned for a range of reforms to regulate working conditions, prevent industrial child labor, censor movies, promote temperance, enact municipal sanitation procedures, and prevent lynching. In 1913, the Southern Baptist Convention established a Social Service Commission, which, like its southern Methodist and Presbyterian counterparts, issued proclamations on current events. Even as they emphasized the primacy of evangelism to the church's mission, then, white southern churchgoers worked to bend the region to their own religious and racial ideals.[14]

Black and white churchgoers also worked to fill the significant gaps in basic health services. Perhaps because of their history of disease and disaster, Memphians devoted disproportionate energy to medical care. The city rebuilt its antebellum hospital in 1898, and the new Memphis General Hospital included wards for black and white patients. In the 1920s, Memphis added separate children's and maternity hospitals. The hospitals accepted a limited number of charity patients in addition to paying ones, the city's only serious effort to address the needs of the poor. Memphis also proudly promoted the Cynthia Milk Fund, an innovative program that provided fresh cow's milk or canned milk to poor infants and children of both races. In a public–private collaboration, the City Health Department took over distribution of the milk in 1921, while the *Memphis Press-Scimitar* and the community fund paid the bills.[15]

In 1911, several small Memphis medical programs merged to create one of the nation's largest comprehensive medical schools. By 1920, Memphis also boasted Southern Baptist and Catholic hospitals, as well as an Episcopalian institution for crippled children, and in 1922, the Methodists chartered a large hospital to serve the tristate region. The white denominational hospitals served only white patients, so African Americans built their own. In 1909, the National Baptists opened a small infirmary, and the following year the Colored Methodist Episcopal Church opened Collins Chapel Hospital. Both accepted patients from all over the region—a necessity, because the Delta provided no hospital care for African Americans until 1928, when the Afro-American Sons and Daughters, a fraternal society, established a hospital in Yazoo City. Whites had more options. In 1913, the King's Daughters, a nondenominational women's society, opened its first hospital in Mississippi. The state's Southern Baptists founded their own hospital in Jackson in 1914. Arkansas Catholics had built that state's first hospital in Little Rock in 1888, and in 1920 it became the first in Arkansas to earn federal accreditation.[16]

Churches and synagogues in Memphis and across the South also built schools, children's homes, nurseries for working mothers, and community centers, along with institutions designed to reach juvenile offenders, pregnant youth, and elderly men and women. The latter institutions often worked closely with public courts and sometimes received public funds. For instance, the juvenile court system in Memphis might send children to the city's industrial school, to a state facility in Nashville, or to the Memphis Convent of the Good Shepherd. The latter provided medical treatment for venereal disease and promised a moral education to girls deemed delinquent or deficient. In the first years of the twentieth century, such casual relationships between public—particularly municipal—and private aid proved common in the region. The two operated in tandem rather than in competition.[17]

This patchwork of progressive institutions allowed reformers and skeptics alike to claim that southerners now cared for their own. They could point to new hospitals and new schools, as well as a patchwork of efforts to accommodate the region's poor. Yet those institutions remained sparse and underfunded, able to serve only a fraction of the population. Schools and hospitals benefited the middle class most, while poor African Americans and rural whites could rarely access any structural assistance at all. Some reformers saw this as a problem to solve; others disagreed. Providing too much comfort to the poor—or any at all—still seemed a far more dangerous proposition than simply letting them suffer.

A New Era of Cooperation

The Great War marked a temporary shift in focus for American believers from reform at home to reform abroad, and after the Allies' victory, the churches parlayed their dramatically expanded wartime work into peacetime institutionalization and consolidation. The National Catholic War Council, convened to drum up support for the war effort and to train military chaplains, became the National Catholic Welfare Council. The Federal Council of Churches joined with the southern Presbyterians to turn its wartime efforts to expand missionary and relief operations around the globe into the ecumenical Interchurch World Movement. Southern Baptists promoted their Seventy-five Million Campaign, declaring that they needed only five years to raise that sum for missions and other denominational work. In 1925, they also established the Cooperative Program, a centralized agency to coordinate funds and work for the denomination's previously distinct missions, education, and service programs. Methodists, Presbyterians, and Catholics expanded their work at a comparable rate, making the 1920s a period of dramatic institutional growth for the churches.[18]

Southern African Americans also worked to build schools, maintain settlement houses, and support their communities, although they faced declining church membership as black southerners moved north and west to pursue jobs and justice. Some denominations took advantage of the Great Migration, however, as their relocated members demanded new churches in their new homes. By 1926, the Church of God in Christ, unrecognized by the 1916 Census of Religious Bodies, claimed 733 churches in thirty-three states and a burgeoning foreign missions program. Its controversial resistance to the Great War seemed prescient during the isolationist 1920s. Whether or not they had supported the war effort, black and white churches anticipated that their wartime growth in numbers and influence would continue indefinitely, and they launched their postwar programs with expansion in mind.[19]

In the South, the postwar years also marked a period of increased interfaith and interracial institution building. Middle-class black and white Atlantans formalized a series of interracial meetings into the Commission on Interracial Cooperation (CIC) in 1919. Concerned about postwar race riots, the moderate CIC soon had state branches across the South working to connect members of the black and white middle class and to craft their ideal of a kinder, gentler Jim Crow. The CIC became a primary means through which middle-class African American and white churches collaborated in charity and reform. In 1920, heads of women's organizations across the South convened in Memphis for the Women's Interracial Conference, at which several prominent black women spoke about the difficulties of living and working in a separate and unequal world. The women concluded the meeting with the creation of women's committees in several state branches of the CIC. They collaborated on health and child welfare reform as they slowly worked toward the larger goal of finding new ways to work together against lynching and racial violence.[20]

Businessmen led the charge for much of the postwar institutionalization of charity in the South, even though women in the churches and in social work continued to provide most of the legwork and much of the fundraising. In the decades since the Civil War, businessmen had sold the churches on the importance of following a corporate model, with its centralized authority, discrete departments, and emphasis on efficiency. Now, many southern charities also followed the example of their northern counterparts and consolidated under umbrella fundraising bodies often promoted by municipal chambers of commerce. These Community Chest programs centralized fundraising for disparate charitable and social work organizations and in many cases linked together Catholic, Jewish, and Protestant welfare groups and institutions. In Memphis, where the briefly resurgent 1920s Ku Klux Klan reflected resentment toward the city's successful Catholics and Jews, Protestant reformers weighed their religious and ethnic prejudices against the clear evidence that Catholics and Jews did a much better job of caring for their own communities.[21]

In 1920, Catholic, Jewish, and Protestant businessmen and social workers together established the Memphis Council of Social Agencies, which coordinated the work of forty white social service organizations in the city. Men ran the council, while women dominated its social and community work. The Industrial Welfare Commission, Memphis's version of the CIC, operated as the city's African American social service clearinghouse, but its leadership focused more on racial harmony than on serving those in need. In 1923, both groups joined the Memphis Community Fund, established to include a diverse range of religious, civic, and municipal charities and reform agencies in a single philanthropy. Like similar organizations across the nation, the community fund further consolidated the fundraising appeals of its member agencies and worked closely with the chamber of commerce to enhance the city's benevolent image. It also operated the Social Service Exchange, which tracked the names of aid recipients and the services provided them. Administered independently, the Memphis Federation of Jewish Welfare Agencies, the Salvation Army, the Good Shepherd Convent, the city's Children's Bureau, and a score of other agencies agreed to fundraise through and report to the community fund.[22]

Memphis and the Delta remained disproportionately dependent on private and voluntary aid and social services as compared to many American communities, even compared to some southern cities like Richmond, Virginia, which boasted robust public agencies. Nationally, public relief spending outpaced private aid by a ratio of three to one, but public welfare in Memphis and the Delta remained limited to veterans' benefits and the same institutions that predated the Great War. Private charities thus maintained a central role in the region, though they too ran chronically short. In 1929, for instance, the total per capita expenditure on both public and private aid in Memphis was just forty-one cents, as compared to a national median of eighty-seven cents. Yet even at that low rate of charitable aid, Memphis outpaced other major southern cities like Houston and Charlotte. With rural areas factored in, the South's average level of aid was only twenty-nine cents per capita. In Memphis, just over sixty-eight percent of relief funds came from private sources. Veterans' benefits were not calculated as relief, so Mothers' Aid for dependent children represented the only significant public expenditure.[23]

Indeed, the most significant development in public aid in the postwar years was the spread of Mothers' Aid funds, enacted in all but three states nationally—and in all three in this study—between 1911 and 1930. The women's groups and reformers who promoted Mothers' Aid stressed the importance of keeping families intact and argued that widows and other single mothers deemed morally fit must have some help caring for their children. Social workers evaluated the eligible mothers before permitting them assistance to ensure "that the home shall be a satisfactory place for the rearing of children," thus providing another means of middle-class control over poor women's lives. Arkansas, Mississippi, and Tennessee Mothers' Aid laws left it up to individual counties to raise money for their own residents, and the juvenile courts worked with local social workers to administer the funds. But rural counties almost always opted out.[24]

Reformers defended Mothers' Aid as a necessary and carefully policed exception to their concerns about direct charity. They argued that these stipends would keep children who had a living parent out of the orphanages. Reformers also hoped to place children without living relatives in family rather than institutional settings, again reflecting an increasing emphasis on the centrality of the family to a functioning society. Yet southern legislatures and county relief offices gave little more than a nod to such arguments. They established Mothers' Aid programs but funded them at such a low rate that they often existed in name only.

In Memphis, Mothers' Aid funds proved grossly insufficient to meet the proposed aim of keeping families together, and in the Delta they generally proved altogether unavailable. At only $4.33 per family per month, Arkansas offered the nation's lowest allotments for qualifying mothers, and not all counties participated. By comparison, Massachusetts, the best-funded state, supported families at a rate of $69.31 a month, and twenty-two states met or exceeded the median rate of $21.78 per month. In Mississippi, where grants averaged $11.11 per month in 1931, only 110 children in the entire state—and in only three counties—received assistance at all. Memphis participated, but selectively. "The Mothers Aid law now operative in many states has done much to keep parent and child together," noted the community fund's leaders in 1931, but they admitted that they did not have the resources to transfer orphans from institutional to family care, and indeed, orphanages remained a central part of the fund's work for years to come. Only 111 families in the city received Mothers' Aid, and they averaged only $30 a month each. Thus, while Mothers' Aid set an important precedent for the provision of public relief, it complemented rather than replaced the charity provided by private agencies—as Kate Abraham's petitions to both public and private agencies indicate. For black mothers in Memphis and the Delta, Mothers' Aid was not complementary. It was irrelevant, because once again they were excluded. Black women who received aid might not serve so cheaply in the homes of the white women who relied on their labor.[25]

Such resistance to improving the lot of the suffering in the South remained widespread. If many Americans seemed unusually cooperative in their attempts to expand charity and consolidate religious and community work after the Great War, many more wanted nothing to do with cooperation of any sort. Organizations such as the Memphis Community Fund and the Interchurch World Movement ran into opposition almost as quickly as they coalesced. Even as progressives expanded their numbers and influence, a conservative, isolationist response gained momentum. The Interchurch World Movement failed by 1921, its fundraising efforts inadequate and its participants divided by incompatible visions of social reform. The Southern Baptist Seventy-five Million Campaign met its goal in pledges in 1919, and the denomination quickly began to allocate the promised funds. A recession in 1920–1921 left a thirty percent gap between pledges and receipts, however. The Women's Missionary Union was the denomination's only organization capable of honoring its financial commitment. The Southern Baptists struggled with debt for the remainder of the decade. While some Baptists found ways to continue building schools and hospitals, others complained about the church's fundraising campaigns, bureaucratization, and emphasis on charity at the expense of evangelism.[26]

In Memphis, the community fund met with similar problems. The fund survived the rising tide of nativism and anti-Catholicism during the 1920s, but it dealt with frequent complaints from Protestants that Catholics and Jews received more than their fair share of charity dollars. Community fund workers pointed out that they distributed funds to member charities in the proportion raised from them, that Catholic and Jewish agencies raised more funds, and that those agencies provided a disproportionate share of charity in Memphis to individuals outside their communities. For instance, St. Peter's Orphanage housed two hundred children from a range of religious backgrounds, although the sisters who ran the orphanage provided a Catholic upbringing. The Jewish Neighborhood House housed a well-baby clinic that served both Jews and non-Jews who did not get adequate care at the city's hospitals. The Council of Jewish Women provided other services to non-Jews as well. In 1932, the women established a summer school for poor children that included a hot lunch, a physical exam, and weekly weigh-ins. "There are McGuires, Gianinis, Kellys, Cohns, and Schneiders," reported an observer impressed with the ethnic diversity of the school where "all creeds meet." The observer also reported that during their first four weeks at the school, those hungry children each gained an average of two pounds.[27]

Apart from the minimal services that Jews and Catholics provided, black Memphians too received only the proportion of funds that they raised, their needs often invisible to the community fund's all-white operators. In 1927, only three percent of the fund's outlay supported the category of work designated "Negro Welfare," even though African Americans made up nearly forty percent of the city's population. In 1929, the Industrial Welfare Commission disbanded, leaving the community fund without an African American service agency until 1932, when it established the Community Welfare League, a new division led by black officials. Interracial cooperation, conservative and limited as its aims were, remained little more than an ideal even for the most progressive Memphians.[28]

The community fund also struggled to raise enough money to cover operating costs for its member agencies. It met its fundraising goals in 1923, the year it was founded, a feat it accomplished only once more in the next eighteen years. In 1927, in the wake of the Mississippi River flood that brought thousands of Delta refugees into the city, the fund's fundraising efforts fell so far short that it had to plead for emergency contributions from the city and county to cover the difference.[29]

The campaigns and consolidations of denominational and interdenominational charities and reform organizations in the postwar decade enabled churches to offer social programs that might not otherwise have been possible. At the same time, those programs often proved unsustainable even in relatively prosperous years, and their struggles exacerbated growing ideological differences over the church's primary role in society. They also reflected the middle-class, business-oriented perspective of their organizers, who blamed the poor for their own condition and sought to correct their petitioners rather than to understand them. As a result, they proved as generous with advice about the behavior of aid recipients as they were parsimonious with charity. Charity, they still believed, would likelier corrupt than help the poor, the broken, and the hungry—as dangerous as "the first shot of dope."

"Putting Off the Lord's Cause"

The stock market crash of 1929, the subsequent wave of bank failures, and the drought in the Delta threatened to render the debate over charity moot, because it seemed no one had anything left to give. Charities, churches, and synagogues faced drastic financial losses that forced an immediate re-evaluation of priorities. Southern churches and denominations had expanded their charitable work in the 1920s with borrowed money, and now they counted on members to come through in hard times with pledges they had made in better days. Like many of their members, the churches went deeply into debt on the expectation of an ever-expanding economy. They faced a shock at the end of the decade when credit dried up, offering plates returned empty, and pledges went unmet. Unable to maintain the depth and breadth of their charitable, educational, social, and evangelistic services, church leaders and church members now eliminated even work they considered vital.

Southern religious leaders continued to hope that God would save their religious work from ruin, but conditions only worsened. The collective declaration that "the material depression will never be lifted except on the basis of a spiritual revival" reflected religious leaders' sincere belief that American society was morally adrift. It also reflected the reality that the churches could not continue essential efforts. Between 1929 and 1932, national income dropped by more than fifty percent. Wage earners' income sank by sixty percent; salaried workers' by forty percent. Until 1933, church giving held steady as a proportion of national income, but a fifty percent loss nonetheless proved crippling. The Southern Methodists, the region's second-largest white denomination, actually saw a small but steady increase in offerings between 1924 and 1930, but between 1930 and 1933, the denomination's total contributions plummeted. More ominously, the churches cut benevolent spending by more than fifty percent, while cutting congregational expenses forty percent. When the money ran out, the churches turned their spending inward, not outward.[30]

The Methodists had started the decade on relatively solid footing; the Southern Baptists and the National Baptists, the two largest denominations in the region, were in debt from the start. The Southern Baptists had operated at a deficit throughout the 1920s, but that debt ballooned by 1930, particularly after the treasurer of the Home Missions Board embezzled $900,000 and fled to Canada. Soon, the denomination cut home missions to the bone, recalling all but 160 of 1,600 men and women who worked in African American schools, on Indian reservations, and in city aid agencies. Southern Baptists also slashed foreign missions and education funding, and they stopped providing support to troubled state-level denominational agencies.[31]

In 1931, Southern Baptists announced a twenty-five percent decrease in total denominational resources from 1928. The president of the convention admitted, "We are putting off the Lord's cause while we try to settle with our other creditors." It was no accident that the president ended his humble plea by calling for a "great, profound, searching revival" to "fill our coffers with money, our schools with students, our pulpits with men afire with God and our pews with people imbued with the spirit of love and sacrifice which was in our Lord Jesus Christ." For those already in the pews, the Southern Baptist Convention devoted some of its meager resources to publishing a series of bulletins on "Tithing in Hard Times." The denomination just had to find money somewhere.[32]

In Memphis and the Delta, state and local associations fared even worse than national and regional bodies. The National Baptist Convention of Tennessee stopped funding all missions and education programs in the early 1930s—the two functions the denomination described as most essential to its mission. The hospital it had opened in Memphis in 1909 closed. The denomination almost lost Howe Institute, which had already absorbed Roger Williams College, the church's other school for ministers. The African American Northern Methodist district of upper Mississippi—a relatively middle-class denomination—reported a seventy-five percent drop in giving between 1927 and 1931 and provided no funds to church-supported Rust College, which also nearly folded during the depression.[33]

In Arkansas, the Southern Baptists lost $54,000 in a bank failure, defaulted on 1931 bond payments against their million-dollar debt, closed two of the state's four denominational colleges, and spent the decade focused on paying its creditors rather than aiding its members. In many cases, its creditors *were* its members, some of them poor women and men who had believed investing in their church to be a safe choice. "I was foolish to ever trust anything said by churches," complained one bondholder, who along with the rest settled for a return of thirty-five cents on the dollar, finally paid off in 1938.[34]

Women's clubs, fraternal orders, and social agencies lost ground as well. Memphis's influential Nineteenth Century Club had 1,400 members in 1926, but by 1929 its membership lagged, those still enrolled stopped paying their dues, and the organization retreated from its reform work. Fraternal orders peaked in influence in the late nineteenth century, but many had already collapsed in the two decades before the depression, leaving members without the services they had purchased. Other orders remained active but in the 1920s lost ground to corporate insurance companies like the Universal Life Insurance Company in Memphis, one of the city's largest black-owned businesses. By 1935, researchers in seven Arkansas counties who examined ten plantations and ten rural communities found that seven communities had burial associations and two had insurance societies, but that only one fraternal order remained. It "offered death benefits but no other activity." For rural Delta residents, there were few places left to turn for help.[35]

Just as the churches and mutual aid societies were going broke, their charitable institutions and social services faced growing demand. Orphanages, for instance, housed not only orphans but also children whose parents could not care for them. With few day nurseries or other forms of childcare available, many working mothers, widows, and parents with more children than food relied on orphanages for temporary care and feeding of their children. Demand increased dramatically with the drought and widespread starvation. If separation from one's child was difficult, watching that child die of hunger was far worse. But even in the relatively flush 1920s, the region's orphanages were inadequate, sometimes dangerous places plagued with reports of abuse and neglect and operated with little outside oversight.[36]

The worst orphanage disaster of the decade happened just before the depression began. The Industrial Settlement Home, a private African American children's home and reformatory in Memphis supported by several local churches, burned to the ground in August 1929. The home received children from the juvenile court system, and its matron had an upstanding reputation in the city. Yet just days before the fire, the fire marshal had declared the house a fire hazard and warned the matron that she must evacuate within a week or face eviction. The fire began early on a Sunday morning when the children were still in bed, and though the matron reported to the responding firefighters that all the children were accounted for, they were not. Eight of the orphanage's youngest charges, boys from two to six years old, died huddled together in a second-floor bathroom. "The fire didn't enter the room," the local paper reported, "but it was just like they had been put in an oven."[37]

Only in the ensuing investigation did the public learn that the home had been declared a fire hazard and that it was so overcrowded that children regularly slept in closets and bathrooms. Doctors found many of the eighty surviving children to be chronically malnourished. They also discovered scars marking their backs and reported several unusual cases of ankylosis of the fingers—swelling and stiffness that in this case resulted from partially healed sprains and fractures. Reports soon surfaced that the matron had punished unruly children by twisting their arms behind their backs or pinning down their hands to pound them with the heel of her shoe. A fifteen-year-old girl new to the home soon confessed that she had set the fire to escape a beating. In the ensuing trial, the secretary of the Tennessee Children's Home testified that the surviving children told her the matron had whipped them merci-lessly, burned them with hot pokers, and forced them to stand barefoot in glowing ashes.[38]

Perhaps it was in part because of the Memphis orphanage disaster that St. Raphael's, an Arkansas Catholic home opened in 1932 to house black orphans, failed even in the depths of the depression. White denominations throughout the Delta reported that their children's homes were bursting at the seams, and some worried that few similar institutions were available for orphaned black children. But St. Raphael's closed in 1937 because of "the unexpected difficulty in obtaining orphans." The 150-bed facility housed only twenty-two children when it shut down, and church leaders concluded that "blacks, unlike whites, were unwilling to place their children in an insti-tution run by whites whom they did not know or trust and operated by a Church they did not belong to." The legacy of slavery was strong in the Delta, and the Catholic Church was weaker among African Americans in Arkansas than it was in Mississippi. Black Arkansans were justifiably suspicious of the treatment black children would receive at the hands of white strangers. African American families also proved much likelier to take in orphans on their own. One Mississippi extension agent working on a nutrition study in the Delta noted offhandedly, "[T]he majority of negro homemakers will usu-ally find a place for another child, will accept him, and treat him as one of their own." Indeed, the eighty families she studied had taken in a total of twelve children. In this way, African Americans kept children in their com-munities from contact with institutions they distrusted.[39]

Abuse in white children's homes also proved common. The Mississippi Baptist orphanage in Jackson endured its own scandal on the eve of the depression. In the summer of 1929, a neighbor of the orphanage phoned one of its trustees to report that one of the older girls there had been badly beaten. The trustee investigated, and the girl reported that the superintendent had punished her for failing to scrub pots and pans. The man grabbed his young charge by the neck, attempted to choke her, and finally hit her so hard with a board that it snapped in two. In a separate incident in October, a con-cerned relative reported that two of the orphanage's matrons had beaten her sixteen-year-old niece. Lucile Cochran had angered the matrons by arguing with other residents of the orphanage, and the matrons responded by shaking and slapping her. Deeming her unsuitably repentant, the two women then whipped Cochran with a leather strap. A group of Baptist women who came to investigate later that day examined Cochran. They reported that "one side of the lower back part of her body was almost a solid mass of black and blue bruises, and that on other parts of her body were red streaks showing where the blood had been drawn, where the edge of the leather strap would strike." In January, a grand jury in Hinds County indicted the orphanage superintendent for administering excessive corporal punishment. Baptist leaders also fired the matrons responsible for Cochran's beating.[40]

Denominational leaders then considered the matter closed. Some Southern Baptists even suggested that Cochran and the other girls "made a serious mistake in disrespecting authority and not giving ready obedience, this contributing a large share in bringing about this ugly situation." Their solution: kick the older children out of the orphanage. Meanwhile, the orphanage superintendent retained his job until April. When further details about the two beatings emerged, an outcry from church members finally pushed the orphanage trustees to request the superintendent's resignation. Perhaps the orphanage strengthened its standards and oversight in the following years, but its proudest claim in 1933 did not bode well for the children who remained in the Baptists' care. Looking for the silver lining after the orphanage's money vanished in a bank failure, the new director emphasized its efficiency and boasted that his facility "is operated cheaper than any other similar Home in the South."[41]

In the early 1930s, reports from even well-functioning children's homes proved grim. They took in as many children as they could but turned away still more. St. Raphael's in Arkansas seemed to be the only exception to the overcrowding. Father Clerico, the Greenwood priest, requested room for three children in Mississippi's white Catholic orphanage in March 1930. Bishop Gerow replied, "I have been refusing many, many applications of late simply because of the crowded conditions of our orphanages. I believe in the last two months I have refused on an average of a child every two days." When they could make room for new children, many homes became increasingly strict about admitting those who had surviving family members who had cared for them in better times but deemed them too burdensome when times were hard. Children's homes also turned down children who were too old, too young, too sick, or too difficult. Just as the proportion of hungry, homeless, and unwanted children in Memphis and the Delta soared, the institutions that once would have taken them in now turned them away.[42]

"Nothing to Eat and No Body Help Me"

Kate Abraham and Father John Clerico's correspondence with Bishop Richard Gerow opens a window into the instability of life in the Delta in the early years of the Great Depression. It also provides a valuable glimpse of the limited range of charitable and social services offered to men, women, and children who asked for assistance, as well as the rationale behind those limits.

Because Abraham was a widowed mother, she qualified for Mothers' Aid—Mississippi's only form of state relief—at a sum determined by a social worker who visited her home. Abraham's options would have been different had she lived in a tenant house a few miles outside her hometown of Greenwood, where town church agencies often had little reach, and different still had she lived in Memphis, where the community fund centralized many social services. Had Abraham been African American rather than Syrian, she would have turned to yet a different set of resources for aid. A snapshot of the choices available to struggling citizens of the region in the first years of the depression highlights the changes that followed, first as the nation sunk into economic crisis, and then as Americans elected a president who promised to use the power of the state to alleviate their suffering.

Located on the eastern edge of the Mississippi Delta in Leflore County, Greenwood was a prominent town with a population of just over eleven thousand in 1930. Greenwood's Grand Boulevard boasted stately homes behind neat lines of oak trees on one side of the Yazoo River, and on the other a large cotton market, a busy downtown, and a broad range of churches and civic organizations. Like many larger Delta towns, its diverse population included whites and African Americans alongside a significant community of two hundred Jews, classified as white under Jim Crow. Smaller Chinese, Italian, Syrian, and Lebanese populations occupied a more ambiguous racial status, usually operating on the white side of the racial divide for daily business and sometimes for education but remaining in distinct ethnic communities. Many of the Italian, Syrian, and Lebanese residents of Greenwood owned or operated small retail businesses and attended the Immaculate Heart of Mary Catholic Church, the city's white parish, presided over by Father John Clerico. Kate Abraham was thus part of overlapping, thriving ethnic and religious communities in Greenwood. Abraham and other inhabitants of sizable Delta towns could rely on a wider network of support than could many families in the countryside. But her letter to Bishop Gerow shows just how inadequate that network proved.[43]

Father Clerico's response to Bishop Gerow's inquiry about Abraham outlines the most significant sources of assistance available to Greenwood residents who had fallen on hard times. There, and across the nation, people first turned to their extended families for help. Kate Abraham references only her son and her dead husband, suggesting that she had few family ties in town. Clerico noted, however, that Abraham "has been given help by her own people." American ethnic communities had long worked to support their own, determined not to appear burdensome to the white majority. In Memphis and the Delta, the large African American population also worked particularly hard to maintain independent institutions and aid societies, knowing that assistance from whites came sporadically and grudgingly. For Kate Abraham, the Catholic Church represented the best opportunity for support when aid from the Syrian community, which numbered just under one hundred members, was inadequate to feed and clothe her son and herself. Still, Abraham also found it necessary to seek aid from the American Red Cross, a local Southern Baptist minister, the Catholic Knights of Columbus in nearby Greenville, and her bishop in Natchez.[44]

Kate Abraham could not find adequate assistance from private or public sources in Greenwood because her range of needs did not fit with the available resources and programs. Even if she were one of the few women to receive Mothers' Aid from the county, as her priest indicated, that fund averaged only eleven dollars a month per family. A parent with only one child would have received much less. Church and civic aid groups collected used clothing, prepared meals, and sometimes provided small sums of money to families who lost a home, part of a year's crop, or a wage-earning family member. But their resources were minimal and best suited to cases of acute, rather than chronic, need. The Woman's Auxiliary at Greenville's First Presbyterian Church reported each year between 1930 and 1933 that requests from its "benevolent budget" were "unusually great." Yet its members were proud to report meeting those requests "most efficiently through untiring and sympathetic personal effort," all on a budget of around a thousand dollars a year. As much as they talked about the church's obligation to help those in need, particularly widows and orphans, most churches and aid societies had neither the resources nor the will to provide long-term support even to a widowed mother and her son.[45]

What they could not contribute in funds, church societies often made up for in advice. Kate Abraham was poor, temporarily homeless, and, as a woman and ethnic minority in the worst year of the depression, probably unable to find work. But she had a son old enough to work, although in 1933 he too would likely have joined the quarter of Americans who fruitlessly sought jobs. Father Clerico noted that the youth had recently turned seventeen, and that Abraham chose to send him to school instead of into the struggling workforce. In better times, Delta children might work as farmers, gas station attendants, and errand runners by the time they reached elementary school, and many left grade school to support their families. But for Abraham, education appears to have been more important, and probably more practical. Furthermore, Mothers' Aid was often available only as long as the children were in school. Either through aid, occasional work, or some combination thereof, Abraham found a way to keep her son in school longer than could many parents in similarly dismal situations—even against the wishes of her priest.[46]

Abraham also appealed to the Knights of Columbus, a Catholic fraternal order and one of the region's many mutual aid societies. Fraternal orders, which despite their name often included women or women's auxiliaries, grew rapidly in the nineteenth- and early-twentieth-century South. Sometimes part of national orders like the Masons or the Elks and sometimes part of local orders, most were organized by race, ethnicity, and sometimes denomination. They offered health and life insurance to members, as well as a gathering place and community. Some also built hospitals and health clinics, orphanages, and homes for the elderly—all offered to members at discounted rates. Two Delta fraternal orders, the Woodmen of Union in Yazoo City and the Knights and Daughters of Tabor in Mound Bayou, helped to establish the region's first two black hospitals. For residents of many Delta towns and even more so for rural African Americans, those orders that survived the depression provided the only reliable source of support during hard times. Still, they limited their aid to members, which meant that the very poorest were once again excluded. Even if Abraham's husband had been a member of the Knights of Columbus, the organization was not prepared to provide comprehensive support for a widow and her son.[47]

After a distressed man came to his office to seek assistance, the editor of the local paper in Ruleville, Mississippi—a much smaller town than Greenwood with just over a thousand residents—began to think about where a person in need might turn for help. The petitioner had a wife and children to support, but he had no money and his landlord had just threatened to evict him for unpaid rent. The Red Cross had provided his family with a little food, but that was gone and they were still hungry. Like so many others, this man had sought work for weeks but found none. He was healthy, but his family was not. It was a familiar story to the editor, but this time he began to imagine himself in the other man's shoes. "What Would You Do," he asked, "if you were flat broke, without credit, and a family to feed, and some of them sick? Don't own your own home, have nowhere to move, and can't get employment?"[48]

The editor did not have an answer. He turned to his readers for "suggestions that will help many people in this community." That the editor of the local paper, who printed weekly reports on local religious and civic work, did not know where a person in need could go demonstrated the total absence of a support network for suffering men and women. If they did not have family or friends to help them out, those in need had little choice but to knock on doors and plead for aid. Their last resort was the charity of strangers who were as likely to scorn them as to help them—strangers who, secure in their own homes with stocked cupboards, declared they would sooner starve than accept charity.[49]

As hard as it was in town, the man who walked into the editor's office would have found aid still more difficult to come by had he lived on a farm outside Ruleville, or elsewhere in the countryside. Small landowning farmers often had cars or trucks and could drive into nearby towns frequently enough to become members of local civic clubs and churches, and thus part of the town support network. But many small farmers lived too far from town or lacked adequate resources to connect with the town population. Churches and, to a lesser degree, burial and insurance societies could sometimes help out their struggling members in a pinch, but even smaller rural churches that operated women's aid societies and social organizations had far more needy members than available resources. Many rural churches could scarcely afford to pay a part-time minister and maintain a rough frame building, and their resources dwindled as wealthier residents of the countryside began to worship in town.[50]

Tenants and sharecroppers on Delta plantations sometimes attended better-equipped churches maintained by plantation owners, and these same planters sometimes offered their own form of support to workers in need of assistance. When a family member fell ill or needed treatment for an injury and could not afford the doctor's fee, the plantation owner paid the bill and then added the debt to the family's tab. Not all planters deemed it worthwhile to maintain their workers' health or to furnish them with food and shelter adequate to sustain them, however. Sharecropping families often had no source of outside aid when crisis struck.[51]

"Memphis Cares for Her Own"?

For a struggling Delta farmer, Memphis seemed a step up. Indeed, by 1930, more than 60,000 of the city's 253,142 residents were Mississippians by birth and another 15,000 hailed from Arkansas. More than 40,000 more people moved to Memphis during the 1930s, many of them from the Delta cotton fields. The city boasted more schools, more charities, more potential employers, and more independence than the countryside. But Memphis also had more people looking for assistance. By 1932, at least 17,000 residents of the city were out of work, and that number excludes the flood of new migrants to the city. More than a third of Memphis manufacturing firms closed in the early 1930s, including two of the largest. The total income of Memphis workers dropped fifty-five percent between 1929 and 1933. Those who remained employed now worked for drastically reduced wages, or for none at all. Memphis's school system went bankrupt in 1932, and teachers often went months without pay or received only city-issued scrip.[52]

The Memphis Community Fund weathered one crisis after another during the depression. Middle-class Memphians extolled the virtues of their city's charities and complained about the influx of rural Deltans who took advantage of their generosity. But working-class Memphians and the city's Delta refugees saw little evidence of that generosity during the worst years of the depression.[53]

Black Memphians turned to whites for assistance only as a last resort. The city's black churches tried to establish programs for struggling community members. Some black clergy counted on their good relationships with Ed Crump to secure jobs for members, while others ran soup kitchens and community centers. As in the Delta, the city's fraternal orders proved a valuable resource for their members but offered little to nonmembers. For black Memphians, church and fraternal aid was the primary resource in times of need, because Mothers' Aid in the city was for whites only and the community fund too disproportionately served whites.[54]

Struggling whites also turned to churches for aid. As the depression deepened, Memphis churches, like those in the Delta, initiated small-scale programs to help the men and women who came their way. In December 1930, several Memphis churches established an "adopt a family" program to "take up the burden of caring for the unemployed" through the winter. Churches of several denominations agreed to adopt a few families each, and local merchants provided discounted food and fuel to the program. The churches funneled the money through the Mayor's Relief Committee, a small-scale municipal relief program that also hired unemployed men to sell apples on street corners. By the end of December, the program had adopted one hundred families—a fraction of those in need after the long drought in the Delta. Such small-scale efforts on the part of local churches undoubtedly made a difference for those they served, but they also created the illusion that occasional contributions to local relief were adequate. Churches could emphasize the few families they helped, rather than the many they did not. As a cartoon in a Memphis Community Fund publication put it, "One reason folks is got dey own lil 'pet charities,' dey's lak enny other lil' pet—hit don' cos' much to *feed* em!" The delivery was crude and its minstrel character starkly illustrated Memphis racial attitudes, but the message was clear.[55]

The primary resources for those in need in Memphis were the agencies supported by the city's community fund. Each of these agencies provided a different form of aid—some offered financial relief, but more emphasized social service or even recreation. Many proved indifferent, if not downright hostile, to poor whites from the Delta and to African Americans. In 1932, the fund printed a pamphlet entitled *Where to Send People for Help*, which began with a warning: "IMPORTANT: Do not give strangers money. Send them to the agencies." Broken down into categories by age, gender, race, religion, and type of need, the pamphlet suggested that Memphians had an answer to every need. For instance, the Salvation Army provided food and temporary shelter to homeless men, the Ella Oliver Refuge took in young expectant mothers who lacked family support, and the Bureau for the Blind and Disabled visited and provided financial support to needy clients. But most community fund agencies served whites only. Even for whites, most of the agencies that operated under the aegis of the community fund served specific populations, leaving the Salvation Army as the primary source of support for those who simply needed help finding work or regular meals.[56]

The Protestant, Catholic, and Jewish agencies that made up the community fund each demonstrated distinct priorities in their efforts to reform the behavior of Memphians. The Federation of Jewish Welfare Agencies, which primarily served Jewish clients but also offered infant care and food relief to black and white neighborhood children, emphasized the maintenance of Jewish culture and traditions. Although their resources ran low during the Great Depression, the substantial Jewish middle class meant that Jews in Memphis proved more able than Catholics or Protestants to support members of their own community. Protestant and Catholic agencies worked to convert the men and women they served, and nearly all the community fund's organizations dispensed advice about thrift, cleanliness, and respectfulness along with food and shelter. The Convent of the Good Shepherd, a "home and school for misguided girls," including young mothers and girls who had clashed with the law, proudly described its work of "re-education and re-adjustments" designed to "[shield the girls] from the scorn of the world" while it helped them "[develop] into desirable citizens of the community, both morally and socially." For the Convent of the Good Shepherd, like most agencies in the community fund, charitable and evangelical efforts were one and the same.[57]

Few other options were available. Apart from Mothers' Aid and charity care at Memphis General Hospital, the city of Memphis provided almost no public aid for its destitute citizens in the early years of the depression. Between 1930 and 1932, Mayor Watkins Overton ran a limited work program, the Mayor's Commission on Relief and Unemployment, which allowed wealthier Memphians to rent the labor of an unemployed city resident, who received payment in food and fuel. Unemployed white men could also petition to sell apples, while unemployed black men generally had to pick cotton on nearby plantations instead (Figure 3.1). Relief for the hungry, the homeless, and the unemployed came from private citizens in Memphis if it came at all.[58]

Although the directors of the agencies that participated in the Memphis Community Fund included a broad range of social workers, religious leaders, and businessmen, the fund itself maintained a close relationship with the Memphis Chamber of Commerce. Thus, the character-building emphasis of its member agencies blended with the boosterism of its chamber of commerce affiliation in a way that often downplayed the real suffering of Memphians. Fundraising pamphlets emphasized the tremendous good done by the Salvation Army, the children's homes, and the Family Welfare Agency, but they left unmentioned the thousands of Memphians unserved by the fund because of its chronic shortage of income. A reader of community fund literature (Figure 3.2) plastered with slogans such as "Memphis Cares for Her Own" and "It Shall Be Done!" could hardly be blamed for believing that every hungry person in the city could fill up at the Salvation Army's soup kitchen.[59]

Indeed, the Salvation Army filled many a hungry stomach in Memphis. Founded in England in 1865 by William and Catherine Booth, the Salvation Army focused its work on the urban poor. Its message spread across the United States between the Civil War and the Great Depression. The Salvation Army's dual mission of meeting the physical and spiritual needs of men and women neglected by the rest of society made it one of the most important sources of support for the needy during the depression. Its mission in Memphis included

FIGURE 3.1 Throughout the 1930s, the city of Memphis sent black men and some black women who sought relief to work as low-wage day laborers on Arkansas cotton plantations. Here, those workers board trucks that will drive them to the plantations.

Photo by Dorothea Lange, summer 1937, courtesy of the Library of Congress Prints and Photographs Division

the city's most comprehensive soup kitchen and a shelter for homeless white men. In December 1929, just after the depression began, the Salvation Army served 1,700 meals. The following December, in the midst of the drought, the number of meals served nearly quadrupled. The ranks of the hungry continued to grow. In March 1931, the agency provided 10,250 meals. The men's shelter soon overflowed as well, and the Salvation Army drained its swimming pool to make room for pallets on the pool floor. A visitor later reported, "The pungent odor of perspiration, of pungent old clothes on human beings, smote you as you opened the door." There he encountered "ragged men—old men with resignation written over their faces, young men whose somber faces belied their age."[60]

FIGURE 3.2 "Memphis Cares for Her Own." The cover of the 1927 Memphis Community Fund pamphlet depicts a woman caring for the three groups deemed both the neediest and the most deserving of aid: infants, children, and the elderly—all white. The pie chart on the back cover shows the allocation of resources. "Negro Welfare" represents one of the smallest slivers, only three percent of donations. African Americans made up nearly forty percent of the city's population.

Image courtesy of the Memphis and Shelby County Room, Memphis Public Library and Information Center

The community fund's other agencies struggled to keep up with demand as well. The Family Welfare Agency continued to counsel families of both races on available community resources, nutrition, and behavior and sometimes provided a limited level of financial support. Its caseload increased from just over 1,600 families in 1929 to nearly 3,500 in 1930. In 1932, a group of Catholic men formed a branch of the St. Vincent de Paul Society, which joined the community fund and raised just over seven thousand dollars to aid another 500 families, some of them non-Catholic. The Travelers' Aid Society, reorganized and expanded in 1932, provided families, women, and children new to the city with food, shelter, and guidance.[61]

In 1930, the community fund estimated its total expenses for the next year to be $528,598. Directors expected that $8,865, or 1.7 percent, of that money would go the Charles Wilson Home, an orphanage for black children that had replaced the orphanage burned in 1929 and the only community fund agency that offered significant support for the 96,550 black residents of the city. Black churches and businesses struggled mightily during the depression, but they remained the primary source of support for the hungry and the homeless.[62]

In 1932, the community fund's directors acknowledged that they should include black Memphians. Together with a committee of black ministers and businessmen, they added a new agency, the Community Welfare League. Its small budget raised entirely by African Americans, the league provided flour and clothing, which it handed out alongside the Red Cross. White community fund leaders satisfied themselves that they were doing their part, and black families still went hungry. The Memphis Community Fund continued to tout its hard work on behalf of less fortunate Memphians, and many of its member agencies did as much as they could on limited budgets. But with little help from the city, the state, or the federal government in the early 1930s, the community fund simply could not take care of the thousands of hungry and cold men, women, and children in Memphis. Although they boasted of the work they accomplished on minimal funds, community fund leaders also showed increasing desperation in their pleas for community donations. The 1927 slogan "Memphis Cares for Her Own" reappeared in 1933 with a dire adjustment. That year, the bulletin entreated "Memphis Must Take Care of Its Own."[63]

"Murdered by Society"

But Memphis did not take care of its own, and neither did the Delta. Hungry people continued to ask for help, and now the people they asked also began to ask for help. The women who ran church aid societies and worked with city charities, some of the businessmen who led the community fund, and even many clergy who remained committed foremost to evangelism now asked that the state step in to relieve the burden on the churches and private agencies. Even in Memphis and the Delta, social workers and the occasional liberal reformer had long pushed the federal government to aid the poor, but only in the early 1930s did such demands become as commonplace as they were controversial. For many, the question was no longer whether the government should step in to help. Instead, citizens began to ask whether the government should establish systems to protect the poor, the very young and very old, and the sick and injured, or whether it should throw out the broken capitalist system altogether.

The change in attitudes took place slowly in the churches, and it first man-
ifested in a growing consensus among major denominations that they had to
do something for the poor, and not just among their own membership. Black
denominations made this shift more quickly than white ones, in part because
they had a longer tradition of social Christianity and in part because they
saw more suffering from the start. Complaints common through 1929, about
denominations "beset with 'Social Service' advocates," whose commitment
to the body and not just the soul made them "very disloyal to the church,"
vanished in the following years. Soon, even those who proclaimed "the greatest need of all men regardless to age, race or station, is a new spirit" conceded
that the churches must "be awake to the need of the people, who cry daily for
sustenance for the body, food, clothing, shelter, medicine."[64]

White churches debated the question of church charity more heatedly,
but even Southern Baptists opposed to the denomination's social service
work now softened their language. "We are majoring where [Christ] told
us to minor and minoring where he told us to major," worried Mississippi
Southern Baptist Plautus I. Lipsey in 1931. "When we in reality evangelize
Mississippi, we shall lighten our social service burden." The argument that
evangelism would prevent the need for charity was not dead, but its tone had
changed.[65]

That same year, a Memphis layman proclaimed both his enthusiasm and
his concern about what the depression meant for the church, which "never
had such a challenge as it has today." He pointed to the nation's "seething
unrest" and the millions of people unemployed and "on the verge of starvation through no fault of theirs." He wondered, "Is Christianity able to solve
the economic problem that perplexes the wisest among us?" Perhaps the early
church might serve as a model, as its members "were filled with the benevolent impulse to relieve the want around them and pooled their possessions."
Thus, "the remedy which Christianity offers for this unrest and distress is
the great principle of brotherly love, a principle that organizes the church
into a vast relief society." The church should also "compel by its spiritual earnestness those who have an abundance of this world's goods to release their
possessions for the common good." Yet this layman could imagine no place
for the state in such compulsion: "Not a dole, not charity, not free bread." He
concluded, "[I]f Christianity can't take care of the want of the world, it is a
failure."[66]

By this layman's standards, American Christianity was destined to fail.
The separation of church and state meant that churches could operate without interference from the state, but it also meant that they operated as purely

voluntary organizations. Thus, people could attend or avoid attending, tithe or abstain from tithing as they saw fit. Churches could expel those members who did not cooperate and they could try to compel people to give a set portion of their income to church causes. But in the end, church members had full freedom to choose whether they would attend services, give money, and invest in church programs and charities. The Memphis layman argued that the church could compel sacrificial giving among its members "by its spiritual earnestness," and religious leaders in the depression put tremendous efforts into fundraising. But voluntary giving, no matter how earnest, was utterly inadequate to meet the desperate and growing needs of Americans.[67]

As people demanded more of the churches, it soon became clear that the churches were simply not up to the task. In 1932, a Mississippi Southern Baptist penned an essay about the Thomas family, a churchgoing couple with four children. "[I]nspired at every turn by his beautiful, faithful, and loving wife, and the hopes he entertained for his children, Mr. Thomas toiled on" at a backbreaking job until he contracted tuberculosis and had to go to a sanitarium. Mrs. Thomas took a job to support the children but could not earn enough to keep their home or feed the children, who "[f]or lack of nourishment . . . were fading and becoming nervous and irritable." Then Mrs. Thomas received the news that her husband had died in the sanitarium. For the first time since Mr. Thomas's illness, their minister came to visit. No one else from the church called, and its members "treated her sorrowful plight as a matter of course."[68]

Finally, Mrs. Thomas and her children grew so hungry and desperate that she wrote to her minister for aid. Although "[a] small weekly dole was reluctantly granted her," no one offered "the Christian sympathy and love she so deeply longed for." Soon, the Thomas family fell behind on rent in the "dingy quarters" they had rented from a deacon in the church. Mrs. Thomas came home from a long winter day's work to find an eviction note on the door and "her dear little children hungry and starving." That night, she kissed her sleeping children, lay down in bed, and drank poison. Only after their mother's death did the children inspire "an outburst of sympathy" among church members, who put them in an orphan home. "Such tragedies as I have depicted are being enacted every day in full view of Him who said, 'Inasmuch as ye did it not to one of the least of these, ye did it not to Me,'" reported the author sorrowfully. "'Murdered by society' is a fitting epitaph for Mrs. Thomas and other countless souls who have lost hope in the shadow of church spires."[69]

To those who might argue that communities must care for their own, the Thomases' story—whether historical or apocryphal—illustrated that many communities did no such thing. The Thomas family was Christian, hard-working, and connected to the community, and Mr. Thomas was "counted a valuable member of the church." The church helped, but minimally and belatedly. The essay's explicit message was aimed at the church, but it also indicted a labor system that worked a man to death and then failed to provide for work-related illness and a social system that left a widowed mother of four without adequate support. These were themes that advocates of workman's compensation, Mothers' Aid, family welfare programs, and other federal protections for workers and families repeatedly stressed.[70]

What this Southern Baptist suggested obliquely, the executive secretary of the conservative, business-driven Memphis Community Fund said outright. In 1931, the community fund pared its fundraising goals to a minimum, and it still brought in only $462,344 of the needed $609,553—a twenty-four percent shortfall. In his annual report to the Memphis Chamber of Commerce and others interested in the fund's work, Charles O. Lee excoriated "the men and women of wealth within our city" who had the resources to "lay into the coffers of these agencies practically any reasonable amount for their support." Lee knew his audience, and he addressed the city's businessmen, who contended that the only way to alleviate poverty was to plow more money into business. "I am heartily in favor of bigger and better smokestacks, of more beautiful and taller skyscrapers, of ribbons of concrete threading our country from coast to coast . . . the more the better," he warned. "But man or city which becomes intoxicated for the possession of these while hunger dwells unrequited, while the lives of little children are blighted for want of a chance, is a man or city in which life becomes a hollow mockery and which ultimately loses the material things he has grasped, as he has sluffed off the spiritual."[71]

On the question of the responsibility of the state to the poor—territory Memphis social workers and charities had so long hesitated to tread—Lee now dove in. He cited a Russell Sage Foundation study of 128 aid agencies in several cities, which showed that those agencies had collectively increased spending from just over a million dollars to just under five million between January 1929 and January 1931. The number of families aided likewise increased fivefold, from 50,000 in January 1929 to 250,000 in January 1931. Yet the agencies utterly failed to meet the yawning need before them. "The tremendous increase in relief requirements has also sharpened up the discussions over the entire nation on the relative responsibility between tax support and private support for Family Welfare," Lee noted. He then reported without comment—though in obvious agreement—that the Association of Community Chests and Councils bulletin of April 1931 had concluded, "Communities can carry their immensely greater loads only as public resources assume responsibility for a large part of them."[72]

What for Lee seemed something of a revelation was to many black southerners more painfully obvious. Whites had excluded African Americans in the region from Mothers' Aid and other public programs that might provide a way out of household and plantation labor. Indeed, the community fund—and Lee himself—consistently downplayed its already minimal work for African Americans to donors who believed that the fastest way to corrupt starving black children was to put food in their stomachs and clothes on their backs.

In early 1931, Nannie Helen Burroughs of Washington, DC, long-standing and popular head of the Woman's Convention of the National Baptist Church, wrote a public letter to black leaders. The letter drew on the church's long self-help tradition, but it also pushed black leaders to make public the injustices of Jim Crow capitalism. Burroughs asked why African American religious, fraternal, and welfare organizations "are so impotent in the present economic crisis" and answered that they spent too little time among the suffering. Probably influenced by an Urban League study that showed that a quarter of black adults in the cities were now unemployed, Burroughs prodded black leaders to impress upon all Americans the "moral and social injustice and danger of a permanent boycott against Negro labor." She concluded with a challenge: "If we have leaders now is the time for them to go to leading the people and stop bleeding the people."[73]

The National Baptist Convention's clergy responded with outrage to what they considered a personal attack by Burroughs—whom they already resented because she had determinedly kept the Woman's Convention separate from their authority. But the clergy ignored Burroughs's central argument about the dangers of accepting a system that pushed black workers out of their jobs as soon as white workers were desperate enough to take them. Instead they defended their own charitable acts. This in turn prompted the editor of the *National Baptist Voice* to jump into the debate to return the discussion to "the corrupt capitalistic social order that has brought about all this suffering and distress." He drew the line from charity to capitalism plainly: "These ruthless money-makers are financing our charitable agencies which are caring for the victims of the pitiless economic struggle. We will miss the point altogether if we fail to see that charity does not make for economic justice."[74]

Few white leaders in women's organizations and even fewer in the pulpits dared speak so plainly about the problems with charitable givers—though they worried plenty about the souls of the recipients. Yet the growing unease about the adequacy of churches, charities, and voluntary agencies in serving the needy necessarily prompted a related conversation about the justness of a government that supported struggling industries but ignored the millions of workers put out by those industries. Former Memphis resident and Baltimore *Afro-American* editor William N. Jones did not mince words: "The 'dole' is a step towards a more socialistic or communistic system, while the charity idea is purely capitalistic. What the astute and far-seeing captains of industry fear is any extension of the doctrine that a workingman is entitled to share in the reserves of what he has produced."[75]

BY MARCH 1933, when Kate Abraham wrote to Father Clerico, federal aid had finally arrived in Memphis and the Delta. In January 1932, the Hoover administration established the Reconstruction Finance Corporation (RFC), which Congress authorized to provide emergency loans to banks and corporations. Hoover's first attempt to use the power of the government rather than the power of moral persuasion to address the Great Depression represented a departure in federal policy, but it still did little for the hungry and unemployed. Then, in July 1932, Hoover signed the Emergency Relief and Construction Act, which expanded the RFC's powers so that it could also provide a total of $300,000,000 in loans to states and municipalities for public works projects that would employ out-of-work citizens. Arkansans, already in debt, readily took on the additional loans and set up county agencies to provide relief, and Mississippians soon followed. Political wrangling between Memphians and the governor delayed that city's participation until January 1933, but that winter several thousand men—half of them African American—began work on highway and drainage projects around the city.[76]

Hoover's RFC would not have helped Abraham: the municipalities and counties that took RFC loans could employ only a fraction of the men who needed it, and women were generally excluded. But the program proved popular, and it anticipated the far more extensive public programs of Hoover's successor, whom the region's liberal reformers and conservative religious leaders alike helped elect. Roosevelt's presidency would represent both a realization of these leaders' growing demands for government intervention and a new challenge to churches still trying to find their way in the crisis.

PART III

The New Deal

December 1932

Hopeful out-of-work Arkansans began to appear before brand-new county committees organized to distribute Hoover's Reconstruction Finance Corporation (RFC) work relief in the fall of 1932. Finally, the federal government had acknowledged the urgency of their need, and the state of Arkansas welcomed the RFC loans despite its own financial troubles. Those loans came with rules that promised not just work, but work for black and white men both at decent, albeit hardly generous, wages—twenty cents an hour for unskilled labor, and up to forty cents an hour for skilled workers. Eight hours a day at that rate and a man could put a little food on the table and maybe even a new pair of shoes on one of the kids' feet. It seemed almost too good to be true.

Of course it was. Surely men's hearts sank when they showed up to inquire about work and saw the same planters who distributed—and more often withheld—Red Cross relief also serving on the RFC committees. If Arkansas planters had any particular genius, it was too often aimed at slashing a poor man's wages. After all, higher wages off the plantation meant fewer desperate cotton pickers on it.

True to form, each county's planter-led committee crafted its own clever work relief plan—with emphasis on the work rather than the relief. In Phillips County, the committee assigned unemployed men to paint the county courthouse in Helena. Such skilled work usually brought forty cents an hour, but the committee set the rate at twenty. Wealthy locals were so pleased to find skilled men working for such low wages that they showed up at the courthouse and told them they would pay the same rate for the men to come paint their houses too. It looked like the RFC would bring down already-low wages in the county, which suited those paying them just fine.

Meanwhile, the Arkansas County RFC committee assigned its applicants unskilled tasks with a going rate of twenty cents an hour. But that seemed too generous. So the committee put the unemployed to work eight hours a day, just like the RFC required, but paid the men for only five of those hours—making for five dollars a week per worker rather than the expected eight. Members of both committees paid themselves handsome administrative salaries.

Planters in Crittenden County, home to some of Arkansas's largest plantations, landed on a work relief strategy that their counterparts across the river in Mississippi would soon imitate. These planters claimed that cotton prices were so low and their tenants so demanding that they could not manage to keep them all fed that winter. So they put their own tenants on RFC road jobs two days a week and on the plantations three days a week. The visiting RFC representative fumed, "This is of course equivalent to the R.F.C.'s subsidizing plantation labor this winter and thus relieving the landlords of responsibility." It was another hard fall for both tenants and planters, and at $6.52 a pound, cotton now cost more to grow than it could bring on the market. The future looked bleak to the planters, no doubt, and they had reason to worry that RFC wages might lure away workers who had not seen cash in years. But once again, the Delta's wealthy had found a way to prosper by taking from the poor. Hoover's administration proved no more an obstacle to them than did the local bureaucracy. So long as the federal government heeded their demands for local control, federal funds suited them well.[1]

Frustrated tenants now had fewer avenues of escape. A couple of years ago, a man might go to Memphis to wipe the dust from his boots and find work on the docks, or maybe in a factory. Women had fewer options. In the city, women might once have found some relief from farm labor, and maybe there would be time for the kids to go to school. Not now, though. The RFC jobs went only to men, and the garment factory jobs in town and in Memphis were mostly gone. The people of Memphis met migrants at the train station, or on the highway, and begged them to go back whence they came. The Depression wiped out the city's industries, and even its teachers worked for free half the time—and if they were black, about all the time. The city was broke, and too full of unemployed workers already. Some migrants stayed, though, and soon enough Memphians found a use for some of them: planters drove big trucks into Memphis to load up black men and ship them right back to the plantations. There, they chopped and picked cotton for less than a dollar a day. Boss Crump, once a plantation boy himself, knew how to take care of his most important constituents.[2]

A change was afoot, however. Crump had helped to elect a new president, the first Democrat in a decade. This one promised a "new deal for the American people." But for which ones?[3]

4

A Political Deal or Divine Providence?

INAUGURATION DAY OF 1933 dawned with a cloudy chill. President-elect Franklin Delano Roosevelt and his family began the morning with a brief prayer service at Saint John's Protestant Episcopal Church. The damp gray lingered as Roosevelt rode beside President Hoover to the Capitol. A Mississippi admirer later wrote to Roosevelt that just before he took the oath of office, "the clouds were especially heavy." But "when you came and put your hand on [the Bible] when you were taking the oath, the sun broke through the clouds and gave a ray of light through upon you. I said then, and I still say, that the Supreme Power above blessed your administration."[1]

Roosevelt took the oath of office on no ordinary King James Bible, but on a 247-year-old Dutch family Bible opened to 1 Corinthians 13. This much-used passage extolling the virtues of charity would have been familiar to Protestants everywhere. It set the tone for an inaugural address packed with so many scriptural allusions that the National Bible Press distributed a reference chart mapping Roosevelt's words to relevant verses.[2]

"We are stricken by no plague of locusts," Roosevelt said, his words carried across the radio waves to tens of millions of Americans. He blamed the Great Depression on "unscrupulous money changers" who had destroyed the nation's economy and then "fled from their high seats in the temple of our civilization." The president echoed the revivalist language of the contemporary clergy when he declared, "These dark days will be worth all they cost us if they teach us that our true destiny is not to be ministered unto but to minister to ourselves and to our fellow men." Roosevelt laid out a few general principles he planned to pursue in coming days, and he linked them to "old and precious moral values." He asked "the blessing of God" on the nation and concluded, "May He protect each and every one of us. May He guide me in the days to come."[3]

The New York governor sailed into the White House with the overwhelming support of the solidly Democratic South. Three and a half years into a depression that grew only greater, southerners had turned on Hoover and begun to relinquish their commitment to voluntarism. Local charities and churches, denominations, cities, and even states were either broke or headed there. Bank failures sped the disaster and punished even those who had pinched pennies for decades. Americans were hungry, sick, out of work, and about out of hope. This new president promised to change all that, though he had yet to say much about how.

Once in office, he wasted little time. Between his inauguration on March 4 and the middle of June, a period that would become known as the First Hundred Days, Roosevelt pushed a torrent of legislation through Congress. He called a special session of Congress on March 9 to pass the Emergency Banking Relief Act, which extended a bank holiday he had declared at his inauguration and provided emergency currency and federal oversight to banks on the brink. On Sunday, March 12, Roosevelt gave a fireside chat encouraging Americans to return their savings to the banks. When banks began to reopen on March 13, lines of depositors waited. By June, Roosevelt had signed legislation to provide relief to struggling businesses, workers, farm owners, homeowners, cities, and states. Roosevelt's often-contradictory new policies began to transform the federal government from a distant power into a visible and generally welcome source of support for the hungry, homeless, and unemployed.[4]

Prohibition also ended on Roosevelt's watch, and with his endorsement. While Catholics and Jews applauded repeal, white southern Protestants were dismayed. Prohibition's fiercest defenders in the South opposed Roosevelt's presidency, and they spent most of 1933 waging battles against the ratification of the Twenty-First Amendment. Some of those opponents never forgave the president. But most of the women who had fought so hard for the Eighteenth Amendment and the clergy who joined them celebrated Roosevelt's election and his swift efforts to resurrect the national economy even as they lamented the end to the great Protestant experiment in moral legislation.

Rather than take offense at federal programs that instantly dwarfed their own hard-won contributions, religious leaders and social reformers took credit for them. The National Recovery Administration (NRA), which required industries to set codes that regulated wages and working conditions and acknowledged workers' right to organize, drew a quick and

enthusiastic response from liberal southern Protestants who saw its antecedents in the Social Creed of the Churches and from Catholics who linked it
to papal decrees. Jews pointed to the connections between the New Deal
and the teachings of Ancient Israel's prophets. Conservative Protestants
applauded the New Deal as well and declared that Roosevelt drew his inspiration straight from the Bible. Roosevelt's use of religious language in public
addresses and his efforts to cultivate friendship among Protestant, Catholic,
and Jewish leaders only confirmed their certainty that the new president had
heard and heeded their demands.

There were dissenters, of course. Premillennialists worried that the NRA's
blue eagle symbol resembled the mark of the beast, a symbol of the antichrist.
Christian and Jewish Socialists wanted a president who would revolution-
ize American capitalism, not revive it. As one group of southern Christian
socialists put it, "We believe that the objectives of the New Deal can not be
achieved under the profit economy, and that these short-comings of the New
Deal are inherent in the capitalistic system." Staunch Republicans declared
that capitalism was not the problem at all and that expanding the government would cripple the nation rather than save it.

Even those who supported Roosevelt's ideals had doubts about the execution of some of the administration's programs. Black clergy and some liberal
whites pointed out that southern white elites easily bent federal programs to
white supremacy because Roosevelt yielded too readily to their demands for
local control over federal funds. White supremacists, for their part, balked
at any suggestion that New Deal programs include African Americans. They
declared that to do so would destroy the South's racial harmony and the low
wages that made it competitive with the rest of the country.[5]

While the NRA provoked discussion, the Federal Emergency Relief
Administration (FERA) moved religious leaders in the South to action.
FERA provided both direct relief and work relief in the form of matching
grants to the states. Its programs most clearly took over where religious and
private aid fell short, and again southern religious leaders generally applauded
its arrival. Some tried to yoke the churches and the expanded federal state
together to extend ongoing working relationships between local governments
and private relief organizations. For instance, the Memphis Community
Fund distributed Reconstruction Finance Corporation (RFC) funds first
under Hoover and then under Roosevelt. But in June 1933, FERA head
Harry Hopkins established a policy requiring that public agencies administer public relief. As the Roosevelt administration separated public and private
relief operations, many private organizations faced collapse. Other religious

agencies worked from the start to differentiate their work from New Deal aid, to carve out a new place in a world where they played a complementary rather than central role in the care of needy humanity. Some, like Catholic Charities, managed to circumvent the new rules and reinvent themselves as public agencies.

Those southern religious leaders who saw in the New Deal a reflection of their own religious values readily adapted to the state's expanded moral authority, whether they tried to take part in it or merely took credit for it. Some even invited the state to do more—to provide health care, to attend to delinquents in local communities. African Americans pushed the Roosevelt administration to live up to its Christian rhetoric and intervene when southern white administrators excluded black workers from relief or gave them only the most demeaning work. At the same time, white southern Protestants struggled to balance their concerns over their own waning moral authority with their gratitude for the relief New Deal programs brought. Some, like Mississippi Southern Baptist Plautus Lipsey, asked with alarm, "Must the government do our religious work for us?" The government was doing far more than the churches ever had, Lipsey understood, and he deemed that work necessary. But he and many of his colleagues wondered what was left for the churches. Even as they applauded the New Deal, then, southern clergy sought to correct what they regarded as its inadequacies or its excesses, and they struggled to retain their own moral authority as the federal government moved into Americans' daily lives.[6]

"A Day of National Consecration"

American Catholics and Jews supported Roosevelt from the start, but Protestant leaders were slower to warm to him. The presidential election of 1932 seemed a repudiation of the Protestant establishment's proudest achievement. Hoover had upheld Prohibition as president, but he did not promise to preserve it through his second term; Roosevelt promised to support an amendment to overturn it the moment he entered office. Unhappy with both options, Protestant leaders toned down the open politicking and anti-Catholic vitriol that had preoccupied them four years earlier.[7]

Even southern Prohibitionists found it difficult to support Hoover. Once lauded as a hero in Memphis and the Delta for directing relief operations in the aftermath of the 1927 flood, Hoover had lost all but his most loyal supporters in the region as the depression worsened. While some southern clergy deemed him the lesser of two evils, more returned to their Democratic loyalties. Like many of his colleagues, Daniel B. (D. B.) Raulins, Southern Methodist minister and editor of the Methodist journal for Mississippi and Louisiana, refrained from promoting either candidate. Raulins complained that for Hoover "politics is bigger than patriotism." The most glowing appraisal the disgruntled Methodist could muster for the sitting president was, "He is unwilling to risk his chances on either the wet or the dry side. He is amphibious."[8]

Hoover also made miscalculations that cost him any remnant of southern support. In 1932, several hundred Great War veterans descended on Memphis on their way to Washington, DC, to demand early payment of their bonus for wartime service. Memphians shuttled the Bonus Army off to Nashville. By summer, the veterans with their wives and children arrived in the capital and built a large camp in Anacostia Flats, outside Washington, where they stayed when Hoover denied their request for the bonus. When they resisted eviction by the city police, Hoover sent in General Douglas MacArthur, who brought along both infantry and cavalry. Bayonets out, the soldiers tear-gassed the veterans before burning down their makeshift village. The callous treatment of the nation's veterans at the hands of its standing army destroyed what remained of Hoover's reputation.[9]

But Roosevelt was not the only alternative. Some black religious leaders and a smattering of white clergy in the South also considered a third candidate for president. Socialist Norman Thomas stopped in Memphis to speak in September of 1932, and he drew an estimated crowd of 2,500. Thomas vowed to nationalize all major corporations, institute a five-day workweek, provide unemployment and old-age insurance, and launch an extensive public works program. The wet ex-preacher won over Clay East and Harry Leland (H. L.) Mitchell from Tyronza, Arkansas, who drove into the city to hear him. Soon, Mitchell organized a Socialist Party chapter among white sharecroppers in Tyronza. But Mitchell was in the minority. While many white southerners expressed some agreement with Thomas that the Great Depression resulted from problems inherent to capitalism, few agreed with his commitment to racial equality. Thomas won nearly 900,000 votes in 1932 (2.2 percent of the total), but only 20,000 of those came from the South. Southern white clergy who supported Thomas remained on the margins—and not long in the pulpits—of their denominations.[10]

Black clergy more readily expressed their admiration for the Socialist candidate. In October of 1932, the *National Baptist Voice* described the platforms on Prohibition and race of all nine presidential candidates. The paper also included three essays, one in support of each of the major candidates, including Thomas along with Roosevelt and Hoover. Southern African Americans noted that the Socialist Party platform promised "[t]he enforcement of Constitutional guarantees of economic, political, and legal equality for the Negro," as well as "the enactment and enforcement of drastic anti-lynching laws." Only the Communist candidate, whose running mate was a black Alabamian, matched the Socialists' egalitarian commitments. Still, most black clergy and churchgoers retained their traditional Republican allegiances and supported Hoover, although that support could rarely translate into votes at white-controlled southern polls.[11]

If southern clergy could not agree before November about which candidate least contradicted their religious priorities, many concluded in the months following his election that Roosevelt was the man for the job after all. Roosevelt carried fifty-seven percent of the popular vote and won at least sixty percent of the vote in every southern state. In Mississippi and Arkansas, two states with a poll tax and other voter restrictions that cut African Americans and many poor whites out of the electorate, Roosevelt won ninety-six and eighty-six percent of the total vote, respectively. Still concerned about Prohibition, white clergy who complained too much about Roosevelt's overwhelming victory risked calling attention to the fact that not many southerners were listening to them. Even as they challenged his platform, then, white clergy looked for evidence of Roosevelt's commitment to both spiritual and material recovery.[12]

The long four months between Roosevelt's election and his March 4 inauguration were calamitous ones around the world. Natural disaster and Soviet policy combined to kill between three and seven million people in a famine in Ukraine and the Caucasus. In March 1933, Hitler moved to take control of Germany, and he soon began to target Communists, Jews, and political opponents. Japan left the League of Nations, and war debts continued to depress the European economy. Desperate and hungry workers led strikes across the United States. In Memphis, police spooked by the specter of revolution launched a renewed effort to intimidate the city's black citizens, and six officers murdered nineteen-year-old Levon Carlock on rumors that he had had sex with a white prostitute. What hope they had left, Americans had to put somewhere, and many put it in Roosevelt, whose still-vague promises of "a new deal for the American people" prompted as much anticipation as frustration.[13]

Eleanor Roosevelt helped her husband's case among the clergy in a December 1932 speech and *Forum* essay, "What Religion Means to Me." She opened by calling for "a new standard which will set above everything else certain spiritual values." Recalling "a childhood where religion and religious instruction were part of our everyday life," Roosevelt wrote about a time when "Sunday was, indeed, a day set apart from other days" and reminisced fondly about "the real pleasure of singing hymns on Sunday evening, after supper, as a family." Roosevelt made a nod to ecumenism, claiming, "To me religion has nothing to do with any specific creed or dogma." But her imagery was purely Protestant. Although she connected crisis with religious revival, Roosevelt also spoke of the very real suffering in "these troublous times." She even declared, "It is looked upon today as one of the duties of government to see that no one starves." The essay's subtext established Roosevelt's humanitarian interest even as its religious language emphasized her Christian credentials. At the same time, it marked a state claim on social welfare and relegated the churches to spiritual matters.[14]

Southern clergy generally approved of their soon-to-be First Lady's public discussion of faith. White Methodist editor D. B. Raulins, an increasingly enthusiastic Roosevelt supporter, reported that throughout the article he "could feel her groping for reality in religion, a reality that we might spell with a capital, the Reality that must save our Christianity today." But if Roosevelt's letter won her points, she quickly lost them when she referred in a New York radio address to the young age at which "the average girl of today" must learn "how much she can drink of such things as whisky and gin." Even Raulins said, before speaking up in her defense, that she "does seem to have gone 'out of bounds' somewhat" and worried that she was too "New York minded." In one brief comment, Roosevelt managed to aggravate Protestant fears about urbanization, female sexuality, the temptations facing youth, and, above all, alcohol. Still, many southern religious leaders proved willing to grit their teeth and temporarily reserve judgment in regard to the new president and his family.[15]

The inaugural address impressed even skeptical clergy, as Roosevelt no doubt intended that it would. "This is a day of national consecration," he said. Roosevelt's first words as president could not have been more directly aimed at his hearers' souls. His heirloom Dutch Bible made headlines too, as did his extensive biblical allusions. D. B. Raulins described the inauguration in vivid detail even though he was hundreds of miles away and heard it only over the radio: "I saw Mr. Roosevelt slip away to church," he reported, and listened as "Mr. Roosevelt, in strong and unfaltering tones, repeated the oath after the Chief Justice." Some were less impressed. One Tennessee National Baptist quickly echoed Norman Thomas's concession that the inaugural address "was a good speech; Democrats are usually good talkers." But the compliment was also a critique: "It is going to take more than talk to measure up to the hour."[16]

"As Wet as the Bottom of the Atlantic Ocean"

Roosevelt kept talking, but he also unfolded the New Deal quickly once in office. Already, by the "day of national consecration," the turn of events southern Protestants most dreaded had begun. Roosevelt had promised to fund his expansion of the federal government in part with a liquor tax. Congress set the wheels in motion in late February, before Roosevelt even took office, by passing the Twenty-First Amendment to repeal Prohibition. The amendment then went to the states for ratification. Once in office, Roosevelt made time only to sort out emergency banking measures before he asked Congress to speed up the repeal process by amending the Volstead Act to allow low-alcohol beer in states that permitted it. Congress obliged, and on April 7, some Americans could once again buy beer legally.[17]

White southern Protestant leaders howled, even though most southern states had preexisting prohibition laws that would remain in effect. Prohibition represented for many churchgoers both an affirmation of their political power and a necessary step toward the government's incorporation of Protestant moral imperatives. Identifying alcohol and the shady interests that brewed and distributed it as the root of all modern evil, Prohibitionists had argued that criminalizing the sale of alcohol would shut down the saloons, wipe out gambling and prostitution, and remove the worst temptations of city life from errant fathers and lost young girls alike. Literally sobered by the disappearance of the saloon, the poor whites, immigrants, and African Americans who composed the nation's laboring classes would return to church, renew their relationships with family, and become contributors rather than burdens to society. Prohibitionists acknowledged by the election of 1928 that the amendment was not working out quite as well as they had hoped, but they blamed poor enforcement rather than the legislation itself. They also took credit for the booming 1920s economy—a result, they claimed, of a new national sobriety. The depression dampened Prohibitionist enthusiasm somewhat, especially when Roosevelt proposed that repeal could help fund economic recovery.[18]

The Democrats' case that legalized alcohol sales would redirect revenue from organized crime to government coffers proved persuasive in the face of economic disaster. When Congress passed the Twenty-First Amendment in

February, the bill specified that ratification must happen in state conventions called for that purpose rather than in state legislatures, where Prohibitionist grandstanding could lead to unpredictable results. Upon ratification by thirty-six of the forty-eight states, the amendment would annul Prohibition. As a concession to determinedly dry states and to states' rights advocates in the South, the Twenty-First Amendment also included a clause banning the interstate transportation of alcohol, thereby enabling states that had local prohibition laws to keep alcohol from their borders.[19]

As the Twenty-first Amendment vote reached the states, Protestant leaders focused a disproportionate share of their energy on the immediate goals of preventing its ratification and making sure that their own states remained dry in the event of its passage. For the remainder of 1933, it may have seemed to some white churchgoers in Memphis and the Delta as though their denominational leaders had altogether forgotten the depression in the face of what they deemed a more pressing crisis.[20]

But the tide had already turned against the Prohibitionists. Evelyn Duvall, a white Mississippian, argued even before Roosevelt's election that no one but the clergy really believed in Prohibition anymore, even in the South. "It seems to me that the preachers are sticking their heads in the ground like the ostrich," she opined. "They even talk as if the Eighteenth Amendment has been a glorious success, instead of the greatest farce in the history of the governments of the New World." Duvall echoed common arguments for repeal when she claimed that Prohibition had created "organized gangdom" and encouraged the bootlegger, a "social, economic, and moral gangrene that ought to be burned out with a hot iron." Duvall believed in temperance, but her religious convictions supported the argument for repeal. "The spineless weakling—the cowardly brute—who deprives his wife and children of necessities and pleasures to quench his damnable thirst has no respect for himself, his fellowman, nor his God," she argued. "Do you advocators of the Eighteenth Amendment expect him to have respect for such a little thing as the law?" While many of the white women who had once led the charge for Prohibition remained opposed to repeal, others, like Evelyn Duvall, concluded that legal, regulated alcohol was the morally sound option instead.[21]

Similarly, some African American Protestants enthusiastically participated in the campaign against repeal, but many simply questioned the relative importance of Prohibition when other social problems seemed more pressing. They understood too that support for Prohibition often hinged on racist claims that alcohol rendered black men sexually aggressive and that repeal would unleash a frenzy of attacks on white women. The economic underpinnings of this argument were clear: black southerners must work, not play, and alcohol limited their usefulness to their employers. Prohibitionists also argued that repeal would make it easier for bosses like Crump to buy black votes. Few black clergy focused much energy on the issue either way, as their attention turned to graver concerns in the Jim Crow South.[22]

Russell C. Barbour, a progressive Nashville minister and editor of the Tennessee-based *National Baptist Voice*, the major paper for black baptists, pointed out that white Prohibitionists seemed to waver on the cause as well. Furthermore, many had supported Roosevelt even though they knew he was "as wet as the Atlantic Ocean." Because they "preferred a wet democrat to a dry anything else," Barbour noted, "prohibition leaders have done more to kill the prohibition amendment than any other group." And yet, "Our Southern Baptist Convention friends spent a day on the prohibition question at their Washington Convention, and did not mention the Scottsboro fiasco five minutes." The high-profile trial in which American leftists came to the aid of nine black youths who had ridden the rails in search of jobs and now stood accused of raping two white women near Scottsboro, Alabama, was a rallying point for African Americans. Barbour weighed the Prohibition amendment against the larger issues facing black southerners, and at the same time denounced white baptists' tunnel vision and hypocrisy. To him, arguing about Prohibition in the face of the ongoing disasters of the depression seemed ridiculous at best, heartless at worst.[23]

Barbour pointed out the ever-present threat of unprovoked mob violence and denounced those who pit "nation against nation, race against race, strong against weak." He declared "hate and selfishness" more dangerous evils than drunkenness. He further noted that "the whiskeyheads and drunkards are not doing as much harm as the sober men who are robbing men, women and children out of a living in the factories by sweating them to death for little pay." Barbour concluded with a message for white southerners: "If we would spend half as much time in a militant fight against these two evils [hate and selfishness] as we have spent in emotional effervescence against liquor this world would be made over very soon."[24]

But the white Protestant establishment disagreed. On July 18, Arkansas and Alabama became the first two southern states to hold ratification conventions to vote on the amendment. In preparation for their state's vote on repeal, Arkansas Southern Baptists summed up the primary argument for retaining Prohibition. Alcohol was "The Great Destroyer," one minister argued. "No inherent evil can be legalized. The only effective control of a rattlesnake is to cut off its head. The proper regulation of a mad dog is to shoot him." Whatever the problems with Prohibition, the minister contended, they paled in comparison to the prospect of legalizing sin. Nearly every issue of Arkansas's state Southern Baptist paper urged church members to go to the polls and vote for dry candidates in July. "The 18th Amendment is God's Amendment and God's people will retain it," the editor proclaimed. But he was wrong. Both Arkansas and Alabama voted for the repeal of Prohibition by a three-to-two margin, even as the Arkansas attorney general reminded the populace that his state was still "as dry as a camel's tonsils." Two days later, Tennesseans, led by the wets in Memphis and Nashville, narrowly voted for repeal as well.[25]

In the end, the battle between the wets and the drys was not even close. American voters overwhelmingly agreed with Roosevelt's contention that legal alcohol sales would put much-needed revenue in the hands of the government rather than criminals and concluded that even the poorest sot would find a way to buy alcohol whether it was legal or not. Persuaded in part by the states-rights' provision in the Twenty-First Amendment, even dry states like Arkansas and Tennessee overwhelmingly voted for ratification. Only South Carolina formally rejected the amendment for repeal. Utah became the last of the requisite thirty-six states to ratify the Twenty-First Amendment on December 5, 1933. Mississippi, North Carolina, Louisiana, and Georgia and several midwestern states had not yet held conventions when the amendment passed, and since their votes were no longer required, they abstained from holding conventions at all.[26]

The passage of the Twenty-first Amendment marked the end of one of the Protestants' boldest experiments in shaping federal policy to fit their moral and religious vision for the nation's future. Focused on the immediate consequences of repeal and the host of New Deal policies passed in 1933, many Protestants did not pause to consider the long-term ramifications of the year's events for the churches. They soon lost control of state prohibition policy as well. Statewide prohibition ended in Arkansas in 1935 when legislators decided that an alcohol tax would be the quickest way to pay off state debt. Tennessee followed suit in 1939. Only Mississippi held out, becoming the last state to legalize alcohol in 1966. The Protestants considered the 1920s a period of moral crisis, and no one could disagree that the 1930s were a period of economic crisis. Few blamed Prohibition for creating those problems, but the depression made it clear that the Eighteenth Amendment had not brought the sweeping reforms to American life that many Protestants had anticipated. Even in the South, a Prohibitionist stronghold, the economic appeal of repeal ultimately outweighed the desire for moral control.[27]

"I Have Signed Up for the War Against the Depression"

While the last Prohibitionist holdouts fought repeal, the rest of the nation paid a lot more attention to the unfolding New Deal. The four months between the election and the inauguration brought another nationwide wave of bank failures, and an impasse between the outgoing and incoming presidential administrations left the executive branch largely powerless during that period. Once inaugurated, Roosevelt got to work without pause. On Sunday, his first full day as president, Roosevelt declared a four-day banking holiday and called a special session of Congress for the upcoming Thursday. The hectic Hundred Days had begun, and by their end Roosevelt and a cooperative Congress passed fifteen major pieces of legislation, including banking reform, agricultural regulation policies, employment projects, and programs to mediate between business and labor. Hoover's Revenue Act of 1932, which raised income and estate taxes, helped fund the new programs, as did Roosevelt's promised excise tax on liquor and other luxuries.[28]

Even Protestants preoccupied with Prohibition could not help but comment on the flurry of activity coming from the White House and Congress. The White House had been practically shuttered during the period between Hoover's defeat and his departure from office, and Americans expressed relief simply that it hummed with new life. In May, members of the Social Service Commission of the Southern Baptist Convention wrote to the president a dire warning that the end of Prohibition would be "a calamity to the nation." But they also approved Roosevelt's "earnest effort to relieve the distress of millions of men now without employment." A month later, a Little Rock Southern Baptist and fierce defender of Prohibition paused in the midst of a call for "faith in God and a sober America" to say, "We should whole-heartedly assist and co-operate with our virile president for a new deal. In all things he is right, except in the repeal of the 18th Amendment."[29]

Many black clergy expressed more caution. Any president already so popular among Jim Crow Democrats was worthy of skepticism. Black Democrats were sparse when Roosevelt took office, and for good reason. The Republican Party had welcomed black southerners after emancipation. In the South, Democrats were Confederates, the defenders of slavery, the inventors of Jim Crow, the promoters of lynching. In many southern states like Mississippi, the Democratic Party operated as a private club, its primary restricted to white voters only, and its power nearly absolute. If Republicans had not done much good for southern African Americans, Democrats had done almost

nothing but harm. Roosevelt had powerful—and necessary—white southern allies like Ed Crump of Memphis, who in 1933 sat in the US House of
Representatives, and like Senator Pat Harrison of Mississippi. Even Theodore
Bilbo, Mississippi's bombastic Ku Klux Klansman who served as both a governor of the state and a US senator in the 1930s, was an important Roosevelt
ally.[30]

Yet some southern African Americans expressed tempered enthusiasm
that perhaps this New York Democrat would be different. One National
Baptist warned in April, "The praise of Roosevelt has been so fulsome, so
universal, and so spontaneous that it looked like the American people would
crown him king." At the same time, the skeptic judged Roosevelt "adventur-
ous; unafraid and courageous" and admitted he was "happy that the new
President has had an opportunity to hurl his ideas forward without opposition." Another National Baptist recounted Roosevelt's visit to church just
before his inauguration and exulted, "He is strong and courageous, and he
has a vision, and above all fears God. . . . There is something consoling to know
that we have a new President who does not feel sufficient unto himself."[31]

Religious leaders of both races commented repeatedly on Roosevelt's religious convictions and his frequent biblical allusions in speeches that followed
the inaugural address. Even before the inauguration, one clergyman noted,
"President-elect Roosevelt stated that the dominant strain of his recent campaign was suggested by a country church service." This president, many religious leaders seemed to say, was one of them. His programs represented their
own triumph. When they did comment on specific programs of the New
Deal, they often focused on the resonance between those programs and their
own reform campaigns. At the same time, few of the Hundred Days programs overlapped directly with the limited relief and aid programs offered by
religious institutions. It thus appeared to many religious leaders in Memphis,
the Delta, and nationwide that the state and the churches were working
together to heal a suffering nation rather than competing for the hearts and
minds of desperate Americans.[32]

The National Industrial Recovery Act (NIRA), passed in June 1933,
proved of particular interest to religious southerners. The NIRA represented
Roosevelt's most direct effort to check the power of capital with the power of
the federal government—to salvage capitalism by taming it. The NIRA regulated workers' hours and wages, made provisions for their right to unionize,
and created the NRA. It also established the Public Works Administration
(PWA), which planned public works and infrastructure projects that private companies would bid on and then hire workers to complete. The federal

government for the first time granted workers the right to form labor unions, and then instructed that industry and labor work together to create "codes of fair practices" that would guide production and set wages. Together with labor, each industry would establish its own codes, to be approved by the NRA. Because it minimized industrial competition on the one hand and acknowledged the rights of workers to organize on the other, the NRA won the approval of both industry and union leaders and seemed to herald a new way forward for American capitalism. Those businesses that complied with the NRA pasted a blue eagle on their window to show their cooperation and attract customers.[33]

That the NRA drew support from the churches at all indicated the distance they had traveled since 1929. Churches had readily adopted corporate models and corporate language. They had embraced Bruce Barton's 1925 *The Man Nobody Knows*, which characterized Jesus as the original entrepreneur. Now, they feared that the unchecked power of business had unmade the nation. "We made a god of the business man and the church looked to him for counsel," confessed D. B. Raulins in 1932. "Today we are floundering around the crumbled feet of our god." While Christian socialists and radicals proposed throwing out that god altogether, the NRA proved a more palatable solution to moderates and liberals. Many American religious reformers thus celebrated its arrival.[34]

Critics who otherwise had little to say about the policies of the NRA itself declared the blue eagle—surely to Roosevelt and his cabinet an innocuous, patriotic symbol—an ominous portent straight from Revelation. Calvin B. Waller, minister of the largest Southern Baptist church in Arkansas, reported in September 1933, "Not in decades, perhaps, has there been a more wide-spread interest in the prophetic message of the Bible; especially the Book of Revelation. . . . Men are inquiring everywhere . . . Is the Blue Eagle the Mark of the Beast?" While he reported, "In many quarters of the country this interpretation has been insistently made and thousands have been thrown into confusion," Waller hedged his bets. He argued that the NRA and its blue eagle were not the mark of the beast, but that "it is a preliminary fulfillment of this prophecy." The mark of the beast was a "Tribulation affliction," Waller explained, and tough though times were, the seven-year period of "Satan-controlled earth" had not yet begun. But "The World is certainly getting ready for 'World-Dictator'—Hitler in Germany; Stalin in Russia; Mussolini in Italy; the 'Blue Eagle' in America." With the establishment of the NRA, Roosevelt had secured his place among the ranks of potential antichrists.[35]

But at least at this early phase of his administration, even many premillennialists worked more to alleviate concern over Roosevelt's programs than to raise it. Texas fundamentalist J. Frank Norris—Joe Jeffers's mentor—defended the New Deal in its first years. "To hell with your socialism or what ever you want to call it!" he said to critics who accused Roosevelt of turning too hard to the left, "People are starving!" A Church of Christ minister reassured Arkansans that the NRA was "no cause for alarm." The minister outlined his understanding of the end times before concluding, "Let me suggest that the N. R. A. is a move made by the government officials to bring about better conditions in a social and economic way." Although he believed the end to be near, this minister insisted, "the mark of the beast has to do with religion only," and he thus identified sinfulness in the church, and not the policies of the Roosevelt administration, as the clearest sign of a nation gone astray.[36]

If premillennialists provided the most hostile religious response to the NRA, Catholics proved among the most receptive. Heavily represented in American ethnic communities and in organized labor, Catholics quickly embraced the NRA's blue eagle and accompanying slogan: "We do our part." Indeed, many saw the NRA as their own accomplishment. The National Catholic Welfare Council announced "congratulations for Catholics that some of the most important proposals in the encyclicals are at least partially incorporated in the law." Arkansas Catholics reported as the legislation made its way through Congress, "For the first time, business, labor and the government itself seems to be marching side by side toward the attainment of the ideals of social justice set forth by Pope Leo XIII many years ago." Catholics had long supported organized labor, even in the South, and the promise of its protection in the NIRA was particularly important to many of them. Indeed, one Arkansas priest summed up the whole first New Deal as Roosevelt's "great cause of economic recovery by social justice."[37]

Nationally, Catholics joined with Protestants and Jews to make public both their support for Roosevelt and their claim on his programs. Leaders in the Federal Council of Churches, the National Catholic Welfare Council, and the Social Justice Commission of the Central Conference of American Rabbis together released a statement calling for full cooperation with the NIRA on the grounds that it "has 'incorporated into law' some of the social ideals and principles for which religious institutions have stood for many years." Specifically, the statement congratulated Roosevelt for taking steps toward "a more just and equitable distribution of wealth and income as both a measure of brotherhood and justice" through the NIRA's wage and hour legislation and its support for organized labor. In part prompted by enthusiasm for the New Deal, in 1934, the Methodist Episcopal Church, South became the only white southern denomination to sign on to the revised Social Creed of the Churches, the Federal Council of Churches' statement on economic, racial, and social justice that many saw as a blueprint for the New Deal.[38]

Many other southern Protestants also scorned "those religious people who spend much time on 'beasts' and 'numbers'" and instead claimed a stake in the NRA's success. Vanderbilt social ethics professor Alva Taylor declared it "the greatest opportunity the churches and ministers have ever had to Christianize the social order," although he worried that the churches were not up to the challenge. Taylor represented the southern left, but enthusiasm for the NRA proved more widespread. A Mississippi Methodist declared that the program, "though startling to the conservative spirit, has been interpreted by many preachers as putting into practice many ideas given by Jesus in his Parables." The ever-enthusiastic Methodist editor D. B. Raulins reported in September, as he recalled the churches' significance in drumming up support for the Great War, "We are passing through a period of terrible strain, and it reaches out to us all. It is highly important that we pull together for one another and for all." He declared himself ready for the challenge: "The Blue Eagle is now perched on my door. I have signed up for the war against the depression."[39]

A month later, Raulins proved true to his word. He asked Louisiana and Mississippi Methodists who had complained to him about the blue eagle campaign, "Have you noticed that the NRA program includes three or four items for which the Protestant churches of the Federal Council have been contending for twenty-five years?" He instructed his readers to take out the Methodist Book of Discipline and review its Social Creed. "The abolition of child labor, minimum wage, reduction of hours of labor in industry, economic justice to the farmer, and the right for employee and employer alike to organize for collective bargaining," he reported, "you will find incorporated in the two plans." Even as he paused to register his disagreement with the Roosevelt administration on Prohibition repeal, Raulins expressed enthusiasm for its employment, relief, and social programs. "It is gratifying in the highest degree," reported Raulins, "that our government is actually attempting to try out some of these things for which the Christian church has been contending for a quarter of a century." The NRA was the churches' idea, Raulins insisted, and the churches ought to ensure its success.[40]

Even some southern churchgoers who opposed progressive social activism on the part of the church quickly decided that it was perfectly fine as federal policy. According to one Mississippi Southern Baptist, it might also be a good model for the churches. He proposed a "Baptists' NRA," an approach to missions that would mirror the federal program's national scope, emphasis on recovery, and call for action and cooperation. Similarly, a nearby Methodist proposed that "NRA" could also stand for "New Religious Advance," a religious program to parallel the economic one, focused on "the moral and spiritual life of our people."[41]

But another alternative acronym for the NRA soon proved more accurate. Southern legislators and manufacturers slashed nearly all protections for black workers from the legislation and the NRA codes, and then fired those black workers who might still benefit. In Memphis and the Delta, and around the nation, black workers soon denounced what for them had become the "Negro Removal Act." The NRA excluded agricultural and domestic segments from the codes. It also required industries to plan their employment over a year, which reduced their number of part-time and seasonal jobs, and disproportionately hurt African Americans. The NRA thus left out a majority of southern black women and men from the start. It also allowed more than one hundred industries to set a wage scale with regional differentials. In effect, this meant a lower wage scale for the South, which protested higher wages as the death knell of business that had located there only because of its low-wage, nonunion workforce.[42]

Still, the NRA codes set wages higher than they had been for black workers before, and it prevented direct discrimination by race in wages, though not in hiring. But many companies in the South simply refused to cooperate with the NRA or circumvented the wage codes. Fisher Body Plant in Memphis reclassified its black employees as lumber workers and paid them twenty-three cents an hour rather than the forty cents due them as automobile workers. Other companies summarily fired black workers. The only benefit these companies claimed to see in black labor was the pittance they could pay black workers; if they had to pay more, then they'd just hire whites. In Forrest City, Arkansas, Maid-Well Dress fired all its black workers, including many women who had worked there for years, and whose only real alternative in the city was domestic labor. Several industries in Memphis did likewise or threatened to do so the moment anyone complained about their below-code wages. Mississippi industrialists found another way around the NRA. They declared black workers on the Mississippi Flood Control Project to be contract workers with preset wages and paid them only ten cents an hour rather than the thirty to forty cents the NRA would have otherwise stipulated.[43]

Southern legislators fought for an expanded federal government, but they also demanded that local administrators take charge. In the South, that often meant that Jim Crow's defenders held more power than ever before. Southern white supporters of the New Deal thus believed they had little to fear from the expanded federal government—after all, they got to make the rules. Alabama native and NAACP organizer William Pickens warned of the South's determination to fit the New Deal to Jim Crow capitalism: "Real prosperity for the South without prosperity for its Negro citizens is impossible. But progress always meets the persistent desire to leave the Negro out." Indeed, white southerners who declared the New Deal a religious victory proved most skeptical of it when it seemed that African Americans might benefit.[44]

"The Responsibility of Government"

The NRA was the centerpiece of Roosevelt's economic program, but it was only one of several programs the president and his administration believed necessary to relieve suffering and restore prosperity. In addition to legislation designed to stabilize banks and businesses, the first New Deal included several programs to provide jobs and offer temporary direct relief. The Reconstruction Finance Corporation continued to offer loans for business and works projects, but now the Civilian Conservation Corps (CCC), the NIRA's PWA, and the short-term Civil Works Administration (CWA) provided additional employment on reforestation, road, parks, and public works projects. The Agricultural Adjustment Administration paid farmers to curtail production and plow under crops, and the Tennessee Valley Authority began economic development projects in the southern Appalachian foothills. Soon, FERA, established in May, replaced Hoover's last-ditch RFC loans with grants to states for relief projects. FERA was the first program to put federal funds not only toward employment relief but also toward direct aid for the suffering, in whatever form city and state aid administrators saw fit. It was also the program that most directly engaged with work once conducted by private aid organizations.[45]

Altogether, the Hundred Days of legislation that Roosevelt signed into law marked a shift toward solutions to the depression that might have precedent in Christian and Jewish proclamations but that were almost always controlled by the state—that shift in itself something many religious leaders had urged. Religious, ethnic, and civic organizations could not meet the exigencies of the depression, and now Roosevelt and Congress formalized the transition of responsibility for the unemployed and the destitute from private organizations to the state. The change was more dramatic in the South than in the Northeast and Midwest, where state agencies already took much of the responsibility for relief. The average proportion of private aid—including direct relief and work relief—in the nation's major cities by 1932 was only 18.4 percent, down from 29 percent the previous year, in part because of Hoover's Reconstruction Finance Corporation loans. But in Memphis, 64.8 percent of relief aid remained private in 1932, down from 85 percent the previous year. In the Delta—and much of the rural South—the states still offered virtually nothing to the needy beyond Mothers' Aid and the new RFC funds. Mississippi abandoned even its paltry Mothers' Aid program when New Deal funds arrived. Any other relief available came from private, very often religious, sources. The New Deal tipped that balance drastically in the other direction.[46]

Public relief had already transformed many private agencies. In 1929, before any federal response to the depression, three percent of the total public expenditures on relief in 120 major American cities went through private agencies. For private agencies, this meant that about five percent of total expenditures were of public funds. Although precise proportions are not available for Memphis, the city's juvenile justice system (which handled charity cases, as well as juvenile delinquency) often sent youth to private and religious homes, which in turn received public funds. Otherwise, Mothers' Aid was the only regular public relief available.[47]

In 1927 and again from 1930 forward, however, churches and women's missionary organizations played a central role in the organization and distribution of flood and drought aid through the American Red Cross, which operated in close cooperation with—and with allocations from—the federal government (Figure 4.1). For example, women in the Ruleville Baptist Missionary Society reported in 1932 that a church member had been appointed to join other churchwomen "to ascertain who are the ones most needing some contributions, provided by the Government."[48]

When Hoover authorized the RFC to provide loans to the states for work relief in July 1932, he did not make provisions for the distribution of those loans. In states like Arkansas and Mississippi, which had no centralized welfare board, local committees and private agencies handled the relief

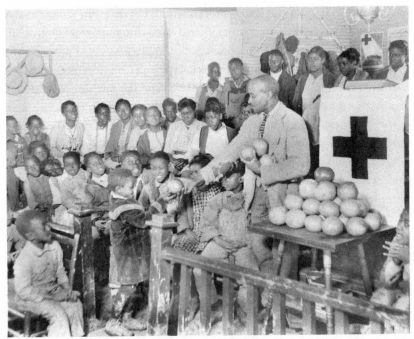

FIGURE 4.1 During the drought of 1930–1931, a teacher in a school that met in a church near Shaw, Mississippi, distributed fruit to schoolchildren. The fruit was part of a donation to the Red Cross from Lake Wales, Florida. In 1933, many of the churches that helped distribute Red Cross aid also sought a role in the distribution of federal aid through the Federal Emergency Relief Administration.

Photo by Lewis Wickes Hine, 1930 or 1931, courtesy of the Library of Congress Prints and Photographs Division.

funds. In Memphis, the community fund distributed part of the RFC relief funds. Agencies like the Salvation Army, the Church Mission of Help, and the Jewish Welfare Board quickly came to rely on federal dollars, particularly as local contributions to private aid dwindled.[49]

Memphis was not alone: by the end of 1932, the proportion of public aid distributed through private agencies in 120 major cities increased to thirteen percent—a ten percent bump in just three years. That year, private agencies handled $27,783,151 in public dollars. Most of those agencies fell into the "nonsectarian" category, which included Family Welfare Agencies and civic groups, as well as religious agencies without particular denominational affiliations. But the Salvation Army, Catholic, and Jewish agencies also received and administered federal relief funds. Because the proportion of public to private aid had increased, this now meant that thirty-six percent of private agencies' relief expenditures came from public funds. The boundaries between public and private blurred both ways—twelve percent of private funds, a total of $6,590,791, went through public agencies. Thus, the RFC erased existing boundaries between public and private relief. In the first few months of 1933, as Hoover lingered in office and as Roosevelt worked his way through the first New Deal, private agencies continued to administer RFC funds at a rate even higher than in the previous year. But that was about to change.[50]

By the time the Federal Emergency Relief Act passed in May 1933, eighteen million Americans—almost one sixth of the population—received some amount of relief, and still more needed assistance they did not receive. The initial FERA allocation amounted to $500,000,000, and in the end FERA spent $3,088,670,625 in grants to the states to aid struggling Americans. Administered at the state and local levels, those funds covered direct relief in FERA's early months, as well as work relief through the Civil Works Administration and other public works programs. Even though FERA was a temporary program—set to end in two years—it dwarfed all prior public expenditures on relief. Roosevelt put Harry Hopkins, an Iowan who had handled his state relief program in New York, in charge.[51]

In June 1933, Hopkins stipulated that as of July 1, only public agencies could administer FERA funds. With so much at stake both financially and politically, Hopkins wanted to avoid the problems and complaints that plagued Hoover's inadequate RFC. Public aid on the RFC's scale was such a novelty that many states—particularly in the South—lacked the infrastructure and experience to administer it, and many simply subsidized private work rather than establishing new public programs. As Josephine Brown, a social worker and FERA field agent, explained, Hopkins's decision meant "the financing and administration of public benefits for persons in need was definitely established as being the responsibility of government and not of private citizens, however organized or however charitably disposed." Leaders of private and religious agencies sometimes transitioned to public positions, while other private agencies—like Catholic Charities in Chicago—gained public certification. Hopkins's decree nonetheless established a clear public–private boundary both for FERA and for subsequent New Deal programs.[52]

For private agencies that had come to depend on public subsidies, Hopkins's new rule spelled disaster. It also led to "considerable delay and confusion" in the transfer of federal funds to public agencies in a dozen cities where private relief predominated, including Memphis and Little Rock. The executive secretary of the Memphis Community Fund declared that without RFC support, "fund agencies will be unable to carry on," and an already-brewing debate over the high cost of administrative salaries in the fund soon divided its supporters. The fund had ended its 1932 fundraising drive with $376,934, which left it $158,066 short of its goal and $38,805 short of the previous year's income. That 1933 amount proved to be a high water mark for the fund, unmatched again until 1941. When a national Community Chest official came to town to evaluate the community fund and declared Memphis "more negligent of its poor and more indifferent to its suffering than any other large city," the city's mayor called him a liar. But the community fund took the advice to heart, at least in part, and its board replaced the entire executive committee. Nonetheless, several participants, including the American Red Cross and the city's only black orphanage, left the fund. The fund's new leaders worked to promote the Community Welfare League, now its only black agency, whose projected budget for 1933–1934 amounted to only $2,600. Again dependent on raising money from Memphians with little interest in their efforts, the participating agencies continued their work as best they could.[53]

New Deal spending made those private contributions look like pocket change. In 1929, Memphians spent $.41 per person on aid for those who needed it, $.28, or 68 percent, of which came from private sources. Informal private aid from churches and women's societies did not factor into that sum and would have tipped the proportion of private aid much higher. At the peak of private giving, in 1931, Memphians raised $.88 per person, $.75, or 85 percent of it, private. Just two years later, Roosevelt's New Deal raised the per capita expenditure on aid to $4.36 per Memphian, but only $.40, or 9 percent, came from private sources. Most of the rest came from the federal government.[54]

By 1934, with the New Deal in full swing, Memphians received $7.21 per capita in aid dollars—including direct and work relief—but contributed only $.12, or 1.6 percent, of the total in private funding. This was a dramatic reversal. For decades, private organizations controlled Memphis relief operations, meager though they were. In just five years, as federal dollars provided the work and food Memphians so desperately needed, private aid dropped from nearly three quarters of relief spending in the city to less than 2 percent. The shift from private to public responsibility for the needy could hardly have been more dramatic (Figure 4.2).[55]

The swing from private to public aid was easier to track in the city, but it was even more pronounced in the countryside, where fewer resources of either kind were available. In the Delta, neither public nor private charity was organized enough to provide accurate data before 1933. By the end of July

	Memphis				Median for 116 Urban Areas			
	Total	Public*	Private	% Private**	Total	Public*	Private	% Private**
1929	.41	.13	.28	68.3	.87	.66	.22	24.2
1930	.55	.13	.42	76.1	1.09	.85	.24	23.9
1931	.88	.13	.75	85.0	2.36	1.62	.45	29.0
1932	.66	.23	.43	64.8	4.81	4.04	.45	18.4
1933	4.36	3.96	.40	9.3	9.52	9.13	.22	5.5
1934	7.21	7.09	.12	1.6	16.51	16.19	.15	1.8
1935	6.51	6.37	.14	2.1	17.37	17.28	.13	1.3
1936	7.67	7.53	.14	1.9	21.48	21.40	.13	.9
1937	5.51	5.35	.16	3.0	18.47	18.41	.13	1.0
1938	8.18	8.04	.14	1.7	26.03	25.98	.13	.8
1939	10.73	10.06	.13	1.2	23.36	23.05	.13	.8
1940	9.80	9.66	.14	1.5	19.15	19.03	.13	1.0

FIGURE 4.2 Per Capita Expenditures on Relief, 1929–1940 (in dollars)

*Includes federal, state, and municipal funds.

**Percentages do not match precisely because they are for total dollars rather than per capita dollars.

Source: Baird, *Public and Private Aid in 116 Urban Areas*, 112–165.

1933, FERA had made grants to every state and the District of Columbia. Between January 1933 and December 1935, eleven states—including Arkansas, Mississippi, Tennessee, and most of the South—received more than ninety percent of their total work relief funds from the federal government. Altogether, FERA grants to Arkansas totaled $46,980,969; to Mississippi totaled $34,793,392; and to Tennessee totaled $37,802,879. Overburdened religious agencies had been among the most vocal advocates for the transfer of welfare from the private realm to the public. Their demands heard, they now had to figure out what the New Deal meant for their people and for their work.[56]

"Must the Government Do Our Religious Work for Us?"

Soon enough, some clergy began to worry that as the federal government accepted its moral responsibility to Americans, it usurped the moral authority of the churches. Because it was the only New Deal agency to provide direct aid to the needy, FERA proved particularly important to religious leaders. People had finally begun to receive the assistance that they so desperately needed and that the churches and civic organizations had proven unable to provide. Now those people began to turn to the state rather than to local religious groups for both material aid and personal guidance. Many religious leaders did the same, expressing hope that the government could salvage charitable operations that the churches had abandoned. Clergy like the Methodist D. B. Raulins continued to celebrate the New Deal as evidence that the churches' "labors have not been altogether in vain." But others who took credit for the New Deal's inspiration also complained that its execution left those most in need without help.[57]

The churchgoers who worked most closely with the poor and suffering more often celebrated the start of the New Deal—including FERA—and pushed for more. Arkansas's Southern Baptist hospital quickly pled its case to the state. The hospital received outside support only from the Women's Missionary Union, and until 1933 compensated for its charity cases by over-charging those who could pay. Its superintendent expressed dismay that "hospitals in Arkansas are not receiving any assistance from any of the government or voluntary Relief agencies, or donations to reimburse them for the immense amount of free service necessarily given to the needy at this time." He lamented "the great number of charity patients dying because they can not get into hospitals for the necessary care and attention." Although he had lobbied within the denomination for funds for his poor patients, the superintendent was more optimistic about the federal government's willingness to help.[58]

Women's societies that had struggled to provide aid likewise proved enthusiastic about the federal government's intervention. "The beginning of the year 1933 was the most trying period many of us had ever encountered," the superintendent of Christian Social Relations for the Mississippi Conference of the Methodist Episcopal Church, South recalled at year's end. "Somehow we carried on, each one trying to help some other less fortunate, until the Federal Government came to the aid of distressed humanity." She specifically applauded the CWA, NRA, and CCC. "Too much cannot be said in praise of President Roosevelt's plans," the superintendent went on. "A nation has been fed through the winter, our young men have been given back their self respect and our children have been released from industry to go to school and be real children." Though she worried about the "mistakes made" as the programs rushed to execution, the superintendent concluded, "We must admit that greater strides toward social justice have been made in this one year than during the entire period of our former history. The women of our auxiliaries have cooperated heartily in all of these measures of the government for the relief of suffering humanity." In short, the government was an ally, rather than an adversary, in caring for the poor, and its help was both necessary and welcome.[59]

Many churchpeople also readily accepted the federal government as a direct partner, even a moral advisor. An Arkansas Sunday school superintendent wrote to the "Welfare Society" in Washington, DC, in 1934 to ask this nonexistent agency to intervene with a pair of tough local children, both under fifteen years of age. "We have two small boys in our Community, that are taught immoral and vicious habits, by their father," the superintendent wrote. The boys had been caught "cigarett smoking, cursing, fighting, stealing, disturbing the public in general, destroying property, they are unruly in school . . . anything to make trouble, they are at it." Once, the Sunday school superintendent might have thought it his place to rehabilitate the unruly youth, or at least to refer them to one of the many church-operated juvenile facilities that dotted the South. But the depression had closed off old options, and the New Deal opened new ones. "If you have a place for such lads, to have them reformed," wrote the superintendent, "the community would be much pleased." He was almost certainly disappointed to receive a quick response from Eleanor Roosevelt's secretary reporting that the federal government could do nothing to address the matter, which instead "would come under the jurisdiction of local authorities."[60]

While this Arkansan welcomed federal intervention in moral questions, many New Deal critics did not. They worried that the state's moral authority would trump the churches'. Interestingly, this concern led to a newfound interest in charity on the part of many religious leaders who had previously proven either indifferent or hostile to social Christianity. When Mississippi Southern Baptist Plautus Lipsey asked in the fall of 1933, "Must the government do our religious work for us?" he acknowledged some need for public education and even public charities. Yet Lipsey warned, "[W]e should not let the state come in to do our work as Christians in looking after the poor." In fact, "Any church ought consider itself discredited which permits some other organization to provide for its dependents."[61]

But it was not charity itself that concerned Lipsey, despite the fact that his denomination repeatedly quashed measures to expand its social mission. "[W]e should be on our guard," he explained, "lest we resign to the government our obligation to take care of the moral as well as physical well being of the people." When care for the needy remained the province of the churches and private organizations, Lipsey rarely described it as a moral or religious obligation. Yet when the state came to the aid of its people, "the preservation and protection of morals" now seemed in peril. After four grinding years, Lipsey could not deny the need surrounding him, nor could he declare that existing agencies met that need. But he worried less about the starvation and suffering around him than about the prospect that the state's generosity might reveal the church's bankruptcy—both financially and spiritually. Thus, for many southerners, the state's generosity was as problematic as it was necessary.[62]

Yet the early New Deal honored local agencies and administrators. NAACP investigator William Pickens had already described the "defensiveness of the South against any remedy of the depression which will incidentally improve the relative position of the Southern Negro." The requirements that public bodies administer FERA funds circumvented some of the racist relief structures in the South. But because FERA was to be a temporary program that required states to match federal funding with their own, Harry Hopkins worked to administer aid through existing state and local public structures rather than to create new ones.[63]

Hopkins also abided by the South's demands for local control, which the region's congressmen understood as the surest way to preserve the existing racial and social hierarchy. Local administrators interviewed families and provided the aid they deemed appropriate. They then reported to administrators at the state level, who in turn had to provide detailed reports of their expenditures to Hopkins and his field representatives. Although the states held the purse strings and chose how to allocate funds once the grants arrived, Hopkins could deny grants to states that did not meet a minimum standard of transparency. Southerners were by now well practiced at circumventing federal policy that did not suit them, however, and they easily manipulated FERA's policies against racial discrimination. Poor whites too suffered from this distribution system, often structured to humiliate those who sought assistance and to deny them when possible.[64]

Arkansas governor Junius Marion Futrell pushed Harry Hopkins to name William R. Dyess of Osceola, a Delta planter, head of state relief. Hopkins conceded, and Dyess then appointed his planter colleagues to head local relief committees in the region. Dyess and most Arkansas administrators privileged work relief over direct relief, providing the latter only to those who could not work, and generally in the form of food and clothing rather than money. As with aid from the Red Cross and the RFC, plantation commissaries distributed much of the direct FERA relief in the Delta and other plantation regions. Petitioners had to walk to the commissaries and accept their supplies in front of everyone around, a humiliating experience designed to deter all but the most desperate—of which Arkansas still had thousands. In Mississippi, planters learned quickly that they could put federal relief to good use: they placed their own workers on federal rolls during the off-months rather than supporting them on credit and then cut off all support when planting and picking season came.[65]

Many residents of the region did not have enough food to survive, and they depended on federal support to avoid starvation. Myrtle Sherwood of Leachville, in the Arkansas Delta, sent a desperate message to Roosevelt in September 1933. "Only last week a child starved to death right here," she wrote. "The father tried to get work. Tried to get credit. Tried to get help from the RFC. But the child was laying on a quilt under a shade tree with death rattles in its throat when the RFC committee arrived too late to save it with food." Sherwood implored the president to step in. "That is only one instant among many," she said. "There are hundreds of destitute familys and food prices going up no money no work, and it raining every day, and the cotton rotting in the fields." Sherwood knew the problem: "You only hear from the people who can talk Big Business. But Please consider the Poor fellow who only ask for the crumbs from the rich mans table." Even the crumbs, she said, "are put out of his reach."[66]

Petitioners for work relief through FERA or its winter jobs program, the CWA, likewise found a system rigged against them—or at least in favor of the administrators and their friends. In Arkansas, FERA administrators declared many tenant farmers and sharecroppers ineligible for work relief because they already had employment, even if they were broke and hungry. They also denied relief to those who declined low-wage farm work. To those who still qualified for work relief, Arkansas planters assigned the standard town improvement and cleaning projects. Some planters put men to work on plantation improvement assignments, pleased that they could now have the government pay men to dig ditches and pave roads through the cotton fields. A field investigator in Mississippi in the winter of 1933 reported that most CWA workers were not the neediest unemployed but instead "successful business men" whose "recent reverses had placed them in the group of CWA prospective workers." The hungriest people remained unaided, and black women in particular were denied CWA work even when they qualified for it. Meanwhile, Memphis CWA administrators who were supposed to put people to work on city projects instead offered their friends and neighbors the domestic services of the African American women who petitioned for aid.[67]

When FERA representative Elmer Scott toured the South to evaluate the program in the spring of 1934, he departed Memphis shaken. This New Deal stronghold had proven hospitable enough, and its business sector was as jovial as ever. Yet the city's businessmen showed an offhanded, genteel disdain for the people they lived amongst. "There is a sinister atmosphere in Memphis,—all the more so because disguised by a deceptive color," Scott reported.[68]

He talked to businessmen, he talked to social workers, and he talked to laborers. He forgot, in his brief report, to name a single one of them, to offer any details to account for his dismay, except to say that no one who was very rich seemed much worried about anyone who was not. "When there was any apparent concern it was in respect to the state of their own immediate affairs," Scott said of the city's industrialists. "They were really very sorry for the mass, but the betterment of the mass could only arise out of the prosperous operation of industry." As for the social workers and the civic-minded members of the middle class, "Even those who showed the most intelligent concern acted as though they were licked."[69]

Scott's report ended with an almost audible sigh. "Memphis gave the distinct feeling that a warm welcome was extended to government concerning itself in the plight of the unemployed, and paying the bills," he wrote, "so long as it is the Federal government." Federal intervention meant that well-off Memphians could carry on with their own concerns and not worry about the poor. Indeed, "the local conscience is atrophical and that in itself is the greatest tragedy." Scott's report focused on political and civic leaders, and he did not address their religious perspectives. But if they accepted Lipsey's framing of the question, "Must the government do our religious work for us?" wealthy and middle-class Memphians seemed to answer with a resounding "yes."[70]

If white religious leaders in the region celebrated the New Deal's accomplishments with varied degrees of enthusiasm, black leaders more often echoed Scott's concerns about local leaders in charge of the programs. One Mississippi minister wrote to Roosevelt to "call attention to the Southern negro who has not had a square deal of the many projects since the depression." Yet black religious leaders also applauded signs that the Roosevelt administration cared more for African Americans' safety and well-being in the South than had previous administrations. In 1934, Harold Ickes, Roosevelt's secretary of the interior and head of the PWA, created an "Interdepartmental Group Concerned with Special Problems of Negroes" to push for inclusion of African Americans in the major New Deal programs. Though the group had little power, its existence seemed a hopeful step. The overall standard of living for black workers who kept their jobs also increased a little as their employers found a way to cheat the government and stopped working so hard to cheat their workers.[71]

Still, the celebration of Roosevelt as a religious figure and the New Deal as a religious accomplishment seemed excessive to many black clergy. Russell Barbour scoffed at another National Baptist who declared, "God brought President Roosevelt to the throne for such a time as this." Barbour described the political wrangling between Roosevelt and his opponents in the Democratic primary and concluded, "We will let you decide whether a political deal or Divine Providence made President Roosevelt."[72]

FOR MANY DESPERATE white southerners, the New Deal seemed an answer to prayer. Like their parishioners and petitioners, religious leaders who questioned Roosevelt's commitment to repeal or his willingness to provide relief to both rich bankers and landless laborers nonetheless celebrated each new program as a step toward recovery. They also took credit, joyful that the state took up the social programs that many churches and synagogues had long promoted.

Yet for black southern religious leaders, the New Deal settled too easily into a Jim Crow mold that defied their understanding of Christian aspirations and principles. The New Deal might benefit black workers, but local administration meant that programs like the NRA and FERA benefited white workers more, and white elites most of all. It thus widened the gulf between the races and between the classes, and it wrote Jim Crow into national policy. Some white southern religious leaders celebrated the New Deal for those very reasons. They lamented their loss of authority as Prohibition ended, but they believed that they could control the New Deal. Though they might relinquish some moral authority to the state, it seemed that the state would preserve the segregated order they valued. For the most part, both groups were right.

But they were not altogether right. Two years later, Roosevelt introduced a new round of legislation, and as he did so he stopped to ask the clergy what they thought of the New Deal. Their answers would show that its legacy was already more complicated than either its boosters or its detractors had anticipated.

5

Not One Cent for Religion

AT THE END of September 1935, tens of thousands of American ministers, priests, and rabbis retrieved from their mailboxes individually addressed letters signed by President Franklin Roosevelt. Perhaps some stood by the mailbox to unseal the envelope that bore a White House return address. Perhaps some arrived home in the evening to find the letter waiting on the table, or in the hand of an excited child or spouse. They had heard Roosevelt's voice over the radio in his Fireside Chats, and some had written to him already. This White House spent far more time than its predecessors corresponding with American citizens, but to receive a personally addressed letter from the president—even a form letter—was at least "a very agreeable surprise."[1]

Two and a half years after the president took office, he wanted to know what the nation's ministers, priests, and rabbis had to say about his New Deal. Roosevelt's letter opened with flattery: "Your high calling brings you into intimate daily contact not only with your own parishioners, but with people generally in your community. I am sure you see the problems of your people with wise and sympathetic understanding." "Because of the grave responsibilities of my office," Roosevelt went on, "I am turning to representative Clergymen for counsel and advice." Specifically, he asked for input about the Works Progress Administration and the Social Security Act, both established earlier that year. "I shall deem it a favor if you will write to me about conditions in your community," the president requested. "Tell me where you feel our government can better serve our people." He closed with an appeal to cooperation: "We can solve our many problems, but no one man or single group can do it,—we shall have to work together for the common end of better spiritual and material conditions for the American people."[2]

It is significant that Roosevelt sought feedback and support from the nation's clergy; it is equally significant that he did so only after enacting the social policies that became the hallmark of his legacy and made the state the primary source of support for needy Americans. Between Roosevelt's inauguration in 1933 and the passage of the Social Security Act in 1935, the new president worked with a Democratic Congress to enact a broad range of relief, recovery, and rehabilitation programs. Many of the first New Deal's temporary programs, like the Federal Emergency Relief Administration (FERA), would soon expire, but the new programs aimed to create a permanent social safety net.

The clergy responded enthusiastically and by the thousands. Their replies to Roosevelt's inquiry reflect equal parts gratitude and apprehension that the president had singled them out to write to him, and they generally took the task seriously. These private letters to the president take both a more positive and a more measured tone than do religious journals, letters to news editors, polls of clerical attitudes, or denominational pronouncements of the same period. White upper and middle-class clergy proved likelier to respond, but replies from black clergy and from bivocational, unemployed, and even destitute preachers poured into the White House as well. Many did not identify their affiliation; those who did were most often part of the region's major Protestant denominations, Catholic, or Jewish. A few women replied too—noting that though Roosevelt had not sought their advice, perhaps he should have. Women also wrote to Eleanor Roosevelt, whom they accurately guessed would be likelier to take their concerns seriously.

The two programs that Roosevelt asked the clergy to evaluate were centerpieces of the second New Deal, another barrage of legislation enacted between 1935 and 1936. The Works Progress Administration (WPA), a comprehensive public works and unemployment relief program and the New Deal's largest agency, drew a less detailed and more ambivalent response, perhaps because ministers seemed uncertain about its relationship to their religious ideals and the churches' work. The clergy showed no such doubts about the Social Security Act, particularly in the South. There, both black and white religious leaders celebrated the program as a victory, even "a Divine Revelation," because of its provisions for the elderly, the orphaned, and the disabled. Two years after the New Deal had begun, many clergy still identified its principles as religious ones, and they celebrated its achievements as their own.[3]

Yet clergy in Memphis and the Delta continued to express concern about the execution of New Deal programs. Two years into the New Deal, they feared their own loss of status relative to the men and women appointed to work for the state. Some believed the poor benefited too much; others the rich. Many white clergy predictably complained that the new programs would do even more than the previous ones to erode white authority over black workers, but more than a few instead joined black clergy in chastising the administration for its continued willingness to leave black southerners out of the New Deal and in poverty. Those on both sides declared that the New Deal's good intentions meant little when political friendships and selfish local administrators corrupted its delivery. Most clergy recognized that the question of local administration was, at bottom, a question of race and the South's determined exclusion of African Americans. Some provided a theological rationale for that exclusion; a few offered prophetic challenges to it.

Southerners' rapid and eager turn from church to state for help on matters both financial and moral illustrated both a general dissatisfaction with southern religious responses to crisis and, to many clergy, an alarmingly reduced role for the church in people's everyday lives. Southerners wrote to the Roosevelts or to members of the administration to report any manner of wrongs, to seek aid, and to ask for guidance in personal matters. Particularly for poor whites and African Americans whose concerns had long fallen on deaf ears, the federal government now represented a new source of help and redress. When clergy found out that church members had written to the president to ask for work or counsel, or to report on events in the community or even the church, many felt sharply a corresponding reduction in their own authority.Concerned clergy argued that Roosevelt could simultaneously reconnect people to their churches and address the corrupt administration of relief programs if only he would make a place for the church in the New Deal administration. For many, this step seemed the logical extension of a program modeled on Jewish and Christian social principles. Ministers offered themselves as administrators of relief and their churches as public works projects. But despite Roosevelt's penchant for biblical language and his generous appointments of Catholics, Jews, and Protestant liberals, New Deal administrators continued to do more to disentangle than to unite church and state, and more to disengage from the work of the churches than to include it. The New Deal funded new schools and community facilities in thousands of communities across the nation, but the churches beside them sat untouched. Even some New Deal supporters lamented the government's willingness to fund a range of public programs while it provided "not one cent for religion."[4]

It seemed clearer than ever to the New Deal's opponents that the expanded federal state encroached dangerously on the churches' moral authority at both the local and legislative levels. A larger and more powerful state, they feared, meant a smaller and less powerful church. The previous two years of federal programming provided them ample evidence for that concern. New Deal supporters saw things differently. For them, the church and state worked separately toward similar aims, and the infusion of their religious principles into the state meant a new era of growth for both church and state. In either case, the ongoing expansion of the state under the New Deal forced religious leaders to rethink the place and power of the church and its relationship to the federal government.

"The Friendship of Christian Ministers"

As clergy crafted their responses to the president, the nation showed signs of slow recovery. Unemployment remained high and national income low, but both had improved since the low point of 1933: unemployment dropped from its peak twenty-five percent in 1933 to twenty percent by the end of 1935, and national income increased by forty percent in the same period. National income remained at only sixty-seven percent of its 1929 total, however, and wages too remained low. The national per capita income—total wages divided by total population—had dropped from $679 in 1929 to $376 in 1933, and by 1935 rebounded to $465. In Mississippi, the state with the lowest income in the country, per capita income had plummeted from a paltry $268 in 1929 to just $126 in 1933, and by the end of 1935 it rose to a still-anemic $177. Arkansas and Tennessee, with slightly higher per capita incomes, followed a similar trajectory, as did the rest of the South. There was reason, then, for both optimism and concern.[5]

Concern had outpaced optimism by 1934, when months dragged by with no significant new action from the White House or halls of Congress. The first New Deal, focused on immediate relief and short-term economic recovery, had garnered mixed reactions during the previous two years. The Supreme Court overturned the unpopular National Recovery Administration in May 1935 and the Agricultural Adjustment Administration in December. Roosevelt also chose to end FERA to focus on work relief rather than direct relief. He faced intense pressure from the left to establish more expansive, long-term programs to restore national confidence and prosperity, while opponents on the right dug in their heels. Workers across the nation went on strike in 1934 to demand union recognition and fair wages. The first round of New Deal legislation had arrested the nation's downward slide, but no end to the depression seemed near when Roosevelt finally took action again in January 1935 and laid out a new blueprint for congressional action.[6]

In April, Roosevelt signed into law a dramatically expanded work relief effort through the 1935 Emergency Relief Appropriation Act, creating the WPA. In a fireside chat after he signed the legislation, Roosevelt explained that the program would "establish the practical means to help those who are unemployed in this present emergency." He also promoted his Social Security program, crafted primarily by Secretary of Labor Frances Perkins and making its way through Congress. Roosevelt claimed that Social Security would "make provisions intended to relieve, to minimize, and to prevent future unemployment." In addition to providing old-age and short-term unemployment insurance through a mandatory and self-sustaining payroll tax, the Social Security Act would establish relief programs for the blind, the elderly poor, and children with only one parent or guardian. The second New Deal also included the Resettlement Administration to aid displaced farmers, the Rural Electrification Administration to bring electricity to the countryside, and the National Labor Relations Act to support organized labor.[7]

It stood to reason, then, that Roosevelt might be particularly eager for feedback on the New Deal in the fall of 1935. By then, the WPA was underway already, as were the relief programs of the Social Security Act. The insurance programs operated on a delayed schedule: the government began to collect Social Security taxes and made emergency lump-sum payments in January 1937; in 1940, the program began to provide monthly benefits.[8]

Two polls conducted just a year before the Roosevelt administration sent out its clergy letter may further explain the administration's particular concern with clerical opinion. The first, conducted by *The World Tomorrow*, the journal of the socialist-leaning, Christian pacifist Fellowship of Reconciliation, asked fifteen questions to just over twenty thousand clergymen to determine "liberal and radical trends within the ranks of Protestant pastors and Jewish rabbis." Of that group, sixty-two percent reported themselves to be pacifists, and twenty-eight percent advocated some form of socialism. "Among all the trades, occupations, and professions in this country, few can produce as high a percentage of Socialists as can the ministry," reported the journal. While the journal did not ask about attitudes toward the Roosevelt administration, it did poll clergymen on whether they preferred the form of capitalism that dominated in the United States prior to 1929 or a "cooperative commonwealth," which could include "drastically reformed capitalism," socialism, communism, fascism, or any other system. Just over half the total clergy polled preferred "drastically reformed capitalism," which put them roughly in line with the Roosevelt administration. Only ten percent of voters deemed pre-1929 capitalism to be "consistent with the ideals and methods of Jesus and the noblest of the Hebrew prophets." The clergy polled represented only about ten percent of American clergy, and they disproportionately came from mainline northeastern and midwestern churches. Pockets of radical activity flourished in the depression South as well, however, and continued to grow in Memphis and the Delta.[9]

The second poll, conducted by the *Literary Digest* in the summer of 1934, drew from a broader sampling of opinion, though its respondents were also likelier than the general population to be highly literate professionals. The *Digest* asked 1,772,163 Americans whether they approved "on the whole the acts and policies of Roosevelt's first year." Based on its simple yes-or-no question, the magazine found that sixty-one percent of Americans supported Roosevelt and only thirty-nine percent opposed him. His approval rating by this measure was nearly four percent higher than his margin of the popular vote in the 1932 election, and Roosevelt performed particularly well among the professionals likeliest to participate in the poll. As the *Digest* put it, "Business Men, Clergy, Physicians, Educators, Lawyers, 17 Colleges, 47 States Vote 'Yes'—State of Vermont and Bankers Vote 'No.'" But clergy approved of Roosevelt's policies at a much lower rate than the general population: only fifty-four percent of the nearly twenty-five thousand clergy polled supported the president. The journal also noted that Roosevelt's overall performance relative to 1932 suffered most in agricultural states and the Deep South—including Arkansas, Mississippi, and Tennessee. The poll's interpreters concluded, "If the farmers have found Roosevelt wanting it is probably not because he is too radical. Their complaint against him, in sum, is quite likely to be that he is too cautious."[10]

Together, these polls suggested that Roosevelt's most serious critics among the clergy, as among Americans generally, came from the left. With the second New Deal, Roosevelt sought to answer critics like Huey Long of Louisiana, Father Charles Coughlin of Michigan, and Dr. Francis Townsend of California, who pushed the government to do more to address the depression and to establish measures to provide a safety net for older and unemployed citizens. Women in the administration, including Frances Perkins, had also pushed Roosevelt to better serve the unemployed. The Works Progress Administration, the Social Security Act, and the National Labor Relations Act addressed their concerns.[11]

Yet protest on the right had increased as well. A Memphis Unitarian wrote gleefully to Roosevelt, "My strongest word of recommendation for you is that my son in law in Wall Street says he knows none there who would not gladly strangle you." Despite the New Deal's procapitalist policies, bankers, manufacturers, and many businessmen despised Roosevelt for his willingness to tinker with the economic system, expand government oversight, and support organized labor. Many of those businessmen had built strong fundamentalist and premillennialist alliances during the 1920s, and together they characterized Roosevelt as an apocalyptic figure, an amalgam of Mussolini, Hitler, and Stalin. One of Roosevelt's advisors warned him in the summer of 1935 that opposition from the evangelical right grew ever stronger. This warning too may have prompted the administration to reach out to the clergy.[12]

Roosevelt's own experience with liberal Protestants, Catholics, and Jews in the administration would have insulated him from fundamentalist critique and further infuriated that base. Roosevelt cultivated a friendly relationship with the Federal Council of Churches, and he met with its leadership annually and issued public statements in support of its social justice work. He also endorsed the interfaith National Committee for Religion and Welfare Recovery's Loyalty Days, which encouraged all Americans to attend a worship service of their choice on a designated weekend. Roosevelt found much in common with Catholic and Jewish social perspectives, and he nurtured the relationship with Catholics that he had begun to build as governor of New York. The president quoted papal encyclicals alongside the Federal Council of Churches' Social Creed, and he spoke before Catholic Charities, which the New Deal administration also incorporated into its work. Two Catholics sat on Roosevelt's cabinet, and so many Jews participated in the New Deal administration that anti-Semites disparaged the New Deal as the "Jew Deal." Catholics and Jews disproportionately supported the president, as did liberal Protestants.[13]

Despite Roosevelt's history of cooperation with American clergy and people of faith, the letter to the clergy was an implicit admission that the president had managed just fine for two and a half years without their formal support. As the administration surely expected, many clergy nonetheless expressed only gratitude for the gesture. "I thank you with all my heart for this kindly notice of us preachers," wrote a Mississippi Southern Baptist. "It is the first time in my long ministry that any great officer of the state has ever given us credit for being worthy of consideration in the most important matter of government." Then again, the minister was not quite sure what the clergy had to offer. "Well, most of us are not doing any great amount of thinking," he admitted. "We are just swept along by the passing wave of public sentiment."[14]

But Roosevelt's letter also stirred outrage. Soon, papers reported that his message was nearly identical to one that Wisconsin Governor Philip La

Follette had sent to that state's clergy the preceding March. Press coverage characterized Roosevelt's letter as a thinly veiled tactic to curry favor in preparation for the next year's election. Many of the respondents noted exactly that. "Is it possible," asked an Arkansas minister, "that you sincerely desire the friendship of Christian ministers whose advice was formerly counted as little?" Others accused the president of making a transparent attempt to shore up a diminishing base of support, and some of the most critical took to the papers to publish their replies for all to see. Joe Jeffers's old nemesis Dale Crowley—acquitted of the murder of one of Jeffers's supporters—penned a sneering response to the president. A fundamentalist who shared Jeffers's anti-Semitism, Crowley contended that Roosevelt had "drowned out the pleas of the thousands of Gospel ministers" who had fought to enact and preserve Prohibition. He further suggested that if Roosevelt really cared what the clergy thought, he would "dismiss all the atheistic, Communistic professors of Columbia University from your Brain Trust" and restore Prohibition.[15]

Crowley and many other clergy doubted that the president himself would ever see their responses. Perhaps they were right. Still, nearly a third of the clergy responded: over 100,000 of 121,700 letters sent to clergymen reached the intended recipients, and nearly 30,000 wrote back. Hundreds of letters arrived at the White House from Memphis and the Delta. Some of those letters amounted to only a paragraph or two, while a few topped twenty pages, but most of them—even critical ones—offered thoughtful evaluations of New Deal programs and detailed, vivid descriptions of their local effects.[16]

The administration assigned Department of Commerce official Aubrey C. Mills to read and evaluate the letters, and his careful underlining, annotations, and tabulations of the letters indicate that their contents mattered to Roosevelt's administration. Mills categorized the 12,096 replies that arrived by mid-November as "favorable," "favorable with criticism," or "unfavorable," He designated a stunning eighty-four percent as either "favorable" (forty-nine percent) or "favorable with criticism" (thirty-five percent). Perhaps Mills's categorizations were generous to his boss—even those letters marked "favorable" sometimes quibbled about Prohibition or about local administrators. Still, a sizable majority of clergy expressed approval of all or part of the New Deal even as they acknowledged that the church had taken a back seat to the state in addressing the social problems of the depression.[17]

The tone of the letter to the clergy set the tone for the responses to it. Even clergy who went on to criticize elements of the New Deal often used religious language to describe Roosevelt himself. Among the several hundred letters from Memphis and the Delta, unflinching critics like Crowley proved the exception. Perhaps the clergy who might deem Roosevelt the antichrist chose not to sit down and write him a letter, but southerners in general proved far more likely to term him a heavenly figure than an apocalyptic one.

The president was, according to various clergy, the "Good Samaritan," "God's prepared man for leadership . . . as truly as Moses was the prepared man for leading the Children of Israel out of bondage," or even a divine figure himself. "Who knoweth but thou didst come into the nation for a day like this?" wrote a Mississippi baptist impressed that the president had "manned the Ship of State so securely" and "succored a bleeding nation." An Episcopalian in the small river port of Rosedale, Mississippi, declared he saw "a striking comparison of the present administration to early biblical records" and a parallel between Roosevelt and God: "You the creator—creating the plan of administration, while we the creature, live according to the plan created." This Episcopalian worried that things might turn out badly for Roosevelt, but it was not his fault. Instead, "We have failed to live according to the principle of life given us by the creator of life." Many saw this latter concern as their opportunity to contribute to Roosevelt's success, and they described his efforts and theirs as cooperative.[18]

Yet the letters may have been on the whole less glowing than the Roosevelt administration anticipated. Even many of those clergy who linked the New Deal to religious principles and the president to religious figures often expressed disappointment with particular programs, and sometimes with the president too. The Twenty-First Amendment garnered the most criticism, and Roosevelt's popular work relief programs met with mixed reviews. Even in Memphis and the Delta, much of the concern about the New Deal continued to come from the left, from clergy who deemed the administration's religious impulses well intentioned but too weak to institute the sweeping changes necessary to set the nation right. Still, critics on the left stressed the opportunity for cooperation between church and state. Those on the right more often described the two as competitors.

"New Provisions for Human Welfare"

A few themes ran through both critical and enthusiastic letters from the clergy: disappointment over the end of Prohibition, joy at the passage of Social Security, and concern about the administration of work relief. On the latter two questions, clerical opinion followed national opinion. On Prohibition, it did not. Protestant clergy complained that the nation was awash in liquor, and that repeal had brought "a fearful tide of misery and suffering which has increased the sadness of homes and hearts." One of the few nonclergy to respond to Roosevelt's letter was an "old-fashioned grandmother" from Blytheville, Arkansas, who deemed it her Christian duty to "[help] the preachers to inform you that [the] Liquor proposition is growing worse every day [and] has been ever since repeal." A few still saw Prohibition repeal as evidence that the president was simply not to be trusted with the nation's moral health. For most, however, that disappointment remained separate from their general attitude toward the New Deal.[19]

The clearest indication that southern clergy still claimed credit for the New Deal came in their assessments of Social Security. "Above all else, as I see it, is your Social Security Program," wrote the editor of the South's major white Methodist journal. "For the first time in our history we have a National Administration that is seeking to realize practically all the objectives of the 'Social Creeds' of the Churches—Catholic, Protestant, Jewish." A Mississippi rabbi believed Social Security to be "drawn up in the spirit of Israel's ancient prophets, those eloquent and fearless protagonists of social justice and righteousness," and he noted that he had recently referred to the program in his Day of Atonement sermon. "It seems a providential affair that with unusual courage and fortitude our Chief Executive has undertaken to translate vision into reality and to suggest new provisions for human welfare," gushed a white Memphis Congregationalist. "My impression, Mr. President, is that under your wise compassionate leadership there is more real religion in our government at the present hour than at any time in its history." For advocates of social Christianity, the government's extension of a social safety net was the clearest indication of its adherence to religious principles.[20]

The old-age pension was the most well-known and popular part of the Social Security Act, and it was the part clergy celebrated most. As a Delta Episcopalian declared, "[A]nything that protects the aged and the incapacitated seems to me and to them a truly Christian work" that "a Christian nation should undertake." An Arkansas Christian agreed: "The greatest benefit of this measure will be spiritual. What people want primarily is security. When they have that there will be manifest a new sense of neighborliness and charity." He declared that Roosevelt's "moral achievements, or failures" would outlast "any economic ones."[21]

Social Security raised questions even for those clergy who supported it as Christian, however. Since it was their idea, many clergy seemed to suggest, they ought to clarify how Roosevelt should handle the program. "As to social security, the idea is basically Christian," instructed a Delta Methodist, "but

I am sure that you do not have to be reminded of the fact that we must guard against taking such good care of the aged poor and otherwise unfortunates, as will put a premium on poverty and cut the ham string of individual effort." Another feared the "high cost to the white population" of Social Security because "one-half of the citizenry pays a very small part of the taxes."[22]

Indeed, Roosevelt had heeded such warnings. He believed that only a conservative social insurance program would make it through Congress and win the support of the public, and he allowed white southerners to write most African Americans out of the program. The Social Security Act's provisions for the elderly and the unemployed mimicked private insurance. The government mandated participation and funded it through a regressive payroll tax. Automatic enrollment meant that beneficiaries soon deemed their aid an entitlement, something to which they had contributed and whose benefits they deserved. Southern legislators refused to allow the bill to cover agricultural and domestic workers, the two primary occupations available to black southerners. They also ensured that states, rather than the federal government, could set the rates for unemployment insurance and Aid to Dependent Children, again bending progressive legislation to Jim Crow economics. The relief programs of the Social Security Act, unlike its social insurance, required an application and evaluation for each recipient. Single mothers—who also faced discrimination in New Deal work relief—were now dependents eligible for relief only through their children. This again meant that black women in the South suffered most, as local relief agents could easily term them unfit mothers and thus deny them access to public assistance.[23]

Clergy concerned about "individual effort" generally approved the legislation, whose conservatism appealed in particular to the white middle class. Poor clergy sometimes regretted the program's limits, as did African American clergy. Yet even they celebrated Social Security as largely Christian. "After considering the comments on the New Social Security Legislation, I think it is a Divine Revelation," wrote N. B. Bynum of Arkansas. "If properly administered every unfortunate citizen will be benefited." Perhaps Bynum already knew that he would be disappointed: "I am not attempting to say that they have not been helped in a general way but my observation lead me to believe if my group (Negroes) had a separate unit and administered by Negroes it would give them better advantage of the appropriations."[24]

Another Mississippian proved more skeptical. He believed that Social Security "will relieve a great deal of suffering and embarrassing, which povity brings to the many aged unfortunate people; providing this Act is carried out with an equally divided share to all povity stricken Americans citizens, regardless of race or color." But thus far "the Southern negro . . . has not had a square deal of the many projects since the depression." Clergy concerned about racial justice thus had to weigh the hope that the New Deal might transform the opportunities available to southern African Americans against clear evidence that it disproportionately benefited whites. For them, the New Deal's Christian promise hinged on the degree to which it accommodated or undercut the economic injustices of Jim Crow.[25]

Clerical questions about the fairness of the Social Security Act proved minor relative to their deeper doubts about the WPA and its administration, yet many claimed the WPA too as a Christian achievement. "The WPA and other relief legislation have been of inestimable blessing and benefit to the people of this community," gushed one Mississippi minister. "It has actually put the daily bread into many mouths, and has helped to inspire hope and confidence during one of our most trying crises." He also deemed the WPA a practical victory: "It has helped to set the wheels of commerce turning again. It has saved many of our most substantial farmers and businessmen from financial ruin."[26]

The WPA still had not begun in earnest, but the Roosevelt administration nonetheless scheduled FERA, and with it all remaining direct relief save that in the Social Security Act, to expire at the end of 1935. For the most part, the clergy who understood this development applauded it, although some still depended on relief and feared for their families as it ended. The WPA provided work primarily to individuals already on the relief rolls, with several limitations: only one member of each family would be eligible, and only about two thirds of those eligible for WPA work would have it. Harry Hopkins directed the new organization, which followed a decentralized model similar to FERA. Yet while the Public Works Administration (PWA) had operated through private industry, the WPA put people to work directly for the government. The WPA paid what Hopkins called "security wages," which would have seemed generous to those previously reliant only on direct relief but remained well below the wages for the same work in private industry. The sudden end to FERA at the start of the WPA meant that Americans who relied on the federal government for food and basic supplies suddenly found themselves without, their need turned back to the cities and states that had failed them before. Roosevelt's correspondence with the clergy took place in the midst of this chaos.[27]

Yet among all but the poorest clergy, fear about the dangers of what they invariably termed "the dole" outweighed concern for those who would lose the support they needed. "It was a grief to me when I saw that America had to resort to direct relief for the dole," wrote the same white clergyman who had warned Roosevelt not to be overly generous with Social Security. "But I rejoice that this is being replaced by putting those that must be helped into work" on projects "that will make our nation in a material way more admirable and will make individual life more pleasant." An ardent African American New Deal supporter wrote his opinion in clearer terms—perhaps based in part on his observations that whites benefited disproportionately: "The Dole system has caused more lazy triffiling people than anything else."[28]

For clergy still wrestling with the tension between long-standing beliefs in individual responsibility and clear evidence of widespread social crisis, work relief provided a safe middle ground that addressed the latter without undermining the former. The Roosevelt administration likewise valorized—even sacralized—labor as the path to individual and national stability. In his first inaugural address, Roosevelt celebrated "the joy and moral stimulation of work," and in his fireside chat after the passage of the WPA, he described unemployment as "enforced idleness which is an enemy of the human spirit." Harry Hopkins, administrator of FERA, repeatedly stressed the temporary nature of direct aid as "a bridge by which people can pass from relief status over to normal self-support."[29]

Many southern clergy expressed at least tepid approval of the WPA, but more doubted that the administration could ensure that its local representatives would administer it fairly. Those who declared the WPA Christian in principle expressed the most alarm that its execution might undermine its intent, though they disagreed about how that might happen. Some middle-class and elite clergy approved of local administration and administrators' efforts to preserve the region's power structure. Yet even many who firmly advocated local control of relief doubted the integrity of the particular local people in control. The poor, African Americans, and others outside the southern establishment more often questioned the very premise of local control and asked Roosevelt to take a firmer stand. As one firm New Deal supporter warned, "[L]ocal administration is one of your handicaps and one of your problems, created by the selfishness of people down the line." Here, the clergy took seriously Roosevelt's request for counsel, and they moved from theological to practical commentary.[30]

Because the WPA had just begun, abuses under FERA often shaped attitudes toward its replacement. One out-of-work white Mississippi Delta minister reported during the transition from FERA to WPA that too many of the government's employees "are in large measure men and women who are otherwise able to live in comfort." "Worse yet," he said, the administrators "hand out relief to families who could well maintain themselves without aid, while many really destitute families not only are refused aid; but are even ridiculed and subjected to humiliation by workers when they ask for aid." Sometimes that aid never made it to anyone in need at all, the minister went on, reporting that "at a certain relief station" near his hometown of Cruger, "merchants have had truck loads of goods, sent by the government for the poor and suffering, and have carried these goods to their stores to sell." And yet, "an educated, intelligent lady told me that many people here will starve this winter unless something is done for them." This minister had yet to receive relief, but he worried more about a neighbor, a black tenant farmer with nine children whom he could not clothe or feed. For this southern liberal, it was hard to celebrate the Christian ideals of a program that local elites could too often harness for their own purposes.[31]

WPA administrators did make an effort to correct concerns about corruption and discrimination that sullied earlier programs, and some religious leaders aided that effort. Before FERA ended, each state that wished to continue to receive federal funds had to establish a welfare board, to which people in need of relief could now turn. Tennessee and Mississippi complied, but the Arkansas legislature balked at any orders from the federal government and by the last day of its legislative session had ignored the welfare board requirement. Pulaski County welfare director Ora Nix phoned Rabbi Ira Sanders of Congregation B'nai Israel in Little Rock, who had established the Little Rock School of Social Work in 1927, to ask for his help. Together, the two interrupted the legislative session and refused to leave until the state complied with federal welfare requirements. It did so and promptly promoted Ora Nix to head the new State Social Welfare Office. In this case, New Deal requirements forced local politicians to act on social reforms that religious progressives and social workers had for many years advocated to no avail.[32]

The return of welfare to the states did not bode well for African Americans in the South, and the Federal Council of Negro Affairs, a group of black advisors to the administration, pushed the president to ensure that the New Deal included all southerners. By 1936, the administration included black leaders in many of the major programs, including the WPA. At that program's start in 1935, Roosevelt issued an executive order barring discrimination, and Hopkins too ordered that aid must be administered fairly. Indeed, the WPA spent millions of dollars in black neighborhoods and employed African Americans at a much higher rate than its first New Deal antecedents. The WPA's arts and writers' programs employed a generation of black southerners—including Mississippi native Richard Wright—who would build their careers on that start.[33]

Yet complaints continued unabated, as did evidence that southern relief administrators used ever more devious means to manipulate federal dollars. "The WPA and the New Deal agencies haven't meant a goddamned thing to the Negroes of Mississippi," reported one Jackson resident. "Mississippi politicians refuse to put up a dollar for work relief for Negroes." In Memphis, black women on relief reported that they continued to be "cut off and sent to do work for some white person at three or four dollars per week"—wages much lower than what the WPA stipulated. When the WPA managed to employ African Americans for public work, planters accused the government of stealing their workers, because the city's black men resisted being loaded by the hundreds onto trucks and sent back to the cotton plantations as day laborers. Poor whites suffered too. Endlessly creative in their use of terminology, Mississippi's business interests diverted WPA funds to build "vocational schools" that upon investigation turned out to be private factories that shipped in prison labor when even work relief recipients would not accept their rock-bottom wages.[34]

While few white southern clergy questioned Jim Crow, many disapproved of the discrimination against both African Americans and poor whites in WPA work. A Jackson minister, a "Southern white man, to the [manor] born," wrote a private plea to Harry Hopkins in 1936 regarding the "very gross discrimination between the races" in Jackson. He reported that "though the negroes constitute more than one-half the population of Mississippi, they have not received one-tenth of the relief funds sent into this state during the past two or three years." He pointed to the unequal funding of black schools as an example—and indeed, Mississippians applied $8 million in New Deal funds (much of it WPA funding) to white schools in the state and only $400,000 to black schools. A rural Episcopalian similarly warned Roosevelt, "The charity dollar, will invariably reach the political friend before it reaches the povety stricken tenant. . . . By the time the administrators get through there is little or nothing left, save free advice, for those to whom they are administering." He did not blame the president, or even think there was much he could do. The problem: "America loves the dollar more than the neighbor."[35]

Yet Jim Crow's most strident defenders did not approve of what little help the WPA provided to African Americans. A minister of "nine village and country churches" in the Mississippi Delta warned of "the great danger of abuse and misuse" of aid. The evidence: it helped "possibly a majority of negroes, who are inclined to get out of all work possible as some white people do." At the 1934 annual meeting of the Mississippi Conference of the Southern Methodist Church, middle-class black minister similarly concluded, "The masses of Negroes have always been in a poor economic condition." The only difference for them in the depression: "They don't have as much money to spend for what is called a good time." Some middle-class black clergy downplayed the Depression's effects on the poor, while southern whites claimed that black southerners just did not need much to live on anyway, and that any more would only go to waste.[36]

On the surface, these complaints might seem to have little to do with the status of the churches or the clergy. Rarely did they employ religious language—indeed, such complaints often provided a counterbalance to the explicitly religious celebrations of New Deal policies. Yet they prefaced a deeper set of anxieties about the New Deal's effect on southern religion: first, that the New Deal would fracture the Jim Crow order that the white churches had helped to construct and defend; and, second, that New Deal programs might undermine the power of the churches and sever the ties between clergy and their communities.

"They Now Look to the Government for All"

The clergy reported their concerns to Roosevelt, but so did many, many other southerners who just a few years before would never have dreamed of penning a message to the nation's president. Southerners who felt wronged by their local authorities, including the clergy, now often bypassed them and sent their appeals straight to the top. Some clergy appreciated the help, but many expressed alarm that the once-distant government suddenly threatened to undermine their own power and the central place of the churches in many communities. Long-standing fears about the destabilizing power of modernity and the centralization of authority in a distant capital seemed to be unfolding before their eyes.

Both Franklin and Eleanor Roosevelt encouraged people to write to them, and sometimes they wrote back. Their staff read and sorted the mountains of incoming mail, replied as appropriate, and selected letters for the Roosevelts to read and answer personally. The president cultivated a sense of familiar authority through his fireside chats, broadcast on radios across the nation. Eleanor Roosevelt adopted a still friendlier, more familiar tone in her syndicated "My Day" column, which ran six days a week starting the last day of 1935. Each day, Roosevelt sketched out her travels and encounters with ordinary people, and her thoughts both mundane and profound. Both Roosevelts believed that they could embody the confidence they hoped to restore to American life. Their efforts connected many Americans more closely to the president and First Lady than to their hometown leadership, and the millions of letters to the pair bear out that sense of connection.[37]

Some people wrote in clear desperation. A Great War veteran posted his plea to Franklin Roosevelt just days after the 1932 election. "I did everything to help you get this office that a Negro could do," the soldier wrote. "I am naked and have been hungary for three days. Send me overalls and underwear and send and get me out of Miss. because it is the worst place that I ever been in all my life." When it seemed that no one else could help, Americans like this one could now write to their president.[38]

They could also write to the First Lady. "[W]hen I hear your voice over the radio, I can appreciate you more," wrote Mrs. M. L. Brantley, who lived just south of Memphis. "I sure hope I can hear you and our beloved President every time you are on the air." Brantley wrote in September 1934, several months before Roosevelt unveiled his Social Security plan but just after Eleanor Roosevelt had given a speech in favor of social insurance. She asked the First Lady "to do all in your power to get the 'Old Age Pension,'" but she also simply wanted to chat with the woman who seemed so familiar to her. She spoke of her own poor health, her son's troubles getting to work in Memphis, and her concerns that the president might not win re-election. She also spoke of her reverence for the president. "I pray God he may stay in office till Jesus comes again," she said. "Surely he is God's child to have been spared and brought to this day, to try to help the world in these trying last days." Franklin Roosevelt was, for many Americans, a political authority, a religious figure, and a friend all rolled into one.[39]

People often recognized the humor in the widespread sense of familiarity with the first family, but they simply incorporated it into their communications. A Greenville man wrote to thank Eleanor Roosevelt for a quick reply to a previous inquiry and closed his letter with the note, "I could not resist sending along the enclosed cartoon—one hundred and twenty million Americans feel just like that!" The cartoon featured a middle-aged white couple, the woman asking the man, "Have you written to Roosevelt about our drains being clogged?"[40]

Yet for the poorest and most broken, the opportunity to write to the Roosevelts opened a world of possibility, and there was always hope for a favorable reply. In February 1934, a black farmer from east Mississippi named Sylvester Harris telephoned the White House to plead for help in saving his farm from white creditors. Roosevelt's assistant was unavailable, so the president himself answered the phone, made note of Harris's plea, and person-ally referred him to the newly established Home Owners Loan Corporation. News that the president of the United States had come to the aid of a poor Mississippi farmer swept the South and black papers nationwide. Blues gui-tarist Memphis Minnie sang about it, and at least one clergyman preached about it. "I used to say 'the president,' 'a president,'" the minister said. But Roosevelt was "our president."[41]

Such stories enhanced Roosevelt's reputation among southerners of both races and encouraged still more to reach out to him. Harris's story offered hope that instead of turning to the Red Cross or the planter for help, the poor could now appeal to a higher authority: the federal government. If no one else would listen, they might just call up the president of the United States himself. Indeed, an Arkansas woman wrote to Roosevelt that summer, "Your coming to the aid of the old negro down in Miss. imboldens me to do like-wise. I don't see how you can help, but maybe you will find a way." She com-plained about a Civil Works Administration (CWA) project that promised her an indoor "sanitary closet" but failed to deliver. Administration officials quickly forwarded the message to the Arkansas FERA and WPA administra-tor William Dyess and wrote to her that they had done so.[42]

There was peril too in writing to Roosevelt or members of the administra-tion. As with the previous case, when complaints centered around the deliv-ery of relief or interactions with local government agents, officials sent them back to the states. Repeatedly, southerners asked that their names and the particulars of their situations remain confidential because they feared retali-ation. Even clergy worried that their reports to Roosevelt might fall into the wrong hands. The unemployed Cruger, Mississippi, minister who reported abuses of relief closed with an ominous plea. "Please do not refer my letter to any one here: I might meet a bad end for reporting facts," he wrote. "When good people near me have reported the maladministration of relief workers, the complaints were referred back here, thus making matters still harder for the complainants." Southern elites would not easily relinquish their author-ity. But people continued to write for help. The federal presence in the South meant some hope for redress—or at least recognition—of injustices, and southerners in even the smallest hamlets reoriented themselves to this newly engaged government.[43]

Clergy who wholeheartedly supported the New Deal saw no conflict between their interests and the state's growing power. "I know of no presi-dent in history that the people as a whole has more faith in," wrote an Arkansas Methodist who reported that average wages in his church were only thirty-three dollars per month for families of up two twelve people. His poor and desperate members believed Roosevelt was "doing what you can for humanity" and thought of him as "a big brother beloved." His intervention in local matters could only help.[44]

Clergy often sent detailed lists of names, addresses, and incomes of people in their church who were in need, eager for the government to help where they could not. A white Memphis Methodist tabulated the occupations and financial conditions of all 550 members of his church and added a description of the 55 with a "deficiency, delinquency, or dependency" he believed Roosevelt might address. He listed any assistance they had already received, and in some cases indicated the federal aid he deemed appropriate. To preserve his members' privacy, he provided only their initials and ages as identifying information. A typical description read: "Mrs. L.C.M., widow, 65, Son is one-legged R.R. worker and Drunkard; gives mother meager support; income uncertain." The clergyman hoped that this widowed mother and several more of his church members might soon qualify for Social Security.[45]

Ministers who wrote to Roosevelt about their members' specific needs perhaps hoped to take credit for any aid that eventually arrived, but most seemed only concerned that they knew no other adequate source of help for the suffering. The Memphis Methodist approved of Social Security and saw its precedent in the Social Creed of the Churches, but he also criticized Prohibition repeal and the National Recovery Administration (NRA). Like many of his colleagues, this clergyman stressed the connection of the New Deal to religious principles without claiming any particular place in its execution.[46]

Others disagreed. R. L. Phelps, self-proclaimed "southern Democrat" and former superintendent of the Presbyterian Synod of Mississippi, disapproved of nearly every part of the New Deal except Social Security. He argued that people granted work relief proved so ineffective and defiant "as to forfeit the respect of the substantial citizens." Relief thus caused its recipients "to withdraw themselves from the social life of the community and to form a sort of social nucleus of their own." Of particular concern to Phelps was that, "In some cases children are kept away from school, and children who once went to Sunday school and church now go no more." The state, he concluded, had effectively severed the church's hold on community members, who now had someplace else to find help. "Where they once had community contacts for cooperation and sympathy they now look to the Government for all."[47]

Phelps's letter suggests that the New Deal undercut some of the deference with which the poor approached local people who might have once been their only recourse. There is little evidence that poor children stopped going to Sunday school as a result of federal aid. However, some churches fed children who attended, or provided support only to families who regularly showed up on Sundays. It is possible that federal aid made it easier for poor families to disconnect from middle-class churches where they felt out of place. Now, they had options other than local paternalism, and clergy already inclined to question the New Deal expressed both alarm and outrage.

"*I Don't See Why Any Pastor Would Not Want to Be the Angel of Mercy*"

Many churches and clergy felt their power in their communities dwindle. The depression had brought them low, and they had failed to revive either the economy or their members. But they had hoped to recover their status even as they pushed the state to step in where they failed. Instead, some clergy now worried that the federal government was winning more hearts than they were, and everywhere they saw evidence that people revered the distant president more than any local official. Indeed, many clergy admired him just as much as their parishioners did, and they continued to wholeheartedly celebrate the New Deal. A few opposed it absolutely. But some complained of the federal government's distribution of aid and resources with another plan in mind: they wanted a place for the church and the clergy in the relief work. As one clergyman explained, "The church has always done much of this kind of work and can be of much aid to the state."[48]

Such ideas predated the New Deal and reflected the casual interweaving of church and state in the South. In 1932, a Memphis Nazarene pastor traveled to Nashville to pitch to the governor his plan to "save the state $100,000 through the employment of the ministry to aid in the distribution of charity funds." He proposed that the state assign each pastor a small district in which he would evaluate requests and make recommendations about appropriate aid for petitioners. "Through these contacts he can build character and give spiritual nourishment," the minister added. His plan did not meet the eager reception he anticipated, and now Roosevelt's New Deal more explicitly excluded the churches.[49]

Clergy who invited themselves into the New Deal administration made a simple case: local relief administrators were "very much inclined to the reverse of spirituality and are not really interested in suffering mankind." As a result, "Some are receiving help who do not need it while others are being neglected who are really in distress." The solution was simple. It was "of vital importance" that Roosevelt hire clergy or at least "men who are loyal devout Christians" to receive aid applications and "let these men investigate each case and give a honest, unbiased report or recommendation for help." One minister suggested that the president "appoint at least one representa-tive clergyman in each county of the entire Union to represent and look after the benevolent affairs." Another made a generous offer that his counterparts did not: "If [aid] was administered through the churches it could be done free of charge and save the government [the] added expense" of paying relief administrators.[50]

For members of the Protestant establishment, distributing federal aid seemed a way to regain moral authority; for those outside it, it offered an opportunity to gain a new advantage. Though many clergy did not indicate their denominational affiliation or social class in their letters, both appear widely varied. Clergy who requested a place in New Deal administration came from the city and the countryside, and from towns small and large. Several indicated that they served successful town churches, others appeared to come from poor rural churches, and some indicated that they too were poor. A few were black, but more were white, though many did not directly identify their race. Some probably had prior experience with religious char-ity and the blurred lines between public and private aid in the South. Most expressed mixed feelings about the New Deal as a whole—gratitude for its successes, disgust with its failures, and a certainty that they could do a better job than current relief administrators.

African American ministers differed from their white counterparts in that they generally asked only to serve black applicants for aid, and they stressed the importance of inclusion. As important leaders in many small communities, African American ministers who spoke up about the system-atic exclusion of black community members from relief were sometimes the only such voices administrators heeded. "If it would be possible for you to appoint the Minister in their respective Community or some Minister in each State to administer whatever the Government [deems] appropriate for the benefit of our old age people and cripple children I think that would be another great step forward," wrote a Missionary Baptist from Yazoo City. There, he reported, "the men with money and they with greed and envy keep [help] back by fraud from the suffering children of God."[51]

J. E. Adams, a black minister in the Arkansas Delta, wrote to Roosevelt, "[T]housand of my peoples will Never get any benefit." Adams hoped "it was possible that you could [point] are [our] deal direct from the white house to my peoples through The church." Particularly concerned about those "in all of these far back community, and plantations," Adams argued, "no one are able to see these conditions in the community, and look after them better Then the ministers." Like their white counterparts, black ministers who made such proposals probably had both selfish and unselfish motives. But they wrote as representatives of local African American communities as much as on behalf of their churches. Black clergy and their community members were desperate for the New Deal to be, in Adams's words, "are deal" too.[52]

Given their predilection for bickering and name-calling in other circumstances, the white clergy who wrote to Roosevelt displayed remarkable faith in the ability of their fellow men of the cloth to evaluate and meet the needs of people around them. "Is it not a truth that most of the suffering people of the nation are not church goers?" asked E. B. Rucker, pastor of five rural churches. Rucker thought that the answer to his rhetorical question was obvious and thus that "to get folks to attend church and believing in the teaching of the Bible will put them in an attitude to take the help you may give them and get on their feet."

Like many of his colleagues, Rucker proposed that each pastor inventory his own church and community and apportion aid and advice as he saw fit. "I don't see why any pastor would not want to be the angel of mercy to bring your help to his parish," Rucker explained. "This the man of God will do, he will be fair and without recpect to persons; he will be as economical as possible." Best of all, the minister's aid would "bring the people into a closer relationship with the church thereby developing a citizenry that will be loyal and content, even tho with little." For emphasis, Rucker repeated that, although the funding would come from the federal government, "You are not to [administer] it, but the pastors . . . by reaching them and being the agent in driving the wolf from their doors, will give the preacher a grip that will tie him on to their hearts." Rucker volunteered his own services to Roosevelt, noting with some embarrassment that his family was "a little short" and that he would require help with "expenses."[53]

Rucker's honest message reveals much about the motivations of clergy who wanted a place for the church in the New Deal. Although few black or white clergy acknowledged as forthrightly as Rucker that the positions they sought would strengthen both their own authority and their churches', many surely sought exactly that. Most probably believed sincerely that they would be fair and judicious when they evaluated applicants for aid—more discriminating, certainly, than the local officials whose honesty they doubted. Indeed, their ability to discriminate was precisely what white clergy stressed, and many promised to distribute less aid, not more.

But clergy also wanted the power that came with relief administration, and they understood now better than ever that people would turn to those institutions that came to their aid. These clergy sought to reaffirm their own moral authority, and they deemed it better that people feel indebted to the church than to the state—even if the state paid the bills. Furthermore, many agreed with Rucker that churchgoers made better workers and better citizens than nonchurchgoers. If the New Deal threatened to sever the tie between church and community, they argued, then Roosevelt should undo the damage. "If our government has to see to the Bodly Welfare of those why not Spiritual," asked one minister. "See that those unlearned children attend some religious service on Sunday, to be enlighten is Better Citizenship." Such coercion had long been part and parcel of private and even state aid in the South, and many clergy saw no reason federal aid should be any different.[54]

Significantly, the clergy in Memphis and the Delta who asked for a role in aid distribution did not offer to share that position with the people in their churches most likely to have handled such work before and to have maintained some semblance of it during the depression: members of women's societies. One minister even clarified, "It might not be a bad idea to have some one (not a woman—God bless them, I'm for them; but not in this political 'dog fight') to check up on the leaks of local administration." In fact, women like Ellen Woodward, a Mississippi native who headed up women's work programs in both FERA and the WPA and in 1939 became the WPA's director of Women's and Professional Projects, handled that "dog fight" more successfully than many of their male counterparts. Battles between members of women's societies and the clergy who deemed them too independent and envied their successes were common, however, and it is likely that clergy sought an advantage not only for the church but also within it.[55]

The New Deal presented another practical disadvantage to churches. Until then, in many southern communities, church buildings and schools had often been the only available community meeting places. Now, the WPA promised to bring new school gymnasiums, community theaters, and centers to bring people together in secular settings, without the slightest dependence on the beneficence of religious institutions. Meanwhile, religious facilities were not eligible for WPA construction funds, even if they provided their own supplies.

Some clergy did not accept this distinction between civic and religious space, particularly since their buildings had often served as both. "I call your attention to the fact that there are many churches of the Catholic denomination and of other denominations as well who would gladly undertake the building of new churches, parsonages, teachers' dwellings and recreational halls, if they had only to provide the materials and had the labour supplied by the unemployed through the agency of the United States Government," wrote an Arkansas priest. "My own parish is one example and I know there are hundreds of others who would do likewise." Given the administration's cooperation with Catholic Charities, it is understandable that this priest might not accept that his church should follow different rules.[56]

Even clergy who understood the rules pushed them: "I have been told by workers connected with the recovery program that there are no provisions for the use of funds on Churches, either building or equipment," wrote a white Delta Methodist. "This may be wise and best for all parties concerned." But church buildings had gone without necessary repairs during the depression, even as they housed Red Cross distributions and other quasi-governmental efforts. Clergy were in a bind. "I am wondering if some provision could not be made for furnishing proper building and equipment for Churches to better minister to our people," inquired the Methodist.[57]

By 1935, the new opportunities that the New Deal provided for rural people to gather outside the church alarmed some clergy. A white baptist preacher in Tyronza, Arkansas, voiced some approval of New Deal ideals, but he characterized its effects as generally detrimental. Even in the early 1930s, he reported, people were "attending Satin's play houses and the places of sin" instead of church. God punished them with "this depression and these droughts," but now the government was "spending millions of dollars furnished by our government to build pleasure houses and health resorts and *not one cent* for religion." It amounted to "robbing God of what belongs to him." By cutting the churches out of the New Deal, this pastor believed, Roosevelt angered God and worsened the depression. Furthermore, by helping to strengthen secular community institutions and neglecting religious ones, the president was weakening the churches' hold on Americans. God would only grow angrier.[58]

"Booze Seems to Be About the Only Kind of Spirit You Have"

Another, smaller contingent of clergy was already furious with Roosevelt and certain that God agreed. The president faced opposition from both left and right, but neither the radical left nor the radical right was yet very large in Memphis and the Delta. Some liberal and even radical leftist clergy saw clouds on the horizon for the South, however, and like some of Roosevelt's own advisors, they warned the president that "practically all the leaders in movements to defeat your objectives have prominent connections in the Churches." Indeed, the fundamentalist movement that organized in opposition to the president even before he took office allied with angry businessmen to unite the right's opposition to the New Deal. This over-whelmingly white movement proved most successful outside the South, but it also began to gain ground in Arkansas as a result of work by men like Ben Bogard, Joe Jeffers, and Dale Crowley. Arkansas fundamentalists concentrated in the western part of the state, but some made inroads in the Delta as well, perhaps helped along as frustration mounted over that state's particularly corrupt politicians and their chokehold on relief administra-tion. These clergy did not just worry that the New Deal would sever the bond between people and their churches: they contended that Roosevelt wanted to lead Americans away from Christianity altogether. It was their job to fight back.[59]

By 1935, Joe Jeffers had decamped to Florida, leaving behind Dale Crowley in Jonesboro and Ben Bogard in Little Rock to head up the state's funda-mentalist movement. The two circled in similar orbits, but not in coopera-tion. Crowley's *Back to the Bible Crusader* claimed in its masthead to have the "largest circulation of any newspaper in northeastern Arkansas." The *Baptist and Commoner* and *Orthodox Baptist Searchlight*, affiliated with warring fac-tions of Bogard's American Baptist Association (ABA), was circulated all over the state. ABA churches dotted the Arkansas Delta. Crowley remained a visible presence in Jonesboro until he left Arkansas in 1936 and his church returned to the Southern Baptist Convention.[60]

Yet only a handful of the nearly one hundred letters to Roosevelt from the Arkansas Delta share Bogard and Crowley's personal disdain for Roosevelt and their ferocious hostility to the New Deal—and that handful includes both Bogard's and Crowley's letters. Of nearly two hundred letters from each state that arrived in time for his November tally, Aubrey Mills counted only sixteen in Mississippi and eighteen in Arkansas as wholly unfavorable, and most of these came from outside the Delta. White baptists penned most of the critical letters, though a few Methodists and members of Churches of Christ joined their number, and a few omitted any affiliation. Given the confrontational and political nature of this strain of fundamentalism, it seems that Roosevelt's letter to the clergy should have provided an irresist-ible opportunity to give the president a public flogging. The paucity of such responses suggests that fundamentalists in this Roosevelt-friendly region of the country remained for the time being more concerned with local religious controversies and political battles than with the New Deal.[61]

Delta fundamentalists wrote to Roosevelt as if all the world agreed with them, however, and their unabashedly cantankerous missives anticipated the terms with which religious conservatives would take on the federal government in coming decades. First, most shared their more moderate counterparts' dismay at the end of Prohibition, but the fundamentalists saw this as only one indicator of the president's moral turpitude. One Arkansan fumed, "I do not know of more than ten protestant ministers over the entire nation who thought God would have whiskey thrown back on helpless poor people." He also noted that Roosevelt's son had recently divorced and remarried, and he scolded the president, "I know that if my own children come to failure morally I shall carry the blame in my own heart to my grave, and from this issue I think you ought to step down out of the race for President of our great Home-Loving nation."[62]

In an uncharacteristically brief but typically fiery letter, Bogard himself wrote, "Your personal example demoralizes youth." He claimed to have read reports that on July 22, 1935, Roosevelt, Vice President John Nance Garner, and Arkansas Senator Joe Robinson had "spent the night until the small hours of the morning gambling, playing poker with a ten dollar limit and you cleaned up on the other boys." Bogard claimed that when the story hit the headlines the following morning, "I was astounded, hurt, and the moral conscience of the people was offended all over the land." Bogard may have confused analogy with fact. The news headlines indeed spoke of Roosevelt and Garner playing poker that week, but only in a metaphorical sense, as they faced a tough congressional vote over tax and banking bills. But Bogard's mind was made up: no gambling man should hold the highest office in the land—not even a winning one.[63]

Prohibition and its enforcement were acceptable actions on the part of the government, because "God and morality have a definite place in the building of a nation"; any other centralized effort on the part of government was just Communism and a threat to the churches. As one breathlessly angry clergyman declared: "With conditions in regard to unemployment growing worse instead of better; with the increase of deaths due to drunkenness; with tendencies in your administration toward the nationalization of all the means of production, which is only another word for Communism; with the lust for power beyond what an ordinary man should desire which has been so much in evidence in your administration; with the attack which you have made on the Constitution of our country; with the recognition of God-hating,

Church-destroying, home-disrupting, Communistic Russia—it is little wonder that not only Christian ministers but Christian laymen all over this section, as well as all over the Nation are seriously alarmed and aroused." The Protestant establishment might celebrate the New Deal's Christian underpinnings, but its members had been misguided for a long time. The fundamentalists would not be Roosevelt's dupes.[64]

Roosevelt's fundamentalist opponents in the Delta tied economic regulation, federal spending on relief and works programs, and new agricultural controls to Communism, but they generally spoke in practical rather than premillennial terms. Crowley's paper carried an announcement of an upcoming sermon, "Is Mussolini the Anti-Christ?" alongside his letter to Roosevelt. Yet even he avoided drawing the kind of direct parallel between Roosevelt's administration and biblical prophecy that proved so common among fundamentalists elsewhere. Roosevelt's opponents in Memphis and the Delta nonetheless declared their loyalty to unfettered capitalism and their conviction that, in seeking to rein it in, Roosevelt stood in violation of the Constitution and threatened the very foundations of the nation.[65]

"I am a Democrat, but not one of the fool kind," wrote one white Mississippi baptist. He declared, with more venom than accuracy, "The South emerged from the ruins of the civil war . . . without a single dollar of relief from the federal government" when "conditions were ten times worse." Like his colleagues, this Mississippian avoided direct references to race, though Crowley shared at least some of Jeffers's anti-Semitism and anti-Catholicism, and Bogard had joined the Ku Klux Klan in the 1920s. But they echoed the critiques of clergymen particularly concerned with loss of control over black southerners. Now, thanks to the New Deal, "people by the multiplied thousands have quit trying to provide for themselves." Furthermore, Roosevelt refused to leave business "in the hands of those whose right it is to conduct it." One of the few African American Arkansans to denounce the New Deal echoed the latter sentiment, warning Roosevelt, "Let us remember that the rich man did not bring the mass into the condition that they are now in, but the mass brought themselves into this condition by trying to cope with the rich, in buying Auto, grafophones and radios."[66]

J. W. White, from the Delta's northwestern fringe, fired off a ten-page philippic that shared his colleagues' anger at Roosevelt's personal and political decisions but exceeded the rest in its unrelenting ferocity. His message perhaps best demonstrates the direction of southern fundamentalism and explains the response to it on the left. "It's really strange??? you should think of the clergy now at such later hour of staggering folly," opened White. He declared that Roosevelt had "ruined and wrecked the government by borrowing money from the rich . . . and spending it like a madman" and denounced the New Deal as "the cause of, not cure for, poverty." He opposed all taxation and warned, "Since you have made such a shipwreck of everything dear to the hearts of all Americans except foreigners and Socilist Reds at that I suggest you get down on your knees before God and repent of your ungodly deeds and wickedness you have done." This clergyman had a sixteen-year-old son who was paralyzed by polio at age two, but he did not see Social Security as any help. Instead, he asked Roosevelt, "Why have the satanic audacity to talk about the common end of better spiritual conditions of the American people? Are you a joke?" And then he concluded with one: "Booze . . . seems to be about the only kind of spirit you have."[67]

Even though critics like White remained in the overwhelming minority, their objections overlapped with those of the New Deal's business opponents, and their absolute condemnation of the liberal state alarmed Roosevelt's supporters and even his critics on the left. Some of those supporters applauded the president even as they feared that his detractors would prevail. Arkansan T. Steiner wrote, "I have often been astonished at the tremendous and dangerous measures proposed and put afoot at Washington: tremendous because of their possibility for good; dangerous because dependent up on the sound moral character of the nation." He deplored the "critical condition" in which Hoover left the country but lamented, "greed, selfishness, dishonesty will warp every effort on your part." He proposed no religious remedy and hoped only that "such a time will come soon when similar plans can be put into effect." For now, however, "Your program has been like a ballance in which the nation's character has been weighed and found wanting." Steiner's critique sounded like a version of Reinhold Niebuhr's emphasis on original sin and the resultant inadequacy of all political systems, yet he went no further. Perhaps he simply did not want to admit his distaste for the New Deal, but perhaps too he feared its energizing effect on the Delta's more reactionary clergy.[68]

Dissent was in the air, even if only a whisper in Memphis and the Delta, and the Supreme Court's rejection of the NRA had given courage to Roosevelt's opponents and worried his supporters. John Petrie, the Memphis Unitarian who happily announced that Wall Street lined up against Roosevelt, ended his upbeat letter to the president on a note of concern: "You have tried, I believe, to place human welfare first and property interests after—almost a revolution." He hoped that it would not, but "[i]f it comes to a dangerous fight between you and the old methods I shall probably leave my pulpit and campaign for you."[69]

Two Nashville-based church officials warned Roosevelt that his political and religious enemies had joined forces. The editor of the *Christian Advocate*, the Southern Methodist journal, reported that in his pages he "set forth that present day social movements and programs are in line with what the Churches for more than twenty-five years have been declaring as their social objective," and he encouraged Roosevelt to do the same. "Keep these objectives of your Administration before the clergymen and the 'Church Vote' generally," he cautioned. Roosevelt's enemies had too many friends in the churches, and "the opposition of these laymen is having effect."[70]

Southern Baptist statistician and record keeper Eugene P. Alldredge likewise feared that Roosevelt underestimated his enemies. Alldredge deemed Roosevelt a hero who had "labored with equal zeal and wisdom" to institute Social Security and an economic recovery program. But "there is now a nationwide, well-financed and very aggressive campaign under way," he warned, "to smash your whole program of recovery." Not only did Roosevelt's opponents plan to divide Congress and defeat him at the polls, but also they worked "in the meantime to so mislead the great rank and file of the people . . . to deliver this whole nation back into the hands of the great business magnates." In case Roosevelt missed the message, Alldredge repeated it: "Let there be no mistake: *Big Business is out to get you!*" "Do you not yet understand," he went on, mocking the president's detractors, "that more dollars, not more self-sustaining and self-respecting human beings, is the one great purpose for which this Constitution was drawn and this great nation founded?" Perhaps Alldredge was merely more pessimistic than his colleagues, but it was his job to tabulate Southern Baptist demographics and changing attitudes, and his anxious message to Roosevelt suggests that more than a few well-placed members of that denomination had already begun to stir up their membership against the president.[71]

ROOSEVELT SUPPORTERS LIKE Alldredge outnumbered the reactionaries they feared in 1935, and in general the clergy letters from Memphis and the Delta show that Roosevelt stood on solid ground among religious leaders, whatever the polls had reported. Perhaps the relative ambivalence about the New Deal among American clergy in the 1934 *Literary Digest* poll was only a result of the poll's small sample size. Perhaps it resulted from the relatively significant proportion of Christian socialists among the clergy on the left as much as it did from growing numbers of conservative dissenters. It almost certainly resulted from the fact that the journal's polling strategy favored white, northern, middle-class and elite clergy, rather than poor and black clergy who were likelier to share their members' experiences and perspectives on the New Deal. But that poll nonetheless proved troubling to religious leaders like Alldredge, because it affirmed a growing concern that Roosevelt might lose his religious base.

Another *Literary Digest* poll in 1936, this one conducted shortly after the Supreme Court overturned the Agricultural Adjustment Administration, provoked more consternation on the left. It showed that more than fifteen thousand of twenty-one thousand clergy—just over seventy percent—now answered "no" to the question "Do you NOW approve the acts and policies of the Roosevelt New Deal state?" Roosevelt won Mississippi but lost both Arkansas and Tennessee in the poll. The question's phrasing and its requirement for an up-or-down vote, as well as its selective sampling, undoubtedly skewed the results. One clergyman complained, "If I vote 'yes,' I feel that I am repudiating the Supreme Court, and if I vote 'no' I am repudiating a Chief Executive who has steadfastly sought to close the new avenues of oppression which have been opened by modern economic expansion." Indeed, the *Literary Digest* spelled its own demise after another poll that year predicted that Alf Landon would trounce the president in the 1936 election. Roosevelt instead won forty-six of fifty states and sixty-one percent of the popular vote—the largest margin of victory in any presidential election in American history. Ninety-seven percent of Mississippi voters, eighty-two percent of Arkansas voters, and sixty-nine percent of Tennessee voters (a number that reflects the Republican strongholds in East Tennessee more than the heavily Democratic West) stood by the president. If the clergy parted ways with their members, they did not do so by a significant margin.[72]

Nonetheless, the few clergy who opposed Roosevelt in the 1930s South did so vehemently, and many more had begun to worry that the New Deal, as much as the Great Depression, undercut their prestige in their own communities. The slow disintegration of the southern clerical consensus in favor of the New Deal represents an important step in the Protestant establishment's renegotiation of its status in the 1930s. Dismantled by the Depression and rebuilt in partial cooperation with the New Deal, the Protestant establishment now divided over a new question: was the expanded federal state its partner or its competitor? On what terms could it reaffirm or re-establish its essential place in southern communities? Meanwhile, fundamentalists and other believers outside the establishment fought to expand their own power in southern communities.

PART IV

Religion Reinvented

Spring 1936

The president never visited any Delta sharecroppers, but the First Lady did. "My first glimpse of Arkansas was a drive through very rich country just before sun down on my way to the Dyess Colony," she wrote. In this New Deal–sponsored resettlement community in Mississippi County, out-of-luck farming families that had been on relief moved into clean, brand-new houses and cleared twenty- to forty-acre plots of land that they hoped to cultivate and one day purchase from the federal government. Eleanor Roosevelt was pleased to see "four hundred and eighty families actually moved into their homes." Dyess also had a community center, recreation hall, and hospital for families to use, and to which they would contribute.[1]

"The opportunity is here—it is up to you to develop it," Roosevelt said to the 2,500 farmers who gathered at the Dyess administration building for her visit. She praised the farmers' work, encouraged them to "derive gains which may be used to help other people," and then shook hands with everyone assembled. "It was hot as we stood on the steps of the community center and shook hands with them all," recounted Roosevelt in her daily column, "but as I looked into their faces as they came by and at the children who slipped around and in and out, I decided that they had character and courage to make good when an opportunity offered." Finally, she said happily, "that opportunity seemed to be within their reach."[2]

Only white families could apply to move to Dyess, but soon Arkansas would house resettlement projects for black families too. Just a few hundred of the tens of thousands of displaced Arkansas families made it successfully through the application process, however, and even then they had to start over in a new place, with new rules and new neighbors. The work was hard and hot. After an evening just shaking hands at the community center, Roosevelt and her companion on the trip "were gasping for something cold to drink." They enjoyed a "long lemonade" as the train pulled away, while the lucky few at Dyess headed to bed to rest for the long day of work ahead—but finally, it was work on land that might one day be their very own.[3]

Just three months earlier, Catholic activist Dorothy Day had also traveled to the Arkansas Delta, but she saw a very different world. On a seventeen-degree day in early March, Day rode with members of the Southern Tenant Farmers' Union to deliver a carload of supplies she had collected "to bring relief to dispossessed families." Founded in 1934, this local, interracial organization of landless Delta sharecroppers had drawn the attention of the nation's religious left, and Day was curious about its work. She rode in the back seat with Marie Pierce, a member of the union's executive committee.[4]

They stopped first at Pierce's house. After eviction from their home "on account of their work for the union," Pierce and her husband shared a two-room cabin with three other families. Even though the house "was no better than a shack through which the wind tore and nagged at the loose-hung doors," its residents considered their own situation comfortable, because "there was timber on the little piece of land they rented from the Government and they could keep warm." Indeed, Pierce's home appeared luxurious compared to the next encampment of evicted union members that Day's hosts took her to visit. Just south of the town of Earle, five families huddled together in a "little church which was not much more than a shed." Day watched a woman washing clothes just outside, moved by "this attempt at cleanliness in this hovel unfit even for animals."[5]

Yet those families at least had a roof over their heads. That afternoon, outside the town of Parkin, Day's hosts stopped at a roadside tent colony with 108 residents, including four infants "wrapped in scanty cotton blankets" and many small children dressed in raggedy clothes that provided little protection from the chilly day. "They grow cotton but they dress in flour sacks," wrote Day, as impressed with the union's efforts to fight the planter elite as she was aghast at the poverty that surrounded her.[6]

Four years into Roosevelt's administration, many Delta farmers still struggled "to keep body and soul together," as Myrtle Sherwood had put it. The New Deal precipitated new crises on the Delta plantations, but it also brought new solutions to them. Some farmers who had longed for a chance at a new start got it; others found themselves pushed off the land without even the means to escape to Memphis. Reformers who had once sought to help both groups through the churches soon worked to do the same through the state.[7]

6

New Religious Alliances

THE BARCLAY FAMILY sat waiting to make their annual budget in a cramped county relief office in western Arkansas. The woman behind the partition held their fate in her hands, in the words she chose to hammer into the paper wound through her typewriter. Two of the Barclays' four children waited with them, the youngest in her mother's lap. A "bright new 'two bit piece'" kept the tot occupied. She dropped the quarter, and it rolled toward the hidden woman with the clacking typewriter. The typing stopped and a hand emerged with the coin. The mother took it and returned it to the restless child, who dropped it again. This time a "much annoyed" Anna Weir Layne "took the coin into the next room to ascertain who was so loose with money." Her face surely reflecting her disapproval at "this somewhat amazing behavior of a family on relief," Layne met the Barclays, whom she would soon evaluate for resettlement at Dyess Colony in Mississippi County.[1]

It was a curious project, a Federal Emergency Relief Administration (FERA)–sponsored, planned farming community that would eventually house nearly three thousand people, all members of white Arkansas families who relied on federal relief. William R. Dyess, state FERA and Works Progress Administration (WPA) director and a steady ally of the planter aristocracy, dreamed up the colony. In 1934, he purchased fifteen thousand acres of land near his home in Mississippi County and began to build a town there. The town appeared before its residents, who faced a rigorous application process. A few families arrived to clear land that October. In 1935, the colony incorporated. It remained independent of FERA's successors, but the new Resettlement Administration took over the process of family selection in an effort to fill Dyess's brand-new, empty homes (Figure 6.1).[2]

Federally employed family selection specialists, including Anna Layne, scattered across the state to interview relief clients who wished to relocate to Dyess. The specialists helped each family prepare an annual budget

FIGURE 6.1 A farmer and his family resettled at Dyess Colony in Mississippi County, Arkansas.

Photo by Arthur Rothstein, August 1935, courtesy of the Library of Congress Prints and Photographs Division

and visited them at home to evaluate their appearance, intelligence, work ethic, family life, and religious and political behavior. Layne had lived in Helena, a major Mississippi River port town, for nearly thirty years. She disliked her assignment to the hills of western Arkansas, where she forded streams and pushed through brambles to visit homes inaccessible by car. Nevertheless, she thought herself an authority on the appropriate kind of families for Dyess, and she took her evaluations seriously. Layne lacked formal training in social work, though she had extensive background in women's clubs. After each home visit, she helped families complete the six-page application form for Dyess. She then added her own evaluation and recommendation for the senior family selection specialist, who had final say over each family's fortunes. They wanted solid, stable families who would adapt well to home ownership and prove productive and amiable community members. The families must be poor and on relief but healthy and hardworking, and not so ambitious as to seek a life beyond the farm. They must certainly not display "extreme or emotional" tendencies in politics, economics, or religion.[3]

Layne found the families she interviewed so quaint and interesting that she wrote up brief stories about each to enter in a writers' contest at *Reader's Digest*. She also sent a copy to Eleanor Roosevelt. Layne called the Barclays' story "The House of the Wooden Crosses," and in it, she is both actor and omniscient narrator, there to interpret and correct the family's behavior. Her narrative opens in the relief office, where before they even come face to face with Layne, the Barclays have confirmed her suspicion that poor people just cannot be trusted with money. Few people enjoyed a trip to the relief office, where they had to lay out their finances and divulge personal information to middle-class men and women inclined to eye them with some combination of sympathy and scorn. Many had to wait for hours to do so. Layne does not share with her readers how long the Barclays had been sitting in her office, soothing their restless children as best they could while she sat at her typewriter.[4]

Later in the fall of 1935, Layne visited the Barclays at home, where her opinion of the family improved. Their four children appeared "cute, well fed, and well dressed," even though Mr. Barclay "[looked] heavy," and his wife was "a thin person of the 'pine knot' variety." Their rented house "seemed to rise up out of a cornfield," with no yard or farm tools in sight. It was a small home, "of the inevitable batten type, but in excellent repair." Layne had to pause before she could enter the house, because Mrs. Barclay was "tacking a comfort[er] of such gargantuan proportions the frame takes up almost all the space in the room." Together, Layne and the Barclays used strings of calico to wind the handmade comforter's frame toward the ceiling, high enough that they could put three chairs underneath and sit, "canopied like Selassie in his last picture."[5]

As Mr. Barclay stoked the fire, Layne fixed her attention on the mantle above him. In the center rested a framed print of Joshua Reynolds's *The Age of Innocence*, an eighteenth-century painting of a small girl. On either side of the print stood a two-foot-tall wooden cross, painted white. "Sorrow" was lettered in green across one, "Adversity" across the other. The popular Reynolds print placed betwixt the two painstakingly lettered crosses suggests a particular sort of sorrow and adversity: the death of a child, no less wrenching for its prevalence among poor southerners. "Mr. Barclay, will you please tell me why you have those words on the crosses?" Layne recalled asking. "Yes, life is like that, most all sorrow and adversity," answered Barclay.[6]

Indeed, the Barclays had seen their share of troubles, and Mr. Barclay dutifully recounted them to Layne. He and his wife had moved from Mississippi to central Arkansas in 1917, where he mined bauxite until the company that employed him closed. Together with another family, the Barclays then rented a nearby farm, but they had been on the land scarcely a year when a tornado swept away the houses, crops, and livestock. "Eighty chickens were actually blown away and could not be found," a friend of the Barclays later told Layne. The family relocated yet again, but Barclay lamented, "God knows I must not know how to farm. I have been at it all my life and I still have no more money than I had at first." The Barclays and their four children worked hard each year on their rented land, but they relied on federal relief to make it through the winter.[7]

Layne declined to address the circumstances that contributed to Barclay's grave assessment of life. Instead she scolded him, "God made you in his own image and he didn't intend for you to be miserable all the time. He wants you to be happy. . . . All we have to do is to practice the presence of God within our own souls and we will find our best expression in life." If Barclay found Layne's instruction absurd, he did not tell her so, and Layne happily reported, "He seemed to understand very well what I was talking about." In a gesture that perhaps summed up the influence she hoped resettlement would have on the family, Layne directed Barclay to "turn those crosses around and print on one 'Love' and the other 'Joy.'" Surely aware that Layne held his family's hopes in her hands, Barclay consented. Layne turned the conversation back to agricultural matters, and then she took her leave.[8]

In her final assessment of the family, Layne reported, "From the soil, [Barclay] is firmly convinced must come finally the good things of life for his family. They have seldom, if ever, had any money; they only ask for a chance to work and get what they can from the soil." Layne concluded, "They have no thought of ever having an easy life. Mr. Barclay is highly recommended as an honest man and a hard worker."[9]

Anna Weir Layne represented a growing cohort of southerners who discovered in the 1930s that they could pursue many of their religious ideals more effectively as agents of the expanded federal government than through religious or voluntary societies. By the end of the decade, members of the southern Protestant establishment who had claimed common cause with the New Deal often found work further beyond the church walls than they had done before. Others trod a middle ground, critiquing the New Deal even as they sought a home within it. Yet the New Deal state produced new alliances as well, among churches and religious leaders outside the Protestant establishment who found their own voices either in affirmation of or opposition to Roosevelt's policies—and often, both at once. This realignment of southern religion during the Great Depression and New Deal shaped the

churches' response to the looming war and presaged the new shape of southern Christianity in the coming decades.

The Barclays' story and Layne's intervention in it reflect one of the
most urgent problems that residents of Memphis and Delta faced in the
1930s: the rural and agricultural crisis. Both that crisis and the proposed
solutions to it predated the Great Depression by decades. But the depression turned crisis to catastrophe and propelled the Delta into the headlines. Vast swaths of rural America, from the Dust Bowl to the California
berry patches, soon followed. FERA, the WPA, and the Social Security
Act addressed the needs of Americans in both cities and the countryside.
The first New Deal's Agricultural Adjustment Administration (AAA),
Civilian Conservation Corps (CCC), and Tennessee Valley Authority
(TVA) and the second New Deal's Resettlement Administration, Farm
Security Administration (FSA), Soil Conservation Service (SCS), and
Rural Electrification Administration each aimed to address the rural cri-
sis, though in different and often contradictory ways. All these programs
engaged with ongoing rural reclamation efforts begun by members of the
Protestant establishment, including schools for rural clergy and organized
relief efforts for poor farmers. Commission on Interracial Cooperation
(CIC) head Will Alexander emerged from those efforts to help lead the
Resettlement Administration and then the FSA, which employed a disproportionate share of southern Protestant activists. Yet the federal programs
also opened new opportunities for engagement and opposition from religious groups outside the establishment.[10]

Delta believers developed their own responses to the rural crisis, and in
1934 the nascent Southern Tenant Farmers' Union captured the attention
of the Christian left. Radicals from across the region traveled to the Delta to
support the union and to cultivate a new alliance between politically engaged
Christian socialists and local people of both races whose theological conservatism undergirded their social activism. It was a fractious, sometimes ran-
corous set of alliances. Its members proved as ambivalent about the New Deal
as they were about one another. Those conflicts only intensified in 1935, when
northern supporters established the Delta Cooperative Farm in Mississippi
to house select union members in an interracial Christian community. The
project both paralleled and undercut the federal government's simultaneous
efforts to resettle victims of the rural crisis. Both the union and the farm
peaked in the late 1930s and then followed a slow decline. Yet their efforts
reshaped the southern Christian left for decades to come. They fostered a new
kind of Christian activism that took place largely outside the churches even

as it claimed that only through those churches could the South break free of its unjust history.[11]

Once-marginal southern pentecostals also forged their own relationships to the New Deal, separate from and at times in conflict with the Protestant establishment. The "extreme and emotional" faith of people like the Barclays thus found a place in the New Deal coalition, and in Memphis and the Delta the Church of God in Christ (COGIC) led the way. The church's founder, Charles H. Mason, asked Illinois native and COGIC convert Arenia Mallory to take over its crumbling school in Holmes County, Mississippi, just before the start of the depression.

As Mallory worked to raise funds for the school and its students, she developed ties with middle-class women's groups and federal agencies. She worked with National Council of Negro Women (NCNW) head Mary McLeod Bethune to improve conditions for her students, she visited Eleanor Roosevelt at the White House, and she propelled her denomination into the New Deal fold. In this way, denominations formerly outside the power structure in a region dominated by the Protestant establishment now tapped into the wellspring of resources flowing southward even as they maintained an image of independence.[12]

No religious cohort in the South played a more active role in the New Deal's administration than members of the southern Protestant establishment, but those churches nonetheless began to fear that the breadth of the New Deal coalition threatened their singular power in the region. As a result, the major southern churches turned rightward between 1937 and 1941, determined in particular to preserve and rehabilitate the image of Jim Crow. Southern Methodists and northern Methodists reunited in 1939, and together they continued to make progressive proclamations on social questions even as they shunted black Methodists off into a segregated conference. Southern Baptists and Presbyterians also made overtures toward their northern counterparts, who in turn softened their critique of southern segregation. Southern Baptists abandoned a proposal to establish a social service commission and instead created an agency to police the federal government's encroachment on religion. Together with National Baptists and northern Baptists, they stood against a 1939 proposal to include religious employees in Social Security. Once an embodiment of Christian principles, the New Deal now represented a threat to religious freedom.[13]

This turn against the New Deal paled in comparison with a similar but separate protest among fundamentalists. Members of the American Baptist Association (ABA) and the Churches of Christ now fought the New Deal in more organized fashion, and this time many in the southern Protestant establishment supported their arguments for ending once-popular works and relief programs. By the end of the 1930s, then, the southern Protestant establishment and its conservative critics remained at odds, but they shared the alternately engaged and critical attitudes toward the liberal state that would characterize their response to World War II, the Cold War, and the civil rights movement.[14]

"Farm Tenancy and the Christian Conscience"

Shortly after Anna Weir Layne sat in the Barclays' living room and instructed the family to adopt a more optimistic religious outlook, one of her bosses in the Resettlement Administration stood to address a New York City crowd on "Farm Tenancy and the Christian Conscience." Most Arkansans knew Brooks Hays as a twice-failed gubernatorial candidate with a 350-member Sunday school class at Little Rock's Second Baptist Church. Members of the ecumenical, New York–based Christian Rural Fellowship invited the Arkansas New Dealer to talk about his weekday work as special assistant to the administrator of the Resettlement Administration. Speaking in both capacities, Hays simultaneously described the devastation of Southern soil and touted the benefits of redistributing worn-out land to displaced tenant farmers. "The Christian mind rebels against absentee ownership," Hays told his New York audience. "Religion is needed in the delicate task of bending the rigid rules of law pertaining to land, making the rules responsive to human needs." For Hays and many southern Protestant activists in the mid- to late 1930s, participation in the New Deal administration presented an irresistible opportunity to put their religious ideals into practice on a larger scale than they had ever imagined.[15]

Together, Layne, Hays, and their boss, William Winton Alexander, deputy director of the Resettlement Administration and later head of the FSA, represented a new kind of alliance between southern Protestant activists and the federal government. Both Alexander and Hays joined the New Deal administration in 1935 as a direct result of their activism on behalf of black and white southerners displaced by federal agricultural reforms. Alexander, a Methodist minister and head of the CIC until he joined the New Deal coalition, stressed the importance of racial justice in the New Deal's administration, while Hays forged a link between the Roosevelt administration and dissatisfied sharecroppers in Arkansas. Their particular perspectives on rural life and rural Christianity helped to shape the New Deal's approach to the agricultural South after 1935. They also help to explain Layne's particular concern with the Barclays' religious beliefs. Hays and Alexander's work and ideals make sense only in the context of a longer effort on the part of both religious and political leaders to rehabilitate rural America and its residents, an effort that took off under the supervision of the first President Roosevelt.[16]

Theodore Roosevelt established the Country Life Commission in 1908 to address concerns about vanishing natural resources and to study the gap between urban and rural income and development and propose measures to close it. The commission's 1909 report included "the country church" as one of five "corrective forces that should be set in motion" to rescue rural America. Roosevelt explained, "Our object should be to help develop in the country community the great ideals of community as well as personal character. One of the most important adjuncts to this end must be the country church." The report's major recommendations included the establishment of cooperative extension services at land-grant colleges and universities and support for rural sociologists and researchers to gather data and make recommendations about rural life. The report highlighted again the importance of the church when it proposed that seminaries "unite with agricultural colleges in the preparation of the country clergyman." This last proposal established a clear link between the work of the church and state in rural America. Still, rural religious reformers worked primarily within the churches.[17]

Prompted in part by the Country Life Commission's recommendations, the Federal Council of Churches established its own country life program in 1909 and with its affiliated denominations produced mountains of literature recommending strategies to revitalize rural life in general and rural religious life in particular. These efforts took place first in the mainline, northern denominations, and southerners initially eyed their emphasis on the social responsibility of the church with suspicion.[18]

By the 1920s, however, the major southern Protestant denominations' home mission programs also promoted their rural churches as a key resource for stabilizing poor and dwindling rural communities. Threatened by pentecostalism's growth in the South, they warned of the dangerous susceptibility of rural people to the "Holy Rollers." Such movements disrupted rural communities, members of the Protestant establishment warned, and undermined established relationships between rich and poor, white and black, men and women. Denominationally affiliated and racially segregated baptist, Methodist, and Presbyterian churches, they argued, instead built community through education and service, as well as through worship. These reformers sometimes joined forces with the progressives who fought for expanded education and services in the South, as well as for Prohibition and other means of control over individual behavior. But they worked primarily within their churches and local communities.[19]

Denominational efforts to reshape rural churches complemented and overlapped with the work of a growing cohort of academics who studied southern rural life. Members of the North Carolina Institute for Research in Social Science, established by Howard Odum in 1924, conducted intensive work on the modernizing South. Odum's student Arthur Raper moved beyond his mentor's racial conservatism to study lynching and the racially exploitative nature of sharecropping. Raper also worked with Will Alexander in the Commission on Interracial Cooperation, as did Fisk University sociologist Charles Spurgeon Johnson. Johnson examined the effects of Jim Crow capitalism on black southerners' lives and livelihoods. He publicized his findings in academic circles, but also for a wider audience as founding editor and regular contributor to the National Urban League's journal, *Opportunity*.[20]

Odum, Raper, and Johnson all stressed the important role of churches in rural communities and critiqued the priorities and education of the rural ministry. They also helped colleagues work with local land-grant colleges to create the rural ministers' training programs that the Country Life Commission recommended, first for white clergy and later for black clergy. The programs introduced clergy to rural church work and helped them "develop contacts between agricultural leaders, particularly those engaged in extension work, and rural ministers." The Federal Council of Churches coordinated with black clergy and extension workers to disseminate information about Red Cross aid during the drought of 1930. As this work developed, the rural church advocates and their academic colleagues began to critique the plantation system more directly and to advocate for redistribution of state-owned land to landless farmers. It was an old idea, but by the early 1930s, it was infused with new life.[21]

This comprehensive work by the southern left drew Roosevelt's attention at the same time that denominational interest in rural work flagged. Both the southern Presbyterians and the Episcopalians slashed their rural church departments during the cutbacks of the early 1930s. The work that remained only highlighted the distance between the comprehensive proposals of researchers like Raper and Johnson and the narrower interests of the Protestant establishment. Arkansas Episcopalians gave up on building churches in the countryside and instead piloted a "Church on Wheels" program to serve rural communities outside the reach of their overwhelmingly town-based congregations. Southern Presbyterians stopped paying men to serve as home missionaries and instead deployed young women as evangelists to conduct Sunday schools and Bible classes in "needy and spiritually destitute communities." Meanwhile, several denominations adopted the Lord's Acre plan, which encouraged church members to plant gardens on the church grounds or to dedicate the proceeds from a portion of their own farmland to the church. Arkansas Southern Baptists launched the plan in 1934, declaring it the "country church year." It did not last. The program made sense in the small subsistence farms of the Appalachian counties around Asheville, North Carolina, where it began, but in a land full of landless and hungry farmers, it was not viable.[22]

Women's societies engaged in more extensive efforts than their struggling denominations, but they too worked primarily through churches and religious organizations. In 1930, black and white Methodist women collaborated on a leadership training program for black women at Mississippi Industrial College and afterward launched a study and a protest of the state's refusal to fund black schools, particularly in rural areas. A year later, white Methodist and Southern Baptist women organized a state chapter of the Association of Southern Women for the Prevention of Lynching (ASWPL), whose members traveled to churches across the state to denounce mob violence even as they refused to support federal antilynching bills before Congress in 1933 and 1938. While these efforts later seemed tepid and inadequate, they set the stage for cooperative work outside the church, and they helped define the terms on which progressive southern white churchgoers engaged with the New Deal state.[23]

The reform efforts within the churches and religious organizations looked puny compared with the comprehensive rural programs of the first New Deal, but the Roosevelt administration's efforts were also problematic. The first New Deal's environmental and agricultural programs—the CCC, the TVA, the SCS, and the AAA—brought together progressive conservationists, advocates of rural planning, and large-scale farm owners to conserve rural resources, curb falling prices, and address rural poverty. While the CCC and TVA enjoyed widespread public support in the South, the AAA was a practical and political disaster. Critics first expressed dismay at the directive that farmers plow under crops and slaughter animals to curtail overproduction. But it was the policy's favoritism toward farm owners that created the most lasting problems in the South.[24]

Although it was not the Roosevelt administration's intent to push tenant farmers off the land, that is precisely what happened. Planters accepted government subsidies to reduce production and then evicted their superfluous tenants. The AAA's planter-businessmen powerbrokers stymied the liberals in the organization who tried to ensure that sharecroppers received a share of the federal funds. By the time the Supreme Court ended the program in 1935, cotton tenants were in dire straits (Figure 6.2). Between 1930 and 1935, as a result first of the depression and then of the AAA, southern cotton counties lost 18,520 landless farmers. More than half of that loss came from Arkansas (4,431 tenants) and Mississippi (8,958 tenants). Few people aspired to cotton tenancy or wished to maintain that system, but these displaced sharecroppers moved down the ladder rather than up it, forced to work as day laborers or to leave altogether.[25]

Will Alexander and Charles Johnson collaborated in 1935 on one of the most damning critiques of the AAA, and as a result of their work, Roosevelt hired them both. In *The Collapse of Cotton Tenancy*, Alexander, Johnson, and Julius Rosenwald Foundation president Edwin R. Embree wrote, "Federal relief came to the cotton belt, was translated into plantation terms and the system (except for the further displacement and impoverishment of tenants) was bolstered and given a new release on life." They laid out in both anecdotal and statistical detail the ways the AAA benefited the big farmers at the expense of the small, and left the poorest poorer than ever. They also held the legacy of slavery and the animosity of whites responsible for the South's

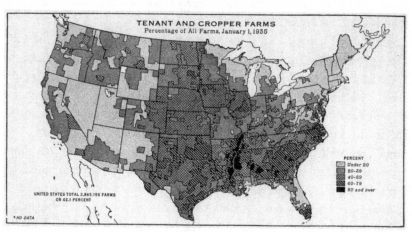

FIGURE 6.2 "Tenant and Cropper Farms," January 1935. Note the density of tenant farms in the Delta region.

Photo from US Department of Agriculture (USDA) pamphlet, *Farm Security: How Can Tenants Find It?* in Farm Tenancy Pamphlets, Gardner Jackson Papers, courtesy of the Franklin Delano Roosevelt Presidential Library, Hyde Park, New York.

problems, rather than pushing the blame onto poor African Americans. The study concluded that "reorganization of farming in the old cotton states" was "the only acceptable and feasible choice" for saving the rural South. Already concerned about the effects of the AAA, the Roosevelt administration helped to fund Johnson's research on southern poverty and made use of his recommendations. The collaboration between a sociologist and a religious reformer in a critique of federal policy was hardly new, but the invitation to those critics to join the New Deal administration and try out their proposed solutions was.[26]

In early 1935, shortly after they released their study, Alexander sat in his Atlanta CIC office with Arthur Raper. The phone rang, and Rexford Tugwell, a Columbia economics professor and one of the liberals on the losing end of the AAA battle, invited Alexander to Washington as his deputy director in a new government venture. As Alexander hung up, he turned to his friend and said, "You criticize them up in Washington and tell them what they ought to do, and then they ask you to come up and help them do it. What do you answer?" Raper told him to go, and he did. Together, Tugwell, an economist, and Alexander, with only a divinity degree from Vanderbilt, set out the parameters of one of Roosevelt's most creative experiments. At Tugwell's urging, the president established the Resettlement Administration by executive order on April 30, 1935. He put the scattershot earlier attempts at land rehabilitation and resettlement under its leadership, and he charged the new organization with correcting precisely those problems that Alexander, Johnson, and Embree had exposed.[27]

Alexander's perspective, developed over years of work with the CIC and a gradual shift from interracialism to integrationism, helped make the Resettlement Administration one of the few programs to recognize the needs of black landless farmers. That organization drew on cooperative farming ideals that Christian socialists and some liberal Protestants in the South had promoted for many years, but also on Tugwell's pragmatic, academic approach to farm economics. The agency thus appealed to a range of southern religious activists, and it also provided a training ground for them. Roosevelt assigned the Resettlement Administration three tasks: to purchase and restore worn-out land, to make loans for rural rehabilitation, and to build new communities to resettle landless farmers. Under Tugwell and Alexander's leadership, the agency emphasized the last of those most emphatically, and by its demise in 1937 it had established ninety-nine resettlement colonies, sixty-one of which were in the South. A dozen of those were in the Arkansas Delta, and two were across the river in Mississippi. One of the Mississippi Delta colonies and three of those in Arkansas were for black farmers, and several others included both black and white farmers on segregated plots. Each colony operated differently, but all aimed to teach farmers new methods of farming and cooperation.[28]

If Alexander shaped the Resettlement Administration's southern and racial policies, his time in Washington, DC dramatically reshaped his own racial politics. Even though planter William Dyess had established Arkansas's first resettlement colony, many southern elites regarded the planned rural communities as an attack on the plantation system—especially when they housed black farmers, promoted solidarity among them, and provided measureable improvements for their lives. The critics were, in part, correct. Too small to overturn the plantation system, the Resettlement Administration nonetheless modeled alternatives to it. But it also hewed to Jim Crow and helped more white farmers than black farmers. Alexander judged its work inadequate and began to publicly question Jim Crow economics.[29]

When Roosevelt subsumed the Resettlement Administration into the new and much larger Farm Security Administration in 1937, Alexander—the agency's newly appointed director—emphasized the importance of aid to black southern farmers. The FSA prioritized rehabilitation loans and programs that allowed for tenants to purchase land. In all regions except Region VI, which covered Memphis and the Delta, the FSA provided loans to black farmers in proportion to their numbers. In Region VI, however, with a larger black population and steady opposition from planters, African Americans represented only twenty-five to fifty percent of beneficiaries in the various loan programs. For all its shortcomings, this agency, headed by a white Georgia Methodist minister, proved to be one of the only New Deal programs to prioritize black southerners.[30]

Alexander's Methodist upbringing and training and his long-standing relationships with rural reformers inside and outside the churches shaped his work with the New Deal administration, but Brooks Hays of Arkansas drew a straighter line between his religious faith and his work for the Roosevelt administration. Hays's interest in politics preceded the New Deal. He narrowly lost two close gubernatorial races in 1928 and 1930, and then lost a congressional race in 1933. Hays was as famous in Little Rock for his large and popular Sunday school class as for his political adventures. Yet he also had a long history in rural church work. In 1927, eight years before his New York speech to the Christian Rural Fellowship, Hays organized a rural life study among Southern Baptists in his home state of Arkansas. In 1934, he convened Arkansas educators and religious leaders for a conference

on African American farm ownership. Hays also served as president of the
Arkansas Conference on Social Work, and in that capacity, he pushed for
more equitable distribution of FERA funds to tenant farmers.[31]

His reputation as an Arkansas liberal cemented, by 1935, Hays accepted an
invitation to conduct an informal investigation for the AAA into deteriorat-
ing labor conditions in the Delta. His brief report proved deeply sympathetic
to tenant farmers even as it hesitated to condemn planters. Most significantly,
it included a recommendation that "available large tracts of land should
be broken up into small farms" on which "capable tenants" could become
owners—a proposal Hays had studied as part of the rural church movement.
When Rexford Tugwell took charge of the Resettlement Administration,
Hays joined him and Will Alexander in Washington, DC as a high-level legal
assistant. There, Hays worked to do what he described to the Christian Rural
Fellowship—to apply his religion in "bending the rigid rules of law pertaining to land, making the rules responsive to human needs."[32]

The presence of liberal Christian activists in the upper echelons of the
Resettlement Administration helps to explain the particular religious concerns that permeated the resettlement application forms and ultimately
helped to include certain kinds of believers and exclude others. Members
of the rural church reform movement who promoted redistributing land
to responsible small farmers believed firmly that these new communities
required a solid and stable church in their midst. They deemed pentecostals both institutionally and individually unstable, even as they hoped that
pentecostal churches might follow the trajectory that once-renegade baptists
and Methodists had followed a decade earlier, if they did not simply fade
away. As one Presbyterian put it, "[W]e must have patience with the 'holy
rollers' during their adolescence while they struggle to become full-grown
denominations." Until those sects passed through their oppositional youth,
rural church reformers saw them as threatening and destructive forces. Their
members would put a fragile new community at risk.[33]

Anna Layne's interrogation of Barclay reflected her own perspective, but
it may also have resulted from a well-meaning effort to shoehorn the family into the Resettlement Administration application's strict requirements.
The application blank required family selection specialists to indicate any
"extreme or emotional" religious beliefs they observed. As an internal memorandum to Region VI specialists explained, "Because of the need of close
community participation and cooperation, families selected should not have
extreme or singular economic, political, religious or social views." Southern

Protestants and Catholics would have recognized that this language aimed to exclude pentecostals and some fundamentalists, as well as socialists and communists, all risky investments for a program already subject to widespread criticism by southern elites. That Layne might deem a religion based on love and joy to be moderate but judge as extreme one that recognized a world full of sorrow and adversity reveals the often-shallow nature of mainstream Christianity in the midst of ongoing crisis. That Layne's perspective on a family's religion helped determine their fate in a government program further demonstrates the degree to which religious and political priorities remained bound together in the Roosevelt administration.[34]

Liberal Christian reformers like Alexander and Hays had already begun to work outside the churches before the Great Depression, and few drew a sharp line between religious and political activism. But most of the avenues through which they pursued those goals—the CIC, the Arkansas Baptist Convention, the rural church movement—organized primarily through churches and relied first on moral suasion, even when they pushed for reforms at the state and federal levels. Religious organizations and ideals, Christian reformers often argued, must lead the way to build a better South. The New Deal reversed those priorities by opening new options to southern Christian activists and allowing them to put their ideas to work as agents of the federal government. Alexander, Hays, Layne, and their contemporaries wove their distinctively southern Protestant values into the government's work and created a new and powerful set of alliances between southern liberal Christians and the federal government.

Revolt Among the Sharecroppers

While Will Alexander and Brooks Hays settled into their new lives in the nation's capital and Anna Layne tramped through the Arkansas hill country, they all kept an eye on another coalition of southern Christians. Indeed, all three owed their jobs in part to the Southern Tenant Farmers' Union (STFU), organized in Poinsett County, Arkansas, in July 1934. The STFU represented a direct and grassroots response to widespread evictions of sharecroppers in the months following the May 1933 enactment of the AAA. As the black and white laborers who founded the union joined forces with an eager cadre of southern Christian socialists and their northern supporters, they captured national headlines. Soon, any well-informed citizen in America had read that the Arkansas sharecroppers who had starved in a drought at the dawn of the Great Depression were in worse shape than ever before, and that it was Roosevelt's fault.[35]

STFU members and leaders coalesced around one key argument. "Since the earth is the common heritage of all," the union constitution read, "we maintain that the use and occupancy of land should be the sole title." This claim, grounded in two contradictory but overlapping theologies of the land, united union members with their Christian socialist promoters and allies and framed the union's work as a prophetic stand against precisely the kind of runaway rural capitalism that Brooks Hays denounced in his speech to the Christian Rural Fellowship. A group of southern Christian socialists and their northern allies moved to support the union, and even helped to draft its constitution. Steeped in both the rural church movement and southern socialism, these reformers sought nationalization of farmland and resources as the way to an equitable and Christian system. Some union members embraced this agrarian Christian socialism, but most did not. Instead, they stressed the "use and occupancy" of land. Inheritors of the turn-of-the-century populist revolt and the self-determination ethos of Garveyism, union members wanted to claim and hold a parcel of land as their own. Like Hays and many rural church reformers, they regarded the land, and the farmer's relationship to it, as a sacred trust that large-scale landowners violated. As union chaplain Arthur Brookins put it in a letter to Roosevelt, "God told man after he had violated the law he must reap the [sweat] of his [brow]." Yet in the South, "we workes the land but the land oner gets the benefit of what we makes." Both union members and their Christian socialist allies wanted large-scale land redistribution, but on very different terms. The Christian socialists wished to abolish ownership; union members hoped instead to partake of it.[36]

The fragile and fractious coalition that came together in the STFU also shared another central belief: the state bore a moral responsibility to its poorest citizens. While Alexander, Hays, and Layne wove their religious priorities into the state, members and boosters of the STFU issued a call to conscience from without. Union members saw the Roosevelt administration as an ally and petitioned the president to redress the injustices of his agricultural policies. Their socialist leaders and supporters declared that the New Deal's commitment to capitalism doomed it to failure, but they too worked to bend its programs toward justice for poor farmers. The STFU nurtured alliances that pushed against every social boundary the plantation South constructed: it drew together black and white sharecroppers, relied heavily on the organizing skills of women, and united middle-class Christian radicals with Bible-thumping preachers and agnostic socialists. Each of these disparate parties was a product of the very Jim Crow capitalism they sought to correct, and distrust and misunderstanding marked their relationships. Yet for a time, their similar theologies of the land held them together and compelled the state to hear their demands.[37]

The union reflected a cooperative venture between Arkansas sharecroppers and Christian socialists from the very start. The STFU's founders gathered at a schoolhouse in Marked Tree, Arkansas, near a plantation whose owner had evicted twenty-three families just after they planted the year's cotton crop. The eighteen black and white men who assembled at this meeting included sharecroppers from that plantation and H. L. Mitchell, a white socialist activist and former sharecropper who ran a dry cleaning business in nearby Tyronza. Several other men present also had a background of resistance. One had been part of the Progressive Farmers and Household Union of America organized fifteen years earlier in Elaine, another black member had been a coal miner and union organizer in Illinois, and another white member besides Mitchell participated regularly in socialist politics. After some discussion, and probably at Mitchell's urging, the men decided they stood a chance against their landlords only if they stood together rather than organizing two separate, segregated unions. Mitchell had pushed for a sharecroppers' union before, and the group elected him president.[38]

Mitchell had little use for Christianity, but he understood its importance to the sharecroppers and he knew that the union needed committed allies. He had already made contact with Ward Rodgers and Claude Williams, two of the Vanderbilt radicals then living in Arkansas. Rodgers helped Mitchell draft the union constitution and arrived almost immediately to help organize, but departed after a sensational arrest at a union rally. Williams, a former fundamentalist preacher who moved leftward after a summer at one of the rural church schools that liberal reformers had established, arrived soon after, as did Howard Kester. Both read their own evolving forms of Christian socialism into the union's membership, even though union members on the whole would later state firmly their preference for small-scale, individual farms rather than the cooperatively operated efforts the socialists envisioned. Rodgers and Williams dove into organizing work, while Kester became one of the union's most important publicists and promoters. His 1936 *Revolt Among the Sharecroppers* presented the union as precisely the kind of organization Kester had sought during his years of activism in the South: a grassroots movement dreamed up by "seventeen ragged and disinherited sharecroppers" that "harbors the faith, the hope, and the collective will of twenty-five thousand black men, white men, Indians, and Mexicans in six southern states of the mid-South and Southwest." Together, they would force the federal government to face the moral bankruptcy of plantation capitalism.[39]

The union's grassroots critique grew from the Delta's mobile religious world. Baptist and holiness ministers quickly proved to be the STFU's best organizers, their congregations a ready source of members and their buildings—for those who had them—the safest space for union meetings. One of the union's most committed black organizers in the first few years, E. Britt McKinney oversaw thirty baptist churches. He owned a small farm, which provided independence, and his likely participation in the Delta's Garveyite movement would have meant that he already promoted an oppositional, independent theology in his congregations. Union member John Handcox reinvented old spirituals as union songs and tapped into a long history of song as a source of unity and an expression of resistance. Women too became important union organizers, their leadership roles in church easily translated to the union context. One of the best white organizers, Myrtle Lawrence, told Mitchell that when she first heard of the union from her preacher, "I thought it was a new church." The union's theology reflected that of the Delta's poor churches: it stressed the importance of commitment to family and community, and it drew on both Old Testament stories of the Israelites and Jeffersonian republican ideals to elevate the land and its humblest workers as uniquely holy and fundamentally important to the nation's moral health.[40]

For three years, STFU organizers spread the union gospel and tried to stay alive while Mitchell, Kester, and Williams broadcast their story across the nation. The union claimed 2,500 members by the time of its first convention in February 1935 and 25,000 members, most of them in Arkansas and Missouri, by January 1936. Union members launched a series of strikes between 1934 and 1936 that resulted in few concessions but plenty of brutal retaliation. Groups of planters who dubbed themselves "night riders" dragged union members from church meetings and shot up their houses. Planters who controlled local New Deal programs tried to break up the union by offering municipal relief jobs to whites who renounced their union membership. They denied all other federal relief to members of both races. Arthur Brookins, union chaplain, and E. B. McKinney, union vice president, fled to Memphis after vigilantes rained bullets into their homes. Brookins was badly beaten, and a bullet whizzed through his daughter's hair. The gunmen missed McKinney but shot two of his friends at his home. When McKinney vanished, the vigilantes advertised that they would give "$25.00 apound for his meat." Mitchell moved the union headquarters to a farm outside Memphis in the face of ongoing threats. Both union members and planters appealed to Henry Wallace and AAA administrators for help.[41]

The AAA continued to favor the planters, but the sharecroppers captivated the nation with their courage in the face of violence and their ability to frame their demands in spiritual terms. The planters' violent reprisals rent the union but also served to highlight its theological critique: the plantation corrupted its masters and enslaved its producers. Cotton tenancy destroyed the sacred land and those who dwelt on it. Kester, Mitchell, and Williams wrote missives to that effect to papers across the nation, and the arrest of sharecroppers and their subsequent trials brought national media to the Delta to witness plantation peonage firsthand. Reporters for the *New York Times, The Nation*, and *The New Republic* helped keep the sharecroppers' critique before the nation. Rural church activists and members of the Federal Council of Churches organized collections of supplies and funds for the union and its members, and they often arrived to deliver them in person. Dorothy Day, Norman Thomas, and activists both religious and political descended on the region to tell its story and to push the government to respond.[42]

Will Alexander and Brooks Hays knew the sharecroppers' plight and wanted to help. Together with Rexford Tugwell and Gardner Jackson (one of the AAA liberals fired for his advocacy on behalf of the sharecroppers), they proved to be the STFU's most useful contacts in Washington. The Resettlement Administration did not take on the plantation system itself, however, and its small-scale rehabilitation and resettlement projects provided relief only to those who made it through the selection process. As violence against the union escalated, administration officials placed an STFU member on the President's Commission on Farm Tenancy, whose 1937 report provided the basis for the FSA's high-risk loans to landless farmers. Some of the sharecroppers evicted in the wake of planter violence found places on Resettlement Administration colonies or received rehabilitation loans through that organization or the FSA. But neither program could help all union members, and neither took on rural poverty in the comprehensive fashion that the STFU had demanded. The STFU had helped to shape New Deal agricultural policy, and yet those policies passed many union members by.[43]

The STFU leaders would have their shot at a cooperative farm. In 1935, a Memphis socialist and a group of Christian socialists from the Northeast together bought a plot of land in Bolivar County, Mississippi, and resettled some of the sharecroppers there. The farm was interracial but segregated, and rather than following the ownership model of the Resettlement Administration, it tried out large-scale cooperative farming. It so angered local landowners that they wrote to the government to oppose a black Resettlement Administration colony proposed for nearby Mound Bayou. In 1937, the farm closed and its residents relocated to Holmes County, not too far from the black FSA community of Mileston. The farm thrived, though its leadership and membership never found common ground on questions of ownership and authority. Although they struggled with internal discord and poverty, the two communities would eventually live up to some of local whites' fears: they provided a modicum of independence to poor farmers and in so doing produced a cadre of confident civil rights activists who for the next several decades would stand firm against Jim Crow.[44]

The STFU's influence peaked in 1936, and it faded into obscurity by the 1950s. The opposition its members encountered from without and the fractures within split the union several times over, particularly after it joined with a Congress of Industrial Organizations (CIO) union in 1937. Yet the coalition that formed the STFU and tested its ideals in the region's cooperative farms forced changes to New Deal agricultural policy and crafted a model for cooperative activism in the harshest of environments. When the resettlement and rehabilitation programs that union members had helped to inspire overlooked them, STFU supporters helped found a colony that sought to live out union ideals. Steeped in the Jim Crow capitalism that their union challenged, STFU members faced extraordinary violence and opposition from without and constant division and confusion from within. Even as their alliances crumbled, STFU members demonstrated the radical potential of Delta Christianity and showed that crosscutting efforts on the part of marginalized southerners could nudge the newly expanded and active federal government to take on the region's most entrenched powers.[45]

"Extreme and Emotional" Religion and the New Deal Coalition

The STFU and its southern Christian sympathizers engaged with the New Deal because these activists sought to transform southern politics, but even some Delta pentecostals who avoided political entanglements found a place in the New Deal coalition. The Delta's homegrown denomination, the Church of God in Christ, had grown rapidly since 1907, when Charles H. Mason broke away from his holiness church in Holmes County to embrace pentecostalism and found a new movement. Major black and white denominations, like the rural church reformers who worked with them, deplored holiness and pentecostal churches—indeed, those were precisely the "extreme and emotional" religious groups that the Dyess administrators sought to exclude. Religious reformers worried about the expansion of pentecostalism even as they predicted the movement's imminent demise or anticipated its absorption into the mainline. Yet when COGIC member and school principal Arenia Mallory formed alliances with Mary McLeod Bethune and other members of the New Deal coalition, she helped to transform the denomination's reputation and influence without abandoning its strict codes of dress and conduct or its ecstatic worship practices.[46]

White rural church reformers and social gospel advocates in the 1920s and 1930s could not decide whether to ignore the holiness and pentecostal churches or to raise alarm at their growth, but black reformers tended toward the latter. Many feared that churches like COGIC, whose members danced in ecstasy, spoke in tongues, and often isolated themselves from their less devout community neighbors, undercut black progress and confirmed whites' characterizations of African Americans as dull-witted, emotional, and untrustworthy. William A. Clark, a Tuskegee educator who wrote for Howard Odum's *Social Forces*, argued that COGIC appealed only to the intellectually stunted. He explained its emphasis on sanctification—the pentecostal belief that ecstatic practice represented the attainment of holiness—as merely "a refuge and parental protection for childminded types as well as those with sick minds." As baptists and others moved "toward the more intellectual and refined types of religious expression," he explained, they "left the less developed Negroes religiously adrift" and susceptible to evangelists like Mason. Reformers like Clark thus understood pentecostalism to be a product of poverty and ignorance, and they contended that its appeal would wane as education and opportunity brought its members into the mainline fold. Arenia Mallory and Charles H. Mason would soon prove Clark wrong, but in the 1930s, pentecostals remained on the margins of American religious life.[47]

Critics like Clark who disparaged COGIC members' ignorance and illiteracy might have been surprised to learn that church members prized literacy and the ability to read the Bible. When Mason moved COGIC headquarters to Memphis in 1907, he left behind St. Paul's Church in Holmes County, Mississippi, still known as the Mother Church. A congregant started Saints School in 1918 as an extension of St. Paul's Bible Bands, which taught both biblical and functional literacy to church members' children. In arguably the worst state for African American public education, denominational schools provided many Mississippi children with their only opportunity to learn basic reading and mathematics. Even by 1940, after an influx of New Deal funds for education, Mississippi had only five black high schools. Forty percent of black grade schools in the state operated from churches, lodges, and private homes. In the 1920s, COGIC's Saints Industrial School was a tumbledown wooden structure that sat on stilts in a field that was muddy when it wasn't dusty. Seven grades met in a single classroom, heated in winter by an iron stove.[48]

In 1930, Mason sent Arenia Mallory, a promising young middle-class convert from Illinois, to help salvage the struggling school. The timing could hardly have been worse: depression and drought wiped out any resources the school and its students had. By fall 1932, the state denominational organization could provide the school's 250 students with only two hundred dollars of support for the year, and only 30 of the students could pay any part of their small tuition fee. Members of the COGIC Board of Education suggested closing down the school, which could no longer pay the debt on its land or cover its minimal expenses.[49]

But Mallory refused to give up so easily. After seeking divine guidance for several days in the school's prayer room, Mallory decided to haul a small band of student singers, dubbed the Jubilee Harmonizers, to Florida to capitalize on wealthy whites' enthusiasm for black spirituals. Singing groups modeled on the famous Fisk Jubilee Singers represented a common method of fundraising for black schools. The practice was a departure for COGIC, however, which generally refrained from fellowship with other denominations. But the school needed outside help to survive. Soon, Mallory reported that Saints students sang before "two of the largest white churches in Florida and the principal hotels" in St. Petersburg, and "they had an open door in Miami among the richest white people." They returned from their trip with enough money to keep the school open even as wealthier white schools in the state shortened the academic year to make ends meet.[50]

The Jubilee Harmonizers began to sing at revivals, church services, and club meetings all over Mississippi, where they collected offerings of food and clothing for the school's poor students. Mallory took them on trips across the nation as well, later recalling, "We would go, on credit, with $1.50 in pockets, and ask God where we were to go, put our bills on the bed and in front of Him and ask Him to please help us." She even took the Jubilee Harmonizers to Abyssinian Baptist Church in New York, she explained simply, "because it was the largest protestant church in America." They sang at three services and left the church with eight thousand dollars in donations—enough to construct one of many new buildings on the Lexington campus. Mallory described the band's success as God's work, but she knew that her own remarkable ability to make contacts with important people across the country made God's work a lot easier. By 1935, Saints Industrial School was Holmes County's only black high school, its only black school staffed by college-educated teachers, and the only one with its own bus. Still, the school retained its separate, distinctive nature. Mallory dressed in the Victorian style that COGIC required, and she held Saints students to the church's strict moral standards. Even as she pushed the denomination to embrace education and public engagement, she demonstrated that connections outside the church did not require dramatic changes to practices within it.[51]

Mallory's fundraising prowess turned her school into one of Mississippi's most successful by the end of the 1930s, but her knack for befriending well-connected reformers helped to reshape the denomination's fortunes. One of Mallory's most important new friends was Mary McLeod Bethune, whom Mallory most likely met on one of her singing tours. Bethune, founder of her own school in Florida, organized the NCNW in 1935. The NCNW brought together existing black women's organizations and advocacy groups to push for black women and children's rights and welfare. Bethune's own holiness background drew her close to Mallory, who became a charter member of the NCNW and brought other COGIC women into the organization with her.[52]

Although COGIC leaders did not at first acknowledge this relationship because the church frowned on secular work, Bethune and the NCNW pulled Mallory and the denomination into the circle of black New Deal reformers. Already an advisor to Roosevelt and a good friend of the First Lady, in 1936, Bethune became director of the National Youth Administration's Division of Negro Affairs. In her company, Mallory too visited the White House several times, and in September 1938, five Jubilee Harmonizers sang before the president and First Lady. Eleanor Roosevelt described both the school and Mallory in that evening's *My Day* column, reporting to her readers across the nation that all who listened "were deeply touched by their performance." But Mallory's connections with the Roosevelt administration were not just social. She joined Bethune in advocating for places for black women and children in New Deal programs, and she later pushed the denomination toward a more active role in supporting US entry into World War II—a significant reversal for a church famous for protesting the Great War. Mallory also brought more prominent COGIC women, including future Women's Department supervisor Lillian Coffey, into the NCNW and the New Deal coalition.[53]

By the end of the 1930s, COGIC had grown while other denominations struggled. The 1936 Census of Religious Bodies reported a sharp decline in the number of COGIC churches in Tennessee, Arkansas, and Mississippi since 1926, but reports from Memphis in the 1930s suggest a different trajectory. For instance, the Census reported twenty COGIC churches in all of Tennessee in 1926, and only fifteen by 1936. But the Memphis City Directory listed twenty-five Churches of God in Christ in that city alone in 1936, as compared with eight in 1931, when the directory first included the denomination. Perhaps a better measure of COGIC's success in the 1930s is its physical expansion in Memphis. In the mid-1920s, Mason bought a failing black hospital to serve as a convocation center, where thousands of church members gathered each year for their annual meeting. In 1930, Tabernacle Baptist Church, once a showpiece for black baptists in Memphis, went bankrupt. Mason purchased the structure for his own congregation, and when the structure burned to the ground in 1936, he immediately began to plan a grander building to replace it. Church finances were tight during the depression, but the denomination continued to grow across the United States.[54]

Mallory's work may have aided the church's growth, but her more significant contribution was that she helped to link COGIC to the New Deal coalition. As she did so, Mallory demonstrated that COGIC could work with supporters outside the church and even engage with the federal government without abandoning its distinctive theology and worship style. Mallory's relationships with Bethune and other women activists also helped demonstrate to those outside the church that COGIC's members were far more capable and varied than mainline critics like William Clark suggested. As the church faced the coming decades, its ability to draw on outside resources and build relationships within the federal government would further expand its reach. Mallory had demonstrated that the New Deal's expansive coalition could even benefit the pentecostals that some administration liberals dismissed as "extreme and emotional."[55]

New Alliances for the Protestant Establishment

The expansiveness of the New Deal order troubled many members of the southern Protestant establishment. Southern Baptists, Methodists, Presbyterians, and Episcopalians had demanded that the federal government help those men and women they could not, and they had applauded the transfer of charity and social reform from church to state. White religious leaders in the region believed in the New Deal's early years that they could shape the president's program in the South to fit their own priorities, and the president's unwillingness to challenge Jim Crow directly and his overtures to religious leaders reassured them that they were right. But between 1937 and the end of the decade, disputes erupted among the members of the southern Protestant establishment who continued to believe that the New Deal embodied the churches' highest principles and those who believed that it instead undermined their moral authority and threatened the South's racial order. Eventually, the latter found common cause with the small but growing fundamentalist movement in the South, whose members turned their own efforts against the New Deal.

The slow turn against the New Deal reached a critical point in 1937, and not just among Protestant leaders. The Supreme Court's reversal of the National Recovery Administration (NRA) and AAA in 1935 and 1936 had prompted an outcry from administration opponents who argued that the New Deal as a whole was unconstitutional. When Roosevelt responded in 1937 with an attempt first to force the offending justices into retirement and then to pad their number with additional justices, he faced a fierce backlash across the nation. Even some of Roosevelt's allies complained about this naked gambit to consolidate power and compared the court-packing scheme to European totalitarianism. At the same time, Roosevelt reduced federal spending to balance the budget, and in the summer of 1937, the nation faced a brief but deep recession. Even though it followed a reduction in New Deal programming and spending, for many Americans the downturn seemed to undermine the president's argument that the New Deal could save the nation's economic system. Business leaders who had long opposed Roosevelt took advantage of the recession to more openly denounce his policies as unfavorable to industry. The timing of these new disasters could not have been worse for residents of Memphis and the Delta, who were still trying to recover from another devastating flood that drowned downtown Memphis and the Arkansas Delta in January and February 1937, and who had once again required an influx of federal aid (Figure 6.3).[56]

Meanwhile, as Roosevelt stopped bowing to the demands of southerners in Congress, many of the region's political elites turned on him. In 1938, he released *A Report on the Economic Conditions of the South*, a commissioned study that found that southerners still suffered disproportionately from hunger, preventable disease, substandard housing, minimal education, and low wages. Workers in the South earned, on average, $314 per year, while workers outside the region averaged $607 in annual income, making wages in the richest southern state lower than in even the poorest state outside the region. When Roosevelt named the South "the Nation's No. 1 economic problem,"

FIGURE 6.3 In the wake of the 1937 flood in Memphis, a man in a cart passes a billboard boasting of American prosperity and high wages.

Photo by Edwin Locke, February 1937, courtesy of the Library of Congress Prints and Photographs Division

conservative elites in the region responded with outrage. Some began to organize in resistance to further federal intervention in the region, but they need not have worried. Though the report gained widespread public attention, no legislation specific to the South followed. Nonetheless, southern elected officials increasingly stood against the New Deal even as the majority of their constituents remained fiercely loyal to the president. The same applied to the Protestant establishment: the ordinary people in the pews still supported the president, but the clergy divided as they felt their own power threatened.[57]

Perhaps the clearest indication of Protestant leaders' defection from the New Deal was the defensiveness of its supporters. Mississippi Southern Baptist Plautus Lipsey had openly questioned the way New Deal programs transformed the relationship between church and state in 1935 and 1936 even as he expressed his general approval of the New Deal. But by 1938, Lipsey felt compelled to defend it. "The administration at Washington, if I am not deceived, is trying to strengthen the hold of democracy, and loosen the hold of privilege, by legislation," he said in 1938. Yet "the administration is making little, if any, progress at this time." Lipsey blamed not Roosevelt but his opponents: "Every bill which is designed to lay the burden of taxation where it belongs; every measure which seeks to guarantee to the working man his economic rights; every effort to restrain the dictatorship of vast corporate interests—each effort is met by a howl of anguish and rage from the spokesmen of privilege."[58]

Those spokesmen of privilege included many Protestant clergy, who began to see themselves as competitors rather than partners with the state. They had handed off much of the responsibility for charity and social service, and they did not want it back. But they did want the social control that came with that responsibility, and church leaders began to worry that the government instead sought to control them. The Southern Baptists' 1936 debate over establishing a social research agency, combined with their decision to establish a new Committee on Public Relations, illustrates religious leaders' anxiety about the church's place in a transformed society.

The Southern Baptist Commission on Social Service presented detailed reports on a range of moral issues during the 1920s and 1930s. Focused especially on divorce, alcohol, and lynchings, it operated without funding or significant support from the Southern Baptist Convention. In 1932, North Carolinian and social gospeler William Louis Poteat proposed and chaired a committee to recommend a more comprehensive program for the commission. At the convention's 1935 annual meeting, Poteat, the retired president of Wake Forest College, urged the creation of a social research agency to probe social problems at a deeper level than the commission's sermonizing reports. Ultimately, Poteat hoped that the agency would investigate not only alcohol and the disappearance of the home "as a place of discipline and instruction" but also "the plight of tenant farmers," lynchings, and "the need for Christian understanding of the economic life of the Negro."[59]

When Poteat's proposal came to a vote the following year, it sparked heated debate among church members. One Mississippian expressed cautious approval of an organization that might "[stir] up the sincere minds of the people . . . and thus [provoke] right conduct in individuals and right action by groups." But a Memphis evangelist warned, "[T]he social service gospel has always found its rise with those who have largely set aside the evangelical faith. . . . [A] start in that direction never swings back, but always goes on until the evangelical base is forsaken entirely and a 'Christian' socialism becomes the sole objective."[60]

Southern Baptists had long disagreed about the church's responsibility to address social problems, and the Poteat proposal pitted the denomination's progressives and conservatives against one another. When the convention considered bringing the social research agency proposal to a vote in 1936, its leaders quickly determined that the cries of socialism had drowned out those of service. Church finances certainly factored into the decision as well, because Poteat had requested a full-time, funded agency. But the Southern Baptists' interest in formalized social service remained low. They tabled the proposal, prompting National Baptist Russell Barbour to report in protest, "Southern Baptists Table Jesus."[61]

Social service, the Southern Baptists had concluded, was simply not the work of the church. But if social service was not their place, they decided, social critique was. At the same meeting in which they "Table[d] Jesus," the Southern Baptists voted to revive the Committee on Chaplains of Army and Navy and rename it the Committee on Public Relations. This organization would "demand just rights that are being threatened," primarily by the federal government, and would thus stand against the kind of totalitarianism that now held sway across Europe.[62]

Perhaps the National Baptists perked their ears when they heard that Southern Baptists had begun to worry about threatened rights, but their white counterparts were not concerned with the persecution of African Americans and sharecroppers. Instead, Southern Baptists worried about "the denial of free action" on the part of home missionaries whose work overlapped with that of the New Deal. "The historian of the future," explained committee members, "will describe the New Deal as the inauguration of an era in which the Federal Government, in a period of depression, accepted the responsibility of making provision for the material needs of the underprivileged everywhere throughout this country." But rather than easing the churches' burden, the government had created "agencies whose programs are creating for us and for all other evangelical bodies problems that they have never before faced." Unlike the clergy who wrote to Roosevelt asking that he funnel aid through the churches, some Southern Baptists now worried that accepting state funds for church-related purposes would encroach on their own religious freedom.[63]

Specifically, the Committee on Public Relations worried about the use of public dollars for denominational schools and the application of Social Security requirements to the churches. They commended the baptist seminaries that had refused to allow their students to participate in the NYA (National Youth Administration), a WPA agency that paid college students for work-study projects at their schools. The Social Security Act particularly irked Southern Baptists, who struggled to persuade clergy and churches to participate in the denomination's voluntary retirement program. Both Southern and National Baptists bemoaned the absence of a safety net for retired and elderly clergy and church workers, but they lauded the Social

Security Act's exemption of churches from the obligation to pay into mandatory retirement.[64]

When a New York congresswoman proposed bringing churches under the Social Security Act in 1939, Southern Baptists protested that a Social Security tax would render "the church subservient to the state." The measure failed. That same year, the Northern Baptists, the Southern Baptists, and the National Baptists released their first-ever joint statement. "The American Baptist Bill of Rights" called for "absolute religious liberty" and renewed the call for separation of church and state that many baptists feared denominational leaders had abandoned with the arrival of the New Deal. In 1937, the Southern and Northern Baptists had begun collaborating on questions of religious freedom, and in 1942, the National, Northern, and Southern Baptists formed the Joint Conference Committee on Public Relations, an independent governmental watchdog organization in Washington, DC. For Southern Baptists, the new avenue for reform was not through collaboration with the government or independent activism, but in close supervision and critique of the expanded New Deal state.[65]

Although the Southern Baptists expressed more concern over the question of religious freedom than most denominations in the region, other churches also lamented the government's expanded reach. For white southerners, claims about the New Deal's encroachment on religious liberty often masked concern over federal interference in their racial caste system. Despite their relatively liberal reputation, the southern Methodists reaffirmed their allegiance to the racial status quo in their reunification compact with northern Methodists. While the white baptists and Presbyterians of the South had more contentious relationships with their northern counterparts, stretching back to their initial division over slavery, the Methodists had developed an amicable affiliation. Southern black members of the northern Methodist Church were particularly numerous in Mississippi. Unification would bring together the integrated northern church and the white southern church. Southerners defeated attempts at unification in 1920 and 1924 because those attempts failed to provide a satisfactory plan for bringing black and white southern Methodists into the same fold.[66]

In 1935, Methodists drafted a new plan for unification that explicitly created a separate jurisdiction for black churches. It was a compromise on southern white terms, although many southern whites still complained about the prospect of uniting with a church espousing "radical, dangerous, socialistic ideas" about race, labor, and theology. In 1939, the compromise unification passed in both North and South, with dissenting votes coming only from black Methodists and from white Mississippians who opposed any inclusion of African Americans. Many African Americans and some northern whites regretted that "Negro Methodists are relegated to the outer pale beyond the concern of their white brethren professively belonging to the same household of faith" but remained committed to the unified church nonetheless. With the newly formed Methodist Church, southern whites established their control over racial matters, and northern Methodists accepted their conditions. Such was the pattern that the white southern majority hoped to maintain.[67]

No longer at the vanguard of reform, Protestant agencies became government watchdogs, New Deal critics, and guardians of southern white supremacy. As they did so, the most conservative members of those denominations found common political ground with southern fundamentalists who had opposed the New Deal from the start. Two of those movements took root in Arkansas, where Ben Bogard and Dale Crowley had already found success.

Bogard's denomination, the ABA—casually known as the Landmarkers—squabbled internally through the late thirties, but they also reserved some energy to stand against the New Deal. In the fall of 1940, a group of rural church advocates associated with the Federal Council of Churches (FCC) began work with black and white residents of La Forge, Missouri, an FSA farm project just across the border from the Arkansas Delta that was also an STFU stronghold. They tried to incorporate local clergy in their effort and made overtures in particular toward an ABA minister they feared might cause trouble. He refused to cooperate but promised not to interfere. As soon as they arrived, however, the Landmarker "started vigorous opposition" and published a bulletin denouncing the FCC. His opposition stymied their work. For the Landmarkers, who denounced both the FCC and the New Deal as communist inspired, the apparent collaboration between the two must have seemed a deliberate provocation.[68]

In 1941, as the nation's attention turned toward the wars in Europe and Asia, another Arkansas fundamentalist had an opportunity to take his New Deal critique straight to Washington. The Churches of Christ in Arkansas hired a former missionary named George Benson to rescue Harding College, a church-affiliated school in the town of Searcy. Benson, like Arenia Mallory in Mississippi, reached out to well-off acquaintances when he could not raise the money from the churches, and the school thrived under his leadership. Benson's allies were businessmen, and Benson soon concluded that if he could save a struggling college, he could save the government too. In 1941, one of Benson's friends landed him a spot on the floor to testify before the

House Ways and Means Committee about funding the New Deal in the face of increased defense expenditures. Benson delivered a rousing speech that suggested slashing New Deal funding and forcing the government to balance its budget as he had done at Harding. In this way, by the 1940s, southern fundamentalists joined their northern counterparts to capitalize on disaffection with Roosevelt's programs.[69]

Members of the southern Protestant establishment who opposed the New Deal and the fundamentalists thus moved toward common ground on political questions. But neither group gained much traction during the 1930s, when the New Deal's enthusiastic supporters still held sway in southern churches of all but the most oppositional traditions. Yet they had begun to forge a new kind of relationship to the state, one marked by both active engagement with it and fierce criticism of it.

ACROSS THE RELIGIOUS spectrum, from the socialists and liberals who joined or supported the Southern Tenant Farmers' Union to the fundamentalists who testified before Congress about how the government ought to do its business, religious people engaged with the federal government more in the 1930s than they had done before. The southern Protestant establishment retained the largest influence on federal programs administered in the region, its members visible in Congress and in every federal agency and local relief office. Anna Layne's interaction with the Barclays demonstrates the ways the Protestant establishment wrote its priorities into the New Deal—just as its members had expected to do. Yet those churches that had long advocated disengagement from politics, like members of the Church of God in Christ, also found themselves pulled into the New Deal coalition, and that engagement pushed their work in new directions.

If the New Deal did a poor job of redistributing land or financial resources, it did a better job of redistributing moral authority. Members of the Protestant establishment had to share their place in welfare and reform not only with the federal government, whose help they had sought, but also with their religious rivals in the region. Furthermore, the growing claim that groups like the STFU and COGIC made on New Deal resources and relationships centered around a critique of the South's racial and economic order. The southern Protestant establishment divided over this loss of authority, New Deal supporters on the defensive against those who prized the Jim Crow economic order as the wellspring of their own power. Thus emerged the patterns of a religious realignment that would take decades to resolve.

EPILOGUE

The Myth of the Redemptive Depression

IN A PRELIMINARY study of the effects of the Great Depression on religion, sociologist Samuel C. Kincheloe wrote in 1938, "Church leaders and writers have been going through a process of reorientation on the role of the church in modern society, especially in reference to the state." Although Kincheloe could not yet predict where this reorientation might lead, he suggested that it might be part of a longer trend toward "the secularization of church activities."[1]

In one sense, Kincheloe was right. For several decades before the depression, southern churches and religious organizations had engaged in charitable and social reform work that kept pace with the region's urban and industrial growth. That work expanded most dramatically in the wake of World War I. After their growth stalled in the 1920s, churches "hailed the depression with rejoicing," as Kincheloe put it, "since they had the idea that previous depressions had 'driven men to God' and felt that the time was overdue for men again to be reminded of the need to let the spiritual dominate the materialistic order."[2]

Instead of driving people to the churches, however, the Great Depression drove the churches to the state. Religious and municipal charities across the nation went broke. The 1930 drought in the Delta laid waste to the land and wiped out the region's religious and charitable resources, as well as the limited forms of aid in municipal and state coffers. As a result, the region's religious leaders joined its politicians to demand that the federal government intervene.

The South's Protestant establishment applauded the arrival of Franklin Roosevelt into the White House and celebrated the first programs of the New Deal even as it mourned the end of Prohibition. Protestants, Jews, and

Catholics alike cited scriptural precedent for the establishment of the National Recovery Administration and Federal Emergency Relief Administration in 1933. The Social Security Act and Works Progress Administration, established in 1935, assured them that the New Deal state had taken up the cause of the churches. For many, the New Deal did not represent secularization at all, but instead a religious triumph. For white southerners, part of that triumph was in the New Deal's concession to local control and white supremacy.

Yet when it became clear first that New Deal agents like Harry Hopkins would draw a line between the social programs of church and those of the state, and then that Roosevelt's administration would not altogether bend to Jim Crow, white southern Protestant support for the New Deal began to fracture. By the end of the 1930s, many southern Protestant elites denounced the same programs that they had heralded as religious victories in 1933 and 1935. The federal government was no longer a partner but a competitor, and its provisions for the poor and the sick robbed religious leaders of their moral authority while its protections for workers and retirees threatened the churches' autonomy. Eventually, members of the Protestant establishment who turned on the New Deal found common cause with fundamentalists and corporate conservatives who had denounced federal intervention in social welfare from the start.

Southerners as a whole remained loyal to Roosevelt and the New Deal. White Protestant leaders like Will Alexander and Brooks Hays found a more receptive audience for their religious reforms in state halls than in sanctuaries, and they went to work for the federal government. Those outside the establishment, from Charles H. Mason and Arenia Mallory to the members of the Southern Tenant Farmers' Union, likewise formed new alliances with the New Deal state and strengthened their own churches' work through government partnerships. Members of the South's mobile religious communities found that they had a resource and often an ally in the federal government, even as New Deal liberals like Will Alexander and Anna Layne pushed them toward more conventional and private forms of religious expression.

This was no simple process of secularization. Kincheloe was right that the New Deal state assumed responsibilities for social welfare that the churches had once claimed as their own moral obligation. Yet the state also institutionalized many of the ideals that those churches had long promoted, both in its commitment to providing structures of support for those in need and in its partial willingness to mold those structures to the Protestant establishment's moral sensibilities and racial prejudices. Furthermore, the New Deal welcomed religious reformers eager to work as agents of the federal government or to partner with it. Those reformers' religious preferences in turn shaped the course of federal policy for decades to come.[3]

ALTHOUGH IN THE moment and in retrospect, many have described the depression as an era of mainline declension, it was not. Operating on a shoe-string budget, the 1936 Census of Religious Bodies undercounted the three major denominations in the South—Southern Baptists, National Baptists, and Southern Methodists—as well as the Church of God in Christ and other grow-ing churches. In contrast, the churches' own records show that by the late 1930s, southern Protestants were, at worst, treading water. Fundamentalist and pen-tecostal groups grew more quickly than other Protestant denominations—but still only slightly more rapidly than they had in the prior two decades. Overall, church membership inched upward during the depression, from forty-seven percent of Americans in 1930 to forty-nine percent in 1940. By the numbers, the thirties brought neither revival nor declension.[4]

The Great Depression ended in another great war, and during World War II the anticipated revivals began to take shape. Some American churches had embraced pacifism or at least isolationism in the wake of World War I, but many abandoned those stances as they watched the spread of fascism in Europe. After the Japanese bombing of Pearl Harbor on December 7, 1941, churches quickly rallied to support the war effort, just as they had done twenty-four years earlier. The mobilization of industry and troops meant another dramatic expansion of the federal government. Wartime production brought new jobs, and increased national income brought an end to economic hardship for the churches. The longed-for return to the pews began during the war, although wartime rationing meant that physical expansion had to wait. Nationwide, religious contributions grew sixty-four percent from 1941 to 1945. The churches held on to their growing resources until the war ended in August 1945.[5]

At the war's end, churches poured their savings into evangelistic and building campaigns. Between 1940 and 1950, church membership surged from forty-nine to fifty-five percent of Americans. By 1956, sixty-two percent of Americans claimed membership in a church. Churches that had fallen into disrepair during the depression now sparkled with fresh paint or tumbled to the ground to make way for larger facilities, and home and foreign missions programs expanded dramatically. Southern Baptists built 500 new churches and added 300,000 new members between 1946 and 1949, making them the second-largest denomination in the United States after the Methodist Church.[6]

And yet the churches were different. Mainline Protestants of all varieties swept thousands of new members into thousands of new churches, but so did Catholics, Jews, pentecostals, and others outside the establishment. The growth was so widespread and comprehensive that scholars still debate whether the mainline churches or their competitors dominated. New ecumenical organizations sprang up among liberals, as did cooperative efforts among a new constellation of conservative evangelicals. The Federal Council of Churches expanded in 1950 to become the National Council of Churches, and it retained its role as the nation's central ecumenical organization even though southerners kept their distance from it. In 1942, the National Association of Evangelicals (NAE) formed to unite those who judged the Federal Council too liberal. The NAE embraced many southerners, and in 1944, the belligerent Arkansas fundamentalist Dale Crowley resurfaced in Washington, DC to help the group organize the National Religious Broadcasters, a spinoff organization designed to make room on the radio dial for conservative evangelists in the name of religious freedom.[7]

The churches' resurgence in numbers and influence during the 1940s and 1950s followed the pattern of 1930s realignments, but the context had changed dramatically. If the 1930s marked a period of desperate experimentation, a brief alliance between church and state as both confronted widespread suffering, the 1940s and 1950s marked a period of retrenchment. In the wake of World War II, the bright line Harry Hopkins had tried to draw between the functions of church and state blurred once again, as mainline and Catholic religious agencies coordinated with the federal government to supervise and distribute overseas relief. Conservatives protested the alliance and warned that religious agencies that took federal funding would also have to accept federal oversight and control. Yet even as they raised the alarm that religious freedom was under attack, conservative religious leaders tried to shape state programs at all levels, from local attempts to rewrite public school curricula to the NAE's efforts to train conservative evangelicals for public office.[8]

During the decades-long Cold War that followed the fractious wartime alliance between the United States and the Soviet Union, the churches and the state again joined forces, this time in defense of capitalism rather than in an effort to critique or repair it. Christianity and capitalism together stood as a contrast to godless Communism, and nascent alliances between corporate and religious power structures flourished. White southern churches that in the 1930s had offered tentative support to the Southern Tenant Farmers' Union turned on organized labor and cast their lot with industry. An American must be a capitalist, they decided, and so must a Christian.

Corporate powers had worked to link the three concepts—Americanism, capitalism, and Christianity—in the Gilded Age, but not without challenges from both radicals and progressives, who deemed such an alliance unholy. In the Cold War context, however, challenges to capitalism met with charges of treason. When the Catholic Knights of Columbus sponsored a successful campaign to add the words "Under God" to the pledge of allegiance, and when Congress voted in 1955 to add the phrase "In God We Trust" to paper money, the moves seemed inevitable. Religious leaders and corporate leaders together naturalized the alliance between church and state, capital and Christianity. Soon enough, Americans forgot that God had not always been in the pledge and on the dollar.[9]

Dissent thrived in the midst of consensus, however. For African American religious leaders, the postwar atmosphere offered new opportunities even as it closed off old ones. The depression-era grassroots movements for economic and racial justice expanded into a multipronged effort with the beginning of World War II. The black press announced a "Double V" campaign for victory abroad and at home, and religious leaders soon joined the multitudes of African Americans who demanded the political and civil rights denied them in the Jim Crow South. Civil rights activists honed a careful theological critique of a nation that presented itself as a model to the world but denied many of its own citizens the basic protections it promised to citizens of foreign nations. Civil rights leaders downplayed their secular influences and stressed their Christian theology. Even though most black churches remained on the sidelines, the movement nonetheless drew on the faith and rituals at the center of many black southerners' lives. Black Methodists and baptists fought for their rights as citizens alongside independents and pentecostals once scorned as otherworldly. The day before his assassination, Martin Luther King Jr. gave his famous last speech, "I've Been to the Mountaintop," from the pulpit of Memphis's Mason Temple, headquarters of the Church of God in Christ.[10]

Civil rights activists and their powerful opponents made race a central issue in postwar America. National Baptist editor Russell C. Barbour had written in 1938 that where they should "embrace the brotherhood principles of Jesus," American Christians instead "read into the Holy Bible their own wicked prejudices and make God a little tribal deity interested first in the color of skin of his children." White churches before the depression were no more prepared to join a civil rights revolution than they were in the 1940s. But some of them had played an important, if deeply flawed, role in conversations about race and reform. After the depression, white churches had little to offer the growing campaign for racial justice. Some white liberals who had allied with Roosevelt, including Will Alexander and many of the STFU's members and allies, supported the civil rights movement. But they worked almost entirely outside the white churches. Those churches instead accused the New Deal state of undermining Jim Crow, and they declared themselves responsible for repairing the damage.[11]

White Christians in the South could have chosen otherwise. In the summer of 1954, Southern Baptists gathered two weeks after the *Brown versus Board of Education* school desegregation decision and voted to endorse it as consistent with "the Christian principles of equal justice and love for all men." Other major denominations in the region—Catholics, Methodists, and Presbyterians—soon joined them. But their members did not, and white churches in Memphis and the Delta in particular railed against the proclamations of denominational leaders. The southern Protestant establishment had abandoned the New Deal to save Jim Crow, and the campaign to reform America into a more just society surged ahead without it.[12]

In the 1960s, Lyndon B. Johnson again expanded the social safety net to wage his War on Poverty, and religious organizations on the right developed a sharper critique of the state even as they grew to rely ever more heavily on its resources. A Texan, Johnson stepped into office upon John F. Kennedy's assassination in 1963 and in 1964 defeated conservative favorite Barry Goldwater with sixty-one percent of the popular vote, a margin even more overwhelming than Roosevelt's victories in 1932 and 1936. Yet Johnson's support for civil rights and expanded government services cost him the Deep South, including once solidly Democratic Mississippi. Memphis and the Arkansas Delta tipped only slightly in Johnson's favor. Civil rights activists successfully pressured the new president to push the Civil Rights Act of 1964 and the Voting Rights Act of 1965 through Congress, and many southern whites who had remained loyal until then turned on the Democrats with a vengeance. At the same time, however, church–state collaboration in social action increased under Johnson's Great Society programs, which favored cooperation with voluntary agencies over direct federal action. Sectarian hospitals, church-based childcare providers, and other religious social service agencies across the theological and political spectrum found federal support irresistible.[13]

Conservative critics of the welfare state worked steadily to undermine it, and when they rose to power in the 1980s and 1990s, they pushed both elimination and privatization of services. By the 1980s, the National Association of Evangelicals and other conservative organizations that had once spurned government support now embraced tax credits for private childcare, fought for public vouchers to private schools, and relied heavily on federal support for international missionary and relief work. Democrat Bill Clinton signed the Personal Responsibility and Work Opportunity Reconciliation Act into law in 1996, and with it Charitable Choice, a provision that ensured that religious providers received equal consideration in competition for federal funds and removed stipulations that those providers qualify for tax-exempt status. Clinton's successor, George W. Bush, established the White House Office of Faith-Based and Community Initiatives, which allowed churches themselves, and not just religious charities, to receive federal funds. Thus vanished the last vestige of Harry Hopkins's 1930s effort to separate the social programs of church and state.[14]

AS THEY CAMPAIGNED to dismantle the welfare state, conservatives from the late twentieth century forward also worked to reshape Americans' memory of the Great Depression and the New Deal. In these rosy new narratives, the Great Depression brought suffering and sorrow, but also thrift and humility. It did precisely what religious authorities had hoped it would: it stripped away life's superfluities and brought people together, and to God. The Great Depression brought redemption—or it would have, if only Franklin Roosevelt had not interfered.

According to the myth of the redemptive depression, people who wanted assistance could always turn to their families or their churches, until Roosevelt swept in to replace voluntary assistance with state aid that rendered its recipients hopelessly dependent. This argument recast the Depression era as an idyllic world where the deserving poor, left to their own devices, would find their way out of misery without government help. Churches and voluntary societies could handle the few cases of real need, and as they did so, they could also provide the moral guidance that the state did not.[15]

Proponents of this simplistic narrative ignored five decades of bipartisan efforts to expand the welfare state and make it more inclusive, and focused only on denunciations of government expansion first under Roosevelt and then under Lyndon Johnson. At the heart of these denunciations was a claim as strident as it was inaccurate: that recipients of state aid were too often nonwhite and female, that federal funds rendered them chronically dependent, and that hardworking white men had for too long borne the burden of their support. Suffering and poverty were not the problem; federal efforts to alleviate it were.[16]

The myth of the redemptive depression proved so broadly compelling that when the United States faced yet another widespread economic crisis in 2008 Americans responded with a very different set of demands from those they made in the early 1930s. That crisis swept Barack Obama into office in 2009 amidst calls for business relief and jobs programs not unlike those of the New Deal, as well as for health care provisions that represented one of Roosevelt's unfulfilled dreams. Yet any semblance of bipartisan support for such programs fell apart quickly. Even the popular Affordable Care Act emerged from Congress as a program built on private insurance, rather than the single-payer, federally funded effort that Obama had initially proposed. The Tea Party's rapid emergence, its appeal among conservative Christians, and its powerful corporate backing scuttled any further proposals to expand federal services and instead advanced an antistatist economic agenda that now permeates the leadership of both major parties. This approach has proven particularly popular in places like Memphis and the Delta, where the politics of welfare remain highly racialized.[17]

On Easter Sunday in 2012, Billy Graham's son Franklin, head of Samaritan's Purse, summed up a memory of the Great Depression that prevails in conservative circles, and particularly in conservative evangelical churches. "A hundred years ago, the social safety net in the country was provided by the church," he said to Christiane Amanpour on ABC's *This Week*. "If you didn't have a job, you'd go to your local church and ask the pastor if he [knew] somebody that could hire him. If you were hungry, you went to the local church and told them, 'I can't feed my family.' And the church would help you." Graham explained, "But the government took that. And took it away from the church."[18]

Graham has embraced his role as provocateur. He does not speak for a majority of evangelicals, or for a majority of conservatives. Yet his rendition of the New Deal's relationship to American Christianity reflects a careful erasure and repackaging of Great Depression history that infuses Americans' contemporary faith in the voluntary and private sectors and their skepticism of the federal government. Gone from this myth of the redemptive depression are years of suffering so deep and widespread that they left once-hopeful Americans defeated and their churches and communities unable to come to their aid. Gone are the clergy bold enough to admit defeat and call for a social safety net that would prevent the men and women before them from dying of starvation and the diseases of poverty. Gone are the careful negotiations between church and state, and the willingness to try new solutions to economic and social crises. What remains is a nation haunted by a past it refuses to remember.

Major Religious Groups and Denominations in Memphis and the Delta

Denomination or Association	Acronym	Other Names	Racial Composition	Geographic Distribution	Other
American Baptist Association	ABA	Association Baptists, Landmark Baptists	White	Rural Arkansas Delta. Based in Little Rock and more numerous outside the Delta, in Arkansas and Texas	Fundamentalist, premillennialist. Organized in Arkansas in 1924, largely of churches that broke from the SBC beginning in the late nineteenth century
National Baptist Convention of America	NBCA	National Baptists	African American	Distributed throughout the region	Smaller denomination that divided from the National Baptist Convention, U.S.A. in 1915
National Baptist Convention, U.S.A., Inc.	NBC-USA	National Baptists	African American	Distributed throughout the region	The major black baptist denomination
Southern Baptist Convention	SBC	Southern Baptists	White	Distributed throughout the region	The major white baptist denomination in the South
Catholic Church			African American and white; also included recent Italian, Mexican, and Syrian immigrants	Primarily in Memphis and larger Delta towns, but operated rural missions	

Churches of Christ		African American and white; largely white in the region	Distributed throughout the region, but strong in rural areas	Antidenominational and congregationalist; generally fundamentalist
Congregational and Christian Churches	Congregationalists	African American and white; largely white in the region	Primarily in Memphis	Organized in 1931 as a merger of two Congregationalist bodies. Now the United Church of Christ
Disciples of Christ	Christian Church	African American and white; largely white in the region	Distributed throughout the region	Same roots as Churches of Christ; generally less conservative
Protestant Episcopal Church		African American and white; predominantly white	Primarily in Memphis and larger Delta towns	Now the Episcopal Church
Reform Judaism		Predominantly established citizens of German and Western European origin	Synagogues in Memphis and larger Delta towns	Reform Jews operated the Neighborhood House, which served many Memphis children during the depression
Orthodox Judaism		Predominantly more recent Eastern European immigrants	Synagogues in Memphis	Memphis had (and still has) a particularly strong Orthodox Jewish community

(continued)

Appendix (continued)

Denomination or Association	Acronym	Other Names	Racial Composition	Geographic Distribution	Other
African Methodist Episcopal Church	AME		African American	Distributed throughout the region	Founded in Philadelphia, Pennsylvania in 1816; the oldest independent African American denomination
African Methodist Episcopal Church, Zion	AMEZ		African American	Distributed throughout the region	Founded in New York in 1821; had a smaller presence in the region than the AME or CME churches
Colored Methodist Episcopal Church	CME		African American	Distributed throughout the region	Founded and headquartered in Jackson, Tennessee, ninety miles northeast of Memphis. The CME changed its name to the Christian Methodist Episcopal Church in 1954
Methodist Episcopal Church		Northern Methodists	African American and white; largely African American in the region	Primarily in Memphis and Delta towns, but operated rural churches as well	
Methodist Episcopal Church, South	MECS	Southern Methodists	White	Primarily in Memphis and Delta towns, but operated rural churches as well	

Denomination	Abbreviation	Racial composition	Distribution	Notes
Methodist Church	Methodists	African American and white, divided into separate jurisdictions, with the Central Jurisdiction over all African American churches	Primarily in Memphis and Delta towns, but operated rural churches as well	The MECS, MEC, and Methodist Protestant Church (MPC) merged in 1939 to create the Methodist Church, now the United Methodist Church
Assemblies of God	AG	White	Distributed throughout the region	Most widespread white pentecostal denomination in the region
Church of Christ (Holiness) USA		African American	Primarily located in the Mississippi Delta	Based in Lexington, Mississippi; this is the church from which COGIC divided in 1907.
Church of God (Cleveland, Tennessee)	Church of God	White	Based in East Tennessee	Pentecostal denomination headquartered in Cleveland, Tennessee, and the largest of the several denominations to use the title "Church of God"
Church of God (Holiness)		White	More widespread in the upper South; sparse in the Delta	An association of autonomous holiness congregations

(continued)

Appendix (continued)

Denomination or Association	Acronym	Other Names	Racial Composition	Geographic Distribution	Other
Church of God in Christ	COGIC		African American	Distributed throughout the region	Headquartered in Memphis, COGIC was the largest African American pentecostal denomination in the region
					Holiness and premillennialist
Church of the Nazarene		Nazarenes	White and African American; predominantly white	Distributed throughout the region	
Pentecostal Holiness Church, Inc.			White	Distributed throughout the region	
Pilgrim Holiness Church			White	A small denomination; just a few churches in the region	
Cumberland Presbyterian Church	CPC		White	Primarily in Memphis and Delta towns	
Presbyterian Church in the United States	PCUS	Southern Presbyterians	Predominantly white	Primarily in Memphis and Delta towns	

Presbyterian Church in the United States of America	PCUSA	Northern Presbyterians	Predominantly white	Primarily in Memphis and Delta towns	After conservatives in each denomination departed, the PCUS and PCUSA merged in 1983 to become the Presbyterian Church (U.S.A.)
Seventh-Day Adventist Church		Adventists	African American and white	Distributed throughout the region	Premillennialist; distinguished by seventh-day (Saturday) observation of the Sabbath
American Unitarian Association		Unitarians	White	Primarily in Memphis	The Unitarians merged with the Universalist Church of America in 1961 to become the Unitarian Universalist Association.

This is not an exhaustive list of all denominations or religious bodies present in the region. It is a list of the more common religious bodies that appear in this book.

Sources: Compiled from *Census of Religious Bodies*, 1916, 1926, and 1936; Memphis City Directories, 1930–1940; and denominational records.

Notes

INTRODUCTION

1. Franklin D. Roosevelt, "The Forgotten Man," April 7, 1932, reprinted in *The Public Papers and Addresses of Franklin D. Roosevelt*, vol. 1, 1928-1932 (New York: Random House, 1938), 624.

2. Several excellent books engage questions about religion and the Great Depression. Most recently, Kevin Kruse and Matthew Sutton have identified the New Deal as a catalyst for Christian conservatives' engagement in politics. For Kruse, reaction to the New Deal prompted an explicit alliance between religious and business conservatives: Kevin Kruse, *One Nation Under God: How Corporate America Invented Christian America* (New York: Basic Books, 2015). For Sutton, the New Deal provoked premillennial anxieties and action: Matthew Avery Sutton, *American Apocalypse: A History of Modern Evangelicalism* (Cambridge, MA: Belknap Press, 2014). Several studies focus on the experience of the Great Depression among particular traditions. See Kenneth J. Heineman, *A Catholic New Deal: Religion and Reform in Depression Pittsburgh* (University Park: Pennsylvania State University Press, 1999); David Buckelew Hunsicker, "The Rise of the Parachurch Movement in American Protestant Christianity During the 1930s and 1940s: A Detailed Study of the Beginnings of the Navigators, Young Life, and Youth for Christ International" (Ph.D. diss., Trinity Evangelical Divinity School, 1998); Donald Wesley Trotter, "Making Do: Case Studies of Disciple of Christ Congregations in the Great Depression" (Ph.D. diss., University of Tennessee, 1998); Beth S. Wenger, *New York Jews and the Great Depression: Uncertain Promise* (New Haven, CT: Yale University Press, 1996); David J. O'Brien, *American Catholics and Social Reform: The New Deal Years* (New York: Oxford University Press, 1968); William Oliver Paulsell, "The Disciples of Christ and the Great Depression, 1929-1936" (Ph.D. diss., Vanderbilt University, 1965). Relevant studies of the private-public welfare transfer include: Andrew J. F. Morris, *The Limits of Voluntarism: Charity*

and Welfare from the New Deal Through the Great Society (New York: Cambridge University Press, 2009); David T. Beito, *From Mutual Aid to Welfare State: Fraternal Societies and Social Services, 1890-1967* (Chapel Hill: University of North Carolina Press, 2000); Lizabeth Cohen, *Making a New Deal: Industrial Workers in Chicago, 1919-1939* (Cambridge: Cambridge University Press, 1990); Daniel Michael Hungerman, "Public Finance and Charitable Church Activity" (Ph.D. diss., Duke University, 2005). Religious leaders and scholars began to evaluate the effect of the Depression on American religion even before the decade ended. See Samuel C. Kincheloe, *Research Memorandum on Religion in the Depression* (New York: Social Science Research Council, 1937). After the end of World War II, several historians focused on northern liberalism and the Social Gospel in the interwar years. See William R. Hutchison, ed., *Between the Times: The Travail of the Protestant Establishment in America, 1900-1960* (New York: Cambridge University Press, 1989); Paul Allen Carter, *The Decline and Revival of the Social Gospel: Social and Political Liberalism in American Protestant Churches, 1920-1940* (Ithaca, NY: Cornell University Press, 1956); Donald B. Meyer, *The Protestant Search for Political Realism, 1919-1941* (Berkeley: University of California Press, 1961); Liston Pope, *Millhands and Preachers: A Study of Gastonia* (New Haven, CT: Yale University Press, 1942). More recent interpretations argue for the hardiness of liberalism during and after the Depression. See Elesha Coffman, *The Christian Century and the Rise of the Protestant Mainline* (New York: Oxford University Press, 2013); Matthew S. Hedstrom, *The Rise of Liberal Religion: Book Culture and American Spirituality in the Twentieth Century* (New York: Oxford University Press, 2013); David A. Hollinger, *After Cloven Tongues of Fire: Protestant Liberalism in Modern American History* (Princeton, NJ: Princeton University Press, 2013). The most influential examination of the Depression was for many years Robert T. Handy, "The American Religious Depression, 1925-1935," *Church History* 29, no. 1 (March 1960): 3–16. For a re-evaluation of that essay, see Jon Butler et al., "Forum: American Religion and the Great Depression," *Church History* 80, no. 3 (September 2011): 575–610. Jarod Roll argues that the Great Depression precipitated a "spirit-filled rebellion among rural workers of the South." See Roll, *Spirit of Rebellion: Labor and Religion in the New Cotton South* (Urbana: University of Illinois Press, 2010). And for a similar and compelling argument more focused on workers in Memphis and the Delta, see Jarod Roll and Erik S. Gellman, *Gospel of the Working Class: Labor's Southern Prophets in New Deal America* (Urbana: University of Illinois Press, 2011). Fred C. Smith examines the relationship between religion and several planned communities in the Depression South in *Trouble in Goshen: Plain Folk, Roosevelt, Jesus, and Marx in the Great Depression South* (Jackson: University Press of Mississippi, 2014). Jonathan H. Ebel has examined the experience of displaced southerners and westerners in California in "Reforming Faith: John Steinbeck, the New Deal, and the Religion of the Wandering Oklahoman," *Journal of Religion* 92, no. 5 (October 2012): 527–535.

On the lived experience of religion during the Great Depression and beyond, see Robert A. Orsi, *The Madonna of 115th St.: Faith and Community in Italian Harlem, 1880-1950* (New Haven, CT: Yale University Press, 2010 [1985]) and *Thank You, St. Jude: Women's Devotion to the Patron Saint of Hopeless Causes* (New Haven, CT: Yale University Press, 1996). On broader changes to religious institutions in the period, see Randall J. Stephens, *The Fire Spreads: Holiness and Pentecostalism in the American South* (Cambridge, MA: Harvard University Press, 2007); William R. Glass, *Strangers in Zion: Fundamentalists in the South, 1900-1950* (Macon, GA: Mercer University Press, 2001); Grant Wacker, *Heaven Below: Early Pentecostals and American Culture* (Cambridge, MA: Harvard University Press, 2001); Joel A. Carpenter, *Revive Us Again: The Reawakening of American Fundamentalism* (New York: Oxford University Press, 1997). On religious figures who helped shape the course of the nation or the New Deal, see Marie Dallam, *Daddy Grace: A Celebrity Preacher and His House of Prayer* (New York: New York University Press, 2007); Matthew Avery Sutton, *Aimee Semple McPherson and the Resurrection of Christian America* (Cambridge, MA: Harvard University Press, 2007); Jill Watts, *God, Harlem, U.S.A.: The Father Divine Story* (Berkeley: University of California Press, 1995); Leo P. Ribuffo, *The Old Christian Right: The Protestant Far Right from the Great Depression to the Cold War* (Philadelphia: Temple University Press, 1983); Alan Brinkley, *Voices of Protest: Huey Long, Father Coughlin, and the Great Depression* (New York: Knopf, 1982). On the significant theological transformations of the Depression, see Andrew S. Finstuen, *Original Sin and Everyday Protestants: The Theology of Reinhold Niebuhr, Billy Graham, and Paul Tillich in an Age of Anxiety* (Chapel Hill: University of North Carolina Press, 2009); Joseph Kip Kosek, *Acts of Conscience: Christian Nonviolence and Modern American Democracy* (New York: Columbia University Press, 2009); David L. Chappell, *A Stone of Hope: Prophetic Religion and the Death of Jim Crow* (Chapel Hill: University of North Carolina Press, 2005); Patricia Appelbaum, *Kingdom to Commune: Protestant Pacifist Culture Between World War I and the Vietnam Era* (Chapel Hill: University of North Carolina Press, 1999); Richard Wightman Fox, *Reinhold Niebuhr: A Biography* (Ithaca, NY: Cornell University Press, 1997); Heather A. Warren, *Theologians of a New World Order: Reinhold Niebuhr and the Christian Realists, 1920-1948* (New York: Oxford University Press, 1997).

3. On the Great Depression in Memphis and the Delta, see Roll and Gellman, *Gospel of the Working Class*; Roger Biles, *Memphis in the Great Depression* (Knoxville: University of Tennessee Press, 1986); Nan Elizabeth Woodruff, *As Rare as Rain: Federal Relief in the Great Southern Drought of 1930-1931* (Urbana: University of Illinois Press, 1985).

4. Bureau of the Census, *Census of the United States, 1930*. On Memphis and the Delta's plantation history and economy in the twentieth century, see Roll, *Spirit of Rebellion*; Laurie B. Green, *Battling the Plantation Mentality: Memphis and*

the Black Freedom Struggle (Chapel Hill: University of North Carolina Press, 2007); Nan Elizabeth Woodruff, *American Congo: The African American Freedom Struggle in the Delta* (Cambridge, MA: Harvard University Press, 2003); Clyde Adrian Woods, *Development Arrested: The Blues and Plantation Power in the Mississippi Delta* (London: Verso, 1998); John M. Barry, *Rising Tide: The Great Mississippi Flood of 1927 and How It Changed America* (New York: Simon & Schuster, 1997); Jeannie M. Whayne, *A New Plantation South: Land, Labor, and Federal Favor in Twentieth-Century Arkansas* (Charlottesville: University of Press of Virginia, 1996); Michael Honey, *Southern Labor and Black Civil Rights: Organizing Memphis Workers* (Urbana: University of Illinois Press, 1993); James C. Cobb, *The Most Southern Place on Earth: The Mississippi Delta and the Roots of Regional Identity* (New York: Oxford University Press, 1992); Pete Daniel, *Deep'n as It Come: The 1927 Mississippi River Flood* (New York: Oxford University Press, 1977).

5. Nan Elizabeth Woodruff shows the roots of this transition in the 1930–1931 drought, focusing on the political debates surrounding Red Cross intervention in those early years. Woodruff, *As Rare as Rain*, 39–138.

6. Bureau of the Census, *Census of Religious Bodies: 1926, Part I* (Washington, DC: Government Printing Office, 1930): 466–467, 580–582, 632–634. See the appendix for additional details. On relative social status in the region's churches, see Randy J. Sparks, *Religion in Mississippi* (Jackson: University Press of Mississippi, 2001); Wayne Flynt, *Dixie's Forgotten People: The South's Poor Whites*, 2nd ed. (Bloomington: Indiana University Press, 2004 [1979]); and Flynt, *Alabama Baptists: Southern Baptists in the Heart of Dixie* (Tuscaloosa: University of Alabama Press, 1998).

7. On the broader story of African American religion in the Delta between the Civil War and the Great Depression, see John M. Giggie, *After Redemption: Jim Crow and the Transformation of African American Religion in the Delta, 1875-1915* (New York: Oxford University Press, 2007). On black religion, culture, and politics in the interwar period, see Lerone Martin, *Preaching on Wax: The Phonograph and the Shaping of Modern African American Religion* (New York: New York University Press, 2014); Bettye Collier-Thomas, *Jesus, Jobs, and Justice: African American Women and Religion* (New York: Knopf, 2010); Curtis Evans, *The Burden of Black Religion* (New York: Oxford University Press, 2007); Barbara Diane Savage, *Your Spirits Walk Beside Us: The Politics of Black Religion* (Cambridge, MA: Belknap Press, 2008); Judith Weisenfeld, *Hollywood Be Thy Name: African-American Religion in American Film, 1929-1949* (Berkeley: University of California Press, 2007); Paul Harvey, *Freedom's Coming: Religious Culture and the Shaping of the South from the Civil War Through the Civil Rights Era* (Chapel Hill: University of North Carolina Press, 2007); Harvey, *Redeeming the South: Religious Cultures and Racial Identities Among Southern Baptists, 1865-1925* (Chapel Hill: University of North Carolina Press, 1997); Wallace D. Best, *Passionately Human, No Less*

Divine: Religion and Culture in Black Chicago, 1915-1952 (Princeton, NJ: Princeton University Press, 2005); Glenda Elizabeth Gilmore, *Gender and Jim Crow: Women and the Politics of White Supremacy in North Carolina* (Chapel Hill: University of North Carolina Press, 1996); Evelyn Brooks Higginbotham, *Righteous Discontent: The Women's Movement in the Black Baptist Church, 1880-1920* (Cambridge, MA: Harvard University Press, 1993). On COGIC, see Calvin White Jr., *The Rise to Respectability: Race, Religion, and the Church of God in Christ* (Fayetteville: University of Arkansas Press, 2012); Anthea D. Butler, *Women in the Church of God in Christ: Making a Sanctified World* (Chapel Hill: University of North Carolina Press, 2007); Elton Hal Weaver, " 'Mark the Perfect Man': The Rise of Bishop C.H. Mason and the Church of God in Christ" (Ph.D. diss., University of Memphis, 2007).

PART I

1. Margaret Jones Bolsterli, *During Wind and Rain: The Jones Family Farm in the Arkansas Delta, 1848-2006* (Fayetteville: University of Arkansas Press, 2008), 79; Dorothy Dickins, "A Nutrition Investigation of Negro Tenants in the Yazoo-Mississippi Delta," Mississippi Agricultural Experiment Station Bulletin 254, August 1928, 7, 17, 35–37; Dorothy Dickins, "Food and Health," Agricultural Experiment Station Bulletin 255, July 1928, 7, 16–17; Norman Thomas, *The Plight of the Sharecropper* (New York: League for Industrial Democracy, 1934), 9, Reel 1, in Southern Tenant Farmers Union Papers, 1934-1970 (Glen Rock, NJ: Microfilming Corporation of America, 1971) (hereafter STFU Papers); Dorothy Day, "Sharecroppers," 1936, Reel A, Southern Tenant Farmers Union Scrapbook and Newspaper Clippings, 1934-1970 (Chapel Hill: University of North Carolina, 1971–1973) (hereafter STFU Papers-UNC); Cobb, *The Most Southern Place on Earth*, 101–107; Charles Spurgeon Johnson, Edwin R. Embree, and Will Winton Alexander, *The Collapse of Cotton Tenancy: Summary of Field Studies & Statistical Surveys 1933-35* (Chapel Hill: University of North Carolina Press, 1935), 1–33.

2. Biles, *Memphis in the Great Depression*, 50–53; Biles, "The Persistence of the Past: Memphis in the Great Depression," *Journal of Southern History* 52, no. 2 (May 1986): 183–212; James E. Boyle, "Memphis Merchants Exchange Clearing Association," *Annals of the American Academy of Political and Social Science* 155 (May 1931): 173–217; Gilbert Courtland Fite, *Cotton Fields No More: Southern Agriculture, 1865-1980* (Lexington: University Press of Kentucky, 1984), 120; John Kenneth Galbraith, *The Great Crash, 1929* (Boston: Houghton Mifflin, 2009 [1954]), 88–127.

3. "Five Killed, Scores Injured as Tornado Sweeps Through Mississippi and Arkansas," *Atlanta Constitution*, March 7, 1930, 1; "Arkansas Tornado Kills Seventeen," *Chicago Defender*, May 24, 1930, 2.

CHAPTER I

1. Eddie James "Son" House Jr., "Dry Spell Blues, Part II," Paramount Records, 1930; Woodruff, *As Rare as Rain*, 3–21.

2. Woodruff, *As Rare as Rain*, 56–65; Ben F. Johnson III, *Arkansas in Modern America, 1930-1999* (Fayetteville: University of Arkansas Press, 2000), 10–13; Charles O. Lee, *1931 Annual Report, Memphis Community Fund*, Memphis-Charities-Community Fund Clippings File, Benjamin L. Hooks Central Library, Memphis Public Libraries, Memphis, Tennessee (hereafter MPL), p. 2.

3. "Is It the Turning Tide," *Ruleville Record*, December 25, 1930, 2; interview with Irvin Barker by L. A. Sawyer, no date [1938], New Africa, Mississippi, transcript, p. 11, Folder 1, Box 213, Bolivar and Coahoma County Studies, Charles S. Johnson Collection, Special Collections, John Hope and Aurelia E. Franklin Library, Fisk University, Nashville, Tennessee [hereafter Johnson Collection].

4. James Thomas Baker, *Brooks Hays* (Macon, GA: Mercer University Press, 1989), 63.

5. Son House, "Dry Spell Blues, Part II." These last lyrics are from an extended version of the song on *Mississippi Blues, Vol. 2, 1929-1932* (Origin of Jazz Library).

6. Jonathan Daniels, *A Southerner Discovers the South* (New York: The Macmillan Company, 1938), 125. On the ties between Memphis and the Delta, see Biles, *Memphis in the Great Depression*, 15–16; Green, *Battling the Plantation Mentality*, 1–22; Whayne, *A New Plantation South*, 43–44, 114, 123. Laurie Green calls Memphis "the urban heart of the Delta."

7. Biles, *Memphis in the Great Depression*, 6–10; Woods, *Development Arrested*, 42–46.

8. Cobb, *The Most Southern Place on Earth*, 3, 7–15, 29–30; Christopher Morris, *The Big Muddy: An Environmental History of the Mississippi and Its Peoples from Hernando de Soto to Hurricane Katrina* (New York: Oxford University Press, 2012), 117–124; Bobby Roberts, "'Desolation Itself': The Impact of the Civil War," in *The Arkansas Delta: Land of Paradox*, ed. Jeannie Whayne and Willard B. Gatewood (Fayetteville: University of Arkansas Press, 1993), 70–73; Walter Johnson, *River of Dark Dreams: Slavery and Empire in the Cotton Kingdom* (Cambridge, MA: Belknap Press, 2013), 244–279; Woodruff, *American Congo*, 1–21; Woods, *Development Arrested*, 42–61.

9. Biles, *Memphis in the Great Depression*, 13–17, 28; Beverly G. Bond and Janann Sherman, *Memphis: In Black and White* (Charleston, SC: Arcadia Publishing, 2003), 36–48.

10. Woods, *Development Arrested*, 64–81; McMillen, *Dark Journey*, 35–57; Bond and Shermann, *Memphis: In Black and White*, 58–60.

11. Roger Ransom and Richard Sutch, *One Kind of Freedom: The Economic Consequences of Emancipation*, 2nd ed. (Cambridge: Cambridge University Press, 2001 [1997]), 81–105; Steven P. Hahn, *A Nation Under Our Feet: Black Political Struggles in the*

Rural South from Slavery to the Great Migration (Cambridge, MA: Belknap Press, 2003), 216–264, 412–464; Woods, *Development Arrested*, 40–120.

12. James C. Cobb, ed., *The Mississippi Delta and the World: The Memoirs of David L. Cohn* (Baton Rouge: Louisiana State University Press, 1995), 50; McMillen, *Dark Journey*, 111–154.

13. McMillen, *Dark Journey*, 111–154; Woodruff, *American Congo*, 1–37.

14. Cohn, *The Mississippi Delta and the World*, 80.

15. Ibid., 59–77; Kirby, *Rural Worlds Lost*, 38–40.

16. Cobb, *The Most Southern Place on Earth*, 47–61, 69–78, 98–114; Woodruff, *American Congo*, 21–37; McMillen, *Dark Journey*, 111–123; Whayne, *A New Plantation South*, 17–20, 39–46.

17. Rev. Melville Johnson, "The Middle Zone of Economic Living," *New Orleans Christian Advocate*, February 11, 1932, 4; Woofter, *Landlord and Tenant on the Cotton Plantation* (Washington, D.C.: Works Progress Administration, 1936), 220; Cobb, *The Most Southern Place on Earth*, 105–116; McMillen, *Dark Journey*, 123–150; Whayne, *A New Plantation South*, 59–77; Woodruff, *American Congo*, 30–37; Allison Davis et al., *Deep South: A Social Anthropological Study of Caste and Class* (Chicago: University of Chicago Press), 941. Many Delta farmers used the terms *tenant farmer* and *sharecropper* interchangeably by the 1920s. Technically, tenant farmers had more independence than sharecroppers and tended to be white, while sharecroppers were more often black. Tenant farmers paid for the land they rented either with cash or part of their crop and supplied most of their own tools and livestock. If they had leftover crops after paying rent, they could sell them as they chose. Sharecroppers borrowed tools and livestock on credit from owners and planted crops as they were told, often under harsh supervision from plantation managers. The farmer took the cotton to market and paid sharecroppers for any leftover produce after subtracting money for rent, tools, medical care, and housing, with interest. Many tenant farmers and sharecroppers ended a year of hard work with nothing but debt to the planter, and those that made money often had to accept payment in company scrip, redeemable only at the high-priced plantation commissary. Arkansas plantations were particularly notorious for using only company scrip. See Johnson, Embree, and Alexander, *Collapse of Cotton Tenancy*, 6–24; Alex Lichtenstein, "Introduction: The Southern Tenant Farmers' Union: A Movement for Social Emancipation," in *Revolt Among the Sharecroppers*, 2nd ed., by Howard Kester (Knoxville: University of Tennessee Press, 1997), 27–29; David Eugene Conrad, *The Forgotten Farmers: The Story of Sharecroppers in the New Deal* (Urbana: University of Illinois Press, 1965), 4–10.

18. Whayne, *A New Plantation South*, 59–61; Cobb, *Most Southern Place on Earth*, 102–124.

19. Biles, *Memphis in the Great Depression*, 1–16; John McLead Keating, *A History of the Yellow Fever: The Yellow Fever Epidemic of 1878, in Memphis, Tenn.* (Memphis, TN: Printed for the Howard Association, 1879), 101–144; Edward J. Blum, "The

Crucible of Disease: Trauma, Memory, and National Reconciliation during the Yellow Fever Epidemic of 1878," *Journal of Southern History* 69, no. 4 (November 2003): 791–820. For an interesting perspective on the place of the Mississippi River in creating this environment, see Lee Sandlin, *Wicked River: The Mississippi When It Last Ran Wild* (New York: Pantheon, 2010).

20. Biles, *Memphis in the Great Depression*, 13–17, 28; Green, *Battling the Plantation Mentality*, 19–22; Honey, *Southern Labor and Black Civil Rights: Organizing Memphis Workers*, 21–24; Robert A. Lanier, *Memphis in the Twenties* (Memphis, TN: Zenda Press, 1979), 72–74; Robert Alan Sigafoos, *Cotton Row to Beale Street: A Business History of Memphis* (Memphis, TN: Memphis State University Press, 1979). Laurie Green describes the "plantation mentality" that pervaded Memphis, its elites operating like urban planters and members of its black working class often intimidated. See Green, *Battling the Plantation Mentality*.

21. Bond and Shermann, *Memphis*, 68–71; Elizabeth Gritter, *River of Hope: Black Politics and the Memphis Freedom Movement, 1865-1954* (Lexington: University Press of Kentucky, 2014), 1–50; Biles, *Memphis in the Great Depression*, 27.

22. Honey, *Southern Labor and Black Civil Rights*, 3–6, 49–64; Biles, *Memphis in the Great Depression*, 27.

23. Biles, *Memphis in the Great Depression*, 29–47; William D. Miller, *Mr. Crump of Memphis* (Baton Rouge: Louisiana State University Press, 1964), 25–26, 77–223; Dowdy, *Mayor Crump Don't Like It*, 3–24, 54–74; John E. Harkins, *Metropolis of the American Nile: A History of Memphis & Shelby County, Tennessee*, 2nd ed. (Oxford, MS: Guild Bindery Publications, 1982), 114–129.

24. Biles, *Memphis in the Great Depression*, 29–47, 108–120; Honey, *Southern Labor and Black Civil Rights: Organizing Memphis Workers*, 44–52; Gloria Brown Melton, "Blacks in Memphis, Tennessee, 1920-1935: A Historical Study" (Ph.D. diss., Washington State University, 1982), 36–63. For a Depression-era look at black life in Memphis by a Crump ally, see George W. Lee, *Beale Street: Where the Blues Began* (College Park, MD: McGrath Publishing Company, 1969).

25. Fite, *Cotton Fields No More*, 95–109; George Brown Tindall, *The Emergence of the New South, 1913-1945* (Baton Rouge: Louisiana State University Press, 1967), 111–115; Pete Daniel, *Breaking the Land: The Transformation of Cotton, Tobacco, and Rice Cultures Since 1880* (Urbana: University of Illinois Press, 1985), 10–22; Bureau of the Census, *Statistical Abstract of the United States, 1941* (Washington, DC: Government Printing Office, 1942), 741.

26. Woodruff, *American Congo*, 74–91. There are numerous accounts of the Elaine massacre. See also Robert Whitaker, *On the Laps of Gods: The Red Summer of 1919 and the Struggle for Justice That Remade a Nation* (New York: Crown Publishers, 2008); Grif Stockley, *Blood in Their Eyes: The Elaine Race Massacres of 1919* (Fayetteville: University of Arkansas Press, 2001); Grif Stockley and Jeannie M. Whayne, "Federal Troops and the Elaine Massacres: A Colloquy," *Arkansas Historical Quarterly* 61, no. 3 (Autumn 2002): 272–283; Jeannie M. Whayne,

"Low Villains and Wickedness in High Places: Race and Class in the Elaine Riots," *Arkansas Historical Quarterly* 58, no. 3 (Autumn 1999): 285–313; O. A. Rogers Jr., "The Elaine Race Riots of 1919," *Arkansas Historical Quarterly* 19, no. 2 (Summer 1960): 142–150; Arthur Ocean Waskow, *From Race Riot to Sit-in, 1919 and the 1960s: A Study in the Connections Between Conflict and Violence* (Garden City, NY: Anchor Books, 1967).

27. Woodruff, *American Congo*, 74–91.

28. McMillen, *Dark Journey*, 111–154; T. J. Woofter, *Landlord and Tenant*, 104, 196, 198; Johnson, Embree, and Alexander, *Collapse of Cotton Tenancy*, 4–5; Hamilton, "The Causes of the Banking Panic of 1930," 586; Howard A. Turner, "Farm Tenancy Distribution and Trends in the United States," *Law and Contemporary Problems* (1937): 431–432; Howard A. Turner, *A Graphic Summary of Farm Tenure: United States Department of Agriculture Miscellaneous Publication no. 261* (Washington, DC: US Department of Agriculture, 1936), 8–35; Donald Holley, "The Plantation Heritage: Agriculture in the Arkansas Delta," in *The Arkansas Delta: Land of Paradox*, ed. Jeannie Whayne and Willard B. Gatewood (Fayetteville: University of Arkansas Press, 1993), 257–258. On the southern farm crisis and race more generally, see Elizabeth Ann Herbin, "Healing the Land, Healing the South: Reforming the Southern Cotton Farm, 1900-1939" (Ph.D. diss., Columbia University, 2007).

29. Dickins, "A Nutrition Investigation," 9–10; Federal Writers' Project of the WPA, *Mississippi: A Guide to the Magnolia State* (New York: Hastings House, 1938), 102–104, 350.

30. Dickins, "A Nutrition Investigation," 16–33; Joseph Goldberger and Edgar Sydenstricker, "Pellagra in the Mississippi Flood Area: Report of an Inquiry Relating to the Prevalence of Pellagra in the Area Affected by the Overflow of the Mississippi and Its Tributaries in Tennessee, Arkansas, Mississippi, and Louisiana in the Spring of 1927," *Public Health Reports* 42, no. 44 (November 4, 1927): 2706–2725; Cohn, *Where I Was Born and Raised*, 19; Kim Lacy Rogers, *Life and Death in the Delta: African American Narratives of Violence, Resilience, and Social Change* (New York: Palgrave Macmillan, 2006), 22–23.

31. Dickins, "A Nutrition Investigation," 16–17; Goldberger and Sydenstricker, "Pellagra in the Mississippi Flood Area," 2714; Hortense Powdermaker, *After Freedom: A Cultural Study in the Deep South* (Madison: University of Wisconsin Press, 1993 [1939]), 79.

32. Gritter, "Black Politics in the Age of Jim Crow: Memphis, Tennessee, 1865 to 1954" (Ph.D. diss., University of North Carolina, 2010), 1–140; Biles, *Memphis in the Great Depression*, 18–28; Green, *Battling the Plantation Mentality*, 33–38.

33. Ella Oppenheimer, *Infant Mortality in Memphis* (Washington, DC: US Department of Labor, 1937), 1–20; Nick Salvatore, *Singing in a Strange Land: C.L. Franklin, the Black Church, and the Transformation of America* (New York: Little, Brown & Company, 2005), 47–49.

34. James Crawford, "Flood and Thunder Blues," quoted in David Evans, "High Water Everywhere: Blues and Gospel Commentary on the 1927 Mississippi River Flood," in *Nobody Knows Where the Blues Comes From: Lyrics and History*, ed. Robert Springer (Jackson: University Press of Mississippi, 207), 54; Daniel, *Breaking the Land*, 6; Daniel, *Deep'n as It Come*, 2–9, 119–161; Barry, *Rising Tide*, 13–17, 179–209, 308–323, 378–386; William Alexander Percy, *Lanterns on the Levee: Recollections of a Planter's Son* (Baton Rouge: Louisiana State University Press, 1941), 242–269.

35. Donald Holley, *Uncle Sam's Farmers: The New Deal Communities in the Lower Mississippi Valley* (Urbana: University of Illinois Press, 1975), 12–13; Gail S. Murray, "Forty Years Ago: The Great Depression Comes to Arkansas," *Arkansas Historical Quarterly* 24, no. 4 (Winter 1970): 291–312; "Twenty-One Die as Storms Wipe Out Mississippi Town, Hit in Texas and Arkansas," *Atlanta Constitution*, February 26, 1929, 1; "Death Toll High in Pathway of Dixie Storm," *Chicago Defender*, April 27, 1929, 1; Bureau of the Census, *Statistical Abstract of the United States, 1941*, 741.

36. Woodruff, *As Rare as Rain*, 3–19. Nan Woodruff's study of the drought and the federal response to it focuses in particular on Arkansas and examines in close detail the suffering the drought brought to the Delta. Woodruff argues that the response to the drought provided a rehearsal for the expansion of the welfare state under Roosevelt.

37. "Drought: Field Reports from Five of the States Most Severely Affected," *New Republic*, February 25, 1931, 41; Woodruff, *As Rare as Rain*, 16.

38. Elmus Wicker, *The Banking Panics of the Great Depression* (Cambridge: Cambridge University Press, 1996), 38; David E. Hamilton, "The Causes of the Banking Panic of 1930: Another View," *Journal of Southern History* 51, no. 4 (November 1985): 581–608; Daniel C. Vogt, "Hoover's RFC in Action: Mississippi, Bank Loans, and Work Relief, 1932-1933," *Journal of Mississippi History* 47, no. 1 (1985): 35–53.

39. "One-Fourth of a State Sold for Taxes," *Literary Digest*, May 7, 1932, 10; "Tight Credit After Drought Reason Farmers Need Aid," *Washington Post*, January 27, 1931, 8.

40. *Statistical Abstract of the United States, 1941*, 741; "Hunger-1931," *The Nation*, February 11, 1931, 151–152; Woodruff, *As Rare as Rain*, 30–36, 50–52; "$962,000 Is Obtained for Drought Relief," *New York Times*, January 22, 1931, 3.

41. "An Arkansas Farmer Speaks," *New Republic*, May 27, 1931, 40–41; "The Week," *New Republic*, January 14, 1931, 228–229. See also Woodruff, *As Rare as Rain*, 56–64.

42. "Red Cross Remains in Field to Assist Drought-Hit Areas," *Washington Post*, March 15, 1931, M15; "Drought," *New Republic*, 40–41.

43. Holley, "The Plantation Heritage," 261; Woodruff, *As Rare as Rain*, 4–5; "Drought," *New Republic*, 37–38.

44. "A Story from the Orphanage," *(Mississippi) Baptist Record*, March 12, 1931, 3. On nutrition deficiencies, see Dickins, "A Nutrition Investigation," 9–33; Kim Lacy Rogers, *Life and Death in the Delta: African American Narratives of Violence, Resilience, and Social Change* (New York: Palgrave Macmillan, 2006), 22–23. See also Keith Wailoo, *Dying in the City of the Blues: Sickle Cell Anemia and the Politics of Race and Health* (Chapel Hill: University of North Carolina Press, 2001).

45. *1931 Annual Report, Memphis Community Fund*, 2, 9, Memphis Community Fund Clippings File, Memphis and Shelby County Room, MPL; "$962,000 Is Obtained for Drought Relief," *New York Times*, January 22, 1931, 3; Biles, *Memphis in the Great Depression*, 53.

46. "Down on Beale," *Memphis World*, April 19, 1932, 6; "Hunger, Cold Drive Hundreds for Aid at Family Welfare Agency," *Memphis World*, December 16, 1932, 1.

47. "An Arkansas Farmer Speaks," 41.

PART 2

1. Cynthia Jones Sadler, "The Pageantry of Segregation: The Socio-Cultural Impact of the Cotton Makers' Jubilee," *West Tennessee Historical Society Papers* 65 (2012): 88–109.

2. Fite, *Cotton Fields No More*, 44–45; Woofter, *Landlord and Tenant*, 1–42.

3. Bolsterli, *During Wind and Rain*, 78–80; Dickins, "A Nutrition Investigation," 6–7; Daniel, *Breaking the Land*, 4.

CHAPTER 2

1. Dusty Jordan, "Baptists Bring War to Jonesboro," *Craighead County Historical Quarterly* XXI, no. 1 (Winter 1983): 1–9. In 1930, First Baptist Church of Jonesboro had 1,154 members, making it the seventh-largest Southern Baptist church in Arkansas and the second largest in the Delta. E. P. Alldredge, *Southern Baptist Handbook, 1931* (Nashville, TN: Sunday School Board of the Southern Baptist Convention, 1931), 158; "Baptists Staging Capital Revival," *Washington Post*, September 27, 1930, 4; "Religion: Battle of Jonesboro," *Time*, September 21, 1931, 56.

2. Jordan, "Baptists Bring War to Jonesboro," 1–2; On Norris, see Barry Hankins, *God's Rascal: J. Frank Norris and the Beginnings of Southern Fundamentalism* (Lexington, KY: University Press of Kentucky, 1996).

3. Jordan, "Baptists Bring War to Jonesboro," 1; "Religion: Battle of Jonesboro," 56.

4. "An Open Letter to Joe Jeffers, the Funnymentalist Evangelist," *Baptist and Commoner*, September 21, 1932, 14; "Churchmen Militant," *Los Angeles Times*, September 11, 1931, 1.

5. Peter Levins, "What Is Justice in This Case?" *Atlanta Constitution*, May 13, 1934, SM2; Jordan, "Baptists Bring War to Jonesboro," 2.

6. Jordan, "Baptists Bring War to Jonesboro," 2; "What Is Justice in this Case?" SM2.

7. "Churchmen Militant," *Los Angeles Times*, September 11, 1931; "Arkansas Church War," *Outlook and Independent* 159, no. 4 (September 23, 1931): 104.

8. "Religion: Battle of Jonesboro," 56; "What Is Justice in this Case?," SM2; "Churchmen Militant," 1.

9. Levins, "What Is Justice in this Case?," SM2; "Religion: Battle of Jonesboro," 56. See also "Churchmen Militant," 1; "Minister's Arrest Considered After Attack on Authorities," *Atlanta Constitution*, September 13, 1931, 1A. Details of this story vary slightly among news sources, but the Levins article in the *Atlanta Constitution* offers the most extensive retelling.

10. "Troops Withdrawn as Church Dispute Becomes Peaceful," *Chicago Daily Tribune*, September 14, 1931, 16. Reported turnout at Jeffers's services in the fall of 1931 was between one thousand and five thousand people per meeting. "Worshippers' Guns Sought by Troops," *Washington Post*, September 12, 1931, 5; "Machine Guns Sent to Curb Evangelist," *Washington Post*, September 13, 1931, M20; Jordan, "Baptists Bring War to Jonesboro," 2–3.

11. "Troops Withdrawn as Church Dispute Becomes Peaceful," 16; Jordan, "Baptists Bring War to Jonesboro," 3–4; Edward Underwood, *Haunted Jonesboro* (Charleston, SC: History Press, 2011), 105–106; "Blaze Finale in Church Row," *Los Angeles Times*, October 27, 1931, 1.

12. Levins, "What Is Justice in this Case?" SM2; "History of Central Baptist Church, Jonesboro, Arkansas," in Central Baptist Church, Jonesboro, Craighead County, Folder 49, Box 420, Arkansas Church Records, Special Collections, David W. Mullins Library, University of Arkansas, Fayetteville, Arkansas (hereafter Arkansas Church Records); Dusty Jordan, "Baptists Bring War to Jonesboro," 5–8.

13. Bureau of the Census, *Census of the United States*, 1930.

14. Bolsterli, *During Wind and Rain*, 99. On the importance of class and race to the character of southern churches, see Gellman and Roll, *The Gospel of the Working Class*; Roll, *Spirit of Rebellion*; Collier-Thomas, *Jesus, Jobs, and Justice*; Richard J. Callahan Jr., *Work and Faith in the Kentucky Coal Fields: Subject to Dust* (Indianapolis: Indiana University Press, 2009); John Hayes, "Hard, Hard Religion: The Invisible Institution of the New South," *Journal of Southern Religion* X (2007): 1–24; Joe Creech, *Righteous Indignation: Religion and the Populist Revolution* (Urbana: University of Illinois Press, 2006); Wayne Flynt, "Religion for the Blues: Evangelicalism, Poor Whites, and the Great Depression," *Journal of Southern History* 71 (February 2005): 3–38; Flynt, *Dixie's Forgotten People*. For an example of an interracial revival in the Delta (this one conducted by a group of African American churches), see "Satan's Camp Demolished," *Star of Zion*, September 11, 1930, 3. See also Giggie, *After Redemption*, 103–104. Two Southern authors, Richard Wright and Lillian Smith, provide fictionalized but powerful

accounts of the role revivals played in southern communities: Wright, *Black Boy* (New York: Harper Perennial Modern Classics, 1998), 113–118, 151–155; Smith, *Strange Fruit*, 4th ed. (New York: Mariner Books, 1992), 68, 248–250.

15. Henry Cherry, interviewed by Bill Boyd, May 8, 1974, p. 14, transcript, Box 1, Oral History Series, Delta Pine and Land Company Records, Special Collections, Mitchell Memorial Library, Mississippi State University.

16. Bureau of the Census, *Census of Religious Bodies: 1926, Part I* (Washington, DC: Government Printing Office, 1930), 466–467, 580–582, 632–634. See appendix for additional details. The 1926 census is generally deemed the most accurate. On the reliability of the Census of Religious Bodies generally, and the 1936 census particularly, see Kevin Christiano, " 'Numbering Israel': The U.S. Census and Religious Organizations," *Social Science History* 8, no. 4 (Autumn 1984): 341–370; Rodney Stark, "The Reliability of Historical United States Census Data on Religion," *Sociological Analysis* 53, no. 1 (Spring 1992): 91–95.

17. There are exceptions to these generalizations, but this pattern dominated. I have drawn these generalizations from denominational descriptions in the 1936 *Census of Religious Bodies* and an overview of the Arkansas Church Records and the Memphis city directories.

18. Kester, *Revolt Among the Sharecroppers*, 47; Presbyterian Church in the United States, The Committee on Assembly's Work, Department of Home Missions, *Sixty-Fourth Annual Report*, Charlottesville, Virginia, May 22, 1930, 10–11, C. Benton Kline Jr. Special Collections and Archives, John Bulow Campbell Library, Columbia Theological Seminary, Decatur, Georgia (hereafter CTS).

19. A short description of the program and its history appears on the first pages of the only volume it published: *Inventory of the Church Archives of Arkansas: Church of Christ, Scientist* (Little Rock: Arkansas Historical Records Survey, 1941), iv–v. Few historians have used this extensive and remarkable collection of records (56 boxes altogether). Notable exceptions include John Giggie, *After Redemption*, and Jeannie Whayne, *A New Plantation South* and *Delta Empire*. Historians have relied more heavily on four anthropological/sociological studies of the region: Allison Davis et al., *Deep South*; John Dollard, *Caste and Class in a Southern Town*; Charles S. Johnson, *Growing up in the Black Belt*; and Hortense Powdermaker, *After Freedom*. While I reference those occasionally, the church records provide a more nuanced account of Delta religious life. Two historians have recently demonstrated the limits of the spate of sociological and anthropological studies that genericized poor African American religions in the South, pointing instead to the religious diversity in the region and denaturalizing religiosity as a particularly African American quality. See Barbara Diane Savage, *Your Spirits Walk Beside Us*, 20–120, and Curtis Evans, *The Burden of Black Religion*, 216–259.

20. Turner, *Graphic Summary of Farm Tenure*, 47–48; Woofter, *Landlord and Tenant*, 107–124; Wayne Flynt, John Hayes, and Paul Harvey have argued that black and white working-class churchgoers crossed racial boundaries more frequently than

their middle-class counterparts. This was sometimes the case in the Delta, but such boundary crossing was not the norm. See Hayes, "Hard, Hard Religion," 1–24; Harvey, *Freedom's Coming*, 107–168; Wayne Flynt, "Religion for the Blues," 4–38. On the importance of African American fraternal orders in this period, see Peter P. Hinks, Stephen Kantrowitz, and Leslie A. Lewis, *All Men Free and Brethren: Essays on the History of African American Freemasonry* (Ithaca, NY: Cornell University Press, 2013); John M. Giggie, "For God and Lodge: Black Fraternal Orders and the Evolution of African American Religion in the Postbellum South," in *The Struggle for Equality: Essays on Sectional Conflict, the Civil War, and the Long Reconstruction*, ed. Orville Vernon Burton et al. (Charlottesville: University of Virginia Press, 2011), 198–218; Corey D. B. Walker, *A Noble Fight: African American Freemasonry and the Struggle for Democracy in America* (Urbana: University of Illinois Press, 2008); Theda Skocpol, Ariane Liazos, and Marshall Ganz, *What a Mighty Power We Can Be: African American Fraternal Groups and the Struggle for Racial Equality* (Princeton, NJ: Princeton University Press, 2006); David T. Beito, *From Mutual Aid to Welfare State: Fraternal Societies and Social Services, 1890-1967* (Chapel Hill: University of North Carolina Press, 2000).

21. On southern fundamentalism, see Glass, *Strangers in Zion*. On southern pentecostalism, see Stephens, *The Fire Spreads*; Roll, *Spirit of Rebellion*.

22. On Mason and COGIC, see White, *The Rise to Respectability*, 34–54; on Christian, see Giggie, *After Redemption*, 165–166; on Bogard, see J. Kristian Pratt, *The Father of Modern Landmarkism: The Life of Ben M. Bogard* (Macon, GA: Mercer University Press, 2013); Christopher Bart Barber, "The Bogard Schism: An Arkansas Baptist Agrarian Revolt" (Ph.D. diss., Southwestern Baptist Theological Seminary, 2006). On the theology of the 1920s Klan, see Kelly J. Baker, *Gospel According to the Klan: The KKK's Appeal to Protestant America* (Lawrence: University Press of Kansas, 2011).

23. A survey of the Arkansas Church Records demonstrates the fluid membership and affiliations of Delta churches. See, for example, White Hall Missionary Baptist Church, Hilleman, Woodruff County, Folder 18, Box 415; Church of God (Cleveland), Haynes, Lee County, Folder 104, Box 427; Cottage Home Baptist Church (Landmark), Nettleton, Craighead County, Folder 4, Box 413. On denominational fluidity and concerns from denominational leaders, see Hayes, "Hard, Hard Religion," 16–17; Flynt, "Religion for the Blues," 16. On religious mobility and stasis, also see Thomas A. Tweed, *Crossing and Dwelling: A Theory of Religion* (Cambridge, MA: Harvard University Press, 2006), 54–163.

24. On informal churches in the mobile South and the nature of rural churches, see Michael Berger, *The Devil Wagon in God's Country: The Automobile and Social Change in Rural America, 1893-1929* (Hamden, CT: Archon Books, 1979), 128–130; Work et al., *Lost Delta Found*, 229, 237–246; Lawrence J. Nelson, "Welfare Capitalism on a Mississippi Plantation in the Great Depression," *Journal of Southern History* 50, no. 2 (May 1984): 225–250. On the limited resources in

rural Arkansas churches, see John William Jent, *The Challenge of the Country Church* (Nashville, TN: Sunday School Board of the SBC, 1924), 91–94.

25. Assembly of God Pentecost, Greenfield, Poinsett County, Folder 11, Box 412, Arkansas Church Records; (Blytheville) Full Gospel Church (Pentecostal Church of America), Mississippi County, Arkansas, Folder 4, Box 446, Arkansas Church Records.

26. Sanctified, Helena, Phillips County, Folder 152, Box 433, Arkansas Church Records. The term "sanctified" referred often to members of COGIC in particular, but could refer to any pentecostals.

27. Free Christian Church of Christ, England, Lonoke County, Folder 148, Box 433, Arkansas Church Records.

28. Assembly of God Church, Wynn, Cross County, Folder 7, Box 411, Arkansas Church Records; Leachville Pentecostal Holiness Church, Mississippi County, Folder 7, Box 446, Arkansas Church Records. Many of the churches surveyed had women as pastors. See also Leachville Pentecostal Holiness Church, Mississippi County, Folder 7, Box 446, Arkansas Church Records; (Blytheville) Church of Christ Divine, Mississippi County, Arkansas, Folder 99, Box 426, Arkansas Church Records; Federal Writers' Project, *Mississippi*, 24; Giggie, *After Redemption*, 165–166, 182.

29. Original Church of God (Holiness), Jonesboro, Craighead County, Folder 119, Box 429, Arkansas Church Records; Pilgrim Holiness Church, Blytheville, Mississippi County, Folder 11, Box 446, Arkansas Church Records. See also Assembly of God, Wynne (1020 Union Street), Cross County, Folder 7, Box 411, Arkansas Church Records. On the role of women in southern churches, see Butler, *Women in the Church of God in Christ*; Cheryl Townsend Gilkes, *If It Wasn't for the Women: Black Women's Experience and Womanist Culture in Church and Community* (Maryknoll, NY: Orbis Books, 2001); Gilmore, *Gender and Jim Crow*; Higginbotham, *Righteous Discontent*; John Patrick McDowell, *The Social Gospel in the South: The Woman's Home Mission Movement in the Methodist Episcopal Church, South, 1886-1939* (Baton Rouge: Louisiana State University Press, 1982); Mrs. W. D. Pye, *The Yield of the Golden Years: A History of the Baptist Woman's Missionary Union of Arkansas, Written to Commemorate the Golden Jubilee, 1900-1938* (Little Rock: n.p., 1938); Baptist Woman's Missionary Union of Mississippi, *Hearts the Lord Opened: The History of Mississippi Woman's Missionary Union* (Jackson, MS: Purser Brothers, 1954).

30. On COGIC and Charles H. Mason, see White, *The Rise to Respectability*; Butler, *Women in the Church of God in Christ*; Ithiel C. Clemmons, *Bishop C. H. Mason and the Roots of the Church of God in Christ* (Lanham, MD: Pneuma Life Publishing, 1996); Weaver, " 'Mark the Perfect Man"; White, "In the Beginning, There Stood Two: Arkansas Roots of the Black Holiness Movement," *Arkansas Historical Quarterly* 68, no. 1 (Spring 2009): 1–22.

31. On fraternal orders and the blues as related to Delta religion, see John Giggie, *After Redemption*, 53–95; Harvey, *Freedom's Coming*, 158–168.

32. On *Gospel Pearls*, see Jerma A. Jackson. *Singing in My Soul: Black Gospel Music in a Secular Age* (Chapel Hill: University of North Carolina Press, 2004), 14, 64; Harvey, *Freedom's Coming*, 148–152. The literature on Delta blues, gospel, and religion is extensive. See also R. A. Lawson, *Jim Crow's Counterculture: The Blues and Black Southerners, 1890-1945* (Baton Rouge: Louisiana State University Press, 2010); Gayle F. Wald, *Shout, Sister, Shout! The Untold Story of Rock-and-Roll Trailblazer Sister Rosetta Tharpe* (Boston: Beacon Press, 2007); Nick Salvatore, *Singing in a Strange Land*; Michael W. Harris, *The Rise of Gospel Blues: The Music of Thomas Andrew Dorsey in the Urban Church* (New York: Oxford University Press, 1992); William Barlow, *Looking Up at Down: The Emergence of Blues Culture* (Philadelphia: Temple University Press, 1989); William Ferris, *Blues from the Delta* (New York: DeCapo Press, 1978); Anthony Heilbut, *The Gospel Sound: Good News and Bad Times* (New York: Limelight, 2002 [1975]). In *Preaching on Wax*, Lerone Martin has shown that the marketing of black preaching paralleled that of black music in the interwar period: Martin, *Preaching on Wax*, 62–149.

33. John Hayes, " 'Big River': Johnny Cash and the Currents of History," in Pasquier, *Gods of the Mississippi*, 194–198; Federal Writers' Project, *Mississippi*, 18–21; Harvey, *Freedom's Coming*, 148–155. See also Robert Cantwell, *Bluegrass Breakdown: The Making of the Old Southern Sound* (Urbana: University of Illinois Press, 2003); Bill C. Malone, *Don't Get Above Your Raisin': Country Music and the Southern Working Class* (Urbana: University of Illinois Press, 2002).

34. Mamie Lee Ratliff Finger, "Cora Rodman Ratliff, 1891-1958: A Woman of Courage and Vision," September 1989, p. 5, Mamie Lee Ratliff Finger Collection, Folder 1, SMMSS #93-3, Department of Archives and Special Collections, J. D. Williams Library, University of Mississippi, Oxford, Mississippi (hereafter UM); Howard Snyder, "Negro Migration and the Cotton Crop," *North American Review* 219, no. 818 (January 1924): 25.

35. The historiography of the extent and limits of white Protestant activism in the two decades before the Great Depression is immense. A sampling of those texts includes Arthur Remillard, *Southern Civil Religions: Imagining the Good Society in the Post Reconstruction Era* (Athens: University of Georgia Press, 2011); Christopher D. Cantwell, "The Bible Class Teacher: Piety and Politics in the Age of Fundamentalism" (Ph.D. diss., Cornell University, 2011); Michael McGerr, *A Fierce Discontent: The Rise and Fall of the Progressive Movement in America, 1870-1920* (New York: Oxford University Press, 2005); Gaines Foster, *Moral Reconstruction: Christian Lobbyists and the Federal Legislation of Morality, 1865-1920* (Chapel Hill: University of North Carolina Press, 2002); Harvey, *Redeeming the South*; Martin Marty, *Modern American Religion, Volume 2: The Noise of Conflict, 1919-1941* (Chicago: University of Chicago

Press, 1997); T. J. Jackson Lears, *No Place of Grace: Antimodernism and the Transformation of American Culture, 1880-1920* (Chicago: University of Chicago Press, 1994); Ken Fones-Wolf, *Trade Union Gospel: Christianity and Labor in Industrial Philadelphia, 1865-1915* (Philadelphia: Temple University Press, 1989); Ferenc Morton Szasz, *The Divided Mind of Protestant America, 1880-1930* (Tuscaloosa: University of Alabama Press, 1982); Robert H. Wiebe, *The Search for Order, 1877-1920* (New York: Hill and Wang, 1966); Robert Moats Miller, *American Protestantism and Social Issues, 1919-1939* (Chapel Hill: University of North Carolina Press, 1958).

36. In addition to previously mentioned works, on the church's role in southern Progressivism, see Ann-Marie Szymanski, "Beyond Parochialism: Southern Progressivism, Prohibition, and State-Building," *Journal of Southern History* 69, no. 1 (February 2003): 107–136; William A. Link, *The Paradox of Southern Progressivism, 1880-1930* (Chapel Hill: University of North Carolina Press, 1992); Kenneth K. Bailey, *Southern White Protestantism in the Twentieth Century* (New York: Harper & Row, 1964). On the important role of African American women in progressive reforms and creating private alternatives, see Butler, *Women in the Church of God in Christ*; Gilmore, *Gender and Jim Crow*; Higginbotham, *Righteous Discontent*.

37. Jonathan Ebel, "The Great War, Religious Authority, and the American Fighting Man," *Church History* 78, no. 1 (March 2009): 99–133; Jonathan Ebel, *Faith in the Fight: Religion and the American Soldier in the Great War* (Princeton, NJ: Princeton University Press, 2010), 21–53, 104–126; White, *The Rise to Respectability*, 55–76. See also Ray H. Abrams, *Preachers Present Arms* (New York: Round Table Press, 1933); Adriane Lentz-Smith, *Freedom Struggles: African Americans and World War I* (Cambridge, MA: Harvard University Press, 2009).

38. Joe L. Coker, *Liquor in the Land of the Lost Cause: Southern White Evangelicals and the Prohibition Movement* (Lexington: University Press of Kentucky, 2007), 79–174; Link, *The Paradox of Southern Progressivism, 1880-1930*, 31–123; Yao Foli Modey, "The Struggle over Prohibition in Memphis, 1880-1930" (Ph.D. diss., Memphis State University, 1983). See also Ian Tyrrell, *Woman's World/Woman's Empire: The Woman's Christian Temperance Union in International Perspective, 1880-1930* (Chapel Hill: University of North Carolina Press, 1991).

39. On institutionalization and denominational expansion, see Bailey, *Southern White Protestantism*, 44–91; Sydney S. Ahlstrom, *A Religious History of the American People* (New Haven, CT: Yale University Press, 1972), 896–917; Charles E. Harvey, "John D. Rockefeller, Jr., and the Interchurch World Movement of 1919-1920: A Different Angle on the Ecumenical Movement," *Church History* 51, no. 2 (June 1982): 198–209; Harvey, *Redeeming the South*, 104–106.

40. Fite, *Cotton Fields No More*, 101–110; Bailey, *Southern White Protestantism*, 72–129. In the midst of this controversy, H. Richard Niebuhr argued that new sects emerged when more powerful Christian churches failed to maintain a vital, unified

Christianity and neglected the neediest amongst them. See H. Richard Niebuhr, *The Social Sources of Denominationalism* (New York: Meridian Books, 1929).

41. Bailey, *Southern White Protestantism*, 85–87. On Scopes and its meaning, see Edward J. Larson, *Summer for the Gods: The Scopes Trial and America's Continuing Debate over Science and Religion* (New York: Basic Books, 1997); Charles A. Israel, *Before Scopes: Evangelicalism, Education and Evolution in Tennessee, 1870-1925* (Athens: University of Georgia Press, 2004); Cal Ledbetter Jr., "The Antievolution Law: Church and State in Arkansas," *Arkansas Historical Quarterly* 38, no. 4 (Winter 1979): 299–327.

42. Bailey, *Southern White Protestantism*, 92–110. For state-level results, see The American Presidency Project, University of California at Santa Barbara at http://www.presidency.ucsb.edu/showelection.php?year=1928

43. Federal Writers' Project, *Mississippi*, 20. On religious anxieties in the 1920s, see Carpenter, *Revive Us Again*; Israel, *Before Scopes*; Marty, *Modern American Religion*.

44. DuBose, "A New Year Forecast," *Memphis Commercial-Appeal*, December 25, 1930, 8.

45. "Like a Watered Garden," *(Mississippi) Baptist Record*, October 1, 1931, 5.

46. "Spiritual Interests," *Minutes of the Sixty-Second Session of the North Mississippi Conference of the Methodist Episcopal Church, South*, Greenwood, Mississippi, November 4–8, 1931, 38–39, J. B. Cain Archives of Mississippi Methodism, Millsaps-Wilson Library, Millsaps College, Jackson, Mississippi (hereafter Cain Archives). First quotation from last paragraph on p. 38; next quotations from first three paragraphs on p. 39.

47. "Invited to Pray for Rain," *Hartford Courant*, July 18, 1930, 4; "Church Bells Toll Call for Rain Prayers," *Los Angeles Times*, July 26, 1930, 1; "Convinced It Broke Drought, Negro Church to Pray Again," *New York Times*, August 17, 1930, 21; "4,500 Congregate and Pray for Rain," *Washington Post*, August 12, 1930, 5; "Wickedness Destroyed Ancient Countries and Cities—We Should Take Warning," *Washington Post*, August 8, 1930, 6; "Clergymen Differ on Prayer for Rain," *New York Times*, September 7, 1930, N4.

48. "Will He Find Faith?" *(Mississippi) Baptist Record*, September 11, 1930, 1; J. F. Manning, "The Great Drouth," *The Baptist and Commoner*, September 19, 1930, 4; "Shall Next Year Be a Rising or a Setting Sun for Arkansas Baptists?" September 25, 1930, 6; Warren P. Clark, "Why the Drought?" *(Arkansas) Baptist Advance*, August 21, 1930, 4–5.

49. "Will Rogers Finds Still Used as Relief Kitchen," *Washington Post*, January 24, 1931, 2.

50. "Arkansas Moves to Guard Future," *New York Times*, February 15, 1931, 56; Editorial comments, *Ruleville Record*, February 12, 1931, 2; Rev. Walter B. Capers, "The Macedonian Cry," *St. Andrew's Bulletin* II, No. 48 (December 1931), Folder 2, Box 1, St. Andrews Episcopal Church Records, Mississippi Department of Archives and History, Jackson, Mississippi (hereafter MDAH).

51. Sadler, "The Pageantry of Segregation," 88; Biles, *Memphis in the Great Depression*, 66–67.

52. David E. Guyton, "Worse Than Weevils," *Baptist Record*, October 15, 1931, 11; Sadler, "The Pageantry of Segregation," 88–91; Biles, *Memphis in the Great Depression*, 66–67. On the Lost Cause and southern civil religion, see Remillard, *Southern Civil Religions*; Charles Reagan Wilson, *Baptized in Blood: The Religion of the Lost Cause, 1856-1920* (Athens: University of Georgia Press, 2009 [1980]).

53. Presbyterian Church in the United States, The Committee on Assembly's Work, Department of Home Missions, *Sixty-Sixth Annual Report*, Montreat, North Carolina, May 26, 1932, 18–21 (quotation on p. 19 under "Type of Campaign"), CTS; "Signs of a Great Spiritual Awakening Appear," *Arkansas Baptist*, February 2, 1933, 3.

54. "Groping Man Again Turns to Religion," *New York Times*, June 5, 1932, SM6, SM17. On the Protestant denominations and social action in the early 1930s, see Paul Allen Carter, *The Decline and Revival of the Social Gospel: Social and Political Liberalism in American Protestant Churches, 1920-1940* (Ithaca, NY: Cornell University Press, 1956), 123–179; Donald B. Meyer, *The Protestant Search for Political Realism, 1919-1939* (Chapel Hill: University of North Carolina Press, 1961), 238–291; Miller, *American Protestantism and Social Issues, 1919-1939*, 63–127, 274–289.

55. "Voices of Alarm from Widely Separated Sections," *New Orleans Christian Advocate*, August 20, 1931, 1.

56. "Golden Living in a Golden Age," *(Arkansas) Baptist Advance*, February 11, 1932, 1; Roger W. Babson, *Revival Is Coming* (London: Fleming H. Revell Company, 1936).

57. "Golden Living in a Golden Age," 1. For another southern example of the Depression–revival link, see "Attacking the Spiritual Depression," *(Mississippi) Baptist Record*, November 24, 1932, 2.

58. "When Will the Depression End?" *(Arkansas) Baptist Advance*, June 16, 1932, 2. On fears of Communists as agents for civil rights in the South, see Gilmore, *Defying Dixie*; Robin D. G. Kelley, *Hammer and Hoe: Alabama Communists During the Great Depression* (Chapel Hill: University of North Carolina Press, 1990).

59. E. F. Scarborough, Holly Springs District Superintendent's Report, *Official Journal of the Forty-Second Session of the Upper Mississippi Conference of the Methodist Episcopal Church*, Columbus, Mississippi, December 2–6, 1931, 25–27, Cain Archives.

60. "The March of the Hungry," *Star of Zion*, August 6, 1931, 4; "Modern Capitalism," *National Baptist Voice*, March 7, 1931, 8.

61. "Crisis of Capitalism," *(Arkansas) Guardian*, August 8, 1931, 2; Lawrence B. DeSaulniers, *The Response in American Catholic Periodicals to the Crises of the Great Depression, 1930-1935* (Lanham, MD: University Press of America, 1984), 79–116; O'Brien, *American Catholics and Social Reform*, 3–69. On Catholics in

the Great Depression, see also Heineman, *A Catholic New Deal*; John Augustine Ryan, *Social Doctrine in Action: A Personal History* (New York, NY: Harper & Brothers, 1941).

62. "Shallow Religion," *The World Tomorrow*, May 1932, 134; Kirby Page, "Would Jesus Uphold Capitalism?" *The World Tomorrow*, April 1929, 160–163; Brinkley, *Voices of Protest*, 143–168; Anthony P. Dunbar, *Against the Grain: Southern Radicals and Prophets, 1929-1959* (Charlottesville: University Press of Virginia, 1981), 48–82; John Egerton, *Speak Now Against the Day: The Generation Before the Civil Rights Movement in the South* (New York: Knopf, 1994), 2–63; Miller, *American Protestantism and Social Issues*, 63–112; William McGuire King, "The Emergence of Social Gospel Radicalism: The Methodist Case," *Church History* 50, no. 4 (December 1981): 436–449.

63. Reinhold Niebuhr, *Moral Man and Immoral Society: A Study in Ethics and Politics* (New York: Charles Scribner's Sons, 1932), 82, 169–174 (quotations on 170–171); Fox, *Reinhold Niebuhr*, 111–166; Dunbar, *Against the Grain*, 40–41. See also Reinhold Niebuhr, "Is Peace or Justice the Goal?" *The World Tomorrow*, September 21, 1932, 275–277.

64. Alva Taylor, *Democracy and the Labor Movement* (n.p., n.d.), Folder: Alva Taylor publications, Alva W. Taylor Papers, Disciples of Christ Historical Society, Nashville, TN (hereafter DCHS). See also Stanley Lincoln Harbison, "The Social Gospel Career of Alva Wilmot Taylor" (Ph.D. diss., Nashville, TN: Vanderbilt University, 1975). On religion and the labor movement in the South, see Elizabeth Fones-Wolf and Ken Fones-Wolf, *Struggle for the South of the Post-War South: White Evangelical Protestants and Operation Dixie* (Urbana: University of Illinois Press, 2015). On the working-class religious left more broadly, see Heath Carter, *Union Made: Working People and the Rise of Social Christianity in Chicago* (New York: Oxford University Press, 2015); Janine Giordano Drake, "Between Religion and Politics: The Working Class Religious Left, 1880-1920" (Ph.D. diss., University of Illinois at Urbana-Champaign, 2014).

65. Dunbar, *Against the Grain*, 1–17; Egerton, *Speak Now Against the Day*, 77–79; James J. Lorence, *A Hard Journey: The Life of Don West* (Urbana: University of Illinois Press, 2007), 25–34; H. L. Mitchell, *Mean Things Happening in This Land: The Life and Times of H. L. Mitchell, Cofounder of the Southern Tenant Farmers' Union* (Montclair, NJ: Allanheld, Osmun, 1979), 17–38.

66. Roll, *Spirit of Rebellion*, 52–75; Mary G. Rolinson, *Grassroots Garveyism: The Universal Negro Improvement Association in the Rural South, 1920-1927* (Chapel Hill: University of North Carolina Press, 2007), 103–215; John Lawrence Bass, "Bolsheviks on the Bluff: A History of Memphis Communists and Their Labor and Civil Rights Contributions, 1930-1957" (Memphis, TN: University of Memphis, 2009), 80–114; Biles, *Memphis in the Great Depression*, 65; Honey, *Southern Labor and Black Civil Rights*, 53–58; Lewis, *A Biblical People in the Bible Belt*, 98–99; Mitchell, *Mean Things Happening in This Land*, 17–38; Roll, *Spirit of Rebellion*, 28, 52–75.

67. Eddie James "Son" House Jr., "Dry Spell Blues, Parts I and II," Paramount Records, 1930. See also Luigi Monge, "Preachin' the Blues: A Textual Linguistic Analysis of Son House's 'Dry Spell Blues,'" in *Ramblin' on My Mind: New Perspectives on the Blues*, ed. David Evans (Champaign: University of Illinois Press, 2008), 222–257.

68. Paul S Boyer, *When Time Shall Be No More: Prophecy Belief in Modern American Culture* (Cambridge, MA: Harvard University Press, 1992), 75–112. See also Sutton, *American Apocalypse*, 8–46; Brendan Pietsch, "Dispensational Modernism" (Ph.D. diss., Duke University, 2011); Marsden, *Fundamentalism and American Culture*, 118–120; Timothy P. Weber, *Living in the Shadow of the Second Coming: American Premillennialism, 1875-1982* (New York: Oxford University Press, 1979); Ernest Sandeen, *The Roots of Fundamentalism; British and American Millenarianism, 1800-1930* (Chicago: University of Chicago Press, 1970). On the fate of postmillennialism in the twentieth century, see James H. Moorhead, *World Without End: Mainstream Protestant Visions of the Last Things, 1880-1925* (Bloomington: Indiana University Press, 1999).

69. Sutton, *American Apocalypse*, xiii, 114–231; Boyer, *When Time Shall Be No More*, 100–112; Carpenter, *Revive Us Again*, 33, 91–105. *Sword of the Lord* first appeared in 1934. Matthew Sutton has reperiodized premillennialism, demonstrating its continuous influence in the wake of World War I.

70. "These Perilous Times," *The (Delight, Arkansas) Gospel of Light*, July 15, 1932, 1; Revelation 16:1–17.

71. "Vision of Sis. Rosa M. Rosmare," *The Whole Truth* (n.d.), 14, Folder 4, Box 5, Dupree African-American Pentecostal and Holiness Collection, Schomburg Center for Research in Black Culture, New York, New York (hereafter Dupree Collection). (Other content on this page of newsprint indicates that it is from an early 1930s copy of the paper. The church reprinted 1930s papers during the 1980s, but this page is from an incomplete issue.) On pentecostal institutionalization and theology in the 1920s to 1930s, see Stephens, *The Fire Spreads*, 230–282; Sutton, *Aimee Semple McPherson and the Resurrection of Christian America*, 41–45, 185–211; Wacker, *Heaven Below*, 177–216.

72. James D. Vaughan, "No Depression in Heaven," the Original Carter Family, Decca 5242, 1936; Malone, *Don't Get Above Your Raisin'*, 92, 97, 291.

73. Jordan, "Baptists Bring War to Jonesboro," 2.

74. "The End of the Age," (*Mississippi*) *Baptist Record*, August 6, 1931, 14. In *American Apocalypse*, Matthew Sutton argues that premillennialism in this period proved decidedly political—that premillennialists' apocalyptic view of the world drove them into politics, and specifically into action to protest any expansion of government, which to those who believed they were living in the last days represented a move toward the totalitarianism of the antichrist. Southern premillennialists had not yet adopted such a strong antistatist view nor withdrawn their allegiance to the Democratic Party, but they did not shy away from politics.

CHAPTER 3

1. Kate Abraham to Bishop Richard Gerow, March 29, 1933, Clerico, File 11, Bishop Richard Gerow Files and Correspondence, Catholic Diocese of Mississippi, Jackson, Mississippi (hereafter CDM).

2. Father John F. Clerico to Bishop Richard Gerow, April 1, 1933, Clerico, File 11, CDM. The Hoover administration established the Reconstruction Finance Corporation (RFC) in 1932 primarily to make loans to banks to help restore liquidity. The RFC also lent money to state and municipal governments, which used it for small, temporary jobs programs. See Vogt, "Hoover's RFC in Action," 35–53.

3. Walter I. Trattner, *From Poor Law to Welfare State: A Social History of Welfare in America*, 6th ed. (New York: Free Press, 1999 [1974]), 273.

4. Morris, *The Limits of Voluntarism*, xxxi–34; Michele Mitchell, *Righteous Propagation: African Americans and the Politics of Racial Destiny After Reconstruction* (Chapel Hill: University of North Carolina Press, 2004), 141–172; Elna Green, *This Business of Relief: Confronting Poverty in a Southern City, 1740-1940* (Athens: University of Georgia Press, 2003), 85–176; Michael B. Katz, *In the Shadow of the Poorhouse: A Social History of Welfare in America* (New York: Basic Books, 1996 [1986]), 3–212; McDowell, *The Social Gospel in the South*, 6–59.

5. Kennedy, *Freedom from Fear*, 163; Biles, *Memphis in the Great Depression*, 48–68; Johnson, *Arkansas in Modern America*, 14–15; Bureau of the Census, "Chapter D: Labor," *Historical Statistics of the United States: Colonial Times to 1970*, vol. 1 (Washington, DC: Government Printing Office, 1975), 135; *1940 Annual Report, Memphis Community Fund, with Historical Supplement, Memphis, Tennessee*, Mayor Watkins Overton Papers, MPL.

6. G. E. Holley, "Southern Goodwill Industries," *New Orleans Christian Advocate*, May 19, 1927, 14.

7. The historiography of these attitudes and debates is extensive. In addition to the works cited previously, see Matthew Bowman, *The Urban Pulpit: New York City and the Fate of Liberal Evangelicalism* (New York: Oxford University Press, 2014); Mimi Abramovitz, *Regulating the Lives of Women: Social Welfare Policy from Colonial Times to the Present* (Boston: South End Press, 1988); Paul S. Boyer, *Urban Masses and Moral Order in America, 1820-1920* (Cambridge, MA: Harvard University Press, 1978); Frances Fox Piven and Richard A. Cloward, *Regulating the Poor: The Functions of Public Welfare*, 2nd ed. (New York: Vintage Books, 1993 [1971]).

8. Green, *This Business of Relief*, 80–102.

9. Elna Green, ed., *Before the New Deal: Social Welfare in the South, 1830-1930* (Athens : University of Georgia Press, 1999), ix–xviii; Jennifer Ann Trost, *Gateway to Justice: The Juvenile Court and Progressive Child Welfare in Memphis* (Athens: University of Georgia Press, 2006), 65; Theda Skocpol, *Protecting Soldiers*

and Mothers: The Political Origins of Social Policy in the United States (Cambridge, MA: Belknap Press, 1992), 102–151.

10. Giggie, *After Redemption*, 59–95; Stephen Kantrowitz, " 'Intended for the Better Government of Man': The Political History of African American Freemasonry in the Era of Emancipation," *Journal of American History* 96, no. 4 (March 2010): 1001–1026. See also Skocpol et al., *What a Mighty Power We Can Be*; Higginbotham, *Righteous Discontent*.

11. On these relationships across boundaries of class and race, see Nancy Marie Robertson, *Christian Sisterhood, Race Relations, and the YWCA, 1906-46* (Urbana: University of Illinois Press, 2010); Gilmore, *Gender and Jim Crow*; Darlene Rebecca Roth, *Matronage: Patterns in Women's Organizations, Atlanta, Georgia, 1890-1940* (Brooklyn, NY: Carlson, 1994); Elisabeth Lasch-Quinn, *Black Neighbors: Race and the Limits of Reform in the American Settlement House Movement, 1890-1945* (Chapel Hill: University of North Carolina Press, 1993); Linda Gordon, "Black and White Visions of Welfare: Women's Welfare Activism, 1890-1945," *Journal of American History* 78, no. 2 (September 1991): 559–590.

12. Harvey, *Redeeming the South*, 197–226. See also Ralph E. Luker, *The Social Gospel in Black and White: American Racial Reform, 1885-1912* (Chapel Hill: University of North Carolina Press, 1998).

13. Marsha Wedell, *Elite Women and the Reform Impulse in Memphis, 1875-1915* (Knoxville: University of Tennessee Press, 1991), 98–107.

14. J. Wayne Flynt, "Southern Protestantism and Reform," in *Varieties of Southern Religious Experience*, ed. Samuel S. Hill (Baton Rouge: Louisiana State University Press, 1988), 135–157.

15. *Directory: Social Welfare Agencies* (Memphis, TN: Council of Social Agencies of Memphis and Shelby County, 1941), 9–11, 14–15.

16. Harvey, *Redeeming the South*, 209–210; William D. Miller, *Memphis During the Progressive Era, 1900-1917* (Memphis, TN: Memphis State University Press, 1957), 104–126; Bond and Sherman, *Memphis: In Black and White*, 101; Hannah F. Peck, "St. Vincent's Infirmary, 1888-1987: A History of a Roman Catholic Hospital in Little Rock, Arkansas" (Master's thesis, University of Arkansas at Little Rock, 1987); Sparks, *Religion in Mississippi*, 157–158; Wailoo, *Dying in the City of the Blues*, 34–35; Earnestine Lovelle Jenkins, *African Americans in Memphis* (Mt. Pleasant, SC: Arcadia Publishing, 2009), 43; David T. Beito and Linda Royster Beito, " 'Let Down Your Bucket Where You Are': The Afro-American Hospital and Black Health Care in Mississippi, 1924-1966," *Social Science History* 30, no. 4 (Winter 2006): 551–569.

17. Trost, *Gateway to Justice*, 4, 64–67, 136–138; Mazie Hough, "Are You or Are You Not Your Sister's Keeper? A Radical Response to the Treatment of Unwed Mothers in Tennessee," in *Before the New Deal: Social Welfare in the South, 1830-1930*, ed. Elna Green (Athens: University of Georgia Press, 1999), 100–119.

18. Marty, *The Noise of Conflict, 1919-1941*, 215–221; Ahlstrom, *Religious History of the American People*, 889–901; Harvey, *Redeeming the South*, 102–105.

19. Bureau of the Census, *Census of Religious Bodies, 1926: Church of God in Christ* (Washington, DC: Government Printing Office), 5–10; White, *The Rise to Respectability*, 55–94; Milton Sernett, *Bound for the Promised Land: African American Religion and the Great Migration* (Durham, NC: Duke University Press, 1997), 57–121. This growth is consistent with Jon Ebel's characterization of the postwar years as a period of reillusionment rather than disillusionment—the churches now fought the war at home. See Ebel, *Faith in the Fight*, 168–190.

20. *Southern Women and Race Cooperation: A Story of the Memphis Conference, October Sixth and Seventh, Nineteen Hundred and Twenty* (Atlanta, GA: Commission on Interracial Cooperation, 1920); Jacquelyn Dowd Hall, *Revolt Against Chivalry: Jessie Daniel Ames and the Women's Campaign Against Lynching* (New York: Columbia University Press, 1979), 86–106; Gilmore, *Gender and Jim Crow*, 200–202; David Fort Godshalk, *Veiled Visions: The 1906 Atlanta Race Riot and the Reshaping of American Race Relations* (Chapel Hill: University of North Carolina Press, 2005), 187–284; Robertson, *Christian Sisterhood, Race Relations, and the YWCA*, 71–152.

21. Arthur J. Todd, "Some Sociological Principles Underlying the Community Chest Movement," *Social Forces* 10, no. 4 (May 1932): 476–484; Cecil C. North et al., "Discussion of 'Some Sociological Principles Underlying the Community Chest Movement,'" *Social Forces* 10, no. 4 (May 1932): 485–497; Elwood Street, "Professional Guidance for the Small Town Community Chest," *Social Forces* 5, no. 4 (June 1927): 639–640. On the history of charity organization movements in the South, see Trost, *Gateway to Justice*, 66–73; Green, *This Business of Relief*, 109–127. Timothy E. W. Gloege explains the early-twentieth-century alliance of evangelicalism and consumer capitalism in *Guaranteed Pure: The Moody Bible Institute, Business, and the Making of Modern Evangelicalism* (Chapel Hill: University of North Carolina Press, 2015).

22. *Open Your Heart: Memphis Cares for Her Own*, Memphis Community Fund, 1928, Memphis-Community Chest Clippings File, MPL; *1940 Annual Report, Memphis Community Fund*, MPL; *Directory: Social Welfare Agencies*, 32; Biles, *Memphis in the Great Depression*, 48–68; Melton, "Blacks in Memphis," 65–67.

23. Katz, *In the Shadow of the Poorhouse*, 215–216; Enid Baird, *Public and Private Aid in Urban Areas, 1929-1938* (Washington, DC: Social Security Board, 1942), 34–35; Virginia Ashcraft, *Public Care in Tennessee: A History of Public Welfare Legislation in Tennessee* (Knoxville: University of Tennessee Record, 1947), 34–35, 113.

24. US Department of Labor, Children's Bureau, *Mothers' Aid, 1931*, Bureau Publication 220 (Washington, DC: Government Printing Office, 1933), 1.

25. Charles O. Lee, *1931 Annual Report, Memphis Community Fund*, Memphis-Charities-Community Fund Clippings File, MPL, 10; Skocpol, *Protecting Soldiers and Mothers*, 424–479; *Mothers' Aid, 1931*, 7–9, 14, 17, 26.

26. Eldon G. Ernst, "The Interchurch World Movement and the Great Steel Strike of 1919-1920," *Church History* 39, no. 2 (June 1970): 212–223; Charles E. Harvey, "John D. Rockefeller, Jr., and the Interchurch World Movement of 1919-1920: A Different Angle on the Ecumenical Movement," *Church History* 51, no. 1982 (1982): 198–209; Harvey, *Redeeming the South*, 104–105.

27. "All Creeds Meet at Welfare School," *Memphis Commercial-Appeal*, July 9, 1932; *Open Your Heart: Memphis Cares for Her Own*, Memphis Community Fund, 1928, back page, Memphis-Community Chest Clippings File, MPL; *Twelfth Annual Appeal of the Memphis Community Fund*, 1933, 10, Memphis-Memphis Community Fund Clippings File, MPL; Lewis, *A Biblical People in the Bible Belt*, 128.

28. *Open Your Heart: Memphis Cares for Her Own*, Memphis Community Fund, 1928, back page, Memphis-Community Chest Clippings File, MPL; Melton, "Blacks in Memphis," 132–134; Trost, *Gateway to Justice*, 68–70.

29. *1940 Annual Report, Memphis Community Fund*, MPL (pages unnumbered, but the last ten pages outline the annual goal and income of the fund); Trost, *Gateway to Justice*, 68–70. The community fund met its goal in 1930, but only after it reduced the goal to less than its operating costs. See *1931 Annual Report, Memphis Community Fund*, 2.

30. Rosemary D. Marcuss and Richard E. Kane, "U.S. National Income and Product Statistics: Born of the Great Depression and World War II," *Survey of Current Business* (February 2007): 32–46; "Bowing Out 1931," *New Orleans Christian Advocate*, January 7, 1932, 4; Kincheloe, *Research Memorandum on Religion in the Depression*, 17, 23, 28.

31. "Bad Angel," *Time*, October 8, 1928, 35–36; "Eighty-Fourth Annual Report of the Home Mission Board to the Southern Baptist Convention," *Southern Baptist Convention, Memphis, Tennessee, May 9-12, 1929, Reports of Boards, Institutions, Standing Committees, Special Committees with Recommendations for Convention Action* (Nashville, TN: Marshall & Bruce Co.), 203–236; "Historical Note," Home Mission Board Executive Office Files Finding Aid, AR 631-3, Southern Baptist History Library and Archives, Nashville, Tennessee (hereafter SBHLA).

32. E. P. Alldredge, *Southern Baptist Handbook, 1931* (Nashville, TN: Sunday School Board of the Southern Baptist Convention, 1931), 37; "Our Present Denominational Situation," *(Arkansas) Baptist Advance*, August 7, 1930, 1, 9; "Tithing in Hard Times," *(Mississippi) Baptist Record*, July 23, 1931, 7.

33. On baptists, see "Shall Negro Baptists Be Forced into Receivership?" *National Baptist Voice*, February 11, 1933, 1; *Minutes of the Forty-First Annual Session of the Baptist Missionary and Educational Convention of Tennessee*, Macedonia Baptist Church, Jackson Tennessee, October 24-27, 1932, 2, Box 3, Samuel A. Owen Papers, MS #151, Mississippi Valley Collection, Ned R. McWherter Library, University of Memphis, Memphis, Tennessee (hereafter MVC); *Proceedings of the Thirty-First Annual Sessions of the State B.Y.P.U. and State Sunday School*

Conventions, First Baptist Church, Jackson, Tennessee, July 21–24, 1931, 25, Box 3, Owen Papers, MVC; Rev. S. A. Owen and Rev. H. W. Perry to the Baptist Brotherhood of the State of Tennessee, September 18, 1933, Folder 1, Box 1, Owen Papers, MVC; Wailoo, *Dying in the City of the Blues*, 92. On Methodists, see Durant District Superintendent's Report, *Official Journal of the Thirty-Eighth Session of the Upper Mississippi Conference of the Methodist Episcopal Church*, February 1928, 27–28, Cain Archives; Durant District Superintendent's Report, *Official Journal of the Forty-Second Session of the Upper Mississippi Conference of the Methodist Episcopal Church*, Columbus, Mississippi, December 2–6, 1931, 22–23, Cain Archives.

34. C. Fred Williams, S. Ray Granade, and Kenneth M. Startup, *A System and Plan: Arkansas Baptist State Convention, 1848-1998* (Franklin, TN: Providence House Publishers, 1998), 203–223.

35. Wedell, *Elite Women*, 106–107; David Beito, *From Mutual Aid to the Welfare State*, 1–16, 181–221; Melton, "Blacks in Memphis," 89; Landis and George Edmund Haynes, *Cotton-Growing Communities Study no. 2: Case Studies of 10 Rural Communities and 10 Plantations in Arkansas* (New York: Federal Council of Churches, 1935), 9, 21.

36. Green, *This Business of Relief*, 159–160. On orphanages as childcare, see also Timothy A. Hacsi, *Second Home: Orphan Asylums and Poor Families in America* (Cambridge, MA: Harvard University Press, 1998).

37. Trost, *Gateway to Justice*, 82–85; James H. Robinson, "A Social History of the Negro in Memphis and in Shelby County," (Ph.D. diss., Yale University, 1934), 132–163.

38. Allen R. Coggins, *Tennessee Tragedies: Natural, Technological, and Societal Disasters in the Volunteer State* (Knoxville: University of Tennessee Press, 2012), 111–112; "Charge Orphan Home Head with Cruelty," *Chicago Defender*, September 28, 1929, 4; "Indict Tennessee Orphan Home Supt.," *Chicago Defender*, October 26, 1929, 1.

39. Woods, *Mission and Memory: A History of the Catholic Church in Arkansas*, 206–208; Dickins, "A Nutrition Investigation of Negro Tenants in the Yazoo Mississippi Delta," 8–9. For reports on the exhausted capacity of other children's homes in the region, see "Does Jesus Care About the Orphanage?" *(Arkansas) Baptist Advance*, November 24, 1932, 8; "Clean Out Orphanage Debt with Soap," *New Orleans Christian Advocate*, February 5, 1931, 1; "The Jonesboro Orphan Home," *(Delight, Arkansas) Gospel Light*, November 1, 1933, 4.

40. "To the Friends and Supporters of the Mississippi Baptist Orphanage," *(Mississippi) Baptist Record*, February 13, 1930, 9, 16.

41. "Our Orphanage Situation," *(Mississippi) Baptist Record*, February 6, 1930, 6; "Some Facts About the Financial Condition of the Home," *(Mississippi) Baptist Record*, May 11, 1933, 1; Richard Aubrey McLemore, *A History of Mississippi Baptists, 1780-1970* (Jackson: Mississippi Baptist Convention Board, 1971), 288–289.

42. Father John Clerico to Bishop Richard Gerow, March 15, 1930; June 15, 1934; October 26, 1934; Bishop Richard Gerow to Father John Clerico, March 20, 1930; June 18, 1934; November 9, 1934, all in Clerico, File 11, CDM; Trost, *Gateway to Justice*, 63–121.

43. Bureau of the Census, 1930, 1296–1297; *Guide to Greenwood and Leflore County, Miss. for Service Men and Their Families* (Greenwood, MS: Greenwood Chamber of Commerce, 1943), Mississippi Cities and Towns Collection, UM; Paul V. Canonici, *The Delta Italians* (Madison, MS: 2003); Byrd Gibbens, "Strangers in the Arkansas Delta: Ethnic Groups and Nationalities," in *The Arkansas Delta: Land of Paradox*, ed. Jeannie Whayne and Willard Gatewood (Fayetteville: University of Arkansas Press, 1993): 150–183; Lewis, *A Biblical People in the Bible Belt*, 83–126; Lee Shai Weissbach, "East European Immigrants and the Image of Jews in the Small-Town South," *American Jewish History* 85, no. 3 (1997): 231–262.

44. Father John F. Clerico to Bishop Richard Gerow, April 1, 1933, Clerico, File 11, CDM; "Temperance and Social Service No. 2," *Journal of the North Mississippi Conference*, Starkville, Mississippi, November 5–9, 1930, 64. See also Cohen, *Making a New Deal*, 53–97; Wenger, *New York Jews and the Great Depression*, 136–165.

45. *Mothers' Aid, 1931*, 17; "Woman's Work, First Church, Greenville, Mississippi," 13–15, Ladies' Church Histories, CTS. The Woman's Auxiliary did not provide exact numbers for its budget, but members reported in 1932 that they had increased their budget by five percent in large part due to fifty dollars in savings on graduation dresses.

46. Bureau of the Census, 1930, 1296; Kate Abraham to Bishop Richard Gerow, March 29, 1933, and Father John F. Clerico to Bishop Richard Gerow, April 1, 1933, Clerico, File 11, CDM; *Mothers' Aid, 1931*, 4.

47. Beito, *From Mutual Aid to Welfare State*, 1–16, 181–221; Giggie, *After Freedom*, 59–95; Melton, "Blacks in Memphis," 89.

48. Bureau of the Census, 1930, 1316; Editorial, *Ruleville Record*, February 12, 1931, 2.

49. Editorial, *Ruleville Record*, February 12, 1931, 2.

50. Giggie, *After Redemption*, 59–95; William Ainsworth Tyson, "The Rural Church and Its Background: A Survey of Thirty-Nine Counties in North Mississippi" (Master's thesis, Mississippi State College, 1944).

51. Even the most benevolently run plantations created a cycle of dependency. See Lawrence J. Nelson, "Welfare Capitalism on a Mississippi Plantation in the Great Depression," *Journal of Southern History* 50, no. 2 (May 1984): 225–250; Whayne, *A New Plantation South*, 138–183. For an alternative, rosier recollection of plantation generosity, see Frank Perdue's story in Lawrence Gordon, "A Brief Look at Blacks in Depression Mississippi, 1929-1934: Eyewitness Accounts," *Journal of Negro History* 64, no. 4 (Autumn 1979): 377–390.

52. Biles, *Memphis in the Great Depression*, 50–65, 90.

53. *1931 Annual Report, Memphis Community Fund*, 9–10.

54. *Mothers' Aid, 1931*, 10–11; Biles, *Memphis in the Great Depression*, 44, 93.

55. "Pastors Pledge Aid for 'Job Orphans,'" *Memphis Commercial-Appeal*, December 26, 1930, 1, 3; Cartoon in *Community* 2, no. 47 (August 13, 1929), 4, in Memphis-Charities-Community Fund Clippings File, MPL; see also *Directory: Social Welfare Agencies*, which lists numerous churches that provided limited aid through women's societies and social service divisions.

56. *Where to Send People for Help*, Memphis Community Fund, January 1932, Memphis-Charities Clippings File; *It Shall Be Done!* Memphis Community Fund, 1930, Memphis-Community Fund Clippings File; *Share Your Income!* Memphis Community Fund, 1931, Memphis-Community Fund Clippings File; *1931 Annual Report, Memphis Community Fund*, 1–2.

57. *Twelfth Annual Appeal of the Memphis Community Fund*, 1933, 7, 14; Lewis, *A Biblical People in the Bible Belt*, 134–136.

58. *1931 Annual Report, Memphis Community Fund; It Shall Be Done!*; Biles, *Memphis in the Great Depression*, 55–57, 74.

59. *It Shall Be Done!; Open Your Heart: Memphis Cares for Her Own*, 1928, Memphis-Community Chest Clippings File, MPL.

60. *Twelfth Annual Appeal of the Memphis Community Fund*, 1933, 12; *1931 Annual Report, Memphis Community Fund*, 2; "Boys, Old Men—All Poor and Hungry, Swarm to Salvation Army for Shelter," *Memphis Press-Scimitar*, February 9, 1933. On the history of the Salvation Army in the United States, see Lillian Taiz, *Hallelujah Lads and Lasses: Remaking the Salvation Army in America, 1880-1930* (Chapel Hill: University of North Carolina Press, 2001); Diane H. Winston, *Red-Hot and Righteous: The Urban Religion of the Salvation Army* (Cambridge, MA: Harvard University Press, 1999).

61. *1931 Annual Report, Memphis Community Fund*, 1–2; *Twelfth Annual Appeal of the Memphis Community Fund*, 1933, 13; *First Annual Report of Eleven Conferences of the St. Vincent DePaul Society*, and "Catholic Society Secures Aid for Memphis Families," Memphis-Charities-St. Vincent de Paul Clippings File, MPL.

62. *It Shall Be Done!*, 12, 14.

63. *Twelfth Annual Appeal of the Memphis Community Fund*, 4, 21; Melton, "Blacks in Memphis," 132–133; Biles, *Memphis in the Great Depression*, 93.

64. "The Social Aspect of Christianity," *National Baptist Union-Review*, November 23, 1929, 4; "Soul Saving Campaigns and Revivals," *National Baptist Union Review*, November 7, 1931, 1. The *National Baptist Union Review* was the journal of the National Baptist Convention of America, a more conservative splinter of the larger National Baptist Convention, U.S.A., Incorporated.

65. "What Is the Remedy?" and "More About Our Social Service Work," *(Mississippi) Baptist Record*, September 10, 1931, 7.

66. Editorial page, *Memphis Commercial-Appeal*, August 22, 1931, 6.

67. Ibid. On the broader limits to voluntary giving in the twentieth century, see Morris, *The Limits of Voluntarism*; Trolander, *Settlement Houses and the Great Depression*.

68. William James Robinson, "Murdered by Society," *(Mississippi) Baptist Record*, May 19, 1932, 6.

69. Ibid. The passage the author quotes is from Matthew 25:45.

70. Ibid.; Katz, *In the Shadow of the Poorhouse*, 117–255.

71. *1931 Annual Report*, Memphis Community Fund, 4, 6, 9; *1940 Annual Report*, Memphis Community Fund.

72. *1931 Annual Report*, Memphis Community Fund, 7–8.

73. "Leaders Mark Time with Many Idle, Says Nannie Burroughs," *Baltimore Afro-American*, December 6, 1930, 5.

74. "We Take Our Stand," (Editorial), *National Baptist Voice*, January 24, 1931, 8; A. Clayton Powell, "Miss Nannie H. Burroughs Answered," *National Baptist Voice*, December 20, 1930, 1, 13; "Norfolk Pastor Against Soup-House Churches," *National Baptist Voice*, January 24, 1931, 7; "Letter to the Rev. A. Clayton Powell," *National Baptist Voice*, January 10, 1931, 1; "Dr. G. H. Sims Tells Reporters That $30,000 Negro Preachers Should Be in Jail, if Statement Made by Dr. Powell Is True," "People Need Leadership as Much as Food and Money Says the Rev. A. L. James," "Baltimore Ministers Disagree with Dr. Powell," all in *National Baptist Voice*, January 10, 1931, 5, 14; "Miss Nannie H. Burroughs Answers Dr. Powell and Other Leaders," *National Baptist Voice*, January 24, 1931, 1, 13. On the church's rough and sometimes duplicitous treatment of Burroughs, see Bettye Collier-Thomas, *Jesus, Jobs, and Justice: African American Women and Religion* (New York: Knopf, 2010), 127–138.

75. William N. Jones, "The Dole or the American Red Cross," *National Baptist Voice*, February 2, 1931, 8.

76. Corrington Gill, "Unemployment Relief," *American Economic Review* 25, no. 1 (March 1935): 176–185; Kennedy, *Freedom from Fear*, 84–85; Biles, *Memphis in the Great Depression*, 74; Melton, "Blacks in Memphis," 131–132; Martha H. Swain, *Pat Harrison: The New Deal Years* (Jackson: University Press of Mississippi, 1978), 45; Vogt, "Hoover's RFC in Action." Michele Landis Dauber argues that Hoover's conservative response to disaster relief departed from a long-standing national precedent to provide federal aid in disaster. Dauber, *The Sympathetic State: Disaster Relief and the Origins of the Welfare State* (Chicago: University of Chicago Press, 2012).

PART III

1. A. W. McMillen, "Report on Visit to State of Arkansas, November 28, 1932 to December 12, 1932," December 12, 1932 (unpaginated) in folder: Arkansas—Field Reports, 1932-1936, Box 56 (Federal Relief Agency Papers), Harry L. Hopkins

Papers, Franklin D. Roosevelt Presidential Library, Hyde Park, New York (hereafter FDR Library). On cotton prices, see *Statistical Abstract of the United States, 1941*, 741.

2. Biles, *Memphis in the Great Depression*, 56–65. On plantation wages, see also Benson Y. Landis and George Edmund Haynes, *Cotton-Growing Communities*, 14.

3. Franklin D. Roosevelt, Nomination Address, Chicago, Illinois, July 2, 1932, reprinted in *The Public Papers and Addresses of Franklin D. Roosevelt*, vol. 1, *1928–1932* (New York: Random House, 1938), 647.

CHAPTER 4

1. "Roosevelts Attend Presidents' Church," *New York Times*, March 5, 1933, 3; "100,000 at Inauguration," *New York Times*, March 5, 1933, 1; John L. Sutton, Jackson, Mississippi, to Franklin D. Roosevelt, October 9, 1935, 1, Folder: Mississippi, Box 17, President's Personal File 21A-Church Matters, FDR Library.

2. "Editorial Observations," *New Orleans Christian Advocate*, March 9, 1933, 1; "Roosevelt to Take Oath on Old Dutch Bible; Book Will Open at Paul's Words on Charity," *New York Times*, February 28, 1933, 5; "The President and the Bible," *New Orleans Christian Advocate*, May 4, 1933, 8. The King James translation of 1 Corinthians 13 uses the term *charity*; most other translations use the term *love* instead. The King James Version was commonly used in the 1930s, and the news reports referred to the passage as one about "charity" rather than "love."

3. "Text of New President's Address at Inauguration," *Washington Post*, March 5, 1933, 2.

4. Raymond Moley, *After Seven Years* (New York: Harper and Brothers, 1939), 152–155; David M. Kennedy, *Freedom from Fear: The American People in Depression and War, 1929–1945* (New York: Oxford University Press, 2001), 135–140.

5. Conference of Younger Churchmen of the South: "Findings," Monteagle, Tennessee, May 27–29, 1934, Folder 328, Box 9, Howard Anderson Kester Papers #3834, Southern Historical Collection, Louis Round Wilson Library, University of North Carolina (hereafter SHC).

6. "Substituting Government for Religion," *Mississippi Baptist Record*, October 12, 1933, 2–3.

7. Wenger, *New York Jews and the Great Depression*, 133; William B. Prendergast, *The Catholic Voter in American Politics: The Passing of the Democratic Monolith* (Washington, DC: Georgetown University Press, 1999), 26, 111–115; Miller, *American Protestantism and Social Issues*, 118–121; Bailey, *Southern White Protestantism*, 113–114. The exception here was among fundamentalists, who strongly favored Hoover. See Sutton, *American Apocalypse*, 232–262.

8. "Editorial Observations," *New Orleans Christian Advocate*, June 23, 1932, 1.

9. Biles, *Memphis in the Great Depression*, 54; Kennedy, *Freedom from Fear*, 92.

10. "Thomas Urges Vote for Plank, Not Man," *New York Times*, September 4, 1931, 2; Honey, *Southern Labor and Black Civil Rights, 57*; Mitchell, *Mean Things Happening in This Land*, 31; Gilmore, *Defying Dixie*, 185–186; Dunbar, *Against the Grain*, 37–82; Raymond F. Gregory, *Norman Thomas: The Great Dissenter* (New York: Algora Publishing, 2008), 97–110; Fox, *Reinhold Niebuhr*, 135–136; Martin, *Howard Kester and the Struggle for Social Justice in the South*, 44–65.

11. "The Political Platforms on Prohibition," "The Political Platforms on Race Relations," "Why I Expect to Vote for Herbert Hoover," "Why I Shall Vote for Governor Roosevelt," "Why I Shall Vote for Norman Thomas," *National Baptist Voice*, October 18, 1932, 1, 3, 5, 7. The parties with presidential candidates were the Democratic Party, Republican Party, Socialist Party, Workers' (Communist) Party, Socialist Labor Party, Prohibition Party, Farmer-Labor Party, Liberty Party, and Jobless Party. On Socialist and Communist appeals to black southern voters, see Dan T. Carter, *Scottsboro: A Tragedy of the American South* (Baton Rouge: Louisiana State University Press, 1969), 147–155; Gilmore, *Defying Dixie*, 15–105; Kelley, *Hammer and Hoe*, 30–33.

12. Bailey, *Southern White Protestantism in the Twentieth Century*, 114–115; William E. Leuchtenberg, *Franklin D. Roosevelt and the New Deal, 1932-1940* (New York: Harper & Row, 1963), 17; Tindall, *The Emergence of the New South*, 385–390. For state-level results, see The American Presidency Project, University of California at Santa Barbara [accessed July 19, 2014], http://www.presidency. ucsb.edu/showelection.php?year=1932

13. Franklin D. Roosevelt, Nomination Address, July 2, 1932, 647; Timothy Snyder, *Bloodlands: Europe Between Hitler and Stalin* (New York: Basic Books, 2012), 21–58; Leuchtenberg, *Franklin D. Roosevelt and the New Deal*, 18–26; Kennedy, *Freedom from Fear*, 104–105; Ralph J. Bunche, *The Political Status of the Negro in the Age of FDR*, edited and with an introduction by Dewey W. Grantham (Chicago: University of Chicago Press, 1973 [1940]), 493–494; Ira Katznelson, *Fear Itself: The New Deal and the Origins of Our Time* (New York: Liveright, 2013), 97; Honey, *Black Workers Remember*, 36–37.

14. Eleanor Roosevelt, "What Religion Means to Me," *Forum* 88 (December 1932): 322–324; "Editorial Observations," *New Orleans Christian Advocate*, January 5, 1932, 1.

15. "Editorial Observations," *New Orleans Christian Advocate*, January 5, 1933, 1.

16. "Text of New President's Address at Inauguration," *Washington Post*, March 5, 1933, 2; "Editorial Observations," *New Orleans Christian Advocate*, March 30, 1933, 1, 4; "The New Chief," *National Baptist Voice*, March 18, 1933, 2.

17. David E. Kyvig, *Repealing National Prohibition* (Kent, OH: Kent State University Press, 2000 [1979]), 160–182; Daniel Okrent, *Last Call: The Rise and Fall of Prohibition* (New York: Scribner, 2011), 96–116, 330–334.

18. Link, *The Paradox of Southern Progressivism*, 95–123; Anne-Marie Szymanski, "Beyond Parochialism: Southern Progressivism, Prohibition, and State Building," *Journal of Southern History* 69, no. 1 (February 2003): 107–136.

19. Leuchtenburg, *Franklin D Roosevelt and the New Deal*, 46–48; Kennedy, *Freedom from Fear*, 138–139.

20. "Report of the Social Service Committee," *Mississippi Baptist Record*, June 1, 1933, 2; "The Drys Are to Hold Mass Meetings," *Arkansas Baptist*, June 8, 1933, 1; Bailey, *Southern White Protestantism in the Twentieth Century*, 112–115; Biles, *Memphis in the Great Depression*, 70.

21. Evelyn Duvall, "Why I Am in Favor of Repealing the 18th Amendment," *Ruleville Record*, November 3, 1932, 2.

22. Coker, *Liquor in the Land of the Lost Cause*, 123–173. On the racialized nature of temperance campaigns, see H. Paul Thompson Jr., *A Most Significant and Stirring Episode: Religion and the Rise and Fall of Prohibition in Black Atlanta* (DeKalb: Northern Illinois University Press, 2013); David M. Fahey, *Temperance And Racism: John Bull, Johnny Reb, and the Good Templars* (Lexington: University Press of Kentucky, 1996); DoVeanna S. Fulton, "Sowing Seeds in an Untilled Field: Temperance and Race, Indeterminacy and Recovery in Frances E. W. Harper's Sowing and Reaping," *Legacy* 24, no. 2 (2007): 207–224; Hanes Walton and James E. Taylor, "Blacks and the Southern Prohibition Movement," *Phylon* 32, no. 3 (Fall 1971): 247–259

23. Russell C. Barbour, "To Our Prohibition Friends," *National Baptist Voice*, August 12, 1933, 2. On Scottsboro, see Carter, *Scottsboro: A Tragedy of the American South*; James E. Goodman, *Stories of Scottsboro* (New York: Vintage, 1995).

24. Barbour, "To Our Prohibition Friends," 2.

25. John J. DuLaney, "Think of These Things," *Arkansas Baptist*, April 27, 1933, 4; "Be Sure to Pay Your Poll Tax," *Arkansas Baptist*, May 18, 1933, 1; "The Drys Are to Hold Mass Meetings," 1; "Prohibition: Repeal by Christmas," *Time*, July 31, 1933, 12; "Repeal Battle Entering Final Stage in South," *Washington Post*, July 9, 1933, 7.

26. Norman H. Clark, *Deliver Us from Evil: An Interpretation of American Prohibition* (New York: W. W. Norton & Company, 1976), 167–208; Thomas F. Schaller, "Democracy at Rest: Strategic Ratification of the Twenty-First Amendment," *Publius* 28, no. 2 (Spring 1998): 81–97.

27. Biles, *Memphis in the Great Depression*, 70; Johnson, *Arkansas in Modern America*, 17; Ben F. Johnson III, *John Barleycorn Must Die: The War Against Drink in Arkansas* (Fayetteville: University of Arkansas Press, 2005), 74–76; Sparks, *Religion in Mississippi*, 153–154.

28. Anthony J. Badger, *FDR: The First Hundred Days* (New York: Hill and Wang, 2008), 3–82, 167.

29. "Letter to President Roosevelt," *Arkansas Baptist*, June 8, 1933, 1; "The Drys Are to Hold Mass Meetings," 1. See also Bailey, *Southern White Protestantism in the*

Twentieth Century, 113–115; Carter, *Decline and Revival of the Social Gospel,* 119–122.

30. Harvard Sitkoff, *A New Deal for Blacks: The Emergence of Civil Rights as a National Issue: The Depression Decade* (New York: Oxford University Press, 2009 [1978]), 3–43; Katznelson, *Fear Itself,* 83–92, 148–152.

31. "Criticism Must Not Abdicate," *National Baptist Voice,* April 29, 1933, 2; "The New Deal," *National Baptist Voice,* April 8, 1933, 3.

32. "Race Ministers and Leaders Answer DuBois on Negro Church," *National Baptist Voice,* January 21, 1933, 3.

33. Kennedy, *Freedom from Fear,* 177–190; Cohen, *Making a New Deal,* 277–278.

34. Katznelson, *Fear Itself,* 227–247; Cohen, *Making a New Deal,* 277–293.

35. Calvin B. Waller, "The Mark of the Beast," *Arkansas Baptist,* September 28, 1933, 1, 7; E. P. Alldredge, *Southern Baptist Handbook, 1932* (Nashville, TN: Sunday School Board of the Southern Baptist Convention, 1932), 154. See also Matthew Sutton, "Was FDR the Antichrist?," 1064; and *American Apocalypse,* 232–262.

36. Bailey, "Southern White Protestantism," 121; A. H. Bryant, "The N. R. A. No Cause for Alarm," *(Delight, Arkansas) Gospel Light,* October 15, 1933, 2.

37. O'Brien, *American Catholics and Social Reform,* 53; "Toward Encyclical Ideals," *(Arkansas) Guardian,* April 29, 1933, 2; "Support the President," *(Arkansas) Guardian,* August 5, 1933, 2. The encyclical to which the Arkansas priest referred was the 1891 *Rerum Novarum,* which laid out the "Rights and Duties of Capital and Labor," criticized both socialism and capitalism, and supported the right to organize labor unions.

38. "Protestant-Catholic-Jew," *New Orleans Christian Advocate,* August 3, 1933, 3; "Churches Join in Support of Recovery Act," *(Arkansas) Guardian,* July 15, 1933, 1; Carter, *Decline and Revival of the Social Gospel,* 71.

39. "Vandy Prof Calls Clergy NRA's 'Worst Laggards,'" news clipping, n.p., n.d., Folder: Newspaper Clippings—1930–1939, Box 6, Taylor Papers, DCHS; Henry G. Hawkins, Vicksburg, MS, to Franklin Roosevelt, September 30, 1935, Folder: Mississippi, Box 16, President's Personal File 21A-Church Matters, FDR Library; "Editorial Observations," *New Orleans Christian Advocate,* September 7, 1933, 1.

40. "Editorial Observations," *New Orleans Christian Advocate,* October 5, 1933, 1.

41. "Baptists' NRA," *Mississippi Baptist Record,* September 14, 1933, 3; James B. Grambling, "NRA Code for the Church," *New Orleans Christian Advocate,* October 19, 1933, 3.

42. William Pickens, "NRA—'Negro Removal Act,'" *World Tomorrow,* September 28, 1933, 539–540; Robert Rogers Korstad, *Civil Rights Unionism: Tobacco Workers and the Struggle for Cotton in the Mid-Twentieth Century South* (Chapel Hill: University of North Carolina Press, 2003), 127–130; Sitkoff, *A New Deal for Blacks,* 41–42.

43. John P. Davis, "The Maid-Well Garment Case: A Case Study of the Economic and Social Consequences of the New Deal," Arkansas Complaints-S Folder,

Box 20, State Series: March 1933–1936: Arkansas, Records of the WPA/FERA Central Files, Record Group 69, National Archives and Records Administration II, College Park, Maryland (hereafter NARA); Cheryl Lynn Greenberg, *To Ask for an Equal Chance: African Americans in the Great Depression* (Lanham, MD: Rowman & Littlefield, 2009), 47–48; Honey, *Southern Labor and Black Civil Rights*, 25–26; Pickins, "NRA," 539.

44. Pickens, "NRA," 540; Katznelson, *Fear Itself*, 3–25, 133–194.

45. Kennedy, *Freedom from Fear*, 131–159; Leuchtenburg, *Franklin D. Roosevelt and the New Deal*, 41–62. Chapter 5 covers the works programs in more detail, and Chapter 6 addresses the implications of the Agricultural Adjustment Administration for the region.

46. Baird, *Public and Private Aid*, 112–119; Josephine Chapin Brown, *Public Relief, 1929-1939* (New York: Octagon Books, 1971), 30–31.

47. Trost, *Gateway to Justice*, 136–139; Emma A. Winslow, *Trends in Different Types of Public and Private Relief in Urban Areas, 1929-1935* (Washington, DC: Government Printing Office, 1937), 23.

48. "Ruleville Baptist Missionary Society," *Ruleville Record*, November 3, 1932, 1. Woodruff, *As Rare as Rain*, 22–55. On the American Red Cross's quasi-public role, see Julia Finch Irwin, *Making the World Safe: The American Red Cross and a Nation's Humanitarian Awakening* (New York: Oxford University Press, 2013).

49. "Fund Shakeup Nears; R.F.C. Drops Support," *Memphis Commercial Appeal*, June 26, 1933, Memphis Community Fund clippings file, MPL.

50. Winslow, *Trends in Different Types of Public and Private Relief*, 23–26; Brown, *Public Relief*, 171–185.

51. Brown, *Public Relief*, 147–149. Michele Landis Dauber shows how the nation's history of federal disaster relief provided a precedent for FERA and the New Deal's treatment of the Depression as a large-scale disaster. Dauber, *The Sympathetic State*, 79–126.

52. Brown, *Public Relief*, 172–190 (quotation on 190); Winslow, *Trends in Different Types of Public and Private Relief*, 23; Brown and McKeown, *The Poor Belong to Us*, 164–166; Cohen, *Making a New Deal*, 269–270.

53. Brown, *Public Relief*, 187, fn 40; "Fund Shakeup Nears" and "Statement of Fund Expert Draws Attack from Mayor," *Memphis Commercial Appeal*, July 12, 1933, both in Memphis Community Fund clippings file; "1941 Annual Report, Memphis Community Fund," 14–15; "Spurrier Addresses Rotary," *Memphis Councilor* 2, no. 11 (December 1939): 2; *Twelfth Annual Appeal of the Memphis Community Fund*, 1933, 4, 21; Melton, "Blacks in Memphis," 132–134.

54. Baird, *Public and Private Aid*, 86–151.

55. Ibid., 143.

56. *Final Statistical Report of the FERA*, 102–104; Brown, *Public Relief*, 205. The FERA totals are cumulative to 1941, but the vast majority of aid arrived by 1935; the remainder was rolled over as FERA liquidated (see FERA report, 102–104).

57. "Editorial Observations," *New Orleans Christian Advocate*, October 5, 1933, 1.

58. "Are Hospitals to Be Helped," *Arkansas Baptist*, November 16, 1933, 3; "Whose Responsibility Charity," *Arkansas Baptist*, December 7, 1933, 1, 7; "Annual Report of Baptist State Hospital to the Arkansas Baptist State Convention," *Proceedings of the Arkansas Baptist State Convention*, Little Rock, Arkansas, November 15–17, 1932, 34–38, SBHLA; "Baptist State Hospital," *Proceedings of the Arkansas Baptist State Convention*, El Dorado, Arkansas, January 16–18, 1934, 38–40, SBHLA.

59. Mrs. J. Morgan Stevens, quoted in Winnie Phillips, *Methodist Women: A History*, Mississippi Conference, Southeastern Jurisdiction, The Methodist Church, 1928–1968.

60. J. F. Dodd, School Director, Supt. of Sunday School, Alpena Pass, Arkansas, to Welfare Society, Washington, D.C., October 9, 1934, Box 264, Correspondence with Government Departments, Eleanor Roosevelt Papers, FDR Library; Secretary to Mrs. Roosevelt to J. F. Dodd, October 12, 1934, Box 264, Eleanor Roosevelt Papers, FDR Library.

61. "Substituting Government for Religion," *Mississippi Baptist Record*, October 12, 1933, 2–3.

62. Ibid.

63. Pickens, "NRA," 540; Brown, *Public Relief*, 191–217.

64. Brown, *Public Relief*, 191–217.

65. Whayne, *New Plantation South*, 188–190; Johnson, *Arkansas in Modern America*, 16–17; Holley, *Uncle Sam's Farmers*, 31; Cobb, *The Most Southern Place on Earth*, 192–197.

66. Myrtle Sherwood to FDR, September 4, 1933, Arkansas Complaints-S Folder, Box 20, State Series: March 1933-1936: Arkansas, Records of the WPA/FERA Central Files, Record Group 69, NARA.

67. Whayne, *A New Plantation South*, 189; Woodruff, *American Congo*, 155–162; Edith Foster, "Field Report, Mississippi, December 11 and 12, 1933," 1, Folder: Mississippi—Field Reports, 1933-1934, Box 58, Hopkins Papers, FDR Library; Biles, *Memphis in the Great Depression*, 94.

68. Elmer Scott, "Confidential Report on Memphis, Tennessee," April 30, 1934, 1–2, Folder: Confidential Reports by Elmer Scott, Box 62, Hopkins Papers, FDR Library.

69. Ibid.

70. Ibid.

71. I. C. Franklin, Port Gibson, Mississippi, to Franklin D. Roosevelt, October 16, 1935, Folder: Mississippi, Box 30, President's Personal File 21A-Church Matters, FDR Library; Kirby, *Black Americans in the Roosevelt Era*, 24.

72. "God and the President," *National Baptist Voice*, March 10, 1934, 2.

CHAPTER 5

1. J. M. Shumpert, Bude, Mississippi, October 17, 1935, Mississippi Folder, Box 16, President's Personal File 21A-Church Matters, FDR Library (hereafter CL for Clergy Letters; boxes and folders are alphabetical by state. Because all the letters in this collection are addressed to Roosevelt, I have indicated only the names of the letters' authors and not that of the recipient).

2. Franklin D. Roosevelt to the nation's clergy, September 24, 1935, Box 1, CL.

3. N. B. Bynum, Brinkley, Arkansas, October 16, 1935, Arkansas Folder, Box 3, CL.

4. Guy D. Magee, Tyronza, Arkansas, October 14, 1935, Arkansas Folder, Box 3, CL.

5. Bureau of the Census, "Chapter D: Labor," 135; Bureau of the Census, *Statistical Abstract of the United States, 1941,* 346; John L. Martin, "Income Payments to Individuals, by States, 1929-38," *Survey of Current Business* 20, no. 4 (April 1940), 10. Per capita income in Arkansas in 1929, 1933, and 1935 was $300, $141, and $191, respectively. In Tennessee, per capita income in 1929, 1933, and 1935 was $353, $184, and $254, respectively.

6. Kennedy, *Freedom from Fear,* 218–248; McElvaine, *The Great Depression,* 225–250.

7. Franklin D. Roosevelt, Fireside Chat 7: On the Works Relief Program and Social Security Act, April 28, 1935, Miller Center, University of Virginia [accessed June 23, 2015], http://millercenter.org/president/speeches/speech-3304; Kennedy, *Freedom from Fear,* 249–287. On the conservative nature of the Social Security Act in creating a public–private state, see Jennifer Klein, *For All These Rights: Business, Labor, and the Shaping of America's Public-Private Welfare State* (Princeton, NJ: Princeton University Press, 2003), 1–115.

8. Kennedy, *Freedom from Fear,* 249–287.

9. "Clergymen Swinging Leftward," *World Tomorrow* 17, no. 10 (May 10, 1934): 219–221; Kirby Page, "20,870 Clergymen on War and Economic Justice," *World Tomorrow* 17, no. 10 (May 10, 1934): 222–255 (quotation on p. 227). On the Fellowship of Reconciliation, see Kosek, *Acts of Conscience.*

10. "Final Poll Report Totals 1,772,163 Votes," *Literary Digest,* July 7, 1934, 3–4, 35.

11. Alan Brinkley, *Voices of Protest,* 216–268; Katz, *In the Shadow of the Poorhouse,* 229–230.

12. John Clarence Petrie, First Unitarian Church, Memphis, September 26, 1935, Tennessee Folder, Box 30, CL; Matt Sutton, "Was FDR the Antichrist?" 1052, 1064. On alliances between religious and business conservatives, see also Kruse, *One Nation Under God*; Hammond, "God Is My Partner"; and Ribuffo, *The Old Christian Right.*

13. Gary Scott Smith, *Faith and the Presidency from George Washington to George W. Bush* (New York: Oxford University Press, 2006), 203–208; Brown and McKeown, *The Poor Belong to Us,* 151–192. On Roosevelt's faith and public policy—particularly foreign policy—see also Andrew Preston, *Sword of the Spirit,*

Shield of Faith: Religion in American War and Diplomacy (New York: Anchor Books, 2012), 291–326.

14. Josiah Crudup, Belzoni, Mississippi, October 10, 1935, Mississippi Folder, Box 16, CL.

15. Perry F. Webb, Pine Bluff, Arkansas, October 20, 1935, Arkansas Folder, Box 3, CL; Dale Crowley, "An Open Letter to President Roosevelt," *Back to the Bible Crusader*, October 18, 1935, 1–2, Arkansas Folder, Box 3, CL; "Roosevelt's Letter to Clergy Stirs Big Hullabaloo," *Baltimore Afro-American*, October 12, 1935, 5; "Roosevelt Asks Clergy for Advice on Service," *Los Angeles Times*, September 26, 1935, 1; "Roosevelt's Letter Like LaFollette's," *New York Times*, September 28, 1935, 3; Smith, *Faith and the Presidency*, 199–203.

16. Monroe Billington and Cal Clark, "Clergy Reaction to the New Deal: A Comparative Study," *Historian* 48, no. 4 (1986): 509–524.

17. Aubrey Mills, "Supplementary Report on Clergy Letters," Report of Aubrey Mills Folder, Box 35, CL. Mills broke down the responses by state, as well as nationally. See also Monroe Billington and Cal Clark, "Catholic Clergymen, Franklin D. Roosevelt, and the New Deal," *Catholic Historical Review* 79, no. 1 (January 1993): 65–82; Monroe Billington and Cal Clark, "Baptist Preachers and the New Deal," *Journal of Church and State* 33, no. 2 (Spring 1991): 255–269.

18. B. P. Craddock, Potts Camp, Mississippi, September 27, 1935, Mississippi Folder, Box 16, CL; Luke Edwin Alford, Canton, Mississippi, September 28, 1935, Mississippi Folder, Box 16, CL; Harvey Gray, Sarah, Mississippi, September 30, 1935, Mississippi Folder, Box 16, CL; Cecil B. Jones, Rosedale, Mississippi, October 8, 1935, Mississippi Folder, Box 16, CL. See also Bryant Simon, *A Fabric of Defeat: The Politics of South Carolina Millhands, 1910-1948* (Chapel Hill: University of North Carolina Press, 1998), 88–89. Outside the South, clergy more quickly jumped on the anti–New Deal bandwagon. See Sutton, "Was FDR the Antichrist?"

19. Perry F. Webb, Pine Bluff, Arkansas, October 20, 1938, Arkansas Folder, Box 3, CL; Mrs. Print Smith, Blytheville, Arkansas, October 28, 1935, Non-Clergy Folder, Box 36, CL.

20. John S. Chadwick, editor, *Christian Advocate*, Nashville, Tennessee, October 3, 1935, Authors and Educators Folder, Box 35, CL; Meyer Lovitt, Beth-Israel Congregation, Jackson, Mississippi, October 11, 1935, Mississippi Folder, Box 16, CL; Robert A. George, First Congregational Church, Memphis, October 17, 1935, Tennessee Folder, Box 30, CL.

21. S. W. Foster, Episcopal Church of the Redeemer, Greenville, Mississippi, October 14, 1935, Mississippi Folder, Box 16, CL; Joseph Boone Hunter, Pulaski Heights Christian Church, November 8, 1935, Arkansas Folder, Box 3, CL.

22. Henry G. Hawkins, Vicksburg District, MECS, September 30, 1935, Mississippi Folder, Box 16, CL; George D. Booth, First Presbyterian, Natchez, Mississippi, September 30, 1935, Mississippi Folder, Box 16, CL.

23. Katznelson, *Fear Itself*, 259–260; Katz, *In the Shadow of the Poorhouse*, 242–254; Gwendolyn Mink, *The Wages of Motherhood: Inequality in the Welfare State, 1917-1942* (Ithaca, NY: Cornell University Press, 1996), 123–150; Deborah E. Ward, *The White Welfare State: The Racialization of U.S. Welfare Policy* (Ann Arbor: University Press of Michigan, 2005), 98–130.

24. N. B. Bynum, Brinkley, Arkansas, October 16, 1935, Arkansas Folder, Box 3, CL.

25. I. C. Franklin, Port Gibson, Mississippi, October 16, 1935, Mississippi Folder, Box 16, CL.

26. R. G. Moore, Leland, Mississippi, Missionary Secretary, North Mississippi Conference, MECS, Mississippi Folder, Box 16, CL.

27. Katz, *In the Shadow of the Poorhouse*, 231–243.

28. Henry G. Hawkins, Vicksburg District, MECS, September 30, 1935, Mississippi Folder, Box 16, CL; T. E. Williams, Little Rock, Arkansas, October 10, 1935, Arkansas Folder, Box 3, CL.

29. "Text of New President's Address at Inauguration," *Washington Post*, March 5, 1933, 2; Roosevelt, "Fireside Chat 7"; Brown, *Public Relief*, 152; Bruce S. Jansson, *The Reluctant Welfare State: A History of American Social Welfare Policies* (Belmont, CA: Wadsworth Publishing Company, 1988), 129–130.

30. E. G. Evans, Gunnison, Mississippi, October 8, 1935, Mississippi Folder, Box 16, CL.

31. N. H. Roberts, Cruger, Mississippi, October 11, 1935, Mississippi Folder, Box 16, CL.

32. Carolyn Gray LeMaster, *A Corner of the Tapestry: A History of the Jewish Experience in Arkansas, 1820s-1990s* (Fayetteville: University of Arkansas Press, 1994), 314; Mark K. Bauman and Berkley Kalin, *The Quiet Voices: Southern Rabbis and Black Civil Rights, 1880s to 1990s* (Tuscaloosa: University of Alabama Press, 1997), 107.

33. Sitkoff, *A New Deal for Blacks*, 52–55; Lauren Rebecca Sklaroff, *Black Culture and the New Deal: The Quest for Civil Rights in the Roosevelt Era* (Chapel Hill: University of North Carolina Press, 2009), 24–25, 116–117.

34. Bunche, *The Political Status of the Negro*, 564–565, 496; Memphis Welfare Commission to Mayor Watkins Overton, August 30, 1938, WPA-Misc. Correspondence Folder, Box 26, Series 1, Papers of Memphis Mayor Watkins Overton, MPL; "Mr. Hopkins's telephone conversation with Alan Johnstone," [transcript], March 25, 1936, Transcripts of Phone Conversations Folder, Box 75, Hopkins Papers, FDR Library; Chester M. Morgan, *Redneck Liberal: Theodore M. Bilbo and the New Deal* (Baton Rouge: Louisiana State University Press, 1985), 141–143.

35. Rev. J. T. Thomas to Harry Hopkins, January 14, 1935, Mississippi: Complaints Q-T Folder, Box 156, State Series, March 1933-1936, Records of the WPA/FERA Central Files, 1933-36, RG 69, NARA; Cecil B. Jones, Rosedale, Mississippi, October 9, 1935, Mississippi Folder, Box 16, CL; McMillen, *Dark Journey*, 84. On white interracialism in the New Deal, see Gilmore, *Defying Dixie*, 230–246.

36. J. R. G. Hewlett, Charleston, Mississippi, to Franklin D. Roosevelt, October 3, 1935, Mississippi Folder, Box 16, CL; "The State of the Country Covering the Economic Condition of Negroes," *Official Journal of the Sixty-Seventh Session of the Mississippi Annual Conference*, Methodist Episcopal Church, Waveland, Mississippi, October 31-November 4, 1934, 39, Cain Archives.

37. On American familiarity with the Roosevelts and the White House's letter-reading operations, see Dauber, *Sympathetic State*, 10–11; Lawrence W. Levine, *The People and the President: America's Extraordinary Conversation with FDR* (Boston: Beacon Press, 2002); Russell D. Buhite and David W. Levy, *FDR's Fireside Chats* (New York: Penguin, 1993). On Eleanor Roosevelt's "My Day" columns and her relationship with Americans in the Depression, see Eleanor Roosevelt, *My Day: The Best of Eleanor Roosevelt's Acclaimed Newspaper Columns, 1936-1962*, ed. David Emblidge (New York: Da Capo Press, 2001); Blanche Wiesen Cook, *Eleanor Roosevelt: Volume 2, The Defining Years, 1933-1938* (New York: Penguin Books, 2000); Maurine Hoffman Beasley, *Eleanor Roosevelt and the Media: A Public Quest for Self-Fulfillment* (Urbana: University of Illinois Press, 1987).

38. William T. Schmidt, "Letters to Their President: Mississippians to Franklin D. Roosevelt, 1932-1933," *Journal of Mississippi History* 40, no. 3 (August 1978): 252.

39. Mrs. M. L. Brantley, Whitehaven, Tennessee, to Eleanor Roosevelt, September 24, 1934, 2–3, Box 262, Correspondence with Government Departments, Eleanor Roosevelt Papers, Franklin D. Roosevelt Presidential Library, Hyde Park, New York (hereafter Eleanor Roosevelt Papers).

40. The cartoon is by Los Angeles–based Don Herald, a well-known writer and cartoonist. Enclosed with letter from W. L. Francis, Greenville, Mississippi, November 17, 1934, Box 265, Correspondence with Government Departments, Eleanor Roosevelt Papers, FDR Library.

41. Guido Van Rijn, *Roosevelt's Blues: African-American Blues and Gospel Songs on FDR* (Jackson: University Press of Mississippi, 1997), 96–104.

42. Correspondence between Mrs. W. H. Lindsey, Hamburg, Arkansas, and New Deal officials, April 1934; Mississippi: Complaints Q-T Folder, Box 156, State Series, March 1933-1936, Records of the WPA/FERA Central Files, 1933-36, RG 69, NARA.

43. N. H. Roberts, Cruger, Mississippi, October 11, 1935, Mississippi Folder, Box 16, CL.

44. P. F. Scruggs, Duncan Chapel M.E. Church, Little Rock, Arkansas, October 10, 1935, Arkansas Folder, Box 3, CL.

45. C. H. Witt, Parkway Methodist Church, Memphis, Tennessee, October 29, 1935, Tennessee Folder, Box 30, CL.

46. Ibid.

47. Rev. R. L. Phelps, Synod of Mississippi, PCUSA, September 30, 1935, Church Officials Folder, Box 35, CL.

48. J. J. Galloway, Hughes, Arkansas, October 1, 1935, Arkansas Folder, Box 3, CL.

49. "Advances Charity Plans," *Memphis Commercial-Appeal*, October 18, 1932.

50. R. E. Black, V.D.M., Boydsville, Arkansas, October 7, 1935, Arkansas Folder, Box 3, CL; E. T. Short, Jackson, Tennessee, October 28, 1935, Tennessee Folder, Box 30, CL; George W. Bell, Whiteville M.E. Church, September 28, 1935, Tennessee Folder, Box 30, CL. Black's "V.D.M." designation could have one of two meanings. It was an informal way for uneducated clergy to indicate their status, which loosely translated from the Latin meaning "minister of the divine word." It was also a designation that men and women who completed a Jehovah's Witness self-study course could use. There were Jehovah's Witnesses scattered throughout the Delta, although no formal organization existed in Clay County, where Boydsville is located. If Black was a Jehovah's Witness, his proposal to participate with the government is particularly interesting.

51. F. W. Montgomery, Mt. Olive M.E. Church, Yazoo City, Mississippi, October 8, 1935, Mississippi Folder, Box 16, CL.

52. J. E. Adams, Gould, Arkansas, October 24, 1935, Arkansas Folder, Box 3, President's Personal File 21A-Church Matters, FDR Library.

53. E. B. Rucker, Martin, Tennessee, October 21, 1935, Tennessee Folder, Box 30, President's Personal File 21A-Church Matters, FDR Library.

54. Rector J. A. Knight, Leachville, Arkansas, October 6, 1936, Arkansas Folder, Box 3, CL.

55. L. A. Streete, Rosedale, Mississippi, September 26, 1935, Mississippi Folder, Box 16, CL. See also Sarah Wilkerson-Freeman, "The Creation of a Subversive Feminist Dominion: Interracialist Social Workers and the Georgia New Deal," *Journal of Women's History* 13, no. 4 (Winter 2002): 132–154; Martha H. Swain, *Ellen S. Woodward: New Deal Advocate for Women* (Jackson: University of Mississippi Press, 1995); Collier-Thomas, *Jesus, Jobs, and Justice*; Harvey, *Redeeming the South*.

56. Very Rev. Msgr. Walter J. Tynin, St. Joseph's Rectory, Fayetteville, Arkansas, October 14, 1935, Miscellaneous Officials Folder, Box 35, CL.

57. J. M. Harrison, First MECS, Parkin, Arkansas, October 14, 1935, Arkansas Folder, Box 3, CL.

58. Rev. Guy D. Magee, Tyronza, Arkansas, October 14, 1935, Arkansas Folder, Box 3.

59. John S. Chadwick of the *Christian Advocate*, Nashville, Tennessee and Dadeville, Alabama, October 3, 1935, Authors and Educators Folder, Box 35, CL. On this movement's broader sweep, see Kruse, *One Nation Under God*; Sutton, *American Apocalypse*; Darren Grem, "The Blessings of Business: Corporate America and Conservative Evangelicalism in the Sunbelt Age, 1945-2000" (Ph.D. diss., University of Georgia, 2010); Darren Dochuk, *From Bible Belt to Sunbelt: Plain-Folk Religion, Grassroots Politics, and the Rise of Evangelical Conservatism* (New York: Norton, 2011); Bethany Moreton, *To Serve God and Wal-Mart: The Making of Christian Free Enterprise* (Cambridge, MA: Harvard University Press, 2009); Glass, *Strangers in Zion*; Ribuffo, *The Old Christian Right*; Sarah Hammond, "'God's Business Men': Entrepreneurial Evangelicals in Depression and War" (Ph.D. diss., Yale University, 2010).

60. "An Open Letter to President Roosevelt," *Back to the Bible Crusader*, October 18, 1935, 1–2, Arkansas Folder, Box 3, CL; American Baptist Association Folders, Box 413, Arkansas Church Records; Central Baptist Church, Craighead County, Folder 49, Box 420, Arkansas Church Records; Pratt, *The Father of Modern Landmarkism*.

61. Aubrey Mills, "Supplementary Report on Clergy Letters," Report of Aubrey Mills Folder, Box 35, CL; Arkansas Folders, Box 3, CL; Mississippi Folders, Box 16, CL; Tennessee Folders, Box 30, CL.

62. J. L. Rowland, MECS Board of Missions, Wheatley and Walnut Ridge, Arkansas, December 31, 1935, Arkansas Folder, Box 3, CL.

63. Ben Bogard, Little Rock, Arkansas, October 2, 1935, Arkansas Folder, Box 3, CL; "News Behind the News," *Atlanta Constitution*, July 25, 1935, 8; "Garner Has Hole Cards Up Sleeves," *Hartford Courant*, July 25, 1935, 3.

64. J. L. Rowland, MECS Board of Missions, Wheatley and Walnut Ridge, Arkansas, December 31, 1935, Arkansas Folder, Box 3, CL; Perry F. Webb, Pine Bluff, Arkansas, October 20, 1935, Box 3, CL.

65. Dale Crowley, "An Open Letter to President Roosevelt," *Back to the Bible Crusader*, October 18, 1935, 1–2, Arkansas Folder, Box 3, CL. See Matt Sutton, "Was FDR the Antichrist," for comparisons outside the South, and in Texas, where anti-FDR premillennialism had more traction.

66. B. F. Whitten, Coldwater, Mississippi, September 28, 1935, Mississippi Folder, Box 16, CL; E. L. Turner, Wabbaseka, Arkansas, Elliott Chapel Church of Christ, October 1, 1935, Arkansas Folder, Box 3, October 1, 1935 (cross-referenced with Elliott Chapel Church of Christ, Folder 123, Box 430, Arkansas Church Records).

67. J. W. White, Ravenden, Arkansas, November 17, 1935, Arkansas Folder, Box 3, CL.

68. Rev. T. Steiner, Marvell, Arkansas, November 3, 1935, Arkansas Folder, Box 3, CL.

69. John Clarence Petrie, First Unitarian Church, Memphis, September 26, 1935, Tennessee Folder, Box 30, CL.

70. John S. Chadwick of the *Christian Advocate*, Nashville, Tennessee and Dadeville, Alabama, October 3, 1935, Authors and Educators Folder, Box 35, CL.

71. E. P. Alldredge, SBC Department of Survey, Statistics, and Information, Nashville, Tennessee, September 26, 1935, Tennessee Folder, Box 30, CL.

72. "Special Poll of Clergymen on New Deal," *Literary Digest*, February 22, 1936, 8; Miller, *American Protestantism and Social Issues*, 122; Kennedy, *Freedom from Fear*, 278–286; For state-level results, see The American Presidency Project, University of California at Santa Barbara [accessed July 19, 2014]: http://www.presidency.ucsb.edu/showelection.php?year=1936.

PART IV

1. Eleanor Roosevelt, "My Day," June 11, 1936, accessed at the My Day Project of George Washington University [August 1, 2014]: http://www.gwu.edu/~erpapers/

myday/displaydoc.cfm?_y=1936&_f=mdo54354; On Dyess, see Holley, *Uncle Sam's Farmers*, 30–51.

2. "My Day," June 11, 1936; "Colonists Shake Hands with First Lady," *Colony Herald*, June 12, 1936, 1, Folder: Trips, Arkansas, 1936, Eleanor Roosevelt Pamphlet Collection, Eleanor Roosevelt Papers, FDR Library.

3. "My Day," June 11, 1936; "Colonists Shake Hands with First Lady," 1; Holley, *Uncle Sam's Farmers*, 30–51, 112–114, Appendix.

4. Dorothy Day, "Sharecroppers," undated article [March 7, 1936, printed in *America*], STFU Papers-UNC.

5. Ibid.

6. Ibid.

7. Myrtle Sherwood to FDR, September 4, 1933.

CHAPTER 6

1. Anna Weir Layne, Family Selection Specialist, Resettlement Administration, "The House of the Wooden Crosses," 1, from *Little Stories of Folks in Arkansas*, n.p., n.d., Folder: U.S.—Resettlement Administration—Arkansas, in Eleanor Roosevelt Pamphlet Collection, FDR Library.

2. Holley, *Uncle Sam's Farmers*, 28–40; Fred C. Smith, *Trouble in Goshen: Plain Folk, Roosevelt, Jesus and Marx in the Great Depression South* (Jackson: University Press of Mississippi, 2014), 48–77.

3. "A Field Interviewer's Analysis of Prospective Rural Community Colonist," 1–2, Document MA-9-FS-1, Folder 911-045 (Selection: Property Units), Box 151 (Arkansas), FERA Records, RG 96, NARA; "Procedure: Family Selection: Dyess Colony," and telegram from Mrs. Max Layne to Dr. Wendell Lund, December 5, 1935, and T. Roy Reid to Rexford Tugwell, December 23, 1935, Folder 130 (Personnel), Box 150 (Arkansas), FERA Records; Layne, introductory note, *Little Stories of Folks in Arkansas*; Helen M. Winslow, *The Register and Directory of Women's Clubs in America*, vol. 24 (Boston, MA: Helen M. Winslow, 1922), 10, 65.

4. Layne, introductory note and "The House of the Wooden Crosses," 1, both in *Little Stories of Folks in Arkansas*.

5. Layne, "The House of the Wooden Crosses," 1–3.

6. Ibid., 3.

7. Ibid., 1–5 (quotations on 4, 5).

8. Ibid., 4.

9. Ibid., 5.

10. On the New Deal and its aftermath in the rural South, see Pete Daniel, *Dispossession: Discrimination against African American Farmers in the Age of Civil Rights* (Chapel Hill: University of North Carolina Press, 2013); Sarah Phillips, *This Land, This Nation: Conservation, Rural America, and the New Deal* (New York: Cambridge University Press, 2007); Patricia Sullivan, *Days*

of Hope: Race and Democracy in the New Deal Era (Chapel Hill: University of North Carolina Press, 1996); Holley, *Uncle Sam's Farmers*; Paul E. Mertz, *New Deal Policy and Southern Rural Poverty* (Baton Rouge: Louisiana State University Press, 1978). For another perspective on the FSA bureaucrats and religion, see Jon Ebel, "Re-Forming Faith: John Steinbeck, the New Deal, and the Religion of the Wandering Oklahoman," *Journal of Religion* 92, no. 4 (October 2012): 527–535.

11. On the STFU and the cooperative farms, see Fred C. Smith, *Trouble in Goshen*; Robert Hunt Ferguson, "Race and the Remaking of the Rural South: Delta Cooperative Farm and Providence Farm in Jim Crow-Era Mississippi" (Ph.D. diss., University of North Carolina, 2012); Jarod Roll and Erik Gellman, *Gospel of the Working Class*; Roll, *Spirit of Rebellion*.

12. On COGIC and Mallory in the 1930s, see White, *The Rise to Respectability*; Butler, *Women in the Church of God in Christ*. Butler argues that Mallory's work during the Depression was central to creating mainstream acceptance for the church.

13. Peter C. Murray, *Methodists and the Crucible of Race, 1930-1975* (Columbia: University of Missouri Press, 2004); Bailey, *Southern White Protestantism*, 123–129.

14. See Sutton, "Was FDR the Antichrist?"; Pratt, *The Father of Modern Landmarkism*; Greene, "The End of the 'Protestant Era'?"; Dochuk, *From Bible Belt to Sun Belt*.

15. Brooks Hays, "Farm Tenancy and the Christian Conscience," *Christian Rural Fellowship Bulletin*, no. 9 (February 1936): 4, Folder 5, Box 24, Subseries 1, Series 2, Lawrence Brooks Hays Papers, MS #H334, University of Arkansas; James Thomas Baker, *Brooks Hays* (Macon, GA: Mercer University Press, 1989), 35–36; Brooks Hays, *Politics Is My Parish: An Autobiography* (Baton Rouge: Louisiana State University Press, 1981), 72.

16. On Hays's life and work, see previous note. On Alexander, see Sullivan, *Days of Hope*, 24–59, and Wilma Dykeman and James Stokely. *Seeds of Southern Change: The Life of Will Alexander* (New York: W. W. Norton, 1962).

17. Theodore Roosevelt, introduction to Liberty Hyde Bailey, *Report of the Country Life Commission* (Washington, DC: Government Printing Office, 1909), 8; Liberty Hyde Bailey, *Report of the Country Life Commission*, 18, 56–63 (quotation on 62); Liberty Hyde Bailey, *The Country-Life Movement in the United States* (New York: Macmillan, 1911), 1; Scott J. Peters and Paul A. Morgan, "The Country Life Commission: Reconsidering a Milestone in American Agricultural History," *Agricultural History* 78, no. 3 (Summer 2004): 289–316. The 1914 Smith-Lever Act established the cooperative extension agencies, and the American Country Life Commission, founded in 1917, organized data collection.

18. The literature produced by this movement is enormous; the literature about it is more limited. For the latter, see Kevin M. Lowe, *Baptized with the Soil: Christian Agrarians and the Crusade for Rural America* (New York: Oxford University Press,

2015); Curtis Evans, *The Burden of Black Religion*, 216–259; Christopher Hamlin and John T. McGreevy, "The Greening of America, Catholic Style, 1930-1950," *Environmental History* 11, no. 3 (July 2006): 464–499; Robert P. Swierenga, "The Little White Church: Religion in Rural America," *Agricultural History* 71, no. 4 (Autumn 1997): 415–441; Leigh Eric Schmidt, "From Arbor Day to the Environmental Sabbath: Nature, Liturgy, and American Protestantism," *Harvard Theological Review* 84, no. 3 (July 1991): 299–323; James H. Madison, "Reformers and the Rural Church, 1900-1950," *Journal of American History* 73, no. 3 (December 1986): 645–668; Merwin Swanson, "The 'Country Life Movement' and the American Churches," *Church History* 46, no. 3 (September 1977): 358–373. Relevant works by rural church reformers include Benjamin E. Mays and Joseph William Nicholson, *The Negro's Church* (New York: Institute of Social and Religious Research, 1933); John William Jent, *Rural Church Problems* (Shawnee: Oklahoma Baptist University Press, 1935); C. Luther Fry, *The U. S. Looks at Its Churches* (New York: Institute of Social and Religious Research, 1930); Kenyon L. Butterfield, *The Country Church and the Rural Problem: The Carew Lectures at Hartford Theological Seminary, 1909* (Chicago: University of Chicago Press, 1917); Edwin L. Earp, *The Rural Church Movement* (New York: Methodist Book Concern, 1914).

19. "Holy Rollers" was common slang for pentecostals. See, for instance, Jent, *The Country Church*, 183. On the South in the rural church movement, see essays by John Giggie, John Hayes, and Alison Greene in Michael Pasquier, ed., *Gods of the Mississippi* (Bloomington: Indiana University Press, 2013); John Hayes, "Hard, Hard Religion"; Karen Aaron Stone, "Rescue the Perishing: The Southern Baptist Convention and the Rural Church Movement," (Ph.D. diss., Auburn University, 1998).

20. Sernett, *Bound for the Promised Land*, 210–240; Matthew William Dunne, "Next Steps: Charles S. Johnson and Southern Liberalism," *Journal of Negro History* 83, no. 1 (Winter 1981): 1–34; Gilmore, *Defying Dixie*, 226–236; Arthur Raper, *The Tragedy of Lynching* (Mineola, NY: Dover, 2003 [1933]).

21. Benson Y. Landis and John D. Willard, *Rural Adult Education* (New York: MacMillan Company, 1933), 119; Mark Rich, *The Rural Church Movement* (Columbia, MO: Juniper Knoll Press, 1957), 57–154; Ted Ownby, "Gladys Presley, Dorothy Dickins, and the Limits of Female Agrarianism in Twentieth-Century Mississippi," in *Mississippi Women: Their History, Their Lives*, vol. 2, ed. Martha Swain et al. (Athens: University of Georgia Press, 2010), 211–233; Ted Ownby, *American Dreams in Mississippi: Consumers, Poverty, and Culture, 1830-1998* (Chapel Hill: University of North Carolina Press, 1999), 98–109; Landis, *Cotton-Growing Communities*, 45.

22. Margaret Simms McDonald, *White Already to Harvest*, 218-221; PCUS, Committee on Assembly's Work, Department of Home Missions, Sixty-Fifth Annual Report, Montreat, NC, May 28, 1931, 18, CTS; Williams et al., *A System*

and a Plan, 203–223; Ralph A. Felton, *The Lord's Acre* [1946], Folder 11, Box 17, Home Missions Council of North America, National Council of Churches Collection, RG 26, Presbyterian Historical Society, Philadelphia, PA (hereafter PHS); *The Country Church Needs the Lord's Acre Plan*, Folder 20, Box 14, Social Ethics Pamphlet Collection, RG #73, Yale Divinity School Library, New Haven, CT; Rich, *The Rural Church Movement*, 128–129; "Religion: Lord's Acre," *Time*, September 1, 1924, 17; *Minutes of the General Assembly of the Presbyterian Church in the U.S.A., Part II: Report to the Boards to the One Hundred and Forty-Eighth General Assembly*, Syracuse, New York, May 28-June 3, 1936, 119–121; "Seven Necessities for 1934," *Arkansas Baptist*, January 4, 1934, 8; "Sowing and Reaping for the Lord," *Arkansas Baptist*, February 15, 1934, 16.

23. Sparks, *Religion in Mississippi*, 163–165; Collier-Thomas, *Jesus, Jobs, and Justice*, 387–394; Harvey, *Freedom's Coming*, 67–77.

24. Phillips, *This Land, This Nation*, 75–148; Daniel, *Breaking the Land*, 91–109. See also Theodore Saloutos, *The American Farmer and the New Deal* (Ames: Iowa State University Press, 1982).

25. Woofter, *Landlord and Tenant*, 165, 237; Jess Gilbert, "Eastern Urban Liberals and Midwestern Agrarian Intellectuals: Two Group Portraits of Progressives in the New Deal Department of Agriculture," *Agricultural History* 74, no. 2 (Spring 2000): 162–180.

26. Johnson, Embree, and Alexander, *The Collapse of Cotton Tenancy*, 57, 64.

27. Dykeman and Stokely, *Seeds of Southern Change*, 216; Gilmore, *Defying Dixie*, 230–234; Holley, *Uncle Sam's Farmers*, 65–81.

28. Dunbar, *Against the Grain*, 18–83; Gilmore, *Defying Dixie*, 230–23; Phillips, *This Land, This Nation*, 120–122; Biles, *The South and the New Deal*, 48; Holley, *Uncle Sam's Farmers*, 180–181, Appendix.

29. Holley, *Uncle Sam's Farmers*, 179–186; Dykeman and Stokely, *Seeds of Southern Change*, 211–221.

30. Holley, *Uncle Sam's Farmers*, 179–186.

31. Hays, *Politics Is My Parish*, 73; "Report of Rural Church Commission," *Arkansas Baptist Advance*, December 12, 1929, 6–7; "Minutes of the Conference Held at Hendrix College, Conway, Arkansas," April 28, 1934, Folder 14, Box 24, Hays Papers.

32. Hays, "Farm Tenancy and the Christian Conscience," 4; Brooks Hays, "Memorandum for Mr. Porter [Paul Porter]," Folder 1, Box 24, Subseries 1, Series 2, Hays Papers; Hays, *Politics Is My Parish*, 71–73, 120–123; Baker, *Brooks Hays*, 35–37, 42–43; William J. Atto, "Brooks Hays and the New Deal" *(Arkansas) Historical Quarterly* 67, no. 2 (Summer 2008): 167–186.

33. Home Missions Council and Council of Women for Home Missions, *Home Missions and Social Trends: A Report of a Conference Held in the First Presbyterian Church, Baltimore, Maryland, January 9-10, 1939*, 38, Folder 28, Box 16, HMC, PHS; Edmund de S. Brunner, *Rural Social Trends* (New York: McGraw Hill,

1933), 212–213. Many of these reformers drew on H. Richard Niebuhr's *Social Sources of Denominationalism*, which characterized churches like COGIC as the religion of the disinherited. Niebuhr, *The Social Sources of Denominationalism* (New York: H. Holt & Co., 1929).

34. "Procedure: Family Selection: Dyess Colony," FERA Records; Azile Aaron to J. B. Lawson, Inter-Office Memorandum re. Family Selection for Dyess Colony, November 8, 1935, Folder 911:045 (Selection), Box 151, FERA Records.

35. Holley, 83–104; Donald Grubbs, *Cry from the Cotton: The Southern Tenant Farmers' Union and the New Deal.* (Fayetteville: University of Arkansas Press, 1999 [1971]), 30–61, 136–161.

36. "[STFU] Declaration of Principles and Constitution," n.d. [1934], Reel 1, STFU Papers; Arthur Brookins, Memphis, to FDR, November 3, 1935, Tennessee Folder, Box 30, CL; Roll, *Spirit of Rebellion*, 52–131; Roll and Gellman, *Gospel of the Working Class*, 41–70; Alex Lichtenstein, "Introduction: The Southern Tenant Farmers' Union: A Movement for Social Emancipation," in Kester, *Revolt Among the Sharecroppers* (Knoxville: University of Tennessee Press, 1997 [1936]), 15–57; Craig, *Religion and Radical Politics*, 83–173. Roll provides a sophisticated discussion of the STFU's religious orientation, based in a shared "agrarian cosmology" that inherited and built on the producerist vision of the populists (p. 4). He demonstrates that their faith gave the union its form and power, rather than merely driving its work. On populism and religion, see Creech, *Righteous Indignation*.

37. Jason Manthorne, "The View from the Cotton: Reconsidering the Southern Tenant Farmers' Union." *Agricultural History* 64 (Winter 2010): 20–45; Elizabeth Ann Payne, with photos by Louise Boyle, "The Lady Was a Sharecropper: Myrtle Lawrence and the Southern Tenant Farmers' Union," *Southern Cultures* 4 (Summer 1998): 5–27; Roll and Gellman, *Gospel of the Working Class*, 7–70.

38. Kester, *Revolt Among the Sharecroppers*, 56–57; Mitchell, *Mean Things*, 47–49; Clay East, interviewed by Sue Thrasher, September 22, 1973, Interview E-0003, Transcript, 12, 75–76; Southern Oral History Program Collection (#4007), SHC. Jason Manthorne calls into question many of the union's founding myths, particularly those surrounding its racial harmony. See "View from the Cotton," 20–45. Interracial union organizing was not new to the South. See, for instance, Honey, *Southern Labor and Black Civil Rights*, 67–92; Kelley, *Hammer and Hoe*, 1–118.

39. Kester, *Revolt Among the Sharecroppers*, 96; Dunbar, *Against the Grain*, 83–135; Roll and Gellman, *Gospel of the Working Class*, 1–72.

40. Grubbs, *Cry from the Cotton*, 64; Mitchell, *Mean Things*, 117; Manthorne, "View from the Cotton," 38–39; Roll and Gellman, *Gospel of the Working Class*, 41–83; Payne, "The Lady Was a Sharecropper," 10–16; Payne's study of the problematic treatment of Lawrence and other poor union members illuminates the class-based divisions between the union's leaders and its members. On Handcox and his legacy, see Honey, *Sharecropper's Troubadour*.

41. Howard Kester, "Acts of Tyranny and Terror Committed Against Innocent Men, Women and Children of the Southern Tenant Farmers' Union in Northeast Arkansas," 1935, Reel 1, STFU Papers; "Affidavit of Arthur Brookings [sic] of Memphis, Tenn," 1935, Reel 1, STFU Papers; H. L. Mitchell, "The Southern Tenant Farmers' Union in 1935," 1, Reel 1, STFU Papers; *Southern Tenant Farmers' Union Convention Proceedings: Official Report of Second Annual Convention*, January 3–6, 1936, Labor Temple, Little Rock, 1, Reel 1, STFU Papers; E. B. McKinney to H. L. Mitchell, March 8, 1936, Reel 1, STFU Papers. Because of threats of violence, the union membership remained somewhat secret. Organizers later acknowledged that they inflated the membership numbers (Mitchell, *Mean Things*, 82).

42. Manthorne, "View from the Cotton," 34–37; William R. Amberson, "The New Deal for Share-Croppers," *The Nation*, February 13, 1935, 185–187; H. L. Mitchell, "Organizing Southern Share-Croppers," *The New Republic*, October 3, 1934, 217–218; John Herling, "Field Notes from Arkansas," *The Nation*, April 10, 1935, 419–420; "AAA Piles Misery on Share Croppers," *New York Times*, April 15, 1935, 6; "Arkansas Violence Laid to Landlords," *New York Times*, April 16, 1935, 18; "Norman Thomas Visits the Cotton Fields," March 13–15, 1935, Reel 1, STFU Papers; " 'Run Off Farms,' Tenants Declare," *New York Times*, April 20, 1935, 5; Dorothy Day, "Sharecroppers"; Norman Thomas, *The Plight of the Share-Cropper* (New York: League for Industrial Democracy, Marstin Press, 1934).

43. Holley, *Uncle Sam's Farmers*, 82–104, 190–195; Mitchell, *Mean Things*, 101, 173–178; Roll, *Spirit of Rebellion*, 173–180.

44. "The Sharecroppers' Own Farm," *Baltimore Sun*, April 11, 1937, 84; "Evicted Croppers, Negro and White, Start Co-op Farm," *Catholic Worker* 4, no. 3 (July 1936): 1, 3; "Group Sponsored by Quakers Helps Youth Make Contacts," *Christian Science Monitor*, July 27, 1937, 3; Jonathan Mitchell, "Cabins in the Cotton," *New Republic*, September 22, 1937, 175–177; "Delta Co-operative Demonstrates New Way of Life," *Economic Justice* 6, no. 1 (October 1937): 2; "The Delta Cooperative Farm: Sherwood Eddy's Project in Mississippi," *Atlanta Daily World*, December 26, 1937, 6; "Co-op Farmers Live in Same Street, Use 'Mr.' and 'Mrs.,' " *Baltimore Afro-American*, January 1, 1938, 5; Daniels, *A Southerner Discovers the South*, 148–155, 159; Ferguson, "Race and the Remaking of the Rural South," 64–254; Smith, *Trouble in Goshen*, 114–142.

45. Mitchell, *Mean Things*, 171–278; Roll, *Spirit of Rebellion*, 106–180.

46. Anthea Butler stresses Mallory's central role in COGIC's mainstream growth and its maintenance of boundaries despite a new emphasis on education and middle-class values. For the most part, I follow her argument here. Butler, *Women of the Church of God in Christ*, 96–116.

47. William A. Clark, "Sanctification in Negro Religion," *Social Forces* 15, no. 4 (May 1937): 544–551 (quotations on 549). See also Mays and Nicholson, *The Negro's Church*. Historians have debated to what degree early pentecostals were

in fact poor or marginal. See Stephens, *The Fire Spreads*; Sutton, *Aimee Semple McPherson*; Wacker, *Heaven Below*; Blumhofer, *Restoring the Faith*.

48. Mallory first went to Lexington in 1926 but had to leave when she married a non–church member. She returned in 1930. On COGIC's history, see Clemmons, *Bishop C. H. Mason and the Roots of the Church of God in Christ*, 62–100; White Jr., "In the Beginning, There Stood Two: Arkansas Roots of the Black Holiness Movement," 20–22. On education in Mississippi, see McMillen, *Dark Journey*, 81–83; "Public Education in Mississippi," *School and Society* 51, no. 1321 (April 20, 1940), 510; Federal Writers' Project, *Mississippi*, 118–128. On black education in the region before the Depression, see Katherine Mellen Charron, *Freedom's Teacher: The Life of Septima Clark* (Chapel Hill: University of North Carolina Press, 2010); Adam Fairclough, *A Class of Their Own: Black Teachers in the Segregated South* (Cambridge, MA: Belknap Press of Harvard University Press, 2007); James D. Anderson, *The Education of Blacks in the South, 1860-1935* (Chapel Hill: University of North Carolina Press, 1988); Christopher M. Span, *From Cotton Field to Schoolhouse: African American Education in Mississippi, 1862-1875* (Chapel Hill: University of North Carolina Press, 2009); Heather Andrea Williams, *Self-Taught: African American Education in Slavery and Freedom* (Chapel Hill: University of North Carolina Press, 2007).

49. "Do Not Fail to Read This," *The Whole Truth*, 1982 Souvenir Edition, reprint of an edition from late 1932, 6, Folder 4, Box 5, Dupree Collection. On Mallory, see Dovie Marie Simmons and Olivia L. Martin, *Down Behind the Sun: The Story of Arenia Cornelia Mallory* (Memphis, TN: Riverside Press, 1983), 2–7; Butler, *Women of the Church of God in Christ*, 98–104.

50. "Do Not Fail to Read This,"; Simmons and Martin, *Down Behind the Sun*, 18–21; McMillen, *Dark Journey*, 97–98; Butler, *Women in the Church of God in Christ*, 101–103; Hortense Powdermaker, *Stranger and Friend: The Way of an Anthropologist* (New York: W. W. Norton & Company, 1966), 172. On singers as fundraisers, see Alfterdeen B. Harrison, *Piney Woods School: An Oral History* (Jackson: University Press of Mississippi, 1982), 74; Andrew Ward, *Dark Midnight When I Rise: The Story of the Fisk Jubilee Singers* (New York: Amistad, 2001); Claire Nee Nelson, "Louise Thompson Patterson and the Southern Roots of the Popular Front," in *Women Shaping the South: Creating and Confronting Change*, ed. Angela Boswell and Judith N. McArthur (Columbia: University of Missouri Press, 2006), 204–228.

51. Simmons and Martin, "Down Behind the Sun," 19–21; "Florida News," *Chicago Defender*, May 17, 1930, 20; "Pennsylvania," *Chicago Defender*, September 5, 1931, 15; "Ohio State News," *Chicago Defender*, June 18, 1932, 19; "Arizona State," *Chicago Defender*, July 1, 1933, 22; "Educator Describes Work in Mississippi," *New York Amsterdam News*, September 1, 1934, 7; Butler, *Women in the Church of God in Christ*, 101–116.

52. Butler, *Women of the Church of God in Christ*, 109–124; Collier-Thomas, *Jesus, Jobs, and Justice*, 381–385. Butler describes Bethune and Mallory's relationship in detail and argues that this relationship was significant for both Mallory and COGIC.

53. Eleanor Roosevelt, "My Day," September 29, 1938; Butler, *Women in the Church of God in Christ*, 118–123; Collier-Thomas, *Jesus, Jobs, and Justice*, 381–385.

54. US Bureau of the Census, *Special Reports: Religious Bodies, 1936, vol. II* (Washington, DC: Government Printing Office, 1941), 445; *Memphis City Directory*, 1936, 1417; *Memphis City Directory*, 1931, 1613; Thomas O. Fuller, *The Story of the Church Life Among Negroes in Memphis, Tennessee for Students and Workers, 1900–1938* (Memphis, TN: n.p., 1938), 34–35; Tucker, *Black Pastors and Leaders*, 99–100. On the problems with the 1936 Census of Religious Bodies in the South, see Christiano, "Numbering Israel" and Rodney Stark, "The Reliability of Historical United States Census Data on Religion."

55. Butler, *Women in the Church of God in Christ*, 117–155.

56. Brinkley, *The End of Reform*, 15–30; Gilmore, *Defying Dixie*, 230–233; Welky, *The Thousand-Year Flood*.

57. David L. Carlton and Peter A. Coclanis, *Confronting Southern Poverty in the Great Depression: The Report on the Economic Conditions in the South with Related Documents* (Boston: Bedford Books, 1996 [1938]), 1–2, 19–32, 54–59, 63.

58. Plautus I. Lipsey, "Looking at the World," *Mississippi Baptist Record*, March 17, 1938, 1.

59. *Annual of the Southern Baptist Convention*, 1935, Memphis, Tennessee, 57, 59; Bailey, *Southern White Protestantism in the Twentieth Century*, 124–125; Stricklin, *A Genealogy of Dissent: Southern Baptist Protest in the Twentieth Century* (Lexington: University Press of Kentucky, 1999), 25–26.

60. "Southern Baptists and Social Service," *Mississippi Baptist Record*, May 30, 1935, 4; "The Social Service Program of Jesus," *Mississippi Baptist Record*, August 8, 1935, 9.

61. "Southern Baptists Table Jesus," *National Baptist Voice*, June 13, 1936, 2.

62. *Annual of the Southern Baptist Convention*, 1937, New Orleans, Louisiana, 101.

63. Ibid., 102; David Sehat and Winnifred Fallers Sullivan, among others, describe the conflicted and problematic nature of "religious freedom" as a concept. See David Sehat, *The Myth of American Religious Freedom* (New York: Oxford University Press, 2011); Winnifred Fallers Sullivan, *The Impossibility of Religious Freedom* (Princeton, NJ: Princeton University Press, 2007).

64. *Annual of the Southern Baptist Convention*, 1938, Richmond, Virginia, 117.

65. J. M. Dawson, "Arguments for Including Churches in the Social Security Tax Answered," 2, Box 29, William M. Whittington Collection #MUM00476, UM. See also "Petition to the Members of the 76th Congress by the State Secretaries Association of the Southern Baptist Convention, Tampa, Florida, February 19, 1939, Re. H. R. 101," Box 29, Whittington Collection; *Annual of the Southern*

Baptist Convention, 1938, Richmond, Virginia, 117; Bill J. Leonard, *Baptists in America* (New York: Columbia University Press, 2007), 157.

66. Britton, *Two Centuries of Methodism in Arkansas, 1800-2000*, 215–217; Morris Lee Davis, *The Methodist Unification: Christianity and the Politics of the Jim Crow Era* (New York: New York University Press, 2008).

67. Allen L. Rogers, *Why I Resigned as General Superintendent of the Sunday School of Bethel Methodist Episcopal Church, South*, pamphlet, 1938, Folder 10, Reverend N. G. Augustus Papers, SMMSS76-1, UM; "The Negro and the United Methodist Church," *(Norfolk) New Journal and Guide*, May 27, 1939, 8; Britton, *Two Centuries of Methodism in Arkansas, 1800-2000*, 215–217; Paul A. Carter, "The Negro and Methodist Union," *Church History* 21, no. 1 (March 1952): 55–70.

68. "To the Joint Committee on Sharecropper Work," October 7, 1940, Folder 13, Box 18, Home Missions Council of North America. On Bogard and the American Baptist Association, see Pratt, *The Father of Modern Landmarkism*. On La Forge, see Roll, *Spirit of Rebellion*, 123–129.

69. Moreton, *To Serve God and Wal-Mart*, 164–166; Dochuk, *From Bible Belt to Sun Belt*, 60–66. Both Moreton and Dochuk describe the growing importance of Benson and Harding to corporate fundamentalism.

EPILOGUE

1. Kincheloe, *Research Memorandum on Religion in the Depression*, 53, 58.

2. Ibid., 1.

3. The literature on secularization in the twentieth century is extensive, and I don't mean to engage here in debates about the meaning of the religious or the secular—I mean only to indicate that the transfer of services from church to state in the 1930s defies easy categorization. For more extensive discussion of these processes in the twentieth-century United States and related debates about the meaning of religious freedom, see Chad Seales, *The Secular Spectacle: Performing Religion in a Southern Town* (New York: Oxford University Press, 2014); Sehat, *The Myth of American Religious Freedom*; Kathryn Lofton, *Oprah: Gospel of an Icon* (Berkeley: University of California Press, 2011); Tisa Wenger, *We Have a Religion: The 1920s Pueblo Indian Dance Controversy and American Religious Freedom* (Chapel Hill: University of North Carolina Press, 2009); Sullivan, *The Impossibility of Religious Freedom*.

4. Bureau of the Census, *Census of Religious Bodies: 1926, Part I* (Washington, DC: Government Printing Office, 1930): 466–467, 580–582, 632–634. See the appendix for additional details. The 1926 census is generally deemed most accurate. On the reliability of the Census of Religious Bodies generally and the 1936 census particularly, see Christiano, "Numbering Israel," 341–370; Stark, "The Reliability of Historical United States Census Data on Religion," 91–95; Robert Wuthnow, *Red*

State Religion: Faith and Politics in America's Heartland (Princeton, NJ: Princeton University Press, 2012), 164–165.

5. Statistics from Wuthnow, *The Restructuring of American Religion*, 26. On broader transformations to American Christianity from the 1930s to the 1940s, see Hedstrom, *The Rise of Liberal Religion*, 115–171; Dochuk, *From Bible Belt to Sun Belt*, 46–55; Dan McKanan, *Prophetic Encounters: Religion and the American Radical Tradition* (Boston: Beacon Press, 2011), 136–173; Joseph Kip Kosek, *Acts of Conscience: Christian Nonviolence and Modern American Democracy* (New York: Columbia University Press, 2009), 1–190; Marty, *The Noise of Conflict*, 303–390.

6. Ahlstrom, *A Religious History of the American People*, 952; Wuthnow, *The Restructuring of American Religion: Society and Faith Since World War II*, 14–37. Statistics on 36–37.

7. Hollinger, *After Cloven Tongues of Fire*, 56–76; Sutton, *American Apocalypse*, 285–290; Tona J. Hangen, *Redeeming the Dial: Radio, Religion, and Popular Culture in America* (Chapel Hill: University of North Carolina Press, 2002), 112–158 (Crowley appears on 133–134). On postwar growth and the relative power of the mainline and the right, also see Kruse, *One Nation Under God*; Sutton, *American Apocalypse*; Coffman, *The Christian Century and the Rise of the Protestant Mainline*; Dochuk, *From Bible Belt to Sun Belt*; Kevin M. Schultz, *Tri-Faith America: How Catholics and Jews Held Postwar America to Its Protestant Promise* (New York: Oxford University Press, 2011); Axel R. Schäfer, "The Cold War State and the Resurgence of Evangelicalism: A Study of the Public Funding of Religion Since 1945, *Radical History Review* 99 (Fall 2007): 19–49; Wuthnow, *The Restructuring of American Religion*.

8. Axel R. Schäfer, *Piety and Public Funding: Evangelicals and the State in Modern America* (Philadelphia: University of Pennsylvania Press, 2012), 25–59.

9. Roll and Gellman, *Gospel of the Working Class*, 151–166; Jonathan P. Herzog, *The Spiritual-Industrial Complex: America's Religious Battle Against Communism in the Early Cold War* (New York: Oxford University Press, 2011), 104–108. See also Elizabeth A. Fones-Wolf and Ken Fones-Wolf, *Struggle for the Soul of the Post-War South: White Evangelical Protestants and Operation Dixie* (Urbana: University of Illinois Press, 2015); Kruse, *One Nation Under God*; Molly Worthen, *Apostles of Reason: The Crisis of Authority in American Evangelicalism* (New York: Oxford University Press, 2013); Jason Stevens, *God-Fearing and Free: A Spiritual History of America's Cold War* (Cambridge, MA: Harvard University Press, 2010); Grem, "The Blessings of Business"; Hammond, "God's Business Men"; William Inboden, *Religion and American Foreign Policy, 1945-1960: The Soul of Containment* (New York: Cambridge University Press, 2008); Elizabeth Fones-Wolf, *Selling Free Enterprise: The Business Assault on Labor and Liberalism, 1945-1960* (Urbana: University of Illinois Press, 1994).

10. Sitkoff, *A New Deal for Blacks*, 243–244; White, *The Rise to Respectability*, 113–130 (on King at Mason Temple, see 128–129). See also Savage, *Their Spirits Walk Beside Us*; Charles Marsh, *God's Long Summer: Stories of Faith and Civil Rights* (Princeton, NJ: Princeton University Press, 2008); David Chappell, *A Stone of Hope: Prophetic Religion and the Death of Jim Crow* (Chapel Hill: University of North Carolina Press, 2005); Timothy B. Tyson, *Blood Done Sign My Name: A True Story* (New York: Crown Publishers, 2004); Mark F. Newman, *Divine Agitators: The Delta Ministry and Civil Rights in Mississippi* (Athens: University of Georgia Press, 2004).

11. Russell C. Barbour, "The Wickedness of American Christianity," *National Baptist Voice*, November 12, 1938, 2; Roll and Gellman, *Gospel of the Working Class*, 151–170; Harvey, *Freedom's Coming*, 107–217; Martin, *Howard Kester*, 109–162. An essential work on white religious resistance to civil rights is Carolyn Dupont, *Mississippi Praying: Southern White Evangelicals and the Civil Rights Movement, 1945–1975* (New York: New York University Press, 2013).

12. Jane Dailey, "Sex, Segregation, and the Sacred after Brown," *Journal of American History* 91, no. 1 (June 2004): 119–144; Dupont, *Mississippi Praying*, 63–78; Harvey, 169–217.

13. Ward, *Defending White Democracy*, 168–183; The American Presidency Project, University of California at Santa Barbara, http://www.presidency.ucsb.edu/showelection.php?year=1964; Schäfer, *Piety and Public Funding*, 123–162.

14. Schäfer, *Piety and Public Funding*, 163–214; Bartkowski and Regis, *Charitable Choices*, 1–59.

15. Such narratives proliferated in the welfare reform debates of the 1990s. The most successful example is Marvin Olasky, *The Tragedy of American Compassion* (Washington, D.C.: Regnery, 1992). More recent examples include Burton Folsom, Jr., *New Deal or Raw Deal? How FDR's Economic Legacy Has Damaged America* (New York: Threshhold Editions, 2008); Amity Shlaes, *The Forgotten Man: A New History of the Great Depression* (New York: Harper, 2007); Jim Powell, *FDR's Folly: How Roosevelt and His New Deal Prolonged the Great Depression* (New York: Three Rivers Press, 2003).

16. On the racialized and gendered language surrounding welfare—and its origins in New Deal and Great Society policy—see Ange-Marie Hancock, *The Politics of Disgust: The Public Identity of the Welfare Queen* (New York: New York University Press, 2004); Gordon, *Pitied But Not Entitled*.

17. Theda Skocpol and Vanessa Williamson, *The Tea Party and the Remaking of Republican Conservatism* (New York: Oxford University Press, 2013); Steven Brill, *America's Bitter Pill: Money, Politics, Back-Room Deals, and the Fight to Fix Our Broken Health Care System* (New York: Random House, 2015).

18. Franklin Graham, " 'This Week' Transcript: God and Government," ABC News website, http://abcnews.go.com/ThisWeek/week-transcript-god-government/story?id=13446238#.TySHQ-NSSso [accessed January 28, 2012].

Bibliography

MANUSCRIPT COLLECTIONS
Chapel Hill, North Carolina

Southern Historical Collection, Louis Round Wilson Library, University of North
Carolina
Fellowship of Southern Churchmen Papers
Howard Anderson Kester Papers
Southern Oral History Program Collection Interviews

Clinton, Mississippi

Mississippi Baptist Historical Collection, Leland Speed Library, Mississippi College
Mid-Delta Association File
Washington County Association File

College Park, Maryland

National Archives and Records Administration
Farm Security Administration and Predecessors, Project Records 1935–1940
Federal Emergency Relief Administration Central Files, 1933–1936
Civil Works Administration Central Files

Decatur, Georgia

C. Benton Kline Jr. Special Collections and Archives, John Bulow Campbell Library,
Columbia Theological Seminary
Ladies' Church Histories
Minutes of the Department of Home Missions,

Presbyterian Church in the United States

Fayetteville, Arkansas

Special Collections, David W. Mullins Library, University of Arkansas
 Lawrence Brooks Hays Papers
 Works Progress Administration Church Records

Hyde Park, New York

Franklin D. Roosevelt Presidential Library and Museum
 Eleanor Roosevelt Pamphlet Collection
 Eleanor Roosevelt Papers
 Gardner Jackson Papers
 Harry L. Hopkins Papers
 President's Personal File—Clergy Letters

Jackson, Mississippi

Catholic Diocese of Mississippi
 Bishop Richard Gerow Files and Correspondence
J. B. Cain Archives of Mississippi Methodism, Millsaps-Wilson Library, Millsaps
 College
 Records of the North Mississippi Conference of the Methodist Episcopal
 Church, South
 Records of the Upper Mississippi Conference of the Methodist Episcopal Church
Mississippi Department of Archives and History
 Federal Writers' Project Negro Source Material
 St. Andrew's Episcopal Church Records

Little Rock, Arkansas

Arkansas History Commission and State Archives
 African-American Baptist Associations—Arkansas, microfilm

Memphis, Tennessee

Memphis and Shelby County Room, Benjamin L. Hooks Central Library
 African American Church Histories
 Clippings Files: Memphis Charities, Memphis Community Fund, Salvation
 Army, Travelers' Aid Society, St. Vincent de Paul Society
 Edward Hull Crump Collection

Walter Chandler Papers
Samuel Watkins Overton Papers
Mississippi Valley Collection, Ned R. McWherter Library, University of Memphis
Delta Cooperative Farm Records
Samuel A. Owen Papers
Samuel Watkins Overton Papers
Southern Tenant Farmers' Union Papers
William Amberson Papers

Nashville, Tennessee

Disciples of Christ Historical Society Library and Archives
Alva Taylor Papers
Southern Baptist Historical Library and Archives
Arkansas Baptist Convention Annuals
Pamphlet Collection
Special Collections, John Hope and Aurelia E. Franklin Library, Fisk University
Charles S. Johnson Papers

New Haven, Connecticut

Special Collections, Divinity School Library, Yale University
George Sherwood Eddy Papers
Social Ethics Pamphlet Collection

Oxford, Mississippi

Department of Archives and Special Collections, J. D. Williams Library, University
of Mississippi
Mamie Lee Ratliff Finger Collection
Mississippi Cities and Towns Collection
William M. Whittington Collection

Philadelphia, Pennsylvania

Presbyterian Historical Society
Federal Council of Churches of Christ in America Collection
Home Missions Council of North America Collection

New York, New York

Schomburg Center for Research in Black Culture, New York Public Library

Sherry Sherrod Dupree African-American Pentecostal and Holiness Collection

Starkville, Mississippi

Special Collections, Mitchell Memorial Library, Mississippi State University
A. Eugene Cox Collection
Delta Pine and Land Company Records

MICROFILM COLLECTION

Southern Tenant Farmers' Union Papers

JOURNALS AND NEWSPAPERS

American Mercury
Arkansas Baptist
(Arkansas) Baptist Advance
(Arkansas) Baptist and Commoner
Atlanta Constitution
Atlanta Daily World
Baltimore Afro-American
Baltimore Sun
Catholic Worker
Chicago Defender
Chicago Tribune
Christian Rural Fellowship Bulletin
Christian Science Monitor
The Gospel Light
Literary Digest
Memphis Commercial Appeal
Memphis Councilor
Memphis Press-Scimitar
Memphis World
(Mississippi) Baptist Record
The Nation
National Baptist Union-Review
National Baptist Voice
New Orleans Christian Advocate
New Republic
New York Times
(Norfolk) New Journal and Guide
Pittsburgh Courier

Prophetic Religion
Radical Religion
Ruleville Record
School and Society
Social Forces
Star of Zion
Time
Washington Post
World Tomorrow

PUBLISHED PRIMARY SOURCES AND GOVERNMENT DOCUMENTS

Abrams, Ray H. *Preachers Present Arms*. New York: Round Table Press, 1933.

Agee, James. *Let Us Now Praise Famous Men*. Boston, MA: Houghton Mifflin Company, 1941.

Alldredge, E.P. *Southern Baptist Handbook, 1931*. Nashville, TN: Sunday School Board of the Southern Baptist Convention, 1931.

Amberson, William R. "Report of Survey made by Memphis Chapter L.I.D. and the Tyronza Socialist Party under direction of Wm. R. Amberson." In *Plight of the Share-Cropper*, by Norman Thomas. New York: League for Industrial Democracy, Marstin Press, 1934.

Babson, Roger. *A Revival Is Coming*. New York: Fleming & Revell Company, 1936.

Bailey, Liberty Hyde. *The Country-Life Movement in the United States*. New York: Macmillan, 1911.

———. *Report of the Country Life Commission*. Washington, DC: Government Printing Office, 1909.

Baird, Enid. *Public and Private Aid in 116 Urban Areas, 1929-1938, with Supplement for 1939 and 1940*. Public Assistance Report No. 3. Washington, DC: Federal Security Agency, Social Security Board, 1942.

Baker, O. E. "Rural and Urban Distribution of the Population in the United States." *Annals of the American Academy of Political and Social Science* 188 (November 1936): 264–279.

Bolsterli, Margaret Jones. *During Wind and Rain: The Jones Family Farm in the Arkansas Delta, 1848-2006*. Fayetteville: University of Arkansas Press, 2008.

Boyle, James E. "Memphis Merchants Exchange Clearing Association." *Annals of the American Academy of Political and Social Science* 155 (May 1931): 173–175.

Brown, Josephine Chapin. *Public Relief, 1929-1939*. New York: Octagon Books, 1971.

Brunner, Edmund de Schweinitz. *Rural Social Trends*. New York: McGraw Hill, 1933.

Brunner, Edmund de Schweinitz, and Irving Lorge. *Rural Trends in Depression Years: A Survey of Village Centered Agricultural Communities, 1930-1936*. New York: Columbia University Press, 1937.

Bunche, Ralph J. *The Political Status of the Negro in the Age of FDR*. Edited and with an introduction by Dewey W. Grantham. Chicago: University of Chicago Press, 1973 [1940].

Butterfield, Kenyon L. *The Country Church and the Rural Problem: The Carew Lectures at Hartford Theological Seminary, 1909*. Chicago: University of Chicago Press, 1917.

Caldwell, Erskine. *Tobacco Road*. New York: Scribner, 1932.

———. *You Have Seen Their Faces*. New York: Modern Age Books, 1937.

Carlton, David L., and Peter A. Coclanis. *Confronting Southern Poverty in the Great Depression: The Report on the Economic Conditions in the South with Related Documents*. Boston: Bedford Books, 1996 [1938].

Clark, William A. "Sanctification in Negro Religion." *Social Forces* 15, no. 4 (May 1937): 544–551.

Cobb, James C., ed. *The Mississippi Delta and the World: The Memoirs of David L. Cohn*. Baton Rouge: Louisiana State University Press, 1995.

Daniels, Jonathan. *A Southerner Discovers the South*. New York: Macmillan, 1938.

Davis, Allison, Burleigh Gardner, and Mary R. Gardner. *Deep South: A Social Anthropological Study of Caste and Class*. Chicago: University of Chicago Press, 1941.

Dickins, Dorothy. "A Nutrition Investigation of Negro Tenants in the Yazoo Mississippi Delta." Mississippi Agricultural Experiment Station Bulletin 254, A & M College. Starkville, MS, 1928.

———. "Food and Health," Agricultural Experiment Station Bulletin 255, July 1928.

Dollard, John. *Caste and Class in a Southern Town*. Garden City, NY: Doubleday, 1937.

Dykeman, Wilma, and James Stokely. *Seeds of Southern Change: The Life of Will Alexander*. New York: W. W. Norton, 1962.

Earp, Edwin L. *The Rural Church Movement*. New York: Methodist Book Concern, 1914.

Federal Council of the Churches of Christ in America. *Our Economic Life in the Light of Christian Ideals*. New York: Association Press, 1932.

Federal Writers' Project. *Mississippi: A Guide to the Magnolia State*. 2nd ed. New York: Hastings House Publishers, 1949.

Federal Writers' Project. *Arkansas: A Guide to the State*. New York: Hastings House Publishers, 1941.

Fry, C. Luther. *The U. S. Looks at Its Churches*. New York: Institute of Social and Religious Research, 1930.

Fuller, Thomas O. *The Story of the Church Life Among Negroes in Memphis, Tennessee for Students and Workers, 1900-1938*. Memphis, TN: n.p., 1938.

Gill, Corrington. "Unemployment Relief," *American Economic Review* 25, no. 1 (March 1935): 176–185.

Goldberger, Joseph, and Edgar Sydenstricker. "Pellagra in the Mississippi Flood Area: Report of an Inquiry Relating to the Prevalence of Pellagra in the Area

Affected by the Overflow of the Mississippi and Its Tributaries in Tennessee, Arkansas, Mississippi, and Louisiana in the Spring of 1927." *Public Health Reports* 42, no. 44 (November 4, 1927): 2706–2725.

Hays, Brooks. *A Southern Moderate Speaks.* Chapel Hill: University of North Carolina Press, 1959.

———. *Politics Is My Parish: An Autobiography.* Baton Rouge: Louisiana State University Press, 1981.

Holley, William C., Ellen Winston, and T. J. Woofter. *The Plantation South: 1934-1937.* Washington, DC: Government Printing Office: 1940.

Jent, John William. *The Challenge of the Country Church.* Nashville, TN: Sunday School Board of the SBC, 1924.

———. *Rural Church Problems.* Shawnee: Oklahoma Baptist University Press, 1935.

Johnson, Charles Spurgeon. *Growing up in the Black Belt: Negro Youth in the Rural South.* Washington, DC: American Council on Education, 1941.

———. *Shadow of the Plantation.* Chicago: University of Chicago Press, 1934.

Johnson, Charles Spurgeon, Edwin R. Embree, and Will Winton Alexander. *The Collapse of Cotton Tenancy: Summary of Field Studies & Statistical Surveys 1933-35.* Chapel Hill: University of North Carolina Press, 1935.

Keating, John McLead. *A History of the Yellow Fever: The Yellow Fever Epidemic of 1878, in Memphis, Tenn.* Memphis, TN: Printed for the Howard Association, 1879.

Kester, Howard. *Revolt Among the Sharecroppers.* Knoxville: University of Tennessee Press, 1997 [1936].

Kincheloe, Samuel C. *Research Memorandum on Religion in the Depression.* New York: Social Science Research Council, 1937.

Landis, Benson Y., and George Edmund Haynes. *Cotton-Growing Communities Study No. 2: Case Studies of 10 Rural Communities and 10 Plantations in Arkansas.* New York: Federal Council of Churches, 1935.

Landis, Benson Y., and John D. Willard. *Rural Adult Education.* New York: MacMillan Company, 1933.

Lee, George W. *Beale Street: Where the Blues Began.* College Park, MD: McGrath Publishing Company, 1969 [1934].

Lively, C. E. *Rural Migration in the United States.* Washington, DC: Government Printing Office, 1939.

Lynd, Robert Staughton, and Helen Merrell Lynd. *Middletown: A Study in Modern American Culture.* New York: Harcourt, Brace, and Co., 1929.

Martin, John L. "Income Payments to Individuals, by States, 1929-38." *Survey of Current Business* 20, no. 4 (April 1940): 8–15.

Mays, Benjamin E., and Joseph William Nicholson. *The Negro's Church.* New York: Institute of Social and Religious Research, 1933.

Memphis City Directories, 1929–1941.

Mitchell, H. L. *Mean Things Happening in This Land: The Life and Times of H. L. Mitchell, Cofounder of the Southern Tenant Farmers' Union.* Montclair, NJ: Allanheld, Osmun, 1979.

———. "The Founding and Early History of the Southern Tenant Farmers Union." *Arkansas Historical Quarterly* 32, no. 4 (Winter 1973): 342–369.

Moley, Raymond. *After Seven Years.* New York: Harper & Brothers, 1939.

Moody, Anne. *Coming of Age in Mississippi.* New York: Dell, 1968.

Newell, Bertha Payne. "Social Work of Women's Organizations in the Churches: I. Methodist Episcopal Church South." *Journal of Social Forces* 1, no. 3 (March 1923): 310–314.

Niebuhr, H. Richard. *The Social Sources of Denominationalism.* New York: H. Holt & Co., 1929.

Niebuhr, Reinhold. *Moral Man and Immoral Society: A Study in Ethics and Politics.* New York: Charles Scribner's Sons, 1932.

O'Brien, Robert W. "Status of Chinese in the Mississippi Delta." *Social Forces* 19, no. 3 (March 1941): 386–390.

Oppenheimer, Ella. *Infant Mortality in Memphis.* Washington, DC: US Department of Labor, 1937.

Percy, William Alexander. *Lanterns on the Levee: Recollections of a Planter's Son.* Baton Rouge: Louisiana State University Press, 1941.

Pope, Liston. *Millhands and Preachers: A Study of Gastonia.* New Haven, CT: Yale University Press, 1942.

Powdermaker, Hortense. *After Freedom: A Cultural Study in the Deep South.* Madison: University of Wisconsin Press, 1993 [1939].

———.*Stranger and Friend: The Way of an Anthropologist.* New York: W. W. Norton & Company, 1966.

Raper, Arthur F. *The Tragedy of Lynching.* Mineola, NY: Dover, 2003 [1933].

Roosevelt, Eleanor. *My Day: The Best of Eleanor Roosevelt's Acclaimed Newspaper Columns, 1936-1962.* Edited by David Emblidge. New York: Da Capo Press, 2001.

Ryan, James H. "National Catholic Welfare Council." *Studies: An Irish Quarterly Review* 12, no. 45 (March 1923): 120–131.

Ryan, John Augustine. *Social Doctrine in Action: A Personal History.* New York: Harper & Brothers, 1941.

Shaw, Nate. *All God's Dangers: The Life of Nate Shaw.* New York: Knopf, 1974.

Smith, Frank Ellis. *Congressman from Mississippi.* New York: Pantheon Books, 1964.

Smith, Lillian. *Strange Fruit.* 4th ed. New York: Mariner Books, 1992 [1944].

Snyder, Howard. "Negro Migration and the Cotton Crop." *North American Review* 219, no. 818 (January 1924): 21–29.

Steinbeck, John. *The Grapes of Wrath.* John Steinbeck Centennial Edition. New York: Penguin Books, 2002 [1939].

Street, Elwood. "Professional Guidance for the Small Town Community Chest." *Social Forces* 5, no. 4 (June 1927): 639–640.

Stuenkel, Francelia. "The Organization of Social Service Exchanges." *Social Service Review* 1, no. 3 (September 1927): 414–442.

Thomas, Norman. *The Plight of the Share-Cropper*. New York: League for Industrial Democracy, Marstin Press, 1934.

Todd, Arthur J. "Some Sociological Principles Underlying the Community Chest Movement." *Social Forces* 10, no. 4 (May 1932): 476–484.

Turner, Howard A. *A Graphic Summary of Farm Tenure: United States Department of Agriculture Miscellaneous Publication no. 261.* Washington, DC: US Department of Agriculture, 1936.

———. "Farm Tenancy Distribution and Trends in the United States." *Law and Contemporary Problems* 4, no. 4 (October 1937): 431–432.

US Department of Commerce. Bureau of the Census. *Census of the United States, 1920-1940.* Washington, DC: Government Printing Office.

US Department of Commerce. Bureau of the Census. *Special Reports: Religious Bodies, 1916, 1926, 1936.* Washington, DC: Government Printing Office.

US Department of Commerce. Bureau of the Census. *Statistical Abstract of the United States, 1941.* Washington, DC: Government Printing Office, 1942.

US Department of Commerce. Bureau of the Census. "Chapter D: Labor," *Historical Statistics of the United States: Colonial Times to 1970,* vol. 1 (Washington, DC: Government Printing Office, 1975.

US Department of Labor, Children's Bureau, *Mothers' Aid, 1931,* Bureau Publication 220. Washington, DC: Government Printing Office, 1933.

Watson, Frank Dekker. *The Charity Organization Movement in the United States: A Study in American Philanthropy.* New York: MacMillan, 1922.

Webb, John N. *The Transient Unemployed: A Description and Analysis of the Transient Relief Population.* Washington, DC: Works Progress Administration, 1935.

Whiting, Theodore E., and WPA. *Final Statistical Report of the Federal Emergency Relief Administration.* Washington, DC: Government Printing Office, 1942.

Winslow, Emma A. *Trends in Different Types of Public and Private Relief in Urban Areas, 1929-35.* Washington, DC: Government Printing Office, 1937.

Winslow, Helen M. *Official Register and Directory of the Women's Clubs in America,* vol. 24. Boston: Helen M. Winslow, 1922.

Woodson, Carter Godwin. *The Rural Negro.* Washington, DC: Association for the Study of Negro Life and History, 1930.

Woofter, T. J., Jr. *Landlord and Tenant on the Cotton Plantation.* Washington, DC: US Works Progress Administration, 1936.

———. *Negro Problems in Cities.* Garden City, NY: Doubleday, Doran & Company, 1928.

Work, John W., Lewis Wade Jones, and Samuel C. Adams. *Lost Delta Found: Rediscovering the Fisk University-Library of Congress Coahoma County Study, 1941-1942.* Edited by Robert Gordon and Bruce Nemerov. Nashville, TN: Vanderbilt University Press, 2005.

Works Progress Administration. *Inventory of the Church Archives of Arkansas: Church of Christ, Scientist.* Little Rock: Arkansas Historical Records Survey, 1941.

Wright, Richard A. *Black Boy.* (The Restored Text Established by the Library of America). New York: Harper Perennial Modern Classics, 1998.

SECONDARY BOOKS AND ARTICLES

Abramovitz, Mimi. *Regulating the Lives of Women: Social Welfare Policy from Colonial Times to the Present.* Boston: South End Press, 1988.

Ahlstrom, Sydney E. *A Religious History of the American People.* New Haven, CT: Yale University Press, 1972.

Altenbaugh, Richard J. *Education for Struggle: The American Labor Colleges of the 1920s and 1930s.* Philadelphia: Temple University Press, 1990.

Anderson, James D. *The Education of Blacks in the South, 1860-1935.* Chapel Hill: University of North Carolina Press, 1988.

Anderson, Robert Mapes. *Vision of the Disinherited: The Making of American Pentecostalism.* New York: Oxford University Press, 1979.

Appelbaum, Patricia. *Kingdom to Commune: Protestant Pacifist Culture Between World War I and the Vietnam Era.* Chapel Hill: University of North Carolina Press, 2009.

Ashcraft, Virginia. *Public Care in Tennessee: A History of Public Welfare Legislation in Tennessee.* Knoxville: University of Tennessee Record, 1947.

Atto, William J. "Brooks Hays and the New Deal." *Arkansas Historical Quarterly* 67, no. 2 (Summer 2008): 167–186.

Aucoin, Brent J. "The Southern Manifesto and Southern Opposition to Desegregation." *Arkansas Historical Quarterly* 55, no. 2 (Summer 1996): 173–193.

Auerbach, Jerold S. "Southern Tenant Farmers: Socialist Critics of the New Deal." *Labor History* 7, no. 1 (Winter 1966): 3–18.

Badger, Anthony J. *FDR: The First Hundred Days.* New York: Hill and Wang, 2008.

———. *The New Deal: The Depression Years, 1933-1940.* Chicago: Ivan R. Dee, 2002.

———. "Southerners Who Refused to Sign the Southern Manifesto." *Historical Journal* 42, no. 2 (June 1999): 517–534.

Bailey, Kenneth K. *Southern White Protestantism in the Twentieth Century.* New York: Harper & Row, 1964.

Baker, James Thomas. *Brooks Hays.* Macon, GA: Mercer University Press, 1989.

Baker, Kelly J. *Gospel According to the Klan: The KKK's Appeal to Protestant America.* Lawrence: University Press of Kansas, 2011.

Baldwin, Sidney. *Poverty and Politics: The Rise and Decline of the Farm Security Administration.* Chapel Hill: University of North Carolina Press, 1968.

Baptist Woman's Missionary Union of Mississippi. *Hearts the Lord Opened: The History of Mississippi Woman's Missionary Union.* Jackson, MS: Purser Brothers, 1954.

Barber, William J. *From New Era to New Deal: Herbert Hoover, the Economists, and American Economic Policy, 1921-1933.* Cambridge, MA: Cambridge University Press, 1989.

Barlow, William. *Looking Up at Down: The Emergence of Blues Culture.* Philadelphia: Temple University Press, 1989.

Barry, John M. *Rising Tide: The Great Mississippi Flood of 1927 and How It Changed America.* New York: Simon & Schuster, 1997.

Bauman, Mark K., and Berkley Kalin. *The Quiet Voices: Southern Rabbis and Black Civil Rights, 1880s to 1990s.* Tuscaloosa: University of Alabama Press, 1997.

Beary, Michael J. *Black Bishop: Edward T. Demby and the Struggle for Racial Equality in the Episcopal Church.* Urbana: University of Illinois Press, 2001.

Beasley, Maurine Hoffman. *Eleanor Roosevelt and the Media: A Public Quest for Self-Fulfillment.* Urbana: University of Illinois Press, 1987.

Beigert, M. Langley. "Legacy of Resistance: Uncovering the History of Collective Action by Black Agricultural Workers in Central East Arkansas from the 1860s to the 1930s." *Journal of Social History* 32, no. 1 (Autumn 1998): 73–99.

Beito, David T. *From Mutual Aid to Welfare State: Fraternal Societies and Social Services, 1890-1967.* Chapel Hill: University of North Carolina Press, 2000.

Beito, David T., and Linda Royster Beito. "'Let Down Your Bucket Where You Are': The Afro-American Hospital and Black Health Care in Mississippi, 1924-1966." *Social Science History* 30, no. 4 (Winter 2006): 551–569.

Belfrage, Cedric. *A Faith to Free the People.* New York: Dryden Press, 1944.

———. *South of God.* New York: Modern Age Books, 1941.

Bendroth, Margaret Lamberts. *Fundamentalism and Gender, 1875 to the Present.* New Haven, CT: Yale University Press, 1993.

Berger, Michael. *The Devil Wagon in God's Country: The Automobile and Social Change in Rural America, 1893-1929.* Hamden, CT: Archon Books, 1979.

Best, Wallace D. *Passionately Human, No Less Divine: Religion and Culture in Black Chicago, 1915-1952.* Princeton, NJ: Princeton University Press, 2005.

Biegert, M. Langley. "Legacy of Resistance: Uncovering the History of Collective Action by Black Agricultural Workers in Central East Arkansas from the 1860s to the 1930s." *Journal of Social History* 32, no. 1 (Autumn 1998): 73–99.

Biles, Roger. *Memphis in the Great Depression.* Knoxville: University of Tennessee Press, 1986.

———. *The South and the New Deal.* Lexington: University Press of Kentucky, 1994.

———. "The Persistence of the Past: Memphis in the Great Depression." *Journal of Southern History* 52, no. 2 (May 1986): 183–212.

———. "The Urban South in the Great Depression." *Journal of Southern History* 56, no. 1 (February 1990): 71–100.

Billington, Monroe, and Cal Clark. "Baptist Preachers and the New Deal." *Journal of Church and State* 33, no. 2 (Spring 1991): 255–269.

———. "Catholic Clergymen, Franklin D. Roosevelt, and the New Deal." *Catholic Historical Review* 79, no. 1 (January 1993): 65–82.

———. "Clergy Reaction to the New Deal: A Comparative Study." *Historian* 48, no. 4 (1986): 509–524.

Blackwelder, Julia Kirk. *Women of the Depression: Caste and Culture in San Antonio, 1929-1939.* College Station: Texas A & M University Press, 1984.

Blum, Edward J. "The Crucible of Disease: Trauma, Memory, and National Reconciliation during the Yellow Fever Epidemic of 1878." *Journal of Southern History* 69, no. 4 (November 2003): 791–820.

Blumhofer, Edith L. *Restoring the Faith: The Assemblies of God, Pentecostalism, and American Culture.* Urbana: University of Illinois Press, 1993.

Bond, Beverly G., and Janann Sherman. *Memphis: In Black and White.* Charleston, SC: Arcadia Publishing, 2003.

Boswell, Angela, and Judith N. McArthur, eds. *Women Shaping the South: Creating and Confronting Change.* Columbia: University of Missouri Press, 2006.

Bowman, Matthew. *The Urban Pulpit: New York City and the Fate of Liberal Evangelicalism.* New York: Oxford University Press, 2014.

Boyer, Paul S. *When Time Shall Be No More: Prophecy Belief in Modern American Culture.* Cambridge, MA: Harvard University Press, 1992.

———. *Urban Masses and Moral Order in America, 1820-1920.* Cambridge, MA: Harvard University Press, 1978.

Braude, Ann. "Women's History Is American Religious History." In *Retelling U.S. Religious History*, edited by Thomas A. Tweed, 87–107. Berkeley: University of California Press, 1997.

Brekus, Catherine A., ed. *The Religious History of American Women: Reimagining the Past.* Chapel Hill: University of North Carolina Press, 2007.

Brill, Steven. *America's Bitter Pill: Money, Politics, Back-Room Deals, and the Fight to Fix Our Broken Health Care System.* New York: Random House, 2015.

Brinkley, Alan. *Voices of Protest: Huey Long, Father Coughlin, and the Great Depression.* New York: Knopf, 1982.

———. *The End of Reform: New Deal Liberalism in Recession and War.* New York: Vintage, 1995.

Britton, Nancy. *Two Centuries of Methodism in Arkansas, 1800-2000.* Little Rock, AR: August House Publishers, 2000.

Brown, Dorothy M., and Elizabeth McKeown. *The Poor Belong to Us: Catholic Charities and American Welfare.* Cambridge, MA: Harvard University Press, 1997.

Buhite, Russell D., and David W. Levy. *FDR's Fireside Chats.* New York: Penguin, 1993.

Butler, Anthea D. *Women in the Church of God in Christ: Making a Sanctified World.* Chapel Hill: University of North Carolina Press, 2007.

Butler, Jon, et al. "Forum: American Religion and the Great Depression." *Church History* 80, no. 3 (September 2011): 575–610.

Callahan, Richard J., Jr. *Work and Faith in the Kentucky Coal Fields: Subject to Dust.* Bloomington: Indiana University Press, 2009.

Canonici, Paul V. *The Delta Italians.* Madison, MS: P.V. Canonici, 2003.

Carpenter, Joel A. *Revive Us Again: The Reawakening of American Fundamentalism.* New York: Oxford University Press, 1997.

Carter, Dan T. *Scottsboro: A Tragedy of the American South.* Baton Rouge: Louisiana State University Press, 1969.

Carter, Heath. *Union Made: Working People and the Rise of Social Christianity in Chicago.* New York: Oxford University Press, 2015.

Carter, Paul Allen. "The Negro and Methodist Union." *Church History* 21, no. 1 (March 1952): 55–70.

———. *The Decline and Revival of the Social Gospel: Social and Political Liberalism in American Protestant Churches, 1920-1940.* Ithaca, NY: Cornell University Press, 1956.

Chappell, David L. *A Stone of Hope: Prophetic Religion and the Death of Jim Crow.* Chapel Hill: University of North Carolina Press, 2005.

———. *Inside Agitators: White Southerners in the Civil Rights Movement.* Baltimore, MD: Johns Hopkins University Press, 1996.

Charron, Katherine Mellen. *Freedom's Teacher: The Life of Septima Clark.* Chapel Hill: University of North Carolina Press, 2010.

Chirhart, Ann Short. *Torches of Light: Georgia Teachers and the Coming of the Modern South.* Athens: University of Georgia Press, 2005.

Christiano, Kevin J. "'Numbering Israel': The U.S. Census and Religious Organizations." *Social Science History* 8, no. 4 (Autumn 1984): 341–370.

Clark, Norman H. *Deliver Us from Evil: An Interpretation of American Prohibition.* New York: W. W. Norton & Company, 1976.

Clemmons, Ithiel C. *Bishop C. H. Mason and the Roots of the Church of God in Christ.* Lanham, MD: Pneuma Life Publishing, 1996.

Cobb, James C. *The Most Southern Place on Earth: The Mississippi Delta and the Roots of Regional Identity.* New York: Oxford University Press, 1992.

Cobb, William H. *Radical Education in the Rural South: Commonwealth College, 1922-1940.* Detroit, MI: Wayne State University Press, 2000.

———. "The State Legislature and the 'Reds': Arkansas's General Assembly v. Commonwealth College, 1935-1937." *Arkansas Historical Quarterly* 45, no. 1 (Spring 1986): 3–18.

Cobb, William H., and Donald H. Grubbs. "Arkansas' Commonwealth College and the Southern Tenant Farmers' Union." *Arkansas Historical Quarterly* 25, no. 4 (Winter 1966): 293–311.

Coffman, Elesha. *The Christian Century and the Rise of the Protestant Mainline.* New York: Oxford University Press, 2013.

Coggins, Allen R. *Tennessee Tragedies: Natural, Technological, and Societal Disasters in the Volunteer State.* Knoxville: University of Tennessee Press, 2012.

Cohen, Lizabeth. *Making a New Deal: Industrial Workers in Chicago, 1919-1939.* 2nd ed. Cambridge: Cambridge University Press, 2008 [1990].

Coker, Joe L. *Liquor in the Land of the Lost Cause: Southern White Evangelicals and the Prohibition Movement.* Lexington: University Press of Kentucky, 2007.

Collier-Thomas, Bettye. *Jesus, Jobs, and Justice: African American Women and Religion.* New York: Knopf, 2010.

Conrad, David Eugene. *The Forgotten Farmers: The Story of Sharecroppers in the New Deal.* Urbana: University of Illinois Press, 1965.

Cook, Blanche Wiesen. *Eleanor Roosevelt: Volume 2, The Defining Years, 1933-1938.* New York: Penguin Books, 2000.

Couto, Richard J. *Ain't Gonna Let Nobody Turn Me 'Round: The Pursuit of Racial Justice in the Rural South.* Philadelphia: Temple University Press, 1992.

Cox, Harvey Gallagher. *Fire from Heaven: The Rise of Pentecostal Spirituality and the Reshaping of Religion in the Twenty-First Century.* Reading, MA: Addison-Wesley Publishers, 1995.

Craig, Robert H. *Religion and Radical Politics: An Alternative Christian Tradition in the United States.* Philadelphia: Temple University Press, 1992.

Creech, Joe. *Righteous Indignation: Religion and the Populist Revolution.* Urbana: University of Illinois Press, 2006.

Dailey, Jane. "Sex, Segregation, and the Sacred After Brown." *Journal of American History* 91, no. 1 (June 2004): 119–144.

Dallam, Marie. *Daddy Grace: A Celebrity Preacher and His House of Prayer.* New York: New York University Press, 2007.

Daniel, Pete. *Dispossession: Discrimination Against African American Farmers in the Age of Civil Rights.* Chapel Hill: University of North Carolina Press, 2013.

———. *Breaking the Land: The Transformation of Cotton, Tobacco, and Rice Cultures Since 1880.* Urbana: University of Illinois Press, 1985.

———. *Deep'n as It Come: The 1927 Mississippi River Flood.* New York: Oxford University Press, 1977.

Dauber, Michele Landis. *The Sympathetic State: Disaster Relief and the Origins of the American Welfare State.* Chicago: University of Chicago Press, 2012.

Davis, John H. *St. Mary's Cathedral, 1858-1958.* Memphis, TN: Chapter of St. Mary's Cathedral, 1958.

Davis, Morris Lee. *The Methodist Unification: Christianity and the Politics of the Jim Crow Era.* New York: New York University Press, 2008.

Day, John Kyle. "The Fall of a Southern Moderate: Congressman Brooks Hays and the Election of 1958." *Arkansas Historical Quarterly* 59, no. 3 (Autumn 2000): 241–264.

DeSaulniers, Lawrence B. *The Response in American Catholic Periodicals to the Crises of the Great Depression, 1930-1935.* Lanham, MD: University Press of America, 1984.

Dochuk, Darren. *From Bible Belt to Sun Belt: Plain-Folk Religion, Grassroots Politics, and the Rise of Evangelical Conservatism.* New York: W. W. Norton & Company, 2011.

Dowdy, G. Wayne. "Censoring Popular Culture: Political and Social Control in Segregated Memphis." *West Tennessee Historical Society Papers* 55 (2001): 98–117.

———. *Mayor Crump Don't Like It: Machine Politics in Memphis.* Jackson: University Press of Mississippi, 2006.

Dunbar, Anthony P. *Against the Grain: Southern Radicals and Prophets, 1929-1959.* Charlottesville: University Press of Virginia, 1981.

Dunne, Matthew William, "Next Steps: Charles S. Johnson and Southern Liberalism." *Journal of Negro History* 83, no. 1 (Winter 1981): 1–34.

Dupont, Carolyn Renée. *Mississippi Praying: Southern White Evangelicals and the Civil Rights Movement, 1945-1975.* New York: New York University Press, 2013.

Eason, Andrew Mark. *Women in God's Army: Gender and Equality in the Early Salvation Army.* Waterloo, Ontario: Wilfred Laurier University Press, 2003.

Ebel, Jonathan H. *Faith in the Fight: Religion and the American Soldier in the Great War.* Princeton, NJ: Princeton University Press, 2010.

———. "The Great War, Religious Authority, and the American Fighting Man." *Church History* 78, no. 1 (March 2009): 99–133.

———. "Re-Forming Faith: John Steinbeck, the New Deal, and the Religion of the Wandering Oklahoman." *Journal of Religion* 92, no. 4 (October 2012): 527–535.

Egerton, John. *Speak Now Against the Day: The Generation Before the Civil Rights Movement in the South.* New York: Knopf, 1994.

Eldon G. Ernst. "The Interchurch World Movement and the Great Steel Strike of 1919-1920." *Church History* 39, no. 2 (June 1970): 212–223.

Ellwood, Robert S. *1950, Crossroads of American Religious Life.* Louisville, KY: Westminster John Knox Press, 2000.

Evans, Curtis. *The Burden of Black Religion.* New York: Oxford University Press, 2008.

Evans, David. "High Water Everywhere: Blues and Gospel Commentary on the 1927 Mississippi River Flood." In *Nobody Knows Where the Blues Comes From: Lyrics and History*, edited by Robert Springer, 3–75. Jackson: University Press of Mississippi, 2007.

Fahey, David M. *Temperance and Racism: John Bull, Johnny Reb, and the Good Templars.* Lexington: University Press of Kentucky, 1996.

Fairclough, Adam. " 'Being in the Field of Education and Also Being a Negro . . . Seems . . . Tragic': Black Teachers in the Jim Crow South." *Journal of American History* 87, no. 1 (June 2000): 65–91.

———. *A Class of Their Own: Black Teachers in the Segregated South.* Cambridge, MA: Belknap Press of Harvard University Press, 2007.

Ferris, Marcie, et al., eds., *Jewish Roots in Southern Soil: A New History.* Waltham, MA: Brandeis University Press, 2006.

Ferris, William. *Blues from the Delta.* New York: DeCapo Press, 1978.

Fessenden, Tracy. *Culture and Redemption: Religion, the Secular, and American Literature.* Princeton, NJ: Princeton University Press, 2007.

Finstuen, Andrew S. *Original Sin and Everyday Protestants: The Theology of Reinhold Niebuhr, Billy Graham, and Paul Tillich in an Age of Anxiety.* Chapel Hill: University of North Carolina Press, 2009.

Fite, Gilbert Courtland. *Cotton Fields No More: Southern Agriculture, 1865-1980.* Lexington: University Press of Kentucky, 1984.

Flowers, Elizabeth H. *Into the Pulpit: Southern Baptist Women and Power Since World War II.* Chapel Hill: University of North Carolina Press, 2015.

Flynt, Wayne. *Alabama Baptists: Southern Baptists in the Heart of Dixie.* Tuscaloosa: University of Alabama Press, 1998.

———. *Dixie's Forgotten People: The South's Poor Whites.* 2nd ed. Bloomington: Indiana University Press, 2004 [1979].

———. "Religion for the Blues: Evangelicalism, Poor Whites, and the Great Depression." *Journal of Southern History* 71, no. 1 (February 2005): 4–38.

———. "Southern Protestantism and Reform." In *Varieties of Southern Religious Experience*, edited by Samuel S. Hill, 135–157. Baton Rouge: Louisiana State University Press, 1988.

Folsom, Burton Jr. *New Deal or Raw Deal? How FDR's Economic Legacy Has Damaged America.* New York: Threshhold Editions, 2008.

Fones-Wolf, Elizabeth A. *Selling Free Enterprise: The Business Assault on Labor and Liberalism, 1945-60.* Urbana: University of Illinois Press, 1994.

Fones-Wolf, Elizabeth A., and Ken Fones-Wolf. *Struggle for the Soul of the Post-War South: White Evangelical Protestants and Operation Dixie.* Urbana: University of Illinois Press, 2015.

Fones-Wolf, Ken. *Trade Union Gospel: Christianity and Labor in Industrial Philadelphia, 1865-1915.* Philadelphia: Temple University Press, 1989.

Foster, Gaines M. *Moral Reconstruction: Christian Lobbyists and the Federal Legislation of Morality, 1865-1920.* Chapel Hill: University of North Carolina Press, 2002.

Fox, Richard Wightman. *Reinhold Niebuhr: A Biography.* Ithaca, NY: Cornell University Press, 1997.

Fulton, DoVeanna S. "Sowing Seeds in an Untilled Field: Temperance and Race, Indeterminacy and Recovery in Frances E. W. Harper's Sowing and Reaping." *Legacy* 24, no. 2 (2007): 207–224.

Gage, Beverly. *The Day Wall Street Exploded: A Story of America in Its First Age of Terror.* New York: Oxford University Press, 2009.

Galbraith, John Kenneth. *The Great Crash, 1929.* Boston: Houghton Mifflin, 1972.

Gamble, Richard M. *The War for Righteousness: Progressive Christianity, the Great War, and the Rise of the Messianic Nation.* Wilmington, DE: ISI Books, 2003.

Gaustad, Edwin S., and Leigh Schmidt. *The Religious History of America: The Heart of the American Story from Colonial Times to Today.* San Francisco: Harper, 2002.

Gellman, Erik S., and Jarod Roll. *The Gospel of the Working Class: Labor's Southern Prophets in New Deal America.* Urbana: University of Illinois, 2011.

———. "Owen Whitfield and the Gospel of the Working Class in New Deal America, 1936-1946." *Journal of Southern History* 72 (May 2006): 303–348.

Gibbens, Byrd. "Strangers in the Arkansas Delta: Ethnic Groups and Nationalities." In *The Arkansas Delta: Land of Paradox*, edited by Jeannie Whayne and Willard Gatewood, 150–180. Fayetteville: University of Arkansas Press, 1993.

Giggie, John M. *After Redemption: Jim Crow and the Transformation of African American Religion in the Delta, 1875-1915*. New York: Oxford University Press, 2007.

———. "For God and Lodge: Black Fraternal Orders and the Evolution of African American Religion in the Postbellum South." In *The Struggle for Equality: Essays on Sectional Conflict, the Civil War, and the Long Reconstruction,* edited by Orville Vernon Burton et al, 198–218. Charlottesville: University of Virginia Press, 2011.

Gilbert, Jess. "Eastern Urban Liberals and Midwestern Agrarian Intellectuals: Two Group Portraits of Progressives in the New Deal Department of Agriculture." *Agricultural History* 74, no. 2 (Spring 2000): 162–180.

Gilbert, Jess, and Steve Brown. "Alternative Land Reform Proposals in the 1930s: The Nashville Agrarians and the Southern Tenant Farmers' Union." *Agricultural History* 55 (October 1981): 351–369.

Gilkes, Cheryl Townsend. *If It Wasn't for the Women: Black Women's Experience and Womanist Culture in Church and Community.* Maryknoll, NY: Orbis Books, 2001.

Gilmore, Glenda Elizabeth. *Defying Dixie: The Radical Roots of Civil Rights, 1919-1950.* New York: W. W. Norton, 2008.

———. *Gender and Jim Crow: Women and the Politics of White Supremacy in North Carolina, 1896-1920.* Chapel Hill: University of North Carolina Press, 1996.

Glass, William R. *Strangers in Zion: Fundamentalists in the South, 1900-1950.* Macon, GA: Mercer University Press, 2001.

Gloege, Timothy E. W. *Guaranteed Pure: The Moody Bible Institute, Business, and the Making of Modern Evangelicalism.* Chapel Hill: University of North Carolina Press, 2015.

Godshalk, David Fort. *Veiled Visions: The 1906 Atlanta Race Riot and the Reshaping of American Race Relations.* Chapel Hill: University of North Carolina Press, 2005.

Goodman, James E. *Stories of Scottsboro.* New York: Vintage, 1995.

Goodwyn, Lawrence. *The Populist Moment: A Short History of the Agrarian Revolt in America.* New York: Oxford University Press, 1978.

Gordon, Lawrence. "A Brief Look at Blacks in Depression Mississippi, 1929-1934: Eyewitness Accounts." *Journal of Negro History* 64, no. 4 (Autumn 1979): 377–390.

Gordon, Linda. "Black and White Visions of Welfare: Women's Welfare Activism, 1890-1945." *Journal of American History* 78, no. 2 (September 1991): 559–590.

———. *Pitied but Not Entitled: Single Mothers and the History of Welfare, 1890-1935.* Cambridge, MA: Harvard University Press, 1998.

Graham, John H. *Mississippi Circuit Riders, 1865-1965*. Nashville, TN: Parthenon Press, 1967.

Grantham, Dewey W. *Southern Progressivism: The Reconciliation of Progress and Tradition*. Knoxville: University of Tennessee Press, 1983.

Green, Elna C. *This Business of Relief: Confronting Poverty in a Southern City, 1740-1940*. Athens: University of Georgia Press, 2003.

——, ed. *Before the New Deal: Social Welfare in the South, 1830-1930*. Athens: University of Georgia Press, 1999.

——, ed. *The New Deal and Beyond: Social Welfare in the South since 1930*. Athens: University of Georgia Press, 2003.

Green, Laurie B. *Battling the Plantation Mentality: Memphis and the Black Freedom Struggle*. Chapel Hill: University of North Carolina Press, 2007.

Greenberg, Cheryl Lynn. *To Ask for an Equal Chance: African Americans in the Great Depression*. Lanham, MD: Rowman & Littlefield, 2009.

Gregory, James N. *The Southern Diaspora: How the Great Migrations of Black and White Southerners Transformed America*. Chapel Hill: University of North Carolina Press, 2005.

——. *American Exodus: The Dust Bowl Migration and Okie Culture in California*. New York: Oxford University Press, 1989.

Gregory, Raymond F. *Norman Thomas: The Great Dissenter*. New York: Algora Publishing, 2008.

Gritter, Elizabeth. *River of Hope: Black Politics and the Memphis Freedom Movement, 1865-1954*. Lexington: University Press of Kentucky, 2014.

Grossman, James R. *Land of Hope: Chicago, Black Southerners, and the Great Migration*. Chicago: University of Chicago Press, 1991.

Grubbs, Donald H. *Cry from the Cotton: The Southern Tenant Farmer's Union and the New Deal*. Fayetteville: University of Arkansas Press, 1999 [1971].

Gustafson, Merlin, and Jerry Rosenberg. "The Faith of Franklin Roosevelt." *Presidential Studies Quarterly* 19, no. 3 (Summer 1989): 559–566.

Hacsi, Timothy A. *Second Home: Orphan Asylums and Poor Families in America*. Cambridge, MA: Harvard University Press, 1998.

Hahn, Steven P. *A Nation Under Our Feet: Black Political Struggles in the Rural South from Slavery to the Great Migration*. Cambridge, MA: Belknap Press, 2003.

Hall, Jacquelyn Dowd. *Revolt Against Chivalry: Jessie Daniel Ames and the Women's Campaign Against Lynching*. 2nd edition. New York: Columbia University Press, 1993 [1974].

Hamilton, David E. "Herbert Hoover and the Great Drought of 1930." *Journal of American History* 68, no. 4 (March 1982): 850–875.

——. "The Causes of the Banking Panic of 1930: Another View." *Journal of Southern History* 51, no. 4 (November 1985): 581–608.

Hamlin, Christopher, and John T. McGreevy. "The Greening of America, Catholic Style, 1930-1950." *Environmental History* 11, no. 3 (July 2006): 464–499.

Hamlin, Françoise N. *Crossroads at Clarksdale: The Black Freedom Struggle in the Mississippi Delta after World War II*. Chapel Hill: University of North Carolina Press, 2012.

Hancock, Ange-Marie. *The Politics of Disgust: The Public Identity of the Welfare Queen*. New York: New York University Press, 2004.

Handy, Robert T. "The American Religious Depression, 1925-1935." *Church History* 29, no. 1 (March 1960): 3–16.

Hangen, Tona J. *Redeeming the Dial: Radio, Religion, and Popular Culture in America*. Chapel Hill: University of North Carolina Press, 2002.

Hankins, Barry. *God's Rascal: J. Frank Norris and the Beginnings of Southern Fundamentalism*. Lexington: University Press of Kentucky, 1996.

Harkins, John E. *Metropolis of the American Nile: A History of Memphis & Shelby County, Tennessee*. 2nd ed. Oxford, MS: Guild Bindery Publications, 1991 [1982].

Harris, Michael W. *The Rise of Gospel Blues: The Music of Thomas Andrew Dorsey in the Urban Church*. New York: Oxford University Press, 1992.

Harrison, Alferdeen B. *Piney Woods School: An Oral History*. Jackson, MS: University Press of Mississippi, 1982.

Harvey, Charles E. "John D. Rockefeller, Jr., and the Interchurch World Movement of 1919-1920: A Different Angle on the Ecumenical Movement." *Church History* 51, no. 2 (June 1982): 198–209.

Harvey, Paul. *Freedom's Coming: Religious Culture and the Shaping of the South from the Civil War Through the Civil Rights Era*. Chapel Hill: University of North Carolina Press, 2007.

———. *Redeeming the South: Religious Cultures and Racial Identities Among Southern Baptists, 1865-1925*. Chapel Hill: University of North Carolina Press, 1997.

Hayes, John. "Hard, Hard Religion: The Invisible Institution of the New South." *Journal of Southern Religion* 10 (2007): 1–24.

Hedstrom, Matthew S. *The Rise of Liberal Religion: Book Culture and American Spirituality in the Twentieth Century*. New York: Oxford University Press, 2013.

Heilbut, Anthony. *The Gospel Sound: Good News and Bad Times*. New York: Limelight, 2002 [1975].

Heineman, Kenneth J. *A Catholic New Deal: Religion and Reform in Depression Pittsburgh*. University Park: Pennsylvania State University Press, 1999.

Herberg, Will. *Protestant, Catholic, Jew: An Essay in American Religious Sociology*. Garden City, NY: Doubleday, 1955.

Herzog, Jonathan P. *The Spiritual-Industrial Complex: America's Religious Battle Against Communism in the Early Cold War*. New York: Oxford University Press, 2011.

Higginbotham, Evelyn Brooks. *Righteous Discontent: The Women's Movement in the Black Baptist Church, 1880-1920*. Cambridge, MA: Harvard University Press, 1993.

Hinks, Peter P., Stephen Kantrowitz, and Leslie A. Lewis. *All Men Free and Brethren: Essays on the History of African American Freemasonry.* Ithaca: Cornell University Press, 2013.

Hobson, Fred C. *Serpent in Eden: H. L. Mencken and the South.* Chapel Hill: University of North Carolina Press, 1974.

Holley, Donald. "The Plantation Heritage: Agriculture in the Arkansas Delta." In *The Arkansas Delta: Land of Paradox*, edited by Jeannie Whayne and Willard B. Gatewood, 238–277. Fayetteville: University of Arkansas Press, 1993.

———. "The Second Great Emancipation: The Rust Cotton Picker and How It Changed Arkansas." *Arkansas Historical Quarterly* 52, no. 1 (Spring 1993): 44–77.

———. *Uncle Sam's Farmers. The New Deal Communities in the Lower Mississippi Valley.* Urbana: University of Illinois Press, 1975.

Hollinger, David A. "After Cloven Tongues of Fire: Ecumenical Protestantism and the Modern American Encounter with Diversity." *Journal of American History* 98, no. 1 (June 2011): 21–48.

———. *After Cloven Tongues of Fire: Protestant Liberalism in Modern American History.* Princeton, NJ: Princeton University Press, 2013.

Honey, Michael K. *Southern Labor and Black Civil Rights: Organizing Memphis Workers.* Urbana: University of Illinois Press, 1993.

———. *Sharecropper's Troubadour: John L. Handcox, the Southern Tenant Farmers Union, and the African American Song Tradition.* New York: Palgrave, 2013.

———. *Black Workers Remember: An Oral History of Segregation, Unionism, and the Freedom Struggle.* Berkeley: University of California Press, 2002.

Hough, Mazie. "Are You or Are You Not Your Sister's Keeper? A Radical Response to the Treatment of Unwed Mothers in Tennessee." In *Before the New Deal: Social Welfare in the South, 1830-1930*, edited by Elna Green, 100–119. Athens: University of Georgia Press, 1999.

Hungerman, Daniel M., and Jonathan Gruber. "Faith-Based Charity and Crowd-Out During the Great Depression." National Bureau of Economic Research Working Paper 11332. May 2005.

Hutchison, William R., ed. *Between the Times: The Travail of the Protestant Establishment in America, 1900-1960.* New York: Cambridge University Press, 1989.

———. "Cultural Strain and Protestant Liberalism." *American Historical Review* 76, no. 2 (April 1971): 386–411.

Inboden, William. *Religion and American Foreign Policy, 1945-1960: The Soul of Containment.* New York: Cambridge University Press, 2008.

Irwin, Julia Finch. *Making the World Safe: The American Red Cross and a Nation's Humanitarian Awakening.* New York: Oxford University Press, 2013.

Isetti, Ronald. "The Moneychangers of the Temple: FDR, American Civil Religion, and the New Deal." *Presidential Studies Quarterly* 26, no. 3 (Summer 1996): 678–693.

Israel, Charles A. *Before Scopes: Evangelicalism, Education and Evolution in Tennessee, 1870-1925*. Athens: University of Georgia Press, 2004.

Jackson, Jerma A. *Singing in My Soul: Black Gospel Music in a Secular Age*. Chapel Hill: University of North Carolina Press, 2004.

Jenkins, Earnestine Lovelle. *African Americans in Memphis*. Mt. Pleasant, SC: Arcadia Publishing, 2009.

Johnson, Ben F., III *Arkansas in Modern America, 1930-1999*. Fayetteville: University of Arkansas Press, 2000.

———. *John Barleycorn Must Die: The War Against Drink in Arkansas*. Fayetteville: University of Arkansas Press, 2005.

Johnson, Walter. *River of Dark Dreams: Slavery and Empire in the Cotton Kingdom*. Cambridge, MA: Belknap Press, 2013.

Jordan, Dusty. "Baptists Bring War to Jonesboro." *Craighead County Historical Quarterly* XXI, no. 1 (Winter 1983): 1–9.

Kantrowitz, Stephen. "'Intended for the Better Government of Man': The Political History of African American Freemasonry in the Era of Emancipation." *Journal of American History* 96, no. 4 (March 2010): 1001–1026.

Katz, Michael B. *In the Shadow of the Poorhouse: A Social History of Welfare in America*. New York: Basic Books, 1996 [1986].

Katznelson, Ira. *When Affirmative Action Was White: An Untold History of Racial Inequality in Twentieth-Century America*. New York: Norton, 2005.

———. *Fear Itself: The New Deal and the Origins of Our Time*. New York: Liveright, 2013.

Keith, Jeanette. *Rich Man's War, Poor Man's Fight: Race, Class, and Power in the Rural South During the First World War*. Chapel Hill: University of North Carolina Press, 2004.

Kelley, Dean M. *Government Intervention in Religious Affairs*. New York: Pilgrim Press, 1982.

———. *Government Intervention in Religious Affairs, II*. New York: Pilgrim Press, 1986.

Kelley, Robin D. G. *Hammer and Hoe: Alabama Communists During the Great Depression*. Chapel Hill: University of North Carolina Press, 1990.

Kennedy, David M. *Freedom from Fear: The American People in Depression and War, 1929-1945*. New York: Oxford University Press, 2001.

King, Martin Luther. *A Testament of Hope: The Essential Writings and Speeches of Martin Luther King, Jr.* Edited by James M. Washington. New York: Harper, 1990.

King, William McGuire. "The Emergence of Social Gospel Radicalism: The Methodist Case." *Church History* 50, no. 4 (December 1981): 436–449.

Kirby, Jack Temple. *Rural Worlds Lost: The American South, 1920-1960*. Baton Rouge: Louisiana State University Press, 1987.

Kirby, John B. *Black Americans in the Roosevelt Era: Liberalism and Race*. Knoxville: University of Tennessee Press, 1980.

Klein, Jennifer. *For All These Rights: Business, Labor, and the Shaping of America's Public-Private Welfare State.* Princeton, NJ: Princeton University Press, 2003.

Kleinberg, S. J. *Widows and Orphans First: The Family Economy and Social Welfare Policy, 1880-1919.* Urbana: University of Illinois Press, 2006.

Knock, Thomas J. *To End All Wars: Woodrow Wilson and the Quest for a New World Order.* Princeton, NJ: Princeton University Press, 1995.

Korstad, Robert Rogers. *Civil Rights Unionism: Tobacco Workers and the Struggle for Democracy in the Mid-Twentieth Century South.* Chapel Hill: University of North Carolina Press, 2003.

Kosek, Joseph Kip. *Acts of Conscience: Christian Nonviolence and Modern American Democracy.* New York: Columbia University Press, 2009.

Kruse, Kevin M. *One Nation Under God: How Corporate America Invented Christian America.* New York: Basic Books, 2015.

Kyriakoudes, Louis M. *Social Origins of the Urban South: Race, Gender, and Migration in Nashville and Middle Tennessee, 1890-1930.* Chapel Hill: University of North Carolina Press, 2003.

Kyvig, David E. *Repealing National Prohibition.* 2nd ed. Kent, OH: Kent State University Press, 2000 [1979].

Lambert, Roger. "Hoover and the Red Cross in the Arkansas Drought of 1930." *Arkansas Historical Quarterly* 29, no. 1 (Spring 1970): 3–19.

Lanier, Robert A. *Memphis in the Twenties.* Memphis, TN: Zenda Press, 1979.

Larson, Edward J. *Summer for the Gods: The Scopes Trial and America's Continuing Debate over Science and Religion.* New York: Basic Books, 1997.

Lasch-Quinn, Elisabeth. *Black Neighbors: Race and the Limits of Reform in the American Settlement House Movement, 1890-1945.* Chapel Hill: University of North Carolina Press, 1993.

Lawson, Alan. *A Commonwealth of Hope: The New Deal Response to Crisis.* Baltimore: Johns Hopkins University Press, 2006.

Lawson, R. A. *Jim Crow's Counterculture: The Blues and Black Southerners, 1890-1945.* Baton Rouge: Louisiana State University Press, 2010.

Lears, Jackson. Rebirth of a Nation: The Making of Modern America, 1877-1920. New York: HarperCollins, 2009.

———. *No Place of Grace: Antimodernism and the Transformation of American Culture, 1880-1920.* Chicago: University of Chicago Press, 1994.

Ledbetter, Cal, Jr. "The Antievolution Law: Church and State in Arkansas." *Arkansas Historical Quarterly* 38, no. 4 (Winter 1979): 299–327.

LeMaster, Carolyn Gray. *A Corner of the Tapestry: A History of the Jewish Experience in Arkansas, 1820s-1990s.* Fayetteville: University of Arkansas Press, 1994.

Lentz-Smith, Adriane. *Freedom Struggles: African Americans and World War I.* Cambridge, MA: Harvard University Press, 2009.

Leonard, Bill J. *Baptists in America.* New York: Columbia University Press, 2007.

Lester, Connie L. "Balancing Agriculture with Industry: Capital, Labor and Race in Mississippi's Home-Grown New Deal." *Journal of Mississippi History* 57, no. 3 (Fall 2008): 235–263.

———. *Up from the Mudsills of Hell: The Farmers' Alliance, Populism, and Progressive Agriculture in Tennessee, 1870-1915*. Athens: University of Georgia Press, 2006.

Leuchtenburg, William E. *Franklin D Roosevelt and the New Deal, 1932-1940*. New York: Harper & Row, 1963.

———. *The Perils of Prosperity, 1914-1932*. Chicago: University of Chicago Press, 1993.

Levine, Lawrence W. *The People and the President: America's Extraordinary Conversation with FDR*. Boston: Beacon Press, 2002.

Lewis, Selma S. *A Biblical People in the Bible Belt*. Macon, GA: Mercer University Press, 1999.

Lichtenstein, Alex. "Introduction: The Southern Tenant Farmers' Union: A Movement for Social Emancipation." In *Revolt Among the Sharecroppers*, by Howard Kester. 2nd ed. Knoxville: University of Tennessee Press, 1997 [1936].

Link, William A. *The Paradox of Southern Progressivism, 1880-1930*. Chapel Hill: University of North Carolina Press, 1992.

Loewen, James W. *The Mississippi Chinese: Between Black and White*. Long Grove, IL: Waveland Press, 1988 [1971].

Lofton, Kathryn. *Oprah: The Gospel of an Icon*. Berkeley: University of California Press, 2011.

Lorence, James J. *A Hard Journey: The Life of Don West*. Urbana: University of Illinois Press, 2007.

Lowe, Kevin M. *Baptized with the Soil: Christian Agrarians and the Crusade for Rural America*. New York: Oxford University Press, 2015.

Luker, Ralph E. *The Social Gospel in Black and White: American Racial Reform, 1885-1912*. Chapel Hill: University of North Carolina Press, 1998.

Madison, James H. "Reformers and the Rural Church, 1900-1950." *Journal of American History* 73, no. 3 (December 1986): 645–668.

Maher, Neil M. *Nature's New Deal: The Civilian Conservation Corps and the Roots of the American Environmental Movement*. New York: Oxford University Press, 2007.

Malone, Bill C. *Don't Get Above Your Raisin': Country Music and the Southern Working Class*. Urbana: University of Illinois Press, 2002.

Manthorne, Jason. "The View from the Cotton: Reconsidering the Southern Tenant Farmers' Union." *Agricultural History* 64 (Winter 2010): 20–45.

Marcuss, Rosemary D., and Richard E. Kane. "U.S. National Income and Product Statistics: Born of the Great Depression and World War II." *Survey of Current Business* 87, no. 2 (February 2007): 32–46.

Marsden, George M. *Fundamentalism and American Culture: The Shaping of Twentieth-Century Evangelicalism, 1870-1925*. 2nd ed. New York: Oxford University Press, 1996 [1980].

Marsh, Charles. *God's Long Summer: Stories of Faith and Civil Rights*. Princeton, NJ: Princeton University Press, 2008.

Martin, Robert F. "A Prophet's Pilgrimage: The Religious Radicalism of Howard Anderson Kester, 1921-1941." *Journal of Southern History* 48, no. 4 (November 1982): 511–530.

———. "Critique of Southern Society and Vision of a New Order: The Fellowship of Southern Churchmen, 1934-1957." *Church History* 52, no. 1 (March 1983): 66–80.

———. *Howard Kester and the Struggle for Social Justice in the South, 1904-1977*. Charlottesville: University of Virginia Press, 1991.

Marty, Martin E. *Modern American Religion, Volume 2: The Noise of Conflict, 1919-1941*. Chicago: University of Chicago Press, 1997.

May, Henry F. *Protestant Churches and Industrial America*. New York: Torchbooks, 1967 [1949].

McCloud, Sean. *Divine Hierarchies: Class in American Religion and Religious Studies*. Chapel Hill: University of North Carolina Press, 2007.

McDonald, Margaret Simms. *White Already to Harvest: The Episcopal Church in Arkansas, 1838-1971*. Sewanee, TN: Episcopal Diocese of Arkansas, 1975.

McDowell, John Patrick. *The Social Gospel in the South: The Woman's Home Mission Movement in the Methodist Episcopal Church, South, 1886-1939*. Baton Rouge: Louisiana State University Press, 1982.

McElvaine, Robert S. *Down and Out in the Great Depression: Letters from the Forgotten Man*. Chapel Hill: University of North Carolina Press, 1983.

———. *The Great Depression: America 1929-1941*. New York: Times Books, 1984.

McGerr, Michael. *A Fierce Discontent: The Rise and Fall of the Progressive Movement in America, 1870-1920*. New York: Oxford University Press, 2005.

McKanan, Dan. *Prophetic Encounters: Religion and the American Radical Tradition*. Boston: Beacon, 2011.

McKinley, Edward H. *Marching to Glory: The History of the Salvation Army in the United States*. Grand Rapids, MI: W. B. Eerdmans Co., 1995.

McLemore, Richard Aubrey. *A History of Mississippi Baptists, 1780-1970*. Jackson: Mississippi Baptist Convention Board, 1971.

McLoughlin, William G. *Revivals, Awakenings, and Reform*. Chicago: University of Chicago Press, 1978.

McMath, Robert C., Jr. *American Populism: A Social History, 1877-1898*. New York: Hill and Wang, 1993.

McMillen, Neil R. *Dark Journey: Black Mississippians in the Age of Jim Crow*. Urbana: University of Illinois Press, 1989.

Mertz, Paul E. *New Deal Policy and Southern Rural Poverty*. Baton Rouge: Louisiana State University Press, 1978.

Meyer, Donald B. *The Protestant Search for Political Realism, 1919-1941*. Berkeley: University of California Press, 1961.

Miller, Robert Moats. *American Protestantism and Social Issues, 1919-1939*. Chapel Hill: University of North Carolina Press, 1958.

Miller, William D. *Memphis During the Progressive Era, 1900-1917.* Memphis, TN: Memphis State University Press, 1957.

———. *Mr. Crump of Memphis.* Baton Rouge: Louisiana State University Press, 1964.

Mitchell, Dennis J. *Mississippi Liberal: A Biography of Frank E. Smith.* Jackson: University Press of Mississippi, 2001.

Mitchell, Michele. *Righteous Propagation: African Americans and the Politics of Racial Destiny After Reconstruction.* Chapel Hill: University of North Carolina Press, 2004.

Monge, Luigi. "Preachin' the Blues: A Textual Linguistic Analysis of Son House's 'Dry Spell Blues.'" In *Ramblin' on My Mind: New Perspectives on the Blues,* edited by David Evans, 222–257. Champaign: University of Illinois Press, 2008.

Moore, Deborah Dash. *GI Jews: How World War II Changed a Generation.* Cambridge, MA: Belknap Press, 2006.

Moreton, Bethany. *To Serve God and Wal-Mart: The Making of Christian Free Enterprise.* Cambridge, MA: Harvard University Press, 2009.

Morris, Andrew J. F. *The Limits of Voluntarism: Charity and Welfare from the New Deal Through the Great Society.* Cambridge: Cambridge University Press, 2008.

Morris, Christopher. *The Big Muddy: An Environmental History of the Mississippi and Its People from Hernando de Soto to Hurricane Katrina.* New York: Oxford University Press, 2012.

Murphy, Paul V. *The Rebuke of History: The Southern Agrarians and American Conservative Thought.* Chapel Hill: University of North Carolina Press, 2001.

Murray, Peter C. *Methodists and the Crucible of Race, 1930-1975.* Columbia: University of Missouri Press, 2004.

Namorato, Michael V. *The Catholic Church in Mississippi, 1911-1984.* Westport, CT: Greenwood Publishing Group, 1998.

Nelson, Claire Nee. "Louise Thompson Patterson and the Southern Roots of the Popular Front." In *Women Shaping the South: Creating and Confronting Change,* edited by Angela Boswell and Judith N. McArthur, 204–228. Columbia: University of Missouri Press, 2006.

Nelson, Lawrence J. "Oscar Johnston, the New Deal, and the Cotton Subsidy Payments Controversy, 1936-1937." *Journal of Southern History* 40, no. 3 (August 1974): 399–416.

———. "The Art of the Possible: Another Look at the 'Purge' of the AAA Liberals in 1935." *Agricultural History* 57, no. 4 (October 1983): 416–435.

———. "Welfare Capitalism on a Mississippi Plantation in the Great Depression." *Journal of Southern History* 50, no. 2 (May 1984): 225–250.

Newman, Mark F. *Divine Agitators: The Delta Ministry and Civil Rights in Mississippi.* Athens: University of Georgia Press, 2004.

———. *Getting Right with God: Southern Baptists and Desegregation, 1945-1995.* Tuscaloosa: University of Alabama Press, 2001.

———. "The Arkansas Baptist State Convention and Desegregation, 1954-1968." *Arkansas Historical Quarterly* 56, no. 3 (Autumn 1997): 294–313.

North, Cecil C., C. M. Bookman, Stuart A. Queen, and Elwood Street. "Discussion of 'Some Sociological Principles Underlying the Community Chest Movement.'" *Social Forces* 10, no. 4 (May 1932): 485–497.

Novick, Peter. *The Holocaust in American Life.* New York: Mariner Books, 2000.

O'Brien, David J. *American Catholics and Social Reform: The New Deal Years.* New York: Oxford University Press, 1968.

Okrent, Daniel. *Last Call: The Rise and Fall of Prohibition.* New York: Scribner, 2011.

Olasky, Marvin. *The Tragedy of American Compassion.* Washington, DC: Regnery, 1992.

Olson, James Stuart. "Harvey C. Couch and the Reconstruction Finance Corporation." *Arkansas Historical Quarterly* 32, no. 3 (Autumn 1973): 217–225.

———. *Herbert Hoover and the Reconstruction Finance Corporation, 1931-1933.* Ames: Iowa State Press, 1977.

Orsi, Robert A. *Thank You, St. Jude: Women's Devotion to the Patron Saint of Hopeless Causes.* New Haven, CT: Yale University Press, 1996.

———. *The Madonna of 115th Street: Faith and Community in Italian Harlem, 1880-1950.* 3rd ed. New Haven, CT: Yale University Press, 2010 [1985].

Ownby, Ted. *American Dreams in Mississippi: Consumers, Poverty, and Culture, 1830-1998.* Chapel Hill: University of North Carolina Press, 1999.

———. "Gladys Presley, Dorothy Dickins, and the Limits of Female Agrarianism in Twentieth-Century Mississippi." In *Mississippi Women: Their History, Their Lives,* vol. 2. Edited by Martha Swain et al., 211–233. Athens: University of Georgia Press, 2010.

Parrish, Michael E. *Anxious Decades: America in Prosperity and Depression, 1920-1941.* New York: W. W. Norton & Company, 1994.

Pasquier, Michael, ed. *Gods of the Mississippi.* Bloomington: Indiana University Press, 2013.

Payne, Charles M. *I've Got the Light of Freedom: The Organizing Tradition and the Mississippi Freedom Struggle.* 2nd ed. Berkeley: University of California Press, 2007 [1995].

Payne, Elizabeth Anne, with photos by Louise Boyle. "The Lady Was a Sharecropper: Myrtle Lawrence and the Southern Tenant Farmers' Union." *Southern Cultures* 4, no. 2 (Summer 1998): 5–27.

Pells, Richard H. *Radical Visions and American Dreams: Culture and Social Thought in the Depression Years.* Urbana: University of Illinois Press, 2004.

Peters, Scott J., and Paul A. Morgan. "The Country Life Commission: Reconsidering a Milestone in American Agricultural History." *Agricultural History* 78, no. 3 (Summer 2004): 289–316.

Phillips, Sarah T. *This Land, This Nation: Conservation, Rural America, and the New Deal.* New York: Cambridge University Press, 2007.

Piehl, Mel. *Breaking Bread: The Catholic Worker and the Origin of Catholic Radicalism in America.* 2nd ed. Tuscaloosa: University of Alabama Press, 2006 [1982].

Piper, John F. "The American Churches in World War I." *Journal of the American Academy of Religion* 38, no. 2 (June 1970): 147–155.

Pittman, Dan W. "The Founding of Dyess Colony." *Arkansas Historical Quarterly* 29, no. 4 (Winter 1970): 313–326.

Piven, Frances Fox, and Richard A. Cloward. *Regulating the Poor: The Functions of Public Welfare.* 2nd ed. New York: Vintage Books, 1993 [1971].

Powell, Jim. *FDR's Folly: How Roosevelt and His New Deal Prolonged the Great Depression.* New York: Three Rivers Press, 2003.

Pratt, J. Kristian. *The Father of Modern Landmarkism: The Life of Ben M. Bogard.* Macon, GA: Mercer University Press, 2013.

Prendergast, William B. *The Catholic Voter in American Politics: The Passing of the Democratic Monolith.* Washington, DC: Georgetown University Press, 1999.

Preston, Andrew. *Sword of the Spirit, Shield of Faith: Religion in American War and Diplomacy.* New York: Anchor Books, 2012.

Preston, Andrew, Bruce J. Schulman, and Julian E. Zelizer. *Faithful Republic: Religion and Politics in Modern America.* Philadelphia: University of Pennsylvania Press, 2015.

Pye, Mrs. W. D. *The Yield of the Golden Years: A History of the Baptist Woman's Missionary Union of Arkansas, Written to Commemorate the Golden Jubilee, 1900-1938.* Little Rock: n.p., 1938.

Ransby, Barbara. *Ella Baker and the Black Freedom Movement: A Radical Democratic Vision.* Chapel Hill: University of North Carolina Press, 2005.

Ransom, Roger, and Richard Sutch. *One Kind of Freedom: The Economic Consequences of Emancipation.* 2nd ed. Cambridge: Cambridge University Press, 2001 [1997].

Remillard, Arthur. *Southern Civil Religions: Imagining the Good Society in the Post-Reconstruction Era.* Athens: University of Georgia Press, 2011.

Ribuffo, Leo P. *The Old Christian Right: The Protestant Far Right from the Great Depression to the Cold War.* Philadelphia: Temple University Press, 1983.

Rich, Mark. *The Rural Church Movement.* Columbia, MO: Juniper Knoll Press, 1957.

Robertson, Nancy Marie. *Christian Sisterhood, Race Relations, and the YWCA, 1906-1946.* Urbana: University of Illinois Press, 2010.

Rodriguez, Marc S. *Repositioning North American Migration History: New Directions in Modern Continental Migration, Citizenship and Community.* Rochester, NY: University of Rochester Press, 2004.

Rogers, O. A., Jr. "The Elaine Race Riots of 1919." *Arkansas Historical Quarterly* 19, no. 2 (Summer 1960): 142–150.

Rogers, Kim Lacy. *Life and Death in the Delta: African American Narratives of Violence, Resilience, and Social Change.* New York: Palgrave Macmillan, 2006.

Rolinson, Mary G. *Grassroots Garveyism: The Universal Negro Improvement Association in the Rural South, 1920-1927.* Chapel Hill: University of North Carolina Press, 2007.

Roll, Jarod. *Spirit of Rebellion: Labor and Religion in the New Cotton South.* Urbana, IL: University of Illinois Press, 2010.

———. "Garveyism and the Eschatology of African Redemption in the Rural South, 1920-1936." *Religion and American Culture: A Journal of Interpretation* 20 (January 2010): 27–56.

Roth, Darlene Rebecca. *Matronage: Patterns in Women's Organizations, Atlanta, Georgia, 1890-1940.* Brooklyn, NY: Carlson, 1994.

Rouse, Jacqueline Anne. *Lugenia Burns Hope, Black Southern Reformer.* Athens: University of Georgia Press, 2004.

Royce, Edward. *The Origins of Southern Sharecropping.* Philadelphia: Temple University Press, 1993.

Salmond, John A. "The Fellowship of Southern Churchmen and Interracial Change in the South." *North Carolina Historical Review* 69, no. 2 (April 1992): 179–199.

Saloutos, Theodore. *The American Farmer and the New Deal.* Ames: Iowa State University Press, 1982.

Salvatore, Nick. *Singing in a Strange Land: C. L. Franklin, the Black Church, and the Transformation of America.* New York: Little, Brown & Company, 2005.

Sánchez, Sieglinde Lim de. "Crafting a Delta Chinese Community: Education and Acculturation in Twentieth-Century Southern Baptist Mission Schools." *History of Education Quarterly* 43, no. 1 (Spring 2003): 74–90.

Sandeen, Ernest Robert. *The Roots of Fundamentalism; British and American Millenarianism, 1800-1930.* Chicago: University of Chicago Press, 1970.

Sanders, Cheryl J. *Saints in Exile: The Holiness-Pentecostal Experience in African American Religion and Culture.* New York: Oxford University Press, 1999.

Sanders, Elizabeth. *Roots of Reform: Farmers, Workers, and the American State, 1877-1917.* Chicago: University of Chicago Press, 1999.

Sandlin, Lee. *Wicked River: The Mississippi When It Last Ran Wild.* New York: Pantheon, 2010.

Sarna, Jonathan D. *American Judaism: A History.* New Haven, CT: Yale University Press, 2005.

Savage, Barbara Dianne. *Your Spirits Walk Beside Us: The Politics of Black Religion.* Cambridge, MA: Belknap Press, 2008.

Schäfer, Axel R. "The Cold War State and the Resurgence of Evangelicalism: A Study of the Public Funding of Religion Since 1945." *Radical History Review* 99 (Fall 2007): 19–49.

———. *Piety and Public Funding: Evangelicals and the State in Modern America.* Philadelphia: University of Pennsylvania Press, 2012.

Schaller, Thomas F. "Democracy at Rest: Strategic Ratification of the Twenty-First Amendment." *Publius* 28, no. 2 (Spring 1998): 81–97.

Schmidt, Jean Miller. *Souls or the Social Order: The Two-Party System in American Protestantism.* Brooklyn, NY: Carlson Publishing, 1991.

Schmidt, Leigh Eric. "From Arbor Day to the Environmental Sabbath: Nature, Liturgy, and American Protestantism." *Harvard Theological Review* 84, no. 3 (July 1991): 299–323.

Schmidt, William T. "Letters to Their President: Mississippians to Franklin D. Roosevelt, 1932-1933." *Journal of Mississippi History* 40, no. 3 (August 1978): 231–252.

Schulman, Bruce J. *From Cotton Belt to Sunbelt: Federal Policy, Economic Development, and the Transformation of the South, 1938-1980.* Durham, NC: Duke University Press, 1994 [1991].

Schultz, Kevin M. *Tri-Faith America: How Catholics and Jews Held Postwar America to Its Protestant Promise.* New York: Oxford University Press, 2011.

Seales, Chad E. *The Secular Spectacle: Performing Religion in a Southern Town.* New York: Oxford University Press, 2014.

Sehat, David. *The Myth of American Religious Freedom.* New York: Oxford University Press, 2011.

Sernett, Milton. *Bound for the Promised Land: African American Religion and the Great Migration.* Durham, NC: Duke University Press, 1997.

Shawhan, Dorothy. *Lucy Somerville Howorth: New Deal Lawyer, Politician, and Feminist from the South.* Baton Rouge: Louisiana State University Press, 2006.

Shlaes, Amity. *The Forgotten Man: A New History of the Great Depression.* New York: Harper, 2007.

Sigafoos, Robert Alan. *Cotton Row to Beale Street: A Business History of Memphis.* Memphis, TN: Memphis State University Press, 1979.

Simmons, Dovie Marie, and Olivia L. Martin. *Down Behind the Sun: The Story of Arenia Cornelia Mallory.* Memphis, TN: Riverside Press, 1983.

Simon, Bryant. *A Fabric of Defeat: The Politics of South Carolina Millhands, 1910-1948.* Chapel Hill: University of North Carolina Press, 1998.

Sitkoff, Harvard. *A New Deal for Blacks: The Emergence of Civil Rights as a National Issue.* 2nd. ed. New York: Oxford University Press, 2009 [1978].

Sklaroff, Lauren Rebecca. *Black Culture and the New Deal: The Quest for Civil Rights in the Roosevelt Era.* Chapel Hill: University of North Carolina Press, 2009.

Skocpol, Theda. *Protecting Soldiers and Mothers: The Political Origins of Social Policy in the United States.* Cambridge, MA: Belknap Press, 1992.

Skocpol, Theda, Ariane Liazos, and Marshall Ganz. *What a Mighty Power We Can Be: African American Fraternal Groups and the Struggle for Racial Equality.* Princeton, NJ: Princeton University Press, 2006.

Skocpol, Theda, and Vanessa Williamson. *The Tea Party and the Remaking of Republican Conservatism.* New York: Oxford University Press, 2013.

Smith, Fred C. *Trouble in Goshen: Plain Folk, Roosevelt, Jesus and Marx in the Great Depression South.* Jackson: University Press of Mississippi, 2014.

Smith, Gary Scott. *Faith and the Presidency: From George Washington to George W. Bush.* New York: Oxford University Press, 2006.

Smith, Suzanne. *To Serve the Living: Funeral Directors and the African American Way of Death.* Cambridge, MA: Harvard University Press, 2010.

Snyder, Timothy. *Bloodlands: Europe Between Hitler and Stalin.* New York: Basic Books, 2012.

Span, Christopher M. *From Cotton Field to Schoolhouse: African American Education in Mississippi, 1862-1875*. Chapel Hill: University of North Carolina Press, 2009.

Sparks, Randy J. *Religion in Mississippi*. Jackson: University Press of Mississippi, 2001.

Stark, Rodney. "The Reliability of Historical United States Census Data on Religion." *Sociological Analysis* 53, no. 1 (Spring 1992): 91–95.

Stephens, Randall J. *The Fire Spreads: Holiness and Pentecostalism in the American South*. Cambridge, MA: Harvard University Press, 2007.

Stevens, Jason. *God-Fearing and Free: A Spiritual History of America's Cold War*. Cambridge, MA: Harvard University Press, 2010.

Stockley, Grif. *Blood in Their Eyes: The Elaine Race Massacres of 1919*. Fayetteville: University of Arkansas Press, 2001.

———. *Ruled by Race: Black/White Relations in Arkansas from Slavery to the Present*. Fayetteville: University of Arkansas Press, 2008.

Stockley, Grif, and Jeannie M. Whayne. "Federal Troops and the Elaine Massacres: A Colloquy." *Arkansas Historical Quarterly* 61, no. 3 (Autumn 2002): 272–283.

Stricklin, David. *A Genealogy of Dissent: Southern Baptist Protest in the Twentieth Century*. Lexington: University Press of Kentucky, 1999.

Strub, Whitney. "Black and White and Banned All Over: Race, Censorship and Obscenity in Postwar Memphis." *Journal of Social History* 40, no. 3 (2007): 685–715.

Sullivan, Patricia. *Days of Hope: Race and Democracy in the New Deal Era*. Chapel Hill: University of North Carolina Press, 1996.

Sullivan, Winnifred Fallers. *The Impossibility of Religious Freedom*. Princeton, NJ: Princeton University Press, 2007.

Sutton, Matthew Avery. *American Apocalypse: A History of Modern Evangelicalism*. Cambridge, MA: Belknap Press, 2014.

———. *Aimee Semple McPherson and the Resurrection of Christian America*. Cambridge, MA: Harvard University Press, 2007.

———. "Was FDR the Antichrist? The Birth of Fundamentalist Antiliberalism in a Global Age." *Journal of American History*, 98, no. 4 (January 2012): 1052–1074.

Swain, Martha H. *Pat Harrison: The New Deal Years*. Jackson: University Press of Mississippi, 1978.

———. *Ellen S. Woodward: New Deal Advocate for Women*. Jackson: University Press of Mississippi, 1995.

Swanson, Merwin. "The 'Country Life Movement' and the American Churches." *Church History* 46, no. 3 (September 1977): 358–373.

Swierenga, Robert P. "The Little White Church: Religion in Rural America." *Agricultural History* 71, no. 4 (Autumn 1997): 415–441.

Synan, Vinson. *The Holiness-Pentecostal Tradition: Charismatic Movements in the Twentieth Century*. Grand Rapids, MI: W. B. Eerdmans, 1997.

Szasz, Ferenc Morton. *The Divided Mind of Protestant America, 1880-1930*. Tuscaloosa: University of Alabama Press, 1982.

Szymanski, Ann-Marie. "Beyond Parochialism: Southern Progressivism, Prohibition, and State-Building." *Journal of Southern History* 69, no. 1 (February 2003): 107–136.

Taiz, Lillian. *Hallelujah Lads and Lasses: Remaking the Salvation Army in America, 1880-1930.* Chapel Hill: University of North Carolina Press, 2001.

Taylor, Nick. *American-Made: The Enduring Legacy of the WPA: When FDR Put the Nation to Work.* New York: Bantam, 2008.

Thompson, H. Paul, Jr. *A Most Significant and Stirring Episode: Religion and the Rise and Fall of Prohibition in Black Atlanta.* DeKalb: Northern Illinois University Press, 2013.

Tindall, George Brown. *The Emergence of the New South, 1913-1945.* Baton Rouge: Louisiana State University Press, 1967.

Toulouse, Mark G. "Socializing Capitalism: The *Century* During the Great Depression." *Christian Century* 117, no. 12 (April 12, 2000).

Trattner, Walter I. *From Poor Law to Welfare State: A Social History of Welfare in America.* 6th ed. New York: Free Press, 1999 [1974].

Trolander, Judith Ann. *Settlement Houses and the Great Depression.* Detroit: Wayne State University Press, 1975.

Trost, Jennifer Ann. *Gateway to Justice: The Juvenile Court and Progressive Child Welfare in a Southern City.* Athens: University of Georgia Press, 2005.

Tucker, David M. *Black Pastors and Leaders: Memphis, 1819-1972.* Memphis, TN: Memphis State University Press, 1975.

Tweed, Thomas A. *Crossing and Dwelling: A Theory of Religion.* Cambridge, MA: Harvard University Press, 2006.

Tyrrell, Ian. *Reforming the World: The Creation of America's Moral Empire.* Princeton, NJ: Princeton University Press, 2010.

———. *Woman's World/Woman's Empire: The Woman's Christian Temperance Union in International Perspective, 1880-1930.* Chapel Hill: University of North Carolina Press, 1991.

Tyson, Timothy B. *Blood Done Sign My Name: A True Story.* New York: Crown Publishers, 2005.

Underwood, Edward. *Haunted Jonesboro.* Charleston, SC: History Press, 2011.

Van Rijn, Guido. *Roosevelt's Blues: African-American Blues and Gospel Songs on FDR.* Jackson: University Press of Mississippi, 1997.

VanGiezen, Robert, and Albert E. Schwenk. "Compensation from Before World War I Through the Great Depression." *Compensation and Working Conditions Online*, no. 2001 (January 20, 2003). www.bls.gov/opub/cwc/cm20030124ar03p1.htm

Venkataramani, M. S. "Norman Thomas, Arkansas Sharecroppers, and the Roosevelt Agricultural Policies, 1933-1937." *Arkansas Historical Quarterly* 24, no. 1 (Spring 1965): 3–28.

Vogt, Daniel C. "Hoover's RFC in Action: Mississippi, Bank Loans, and Work Relief, 1932-1933." *Journal of Mississippi History* 47, no. 1 (1985): 35–53.

Volanto, Keith J. "The AAA Cotton Plow-Up Campaign in Arkansas." *Arkansas Historical Quarterly* 59, no. 4 (Winter 2000): 388–406.

Wacker, Grant. *Heaven Below: Early Pentecostals and American Culture.* Cambridge, MA: Harvard University Press, 2001.

Wailoo, Keith. *Dying in the City of the Blues: Sickle Cell Anemia and the Politics of Race and Health.* Chapel Hill: University of North Carolina Press, 2001.

Wald, Gayle F. *Shout, Sister, Shout! The Untold Story of Rock-and-Roll Trailblazer Sister Rosetta Tharpe.* Boston: Beacon Press, 2007.

Walker, Corey D. B. *A Noble Fight: African American Freemasonry and the Struggle for Democracy in America.* Urbana: University of Illinois Press, 2008.

Walker, Vanessa Siddle. *Their Highest Potential: An African American School Community in the Segregated South.* Chapel Hill: University of North Carolina Press, 1996.

Walton, Hanes, and James E. Taylor. "Blacks and the Southern Prohibition Movement." *Phylon* 32, no. 3 (Fall 1971): 247–259.

Ward, Andrew. *Dark Midnight When I Rise: The Story of the Fisk Jubilee Singers.* New York: Amistad, 2001.

Ward, Jason Morgan. *Defending White Democracy: The Making of a Segregationist Movement and the Remaking of Racial Politics, 1936-1965.* Chapel Hill: University of North Carolina Press, 2011.

Ward, Thomas J., Jr. *Black Physicians in the Jim Crow South.* Fayetteville: University of Arkansas Press, 2003.

Warren, Heather A. *Theologians of a New World Order: Reinhold Niebuhr and the Christian Realists, 1920-1948.* New York: Oxford University Press, 1997.

Waskow, Arthur Ocean. *From Race Riot to Sit-in, 1919 and the 1960s: A Study in the Connections Between Conflict and Violence.* Garden City, NY: Anchor Books, 1967.

Watts, Jill. *God, Harlem U.S.A.: The Father Divine Story.* Berkeley: University of California Press, 1995.

Weber, Timothy P. *Living in the Shadow of the Second Coming: American Premillennialism, 1875-1982.* New York: Oxford University Press, 1979.

Wedell, Marsha. *Elite Women and the Reform Impulse in Memphis, 1875-1915.* Knoxville: University of Tennessee Press, 1991.

Weisenfeld, Judith. *Hollywood Be Thy Name: African-American Religion in American Film, 1929-1949.* Berkeley: University of California Press, 2007.

Weissbach, Lee Shai. "East European Immigrants and the Image of Jews in the Small-Town South." *American Jewish History* 85, no. 3 (1997): 231–262.

Welky, David. *The Thousand-Year Flood: The Ohio-Mississippi Disaster of 1937.* Chicago: University of Chicago Press, 2011.

Wenger, Beth S. *New York Jews and the Great Depression: Uncertain Promise.* New Haven, CT: Yale University Press, 1996.

Wenger, Tisa. *We Have a Religion: The 1920s Pueblo Indian Dance Controversy and American Religious Freedom.* Chapel Hill: University of North Carolina Press, 2009.

Whayne, Jeannie M. *Delta Empire: Lee Wilson and the Transformation of Agriculture in the New South*. Baton Rouge: Louisiana State University Press, 2011.

———. "Low Villains and Wickedness in High Places: Race and Class in the Elaine Riots." *Arkansas Historical Quarterly* 58, no. 3 (Autumn 1999): 285–313.

———. *A New Plantation South: Land, Labor, and Federal Favor in Twentieth-Century Arkansas*. Charlottesville: University Press of Virginia, 1996.

Whayne, Jeannie M., and Willard B. Gatewood, eds. *The Arkansas Delta: Land of Paradox*. Fayetteville: University of Arkansas Press, 1993.

Whitaker, Robert. *On the Laps of Gods: The Red Summer of 1919 and the Struggle for Justice That Remade a Nation*. New York: Crown Publishers, 2008.

White, Calvin, Jr. "In the Beginning, There Stood Two: Arkansas Roots of the Black Holiness Movement." *Arkansas Historical Quarterly* 68, no. 1 (Spring 2009): 1–22.

———. *The Rise to Respectability: Race, Religion, and the Church of God in Christ*. Fayetteville: University of Arkansas Press, 2012.

Wicker, Elmus. *The Banking Panics of the Great Depression*. Cambridge: Cambridge University Press, 1996.

Wiebe, Robert H. *The Search for Order, 1877-1920*. New York: Hill and Wang, 1966.

Wilkerson, Kenneth, ed. *Methodism in the Memphis Conference, 1840-1990*. Dallas: Taylor Publishing Company, 1990.

Wilkerson-Freeman, Sarah. The Creation of a Subversive Feminist Dominion: Interracialist Social Workers and the Georgia New Deal," *Journal of Women's History* 13, no. 4 (Winter 2002): 132–154.

Williams, C. Fred, S. Ray Granade, and Kenneth M. Startup. *A System and Plan: Arkansas Baptist State Convention, 1848-1998*. Franklin, TN: Providence House Publishers, 1998.

Williams, Daniel K. *God's Own Party: The Making of the Christian Right*. New York: Oxford University Press, 2010.

Williams, Heather Andrea. *Self-Taught: African American Education in Slavery and Freedom*. Chapel Hill: University of North Carolina Press, 2007.

Winston, Diane H. *Red-Hot and Righteous: The Urban Religion of the Salvation Army*. Cambridge, MA: Harvard University Press, 1999.

Woodruff, Nan Elizabeth. *American Congo: The African American Freedom Struggle in the Delta*. Cambridge, MA: Harvard University Press, 2003.

———. *As Rare as Rain: Federal Relief in the Great Southern Drought of 1930-31*. Urbana: University of Illinois Press, 1985.

Woods, Clyde Adrian. *Development Arrested: The Blues and Plantation Power in the Mississippi Delta*. London: Verso, 1998.

Woods, James M. *Mission and Memory: A History of the Catholic Church in Arkansas*. Little Rock, AR: August House Publishers, 1993.

Worthen, Molly. *Apostles of Reason: The Crisis of Authority in American Evangelicalism*. New York: Oxford University Press, 2013.

Wright, Gavin. *Old South, New South. Revolutions in the Southern Economy Since the Civil War*. Baton Rouge: Louisiana State University Press, 1997.

Wuthnow, Robert. *The Restructuring of American Religion: Society and Faith Since World War II*. Princeton, NJ: Princeton University Press, 1988.

———. *Red State Religion: Faith and Politics in America's Heartland*. Princeton, NJ: Princeton University Press, 2012.

Zwick, Mark, and Louise Zwick. *The Catholic Worker Movement: Intellectual and Spiritual Origins*. Mahwah, NJ: Paulist Press, 2005.

DISSERTATIONS AND THESES

Barber, Christopher Bart. "The Bogard Schism: An Arkansas Baptist Agrarian Revolt." Ph.D. diss., Southwestern Baptist Theological Seminary, 2006.

Bass, John Lawrence. "Bolsheviks on the Bluff: A History of Memphis Communists and Their Labor and Civil Rights Contributions, 1930-1957." Ph.D. diss., University of Memphis, 2009.

Cantwell, Christopher D. "The Bible Class Teacher: Piety and Politics in the Age of Fundamentalism." Ph.D. diss., Cornell University, 2011.

Connell, William Leo. "An Investigation of Catholic Social Teaching in 'The Christian Front': 1936—1942." Ph.D. diss., The Catholic University of America, 1996.

Drake, Janine Giordano. "Between Religion and Politics: The Working Class Religious Left, 1880-1920." Ph.D. diss., University of Illinois at Urbana-Champaign, 2014.

Ferguson, Robert Hunt. "Race and the Remaking of the Rural South: Delta Cooperative Farm and Providence Farm in Jim Crow-Era Mississippi." Ph.D. diss., University of North Carolina, 2012.

Grem, Darren Elliott. "The Blessings of Business: Corporate America and Conservative Evangelicalism in the Sunbelt Age, 1945-2000." Ph.D. diss., University of Georgia, 2010.

Gritter, Elizabeth. "Black Politics in the Age of Jim Crow: Memphis, Tennessee, 1865 to 1954." Ph.D. diss, University of North Carolina, 2010.

Hammond, Sarah Ruth. " 'God's Business Men': Entrepreneurial Evangelicals in Depression and War." Ph.D. diss., Yale University, 2010.

Harbison, Stanley Lincoln. "The Social Gospel Career of Alva Wilmot Taylor." Ph.D. diss., Vanderbilt University, 1975.

Herbin, Elizabeth Ann. "Healing the Land, Healing the South: Reforming the Southern Cotton Farm, 1900-1939." Ph.D. diss., Columbia University, 2007.

Hungerman, Daniel Michael. "Public Finance and Charitable Church Activity." Ph.D. diss., Duke University, 2005.

Hunsicker, David Buckelew. "The Rise of the Parachurch Movement in American Protestant Christianity During the 1930s and 1940s: A Detailed Study of the

Beginnings of the Navigators, Young Life and Youth for Christ International." Ph.D. diss., Trinity Evangelical Divinity School, 1998.

McDonough, Julia Anne. "Men and Women of Good Will: A History of the Commission on Interracial Cooperation and the Southern Regional Council, 1919-1944." Ph.D. diss., University of Virginia, 1993.

Melton, Gloria Brown. "Blacks in Memphis, Tennessee, 1920-1935: A Historical Study." Ph.D. diss., Washington State University, 1982.

Modey, Yao Foli. "The Struggle over Prohibition in Memphis, 1880-1930." Ph.D. diss., Memphis State University, 1983.

Paulsell, William Oliver. "The Disciples of Christ and the Great Depression, 1929-1936." Ph.D. diss., Vanderbilt University, 1965.

Peck, Hannah F. "St. Vincent's Infirmary, 1888-1987: A History of a Roman Catholic Hospital in Little Rock, Arkansas." Master's thesis, University of Arkansas at Little Rock, 1987.

Pietsch, Brendan M. "Dispensational Modernism." Ph.D. diss., Duke University, 2011.

Robinson, James H. "A Social History of the Negro in Memphis and Shelby County." Ph.D. diss., Yale University, 1934.

Ross, James D. "'I Ain't Got No Home in This World': The Rise and Fall of the Southern Tenant Farmers' Union in Arkansas." Ph.D. diss., Auburn University, 2004.

Smith, Fred C. "Agrarian Experimentation and Failure in Depression Mississippi: New Deal and Socialism, The Tupelo Homesteads and the Delta and Providence Cooperative Farms." Master's thesis, Mississippi State University, 2002.

———. "Shadows over Goshen: Plain Whites, Progressives and Paternalism in the Depression South." Ph.D. diss., University of Southern Mississippi, 2008.

Stone, Karen Anne. "Rescue the Perishing: The Southern Baptist Convention and the Rural Church Movement." Ph.D. diss., Auburn University, 1998.

Trotter, Donald Wesley. "Making Do: Case Studies of Disciple of Christ Congregations in the Great Depression." Ph.D. diss., University of Tennessee, 1998.

Tyson, William Ainsworth. "The Rural Church and Its Background: A Survey of Thirty-Nine Counties in North Mississippi." Master's thesis, Mississippi State College, 1944.

Weaver, Elton Hal. "'Mark the Perfect Man': The Rise of Bishop C. H. Mason and the Church of God in Christ." Ph.D. diss., University of Memphis, 2007.

Wilkerson-Freeman, Sarah. "Women and the Transformation of American Politics: North Carolina, 1898-1940." Ph.D. diss., University of North Carolina, 1995.

Youngblood, Joshua. "Realistic Religion and Radical Prophets: The STFU, the Social Gospel, and the American Left in the 1930s." Master's thesis, Florida State University, 2004.

Index

Abraham, Kate, 66–68, 77, 84–86, 98

activists: African American, 7; Catholic, 162; Christian, 58–60, 68, 167, 176–177, 179, 182; civil rights, 182, 198–199; fundamentalist, 42; labor, 59; political vs. religious, 177, 181; Protestant, 48, 167, 169, 226–227n35; rural church, 181; social, 71, 116, 167; southern religious, 68, 167, 169, 174, 177, 182; in STFU (*see* Southern Tenant Farmers' Union); women, 186

acts, congressional: Affordable Care Act, 201; Civil Rights Act, 199; Emergency Banking Relief Act, 102; Emergency Relief and Construction Act, 98; Emergency Relief Appropriation Act, 134; Federal Emergency Relief Act, 121 (*see also* Federal Emergency Relief Administration); Indian Removal Act, 13; National Industrial Recovery Act, 113, 115, 117, 118; National Labor Relations Act, 134–135; Personal Responsibility and Work Opportunity Reconciliation Act, 200; Revenue Act, 112; Social Security Act (*see* Social Security Act); Volstead Act, 108; Voting Rights Act, 199

African Americans: aid denied to or limited for, 29, 70, 72, 85, 89, 92–93, 97, 104, 126, 129, 132, 140, 144, 150 (*see also* relief or relief agencies: racist structures of); children, 22, 29, 81–82, 89 (*see also under* orphanages); churches (*see* churches: African American); Democratic Party and, 113; Great Depression and, 12, 57–58, 61–62, 100, 145; families or mothers, 15, 140; farm or land owners, 21, 176; federal aid or New Deal programs and, 7, 70, 103, 128–129, 132, 140–144, 151, 156; leaders, 24, 68, 97, 128, 143, 180, 185; Memphis (*see under* Memphis); middle or other classes of, 71, 74, 80; migrations of, 16, 20–21 (*see also* Great Migration); millennialism of, 61; music, 24; nationalism of, 59; neighborhoods or towns of, 14–15, 18–19, 143; networks or organizations of, 42, 57 (*see also* fraternal orders; women's societies); NRA and, 117–118, 129; "New Negro," 51; police and, 14, 18, 106; Prohibition and, 108–110, 242n22; Reconstruction-era, 14, 42, 46, 70; Republican Party and, 24, 106, 112; Roosevelt and (*see under*

unions, 6, 55, 59, 113–115, 133,
179, 243n37, 256n38; anti- or
non-, 17, 117; Congress of
Industrial Organizations
(CIO), 182; farmers' (*see*
Southern Tenant Farmers' Union)
Unitarians, 135, 157, 209

Vanderbilt University, 59–60, 116,
174, 179
Vaughan, James D., 62
veterans, 70, 75–76, 105, 146
violence, 19, 70; domestic, 49; mob,
110, 172; racial, 3, 14, 20, 70, 74,
172, 190; against STFU members,
181–182, 257n41. *See also* lynching
Virginia, 25, 75

wage laborers, 42, 47, 91
wages, 79, 133, 147; fair or good, 58, 70,
133, 188; low, 17–18, 68, 91, 99, 103,
117, 127, 144, 187; in Memphis,
17–18, 88, 144; minimum, 116;
plantation, 240n2; NRA, 102–103,
113–115, 117; race and, 70, 117, 144;
RFC, 99–100; WPA, 141, 144
welfare state, 199–200, 220n36,
262nn15–16
white supremacists, 4, 7, 103, 192, 195
widows, 2, 28, 62, 67, 76, 81, 85,
148; Abraham, 66, 68, 84, 86;
Thomas, 95–96
Williams, Claude, 59, 179–181
women, 19, 75, 107, 142; African
American (*see under*
African American); children and, 27,
71 (*see also* Mothers' Aid); churches
or church aid and, 44–45, 48, 74, 79,
83, 85, 93, 98, 172, 185–186, 225n29;
fraternal orders and, 86; Jewish,

78; jobs for or working, 44, 71, 77,
91, 98, 100, 144; New Woman, 51;
poor or middle-class, 76, 80, 165,
168; reform, temperance, or union
campaigns, 49, 72, 74, 102, 109,
178, 180, 227n36; revivals and, 35,
37, 44–45; in Roosevelt/New Deal
administration, 135, 152, 163–165, 185;
Roosevelts and, 131, 146–147; white,
77, 109–110, 172
women's clubs or societies, 48, 74–76,
80, 98, 122, 164, 168, 172, 238n55;
African American, 57, 168, 185;
Association of Southern Women
for the Prevention of Lynching
(ASWPL), 172; church, Jewish, or
missionary, 64, 67, 70–72, 77–78,
86–87, 119, 124, 152; Women's
Christian Temperance Union, 49
Woodward, Ellen, 152
work relief, 90, 98–100, 103, 118–119,
121–122, 126, 127, 140, 201; African
Americans' access to limited, 104,
144; clergy on, 116, 142, 148, 156;
in Mississippi, 144; Roosevelt's
expansion of, 134, 138
Works Progress Administration
(WPA), 131, 135, 147, 163, 167, 190;
African Americans and, 143–144;
Arkansas church survey by, 41–42,
45; creation of, 134, 195; religious
facilities and, 152–153; religious
leaders' view of, 134, 141–42;
women's programs in, 152
World War I, 38, 49, 73–74, 116; veterans
of, 105
World War II, 7, 169, 185, 196–198
Wright, Richard, 144, 222–223n14

Yazoo City, 4, 72, 86, 150

CPSIA information can be obtained
at www.ICGtesting.com
Printed in the USA
BVHW04s0523130618
518894BV00002B/3/P